ROOTS
OF
THE FUTURE

Rabbi
Herbert A. Friedman

gefen גפן
publishing house בית הוצאה לאור

JERUSALEM ◆ NEW YORK

Edition 9 8 7 6 5 4 3 2

Grateful acknowledgment is made to the following for permission
to reprint previously published material:

Every Spy a Prince. Copyright © 1990 by Dan Raviv and Yossi Melman. Reprinted by
permission of Houghton-Mifflin Company.

The Samson Option, Israel's Nuclear Options and American Foreign Policy
by Seymour Hersh, published by Random House, 1991.

History of the Jews in America by Howard Sachar, published by Alfred Knopf, 1992.

Jews and the North American Scene by Seymour Martin Lipset and Earl Raab, published
by Harvard University Press, 1995. *Jews in America* by Arthur Hertzberg, quoted in
Lipset and Raab's *Jews and the North American Scene.*

The Vanishing American Jew by Alan Dershowitz, published by Little Brown and
Company, 1997.

Gefen Publishing House
POB 36004
Jerusalem 91360, Israel
972-2-538-0247
isragefen@netmedia.net.il

Gefen Books
12 New Street
Hewlett, NY 11557, USA
516-295-2805
gefenbooks@compuserve.com

Printed in Israel

Send for our free catalogue

Library of Congress Cataloging-in-Publication Data
Friedman, Herbert A., 1918-
Roots of the future / Herbert A.Friedman
ISBN: 965 229 201 X
1. Friedman, Herbert A., 1918- . 2. Rabbis—Unites States—Biography. 3. Zionists—Unites States—
Biography. 4. Holocaust survivors—Germany. 5. Jews—Persecutions—Poland—Kielce—Public opinion.
6. Public opinion—Poland. 7. United Jewish Appeal—Biography. I. Title.
BM755.F6949A3   1998
966'.092—dc21
[B]   98-35305
                                                                                                                              CIP

History with its flickering lamp
Stumbles along the trail of the past,
Trying to reconstruct its themes,
To revive its echoes and kindle
With pale gleams, the passion of former days.

Sir Winston Spencer Churchill

True redemption will come to the Jew
if he bear his name and every
other burden imposed upon him by
destiny with gleaming courage and
radiant nobleness which, whether or not
they evoke the love of the world
without, will justify the Jew in his
own sight and hallow him anew in
the presence of the Eternal, to whom
alone he is ultimately accountable.

Rabbi Stephen S. Wise

Contents

Few American Jews who had the option to choose their period of life and action would have selected an era other than this. It has been an epoch vibrating with drama, charged with opportunities for service to high causes, yet all under the shadow of tragedies that reach beyond understanding into worlds of anguish and dread. Such was the life depicted in the six decades during which Herbert A. Friedman made his imprint on his generation's life.

The story has humble beginnings in the concerns of a young, Jewish army chaplain organizing the rescue of endangered Jews drifting precariously across the devastated roads in Europe. It springs to life with vaster opportunities for supporting threatened kinsmen on scales previously deemed to surpass fantasy. Friedman was the dynamo under whose directing hand the United Jewish Appeal increased its annual revenues thirty-fold, from $25 million to $750 million, bringing him into intimate contact with the founding fathers of a young nation that knew the exhilaration of having a new creation entrusted in their hands.

Abba Eban has held many high positions in Israel, including deputy prime minister foreign minister, and ambassador to both the United States and United Nations.

Friedman's role was to be permanently mobilized in the service of expanding duties, forever crossing continents and oceans in pursuit of larger issues and broader targets. We see him among suffering Jews in camps euphemistically designed for Displaced Persons, celebrating the seder in Berlin, suffering amid Jews still subjected to pogroms in Poland, trudging across the Alps in quest of freedom and shelter, founding the UJA Education Fund, living and working in Israel – always at the centers of action and hazard.

No one who longed for tranquility would have chosen such a vocation. Friedman suffered the exploits of a Jewish emissary whose charge was "to have no rest himself and to give none to others." For such as these, life is always on the move with one breathless assignment giving way to another. He writes with deep pathos that "when Hitler set out to destroy the world's Jews, I was 15 years old." What worlds of agony are compressed into those 14 words!

What I recall about the author is a constant burst of exuberance, an unfailing humor, with a disposition to see great visions and dream great dreams, with eyes forever fixed firmly on the future, a man of contagious charm with a gift for the easy transfer of his own enthusiasm, always looking to the following day.

"Tomorrow to fresh fields and pastures anew."

The final chapter of the book is somber. Friedman, the stern realist, sketches American Jews as a people hindered by falling birth rates and other afflictions of affluence, destined to be the last generation of "the brilliant American Jewish diaspora" unless those who care act forcefully and soon.

It has always been up to those who care. The demise of Jewry has been so often predicted in the past that it might be premature to doubt the prospect of a new resilience.

– Abba Eban
New York City
December 1997

ACKNOWLEDGMENTS

Thousands of people have entered my life, in Israel, the United States, and many other countries. I owe something to almost every one, for I learned their values, motivations, emotions – and I am a mosaic of them all. I am grateful to every United Jewish Appeal (UJA) prospect I solicited; every local Federation executive director with whom I argued; every lay leader, man and woman, who gave their precious hours, as well as their money, to the cause; every person in an audience who came up to me afterward to compliment or criticize or seek elucidation; and, particularly, every Wexner Heritage Foundation seminar student who spent years reading, discussing, learning in order to improve his or her communal roles. They cannot all be named – but in their nameless multitude they shaped me, and I am grateful beyond words.

★　★　★

I should like to offer my deepest respect and gratitude to Abigail and Leslie Wexner. Their constant support has encouraged and inspired me beyond measure. Leslie is the most thoughtful, generous lay leader I have ever known. His vision on behalf of the Jewish people and Israel is the broadest, his commitment the most constant, his planning the most intelligent. He has given to world Jewry, in addition to other benefactions of note, three major assets: a splendid program for serious adult education; a cadre of professional leaders in the rabbinate and allied fields; and a strengthening of the Israeli senior civil service.

Michael Steinhardt's generosity made possible the editing of this memoir and its preparation for publication. His personal kindness to me is deeply appreciated. On a larger scale, his innovative philanthropies display a far-sighted approach toward the creation of a strong Jewish identity in the next generation.

Roger M. Williams, professional editor and author, has through his skills in pruning, polishing, suggesting and questioning, shaped the manuscript into a book. His careful attention to detail over a long period of months has developed a professional relationship into a personal friendship.

Professor Alvin Rosenfeld's voluntary critique of the text in painstaking detail was the act of a friend whose insights gave me guidance.

Joseph Rackman and Sandy Curtis read the first chapters early on and offered their helpful suggestions, steering me in the right direction.

Very special thanks to Ari Rath, former editor of the Jerusalem Post and a long-time family friend, whose skill with headlines produced the title to this memoir.

To colleagues at the Wexner Heritage Foundation, heartfelt appreciation for their support. I refer to Rabbis Nathan Laufer, Avram (Ramie) Arian, and Shoshana Gelfand; Lori Baron, manager of conferences and publications; assistants Jeanne Forman Shorr and Shelley Wasserman; and support staff, Erica Rosenthal, Cara Stein, and Salome B. Gonzalez.

Sons David and Charles brought me into the modern world of computers by teaching me the rudiments and then responding to my incessant calls for help. Son Daniel and daughters Judith Unice and Joan Bentsen offered their strong encouragement.

And most especially, my wife Francine who steadily, over more than a year, sacrificed her personal time to working time, shepherding 43 chapters through her computer in constantly changing versions that included all sorts of editing and re-writing. Her cogent comments improved ideas and even individual words. Her support has made possible the writing of this volume.

SPECIAL ACKNOWLEDGMENT

I wish to pay tribute to the two deceased men with whom I worked most closely in Germany, Rabbi Philip Bernstein and Major Abraham Hyman.

Phil Bernstein was one of the important Reform rabbis on the American scene in the mid-1940's, resulting in his appointment by the State and War Departments as Advisor on Jewish Affairs (with the simulated rank of major general) to the commander of all U.S. forces in the European theater (USFET).

In the immediate post-war period, the delicate problems involving Jewish survivors of the Holocaust demanded very sensitive handling. Thanks to Bernstein's extraordinary skill in briefing the top generals on the history of European Jewry during the recent Nazi years, plus the fears and hopes of this traumatized refugee population, the Army developed a positive attitude toward the DPs. His explanations of Zionism (i.e., a future state for the homeless survivors) enabled the Army brass to understand the DP mentality. His gentle sincerity, warm personality, and intellectual integrity created an aura of trustworthiness. When problems arose in DP camps, the generals sought his advice and acted on it.

To a large extent, the fate of one-quarter of a million Jews, in 64 camps in Germany and Austria, depended on Bernstein's judgment. He never failed them, and he was a role model for me during all the time I served as his deputy.

The third member of the advisor's office was Abraham Hyman, a lawyer, the officer on the Judge-Advocate General's staff who was in charge of reviewing all death sentences given in Army courts-martial. When a riot occurred one day in a Jewish DP camp in Landsberg between the refugees and U.S. soldiers, the Army recommended that Major Hyman serve as counsel to the DPs to ensure that they had a proper defense. He was a deeply nationalistic Jew, not religious, with a liberal world-view and a very strong conscience. He accepted the assignment to defend them, then joined our office, serving brilliantly. He was finally discharged five years later, long after Rabbi Bernstein and I had left, having himself become the last advisor.

After some years in the United States, during which he worked on my staff at the UJA, he emigrated to Israel with his wife and children, retiring to the kibbutz of which his son was a member. I saw him last shortly before he died at the age of 91.

To FRANCINE,

without whom...

I was arrested once in my life, in Rumania in 1957, by the secret police, on the charge of being a double spy for the Zionists and the CIA. They released me after four days and immediately expelled me from the country.

I smuggled weapons to Palestine, before Israel was born, thus breaking U.S. arms-embargo laws; led convoys of refugees across hostile European borders to freedom; "liberated" crates of medieval religious documents from U.S. Army custody in Germany and transferred them to a professor in Jerusalem; and committed similar, illegal or borderline-legal acts long forgotten.

Those are, I suppose, rather startling admissions for a rabbi. I gained nothing save pride and satisfaction from any of the maneuvers involved. I look back on them now, amazed at how calm I was, and I wonder from what hidden sources the requisite courage emerged. An inner moral summons, not adrenaline alone, seemed to embolden me to react.

In this memoir I will tell these stories, in what I think will be fascinating detail. For now, let me simply point out that I am by temperament neither fearful nor complex, but straightforward, self-confident, given to reaching conclusions quickly and then following through on them. I tend not to spend time and energy analyzing ambiguities but seek to comprehend the essence of a problem and fashion a response. In the telling of the tales summarized above, I think the reader will see strong signs of those traits.

My underlying beliefs were established very early on in life. I was born in 1918, one year after the British Government issued the Balfour Declaration as the enabling document of the future Jewish state. Zionist theory was a living presence in my family's home, synagogue, and circle of friends. At a very young age, I was aware of the excitement and yearning implicit in the movement for Jewish independence. I was a seasoned 14 1/2 year old (sophomore in high school) when Hitler became chancellor of Germany and immediately introduced various anti-Jewish regulations. I understood what was happening and who the good and bad guys were. As Zionism was life giving, Nazism was life destroying.

I felt uneasy and disturbed by the silence all around me. No one, including the Jewish community, was responding to the threat. Only one top-echelon Jewish leader of the day, Rabbi Stephen S. Wise, was calling for massive protest meetings – including parades down Fifth Avenue – and a general economic boycott of Germany. The largest Jewish organizations, such as B'nai B'rith, the American Jewish Committee, Jewish labor unions and many others, were opposing him and urging silence as the best policy. Hitler, they asserted, would become his own worst enemy and would soon pass from power. They quoted Jewish leaders from Berlin who stated that American-Jewish attacks against Germany would only worsen their situation.

Although I comprehended the threat Hitler represented, rationalizations in favor of non-action resounded all around me. That was confusing to a young man such as myself.

One day the air cleared for me. History knocked at the front door of our house, and I witnessed a beautiful, moving example of a fitting and personal response to Hitler. The "teacher" was my mother, Rae.

My mother's sense of duty was as strong as any I have ever encountered. Endowed with a keen conscience, she kept herself and everyone around her on the absolute straight and narrow. Those standards were transmitted not only to me and my brothers Stanley and Sam, but also to a wide circle of friends. She was willing to answer any call. The sisterhood at B'nai Jacob synagogue commanded her loyalty and attention; she held every office in that organization over the course of many decades. No task too unimportant, no person too insignificant, no demand too menial – her reputation was such that every cause came to her attention because every supplicant knew that she would respond affirmatively.

At one meeting of the sisterhood, a representative of the National Refugee Service made an urgent plea for families to take into their homes German-Jewish children whose parents were willing to let them emigrate to the United States, not knowing if they would ever see those children again. The NRS man explained over and over the dangers and evil of Hitlerism, the value placed by Judaism on the saving of a single life, and the time pressure for acting while the small window of opportunity remained open. The congregation's rabbi and his wife added their eloquent voices, urging, even demanding, that the members volunteer their assistance. Of the more than 100 women assembled, all mothers, no more than a dozen raised their hand.

My mother stood and announced that she would take three children. God had been good to her, she said, giving her three healthy sons; this was her opportunity to repay. She added without embarrassment that her family was living in a small apartment, with only two bedrooms, because their house had been foreclosed by the bank during the Depression. Hence, she could take only boys, who could sleep mixed in with her sons.

Mother came home with the affidavit forms, placed them under my father's nose at the kitchen table, and told him of her commitment. Signing the forms, as far as she was concerned, was only a formality. He saw it differently, because of the legal obligations his signature would impose. A soft-spoken and gentle man, he explained to her that an affidavit was legally binding and reminded her of their precarious financial situation. The Depression had reduced his earnings to some pitifully small amount, and he could not envision for an instant how they could handle the additional expense for food, clothing, school, etc., for three more persons.

My mother answered him quietly, but with great passion. Even though we were poor, how could we refuse to save Jewish lives if we were given the chance to do so? She was ashamed of the other sisterhood members. All of them should have volunteered, and she would not hesitate to tell them so at the next meeting. "But if we have enough food for five of us," she asked, "why can't we simply make it do for eight? If I must wash shirts every day for six boys instead of three, what's the difference?"

She refused to debate the financial issue. She demanded that he sign. He hesitated. She insisted. The parental argument raged all night – the only time I remember my parents raising their voices in anger and disagreement. She won. In the morning, my father signed the affidavits, and she proudly took them back to the synagogue.

Five weeks later, we welcomed Walter Krone, Helmut Frank, and Hans Goldschmidt. My parents gave them the same affection as if they had been born into the family, the same share of all rations, and an extra share of psychological attention to overcome their loneliness and fear. In fact, letters from their own parents ceased after a while, and the strong support they received in our house helped them face their future. In later years, whenever my father told the story of what our family had done, he told it with great pride and gave full credit to my mother for her prompt and passionate defense of the endangered, and her instinctive allegiance to what she considered her human and Jewish responsibility.

Aware as I was of the passivity of American Jews at that time, and not knowing the reasons, as I do now in retrospect, I was terribly disturbed by the entire episode. How could good, caring Jews show as little concern as they did? If they *were* concerned, why didn't they act accordingly, especially when a clear opportunity opened in front of their very eyes?

As I mulled over the matter, I decided that my mother's fight with my father symbolized the whole problem, and the only conclusion was therefore to act according to moral Jewish values, without permitting rationalization, delay, or any other diluting factor. When history knocks, you answer. Otherwise, you fail. The lesson I drew from the episode of Walter, Helmut, and Hans in 1936 put me on a course that has endured ever since.

My mother was a remarkable woman in many ways, perhaps due to her upbringing and the closely knit fabric of her family. She was born in a manor house in a clearing in the forest outside of Riga, a city on Latvia's Dvina river, the youngest of 18 children born to the same father and mother within a span of 22 years!

timberland, which he harvested and
a and sold. He was absent for months
ld, waiting for his wife to recover, then
nigsberg in East Prussia), and there

heltered perhaps four-score persons,
the resident rabbi, various teachers for
s, maids and craftsmen, guards, farm
ny mother told me, it was a cheerful,
carried on in a one-household village.
the children, including my mother,
ates during the great waves of the 1880s
escendants were swallowed up in the

★

g as I can remember, my fundamental
redness of Jewish survival, both for the
ge; the value of every single Jewish life,
ler's genocidal attack; the inestimable
l center; the responsibility of every Jew

life, now approaching its ninth decade,
many of the complex challenges that
fore me over this long period. I will

therefore expand on them briefly:

I believe in the uniqueness of the Jewish people.

Jews share the quality of humanness with all others on this planet, yet we are different in many ways. And if we were not, we probably would have disappeared, as have all the others who started on the path of history when we did, almost four millennia ago. There are two elements in our individuality:

the circumstance of our birth as a nation at Mt. Sinai, where we were linked to God and a moral code; and our acceptance of an eternal mission, through the concept of redemption by a Messiah, in which a better world will be born for all humans to enjoy.

I believe in the centrality of a specific land – Israel.

The moral covenant that marked our beginning and the Messianic redemption that will mark our ending are both connected to that small sliver of sacred space at the confluence of three continents. There we wrote the most significant book known to the human race and spawned two globe-girdling daughter religions. The homeland was gained and lost, gained and lost again, but the yearning for it has provided the strength to endure the endless trials of the centuries. Now the land has been gained yet another time, in our era, and, we hope, for *all* time. How miraculous!

I believe in Judaism's gift to humanity.

Along with our separateness and particularity as a special people, we also possess a quality of universalism in its fullest measure. We stress and express, in word and hopefully in deed, the equality of all persons. Our sacred literature teaches that all human beings come from one God. The moral injunctions of our prophets repeatedly state that the stranger shall be treated as the native-born, and the messianic vision of peace, plenty, and health embraces all humankind, not just the Hebrews.

I believe in the Diaspora.

The dispersal of the Jewish people across time and space is an integral part of its creative genius. The Diaspora has been a fruitful hinterland providing intellectual spark and charismatic personalities. At present, the American Jewish future appears cloudy, even dark. But if it brightens, and American Jews maintain their Jewish identity in the midst of unprecedented freedom and affluence, the Diaspora of the future may outstrip all previous ones in achievement.

PREPARATIONS

CHAPTER ONE

MY FAMILY AND FORMATION

My family lived in a small, neat house on Fountain Street in the Westville section of New Haven, Conn. The school was one block away, the grocery store next door to it. Around the corner from our house, the street led to dense woods that contained deer, a pond, an ice house, and many places where my friends and I hid while learning to smoke.

Behind the house stood a one-car garage, big enough for my father's Model A Ford. The car was crucial to his livelihood; he was a traveling salesman who carried his black sample cases as he visited the small dry-goods shops in the towns of southern New England. He went forth methodically every weekday, in all types of weather, never taking a vacation. And when he occasionally ended the day too far away to return home that night, he stayed in the least expensive lodging he could find, seeking early sleep to avoid feeling lonesome. He was never gone longer than one night.

Most of the other men on the block went to work on foot or by trolley, to the arms factories that dominated New Haven or to the small retail establishments. My father, Israel, was considered by the other men white-collar rather than blue, although in fact his earnings were much more uncertain than theirs, for he had no fixed salary and depended on commissions. He did wear a suit and tie to work every day, and presumably these externalities (plus the Model A) defined his status. What really defined him, in our eyes, was his gentle manner, soft-spoken nature, innate kindness, and sense of responsibility.

Israel Friedman was born in Vilna, Lithuania, in 1892, and arrived in the United States during the first few years of the new century on the huge, surging waves of immigration battering at the gates of Ellis Island in New York harbor. On New Year's Day of 1918, in his 26th year, he married, and within a decade bought a house for a family that included three sons. It was the first and last house he ever owned. How proud he must have been to purchase such a precious object, for the unheard-of sum of $12,000, and to feel sufficiently "capitalistic" to commit to the payments of $100 per month. What a great country! What a boundless and bountiful life lay before him and us!

The house had three bedrooms, a complete bathroom with shower, a fireplace in the living room, a sun porch, a furnace in the basement – no prince could want more. His family would be clean, warm, comfortable, and his lovely wife would have a full kitchen with which to keep them all well fed and healthy. It was the fulfillment of the most luxurious dream a man of his time and circumstances could have. And like many dreams, it was to come crashing around his head.

My father bought our house in 1927, when the economy was healthy and growing. He lost it in 1931, when the Depression was in full flower, following the crash two years earlier. As a boy of almost 13, I well remember how he lost it; I was there.

One day around supper time, the bell rang. My father answered to find a deputy sheriff with a paper in his outstretched hand. Nothing was said. My father understood the importance of the moment. He re-entered the house, put on his jacket, and summoned his wife and sons to stand with him on the small front stoop. Thus garbed and strengthened, he asked the formal question; what is this paper? The deputy, who knew him as an honest citizen, was visibly embarrassed, yet exercised his duty by explaining that it was a notice of foreclosure as a result of non-payment. My father had missed three monthly payments because he had earned hardly anything for many months, and even the family diet had long since deteriorated. We all had been living in fear of this moment.

My father asked how much longer we had. The deputy almost begged us to understand there was nothing personal in what he was doing. He was receiving a $5 fee for serving the paper, and he lacked authority to alter the terms very much. Foreclosure called for expulsion within one week; he would try to get us an additional week's grace. The transaction done, we went back into the house; mother gathered the three children into her arms; then kissed her husband and tried to comfort his wounded manhood. From that moment on, she was the dominant personality in our family. She took charge of the major decisions, but was ever careful not to denigrate my father by any word or deed.

After we moved, to a small apartment in a nice neighborhood where many of my parents' friends lived, I announced that I was postponing entry into high school. I would seek a job in order to contribute to the family income. My father looked at me as though I had suddenly become a weird, unknown creature, then laughed uneasily, not knowing quite how to confront me and the situation. He decided to keep it light, shrugging off the suggestion, muttering half-inaudible comments about not being silly.

For my part, I felt patronized by anything less than a serious conversation. Here we were in terrible financial difficulty, and I was making a logical offer to help, to do my share. Immaturely, I escalated my tone and arguments, demanding that I be taken seriously and be allowed to try working at a job. I then made the fatal mistake of stating that school was not important in view of an empty larder.

With that, my father slapped me hard – very hard – across the cheek, as though to shock me back to some reality. Explaining that there were 13 million men out of work, five million of whom were selling apples on the streets, he asked, "If I am unable to earn enough, how do you expect to find any sort of work that would justify dropping out of school?" And then he patiently and lovingly talked about the importance of education to civilization and to the individual – as the only route by which one could move upward on the economic scale. You go on with your education, he said gently, and someday you will be able to help with the family budget. He never hit me again.

I entered tenth grade at Hillhouse High School, on the site where Silliman College of Yale University now stands, in September 1931, a few weeks before my 13th birthday. The next three years were to be the best I had known.

I studied Latin and German, literature and science, history and the social sciences, math and English. We were taught carefully to write and spell. Reading was impressed upon us as the basis of all knowledge; correct grammar marked one as a literate and civilized person. Speaking fluently, writing accurately, thinking logically, and above all reading with comprehension, a student could go forward to conquer a higher education. It was a joy to study in that wonderful school, where respect for intellectual achievement was firmly grounded. I have been thankful all my life for the abilities developed in those years, using that framework.

Extra-curricular opportunities also attracted me, and without my even realizing it, they helped me attain a self-confidence before audiences – a trait that became the basis of my entire public career. In school and out, my activities covered a broad range. Well endowed physically with height, stature, presence, and a rich, resonant voice, I assumed a leading role in the York Square Players, our school dramatic group, and achieved a high degree of onstage comfort. We did great classics and silly pleasantries, all of them fun and a wonderful experience.

I became president of the German Club without knowing that, years later, fate would place me in Germany, and facility with the language would turn out to be a substantial asset in the performance of dangerous and delicate tasks. The debating club became a second home. I loved the cut and thrust of argument and rebuttal. Here the powerful combination of intellect and oratory, brain and voice, provided thrill and pleasure, as well as an intuitive sense of what was necessary to convince others of the merit of one's case. I found, however, that I did much better when defending a position in which I believed heartily. I could then introduce the factor that I discovered was the most persuasive of all: passion, which supported intellect with the warmth of conviction, causing the voice to rise, the eyes to gleam, and the whole power of the body to be engaged. Passionate speaking became another personal trademark in my later life.

During this same period, I was very involved in the youth group of our conservative synagogue, B'nai Jacob, on George Street, which was remarkably advanced for its day and constituency. It had an organ, mixed seating for men and women, English-language readings during the service, an organized administration, a large membership, and a panoply of social-welfare interests beyond the exclusively "religious."

I found a ready place in the organization. The youth group had an active small cadre of boys and girls interested in and capable of traveling around Connecticut to attend similar programs with youth groups at other synagogues. I remember many pleasant trips and spent enjoyable Sundays in panel discussions, debates, and oratorical contests.

I found myself concentrating on the subject of Zionism, which seemed to me to be the right answer for the world's Jews of those perilous times. Hitler became chancellor on January 30, 1933, and Roosevelt was inaugurated the same day. Thus, in the middle of my junior year of high school, at the age of 14, I became aware of the clouds casting shadows on the fate of Jews and the world. Jewish sovereignty, national identity, and independent power, together with all the ancillary benefits they bestowed, were the goals our people should seek to counter threats to their existence.

In conversation as well as debate, I tried to warn against Hitler, while offering the positive solution of an independent Jewish state. Yet I often found myself addressing deaf ears. I was accused of exaggerating the danger of Hitler and overlooking the fact that support of Zionism could be construed as dual loyalty – to the U.S. and a Jewish state. Such was the mood of American Jews of those days.

What was the source of the ideas and conclusions I held so strongly at that early age? Many of them sprang from books, articles, journals and the like, for I was an active reader. But four individuals also had a strong influence. Two of them came from B'nai Jacob, the other two from Yale:

Rabbi Louis Greenberg stands out very clearly. Tall and dignified, impressive, patient and learned, over-worked but always available, he possessed depths I could scarcely imagine. A son of Eastern Europe, he adjusted to America in such full and vigorous measure that he preached his sermons in English, won a place of high repute in the general civic leadership, and ultimately earned a Ph.D. from Yale for *The Jews of Russia*, a two-volume work that remains useful today. Imagine the energy and devotion all that required. It was achieved while tending to a large congregation, without an assistant, and gaining the respect of the city at large. Rabbi Greenberg loved Judaism, taught it with love and skill, portrayed it as the mirror image of the Jewish people, and connected all three – faith, people and land – into an organic whole. This was his Zionism, and it is what I drew from him.

Charles Sudock, B'nai Jacob's cantor, was rotund and so short that he wore built-up heels to go with his tall, octagonal, clerical hat. Even then, he did not reach Greenberg's height. So when the two stood side by side at the altar, Cantor Sudock unsheathed his most powerful weapon, a tremendous *basso profundo* that shook the chandeliers and leveled the playing field between the two. The jolly Sudock captivated us youngsters, telling us about the concert stage and magical tours to far-away places.

He made no attempt to compete with Greenberg's brain or store of knowledge, but he agreed with the rabbi's Zionist conclusions and tried to teach us their importance through tales of the Polish and Russian villages he knew. How wonderful it would be, he pointed out, if Jews could own their land, instead of being tenant farmers for the local baron. Or, how marvelous if Jews could have their own weapons for defense whenever the peasants or Cossacks decided it was time for a little drunken sport or pogrom. Through such homespun homilies and dreams, Sudock turned the grand theories of nationalism and statehood into real-life reasons for espousing Zionism.

Moshe Bar Am, a Palestinian Jew in his mid-30s, was a graduate student at Yale, translating into English and creating a dictionary from Sumerian, Akkadian, and Babylonian cuneiforms, which archeologists had discovered on baked bricks in the Near East. In his day, there were very few scholars anywhere on earth who could read the wedge-shaped marks pressed into the wet clay more than 4,000 years earlier. To support himself during this exotic but non-lucrative pursuit, Moshe gave Hebrew lessons at the rate of 25 cents per hour. That was real money in my family, but my father felt the benefits were worth the price, and so did I. I learned some Hebrew. Mostly, however, I learned about Palestine, how the Jews lived, how the British ruled, how the Arabs resisted, and how it all might turn out.

Isaac Rabinowitz was tall, blond, Germanic looking and Germanic acting in the precision of his movements and exactness of his personality. His job at the Yale Graduate School included the translation and publication (by the university press) of many volumes of the philosophy of Maimonides.

Receiving from him the perspective of a scholar whose expertise was the medieval period, I learned of Spanish poets and Italian cartographers, the Crusades and the Inquisition. That material can make a deep impression on a boy, and it especially made one on me, with my romantic nature.

Those were the influences, the people, the times. High school and synagogue, father and mother, Hitler and Roosevelt – all did their work. The period drew to a close. I was selected as salutatorian of my high school graduating class and, to my delight, I received from Yale one of the prestigious, four-year scholarships the university granted to the local high school to strengthen the gown-town relationship.

My years at Yale were very hard. Needing to earn money, I took on afternoon and evening jobs. They were to be found in the coffee shops and sandwich places, the old Taft Hotel, and, during summers, in the emerging Howard Johnson chain. I often worked eight-hour shifts as a short-order cook, on my feet in a hot greasy kitchen, always finishing late in the evening, exhausted. The best assignment was waiter because it afforded free moments, when the dinner rush died down, to sit, smoke a quick cigarette, and catch one's breath.

Obviously, my studies suffered as a result. Classes began at 8 a.m. and finished by 1 p.m. Work started around 4. That three-hour "window" was my only real opportunity to do homework. Otherwise, I had to try to read and write after midnight, dead-tired. Most mornings, I arrived at class in a state of nervous fright. I was seldom, if ever, fully prepared, and feared being called upon. In spite of those conditions, I acquired a great deal of knowledge, good reading habits, and a love for learning that has endured for a lifetime.

I majored in International Relations, under Professor Arnold Wolfers, enjoyed that subject immensely, and found in it an intellectual path that conformed to my personal Jewish ideology. Unfortunately, the conditions in which I lived and worked doomed me to a mediocre transcript, and I graduated in 1938, at the age of 19, uncertain as to the next move.

I registered at the Columbia University Graduate School of Business in New York, found a counterman's job at a drugstore on Amsterdam Avenue, and started to learn accounting. Its attraction was simple. It was a profession at which I could earn a living. But I rather quickly concluded that I did not want to spend my life practicing accounting. I left Columbia at the end of the year, without earning the master's degree.

I was by now hundreds of dollars in debt, both to Yale and to Columbia, and it was apparent that the liquidation of these obligations had to take first priority. I simply had to stop thinking about career and destiny. My balance sheet was out of balance. So it was back to New Haven, to look for a job.

Two friends of my father's, Dave and Eddie Levine, had a factory in which they made mattresses, blankets, pads for wrapping furniture, and similar items. The Levine Bedding Co. was itself just emerging from the Depression, yet these good men did not hesitate to offer me employment. Their only fear was that I was overqualified, in view of my education, to work on a sewing machine. I assured them that desperate need would enable me to put my brain on hold and make my fingers nimble instead. The pay was 50 cents per hour, $4 per shift; I begged for two shifts per day, 16 hours for $8; working 6 days per week would give me $48. A 96-hour week was grinding, to say the least, but that was a princely sum, and I had nothing else to do with my time. I went back to live in an attic room in the house where my parents now had a comfortable apartment, forgot about books, spent almost no money, and saved enough by the end of the year to pay off all debts. Thank God!

It was September 1939. Hitler had invaded Poland. England and France had declared war. America was neutral, but should she be? Many of my fellow workers were Polish, some even recent immigrants, and their sense of outrage was high, their anguish real. They were careful not to criticize America, but they wondered why their adopted country was not more outspoken against Hitler. They sensed the industrial power of this nation. Here, in our little factory, orders were beginning to come in from the U.S. Army for blankets, sleeping bags, tarpaulins, and similar articles. Our workers executed these army requirements with zeal and enthusiasm. They saw their labor as fighting against Hitler, and they knew workers in other factories who felt the same way. In addition to the Poles, Levine bedding had many others who shared these sentiments: Russians, Slovaks, Hungarians, Jews.

On the other hand, the factory also had many Italians, who respected Mussolini as a leader taking his nation into the modern world (they didn't know or care about Ethiopia). If *Il Duce* was making an alliance with Hitler, that was all right with them: they did not want America to interfere.

Our 50 employees, groping to crystallize their political opinions, arguing, shouting, reading letters aloud to each other from folks back in the old countries, represented in microcosm what was happening all over the nation. America was not destined to enter the war until 27 months later, and then because of the Japanese, not Hitler. But the great majority of Americans were slowly and surely growing aware of the evil of Nazism.

For me, working in that factory was one of the most important educational experiences I could possibly have undergone. It cleared my thinking as to what I should be doing with my life. I should, I realized, be seeking a path toward arousing American Jews to strong action against Nazism and strong support for a sovereign Jewish state in Palestine.

CHAPTER TWO

A YOUNG RABBI WITH BOLD NEW IDEAS

At about the age of 20, I had two firm objectives that in a sense were really one: arousing the Jews of America toward massive efforts of rescue on behalf of Hitler's victims; and infusing much greater strength into the Zionist movement, whose ultimate purpose was to create an independent state for Jews. To work effectively toward such ends, one must have a platform, a place from which to shout, demand, exhort, inspire, educate. What better platform existed than a pulpit?

While my fingers flew automatically at the sewing machines in the Levine Bedding Company, my mind was free to think. Gradually, I concluded that the best route to my goals was the rabbinate. The decision stemmed not from any epiphany, conversion, or revelation of God. It was for me not a theological matter, but a sudden realization that what I really wanted was to become a civil servant of the Jewish people, leading them down the path of their survival. Once that realization dawned, my heart soared, my spirits lifted, and a vision emerged; I knew that this was the culmination of a process that had begun years earlier, with my mother's struggle over the affidavits for the three German boys.

So I returned to school, this time with no debts, but with a feeling of haste and a sense that I must prepare myself well, as quickly as possible. It was the summer of 1940, and Dachau (the first Nazi concentration camp) and

Kristallnacht (the "night of broken glass," when hundreds of synagogues and thousands of Jewish-owned stores were destroyed) were already two years old. Where should I enroll? Of all the Jewish religious movements, the one most natural and congenial for me was the Conservative, with which my home synagogue of B'nai Jacob was affiliated. I thus turned to the Jewish Theological Seminary, located in New York City.

I arranged an appointment with the chancellor, Dr. Louis Finkelstein, and had hardly entered his room before starting to pour out the emotional thoughts underlying my desire to study at the seminary. He interrupted, saying all that could come later; for now, he wanted to pose three significant questions. First, did I observe the Sabbath according to Jewish law? I answered in the negative. (Rabbi Greenberg had never asked me that question). Secondly, did I observe the dietary laws? I explained that our home had been kosher for about the first ten years of my life, but my mother had gradually abandoned the strict practice of the law. Third, did I observe the regulations regarding family purity? I told him I was not married, but if I were, the decision about going to *mikveh* (ritual bath) each month would be my wife's, not mine.

The chancellor then stated that my replies did not satisfy him. A rabbinical student in the Conservative movement should be a strict observer of religious law, he said, and I was therefore not a proper candidate for admission to his seminary. I thanked him for his time, then expressed my own feeling that this was not the proper seminary for me. I was upset that he was not the least bit interested in my thoughts or emotions concerning Hitler or Palestine.

As I walked down Broadway, my mind racing, weighing alternatives, I worked at calming myself. Two other American seminaries offered possibilities. One was the Hebrew Union College in Cincinnati, but that was not even an option. A Reform seminary, it was in my judgment so far to the left as to be almost non-Jewish. The administration and faculty were mainly anti-Zionist and anti-Hebrew, and I knew that the atmosphere of the school would run counter to most of my cherished ideals.

The other prospect was the Jewish Institute of Religion, a school established in Manhattan about 20 years earlier by Rabbi Stephen S. Wise on the premise of *Clal Yisrael* – in today's jargon, pluralism. The faculty was composed of persons from all branches of Judaism, as was the student body.

Some wore *kippot* (small skullcaps) in class, some did not. Every opinion was legitimate. Chapel services were warm and traditional. Wise himself was one of the earliest American Zionist leaders, active since the end of the 19th Century. All that now seemed appealing. So, from Broadway I cut straight over to Central Park West, sought an appointment at the JIR, and quickly enrolled there.

Its two leading personalities were impressive in every regard. They were Rabbi Wise, the president, and Dr. Henry Slonimsky, the dean. Each was powerful, magnetic, charismatic, charming, incandescent, fascinating, stimulating – no words wholly suffice. Wise was the worldly Jewish politician, founder of many organizations – among them the World Jewish Congress and its American branch – chairman of committees, president of fundraising campaigns, intimate associate of mayors, governors, senators, even President Roosevelt. He was also a key player on the international scene, having testified at the Versailles Conference of 1919 and at numerous World Zionist Congresses throughout Europe. He brought to us the wealth of his wisdom, judgment, and experience.

Every Thursday morning at 11, the entire student body, never more than 20 men, convened around the oval conference table for a class entitled "Problems of the Ministry." When we read that listing in the catalog, we assumed it would be our entry into the arcane mysteries of our trade – e.g., how to comfort the dying, conduct a wedding, deal with a synagogue's board of trustees, stick to a budget, or any of the other practical matters of which we were ignorant and therefore afraid.

Instead, the class began with Dr. Wise imperiously ordering the youngest man in the room (always me) to run to the corner for a box of five-cent cigars. Then, when myriad clouds of smoke were fouling the room, he would shout that the windows were to be opened wide. (Much of his life was spent in smoke-filled rooms.) Out of his inner pocket would come the latest telegram he had sent to President Roosevelt or received from Geneva. With it in hand, he was off and running on the latest intrigue or road-block or double-cross in the intricate game of the State Department Arabists who were refusing visas to frantic Jewish refugees, or the British who were appeasing the Mufti in

Jerusalem, or American Jewish organizations that were opposing him because they felt he was too direct and undiplomatic in his demands.

As far as Wise was concerned, if those matters were not in the forefront of a rabbi's mind, that rabbi was merely a sacerdotal clerk. Wise wanted his pupils to help move the Jewish people through history, not merely serve them through the rites of life. In all, he was a towering figure – both physically and spiritually – the best-known and most-respected Jewish public person in the first half of the 20th Century.

Dr. Slonimsky, the dean, was the soul and brain of the school. Tall, white-haired, declaiming as he strode back and forth before his classes, he was as close to the image of a Greek philosopher as a modern man could be. Greek philosophy is actually what Slonimsky had studied at Marburg University in Germany, along with Jewish philosophy under Hermann Cohen.

The dean was in love with *Midrash* (biblical commentary), but also with life. "Judaism is not an ascetic religion," he would thunder. "Taste all of life – art, nature, women, wine, tragedy, comedy – taste it, and then you will know what it is all about, and perhaps you will be able to explain it to your congregants."

Whatever I thought and still think about God, I drew from Slonimsky. He was most troubled by the problem of theodicy, that is, how to reconcile the goodness and justice of God with the existence of evil and suffering in the world. Although the fires of Auschwitz were not yet burning, and the crystals of Zyklon B were still in their canisters in the Rhineland factories, the shadow of destruction hovered over Europe's Jews. And hovering over the head of Slonimsky were some key questions gnawing away at his faith in God.

It was then not fashionable to speak of God as being dead; that phrase lay a quarter-century in the future. Rather, the questions were, does God know?; does He care?; why doesn't He intervene?; does He even exist?; is He powerless? The Orthodox among us were secure in their faith. God was not a mystery for them. But Slonimsky's efforts rescued the faltering and the doubt ridden. Speaking for myself, he gave me a God-concept that has served me all my life and enabled me to work with enthusiasm and optimism, in spite of all the horrors – Jewish and general – that lay ahead in our century.

Slonimsky's theory was simple. He invented the phrase "limited or finite" to describe God. It is not that God is absent or uncaring or occupied with bigger problems or powerless. To remove God completely from the universe would leave man hopelessly and helplessly alone. That's unthinkable. So God must remain as a factor. But man must be realistic and not expect too much. God is not infinite, omnipotent, omniscient. He is limited, limited by the fact that He gave man free will. God does not do the evil – God's creature does, and God, having destroyed man once, promised not to do it again.

Hence, God is limited by his own creation, and cannot prevent or undo or mitigate the evil performed by this creature. God's power is finite, not infinite. The promise that this condition will change is implicit in the word of the prophet Zechariah, who said that in some future day (the time of the Messiah?) God will be One, and His name will be One. But God is not yet One, in spite of the *Shema* (the most basic daily prayer – "Hear O Israel, God is our Lord, God is One"); He is not whole, united, or in full control. Thus his power is not complete, says the prophet, but it will be.

Richard Aldington, the English literary critic, once wrote a paragraph about Slonimsky, describing him as a person who spoke books better than most people wrote them. That was the magic of the man. Words and ideas flowed from him in a rushing, tumbling stream, carrying the listener along as though on a raft racing through a canyon, adrenaline pounding, just missing the rocks, and finally slowing down and drifting into a placid, level pool where he could catch a breath and savor the experience.

We had many other fine teachers, but Wise and Slonimsky left us the richest heritage. When the school disappeared years later, in a merger with the Hebrew Union College after Wise's death, those two men never faded from memory; and their photographs have always remained on my wall. And even though the school ultimately merged, it lasted long enough to do its essential job of permanently influencing the direction of the Reform movement in America, which became more Zionist in its mood and more traditional in its practices.

To its credit, the merged institution was the first rabbinical seminary in the United States to require that its students spend a year in Jerusalem, to learn the land and the language. The Conservative movement followed suit some years later. The 200 or so graduates of the JIR leavened American Reform Judaism.

They influenced their colleagues and congregants, the Central Conference of American Rabbis and the Union of American Hebrew Congregations. They introduced to the Reform ranks a healthy respect for Jewish tradition and for those who practice it.

In June 1941 I married Elaine Schwartz of Meriden, Connecticut, whom I had met back in our high school days when I visited the synagogue youth group in her community. During the years I attended Yale, she was at Wellesley, and then went on to the Yale school of drama. After her graduation, we rented a one bedroom apartment on West 74th Street and set up housekeeping.

Dr. Wise was a one-man placement office, seeking opportunities for his "boys" to obtain pulpits. By the summer of 1943, my class had been at its studies for three full years, with no vacations, and was more than ready to be placed. Several of us were eager to volunteer for military chaplaincies. But even that required one year of practical experience in a congregation before the War Department would grant a commission.

In July, Wise told me I was going to Denver's Temple Emanuel, as assistant to the senior rabbi, Abraham Feinberg. He told me nothing of Feinberg and the congregation, only that this was the choicest assignment at his disposal, and since I was one of his favorite students, he wanted me to have it. He hinted mysteriously that there might be more favorable future developments.

The Denver congregation was one of the oldest and largest reform temples in the country. It had been established by Simon Guggenheim and other German Jews in 1874, two years before Colorado became a state. In 1889, Rabbi William S. Friedman became the spiritual leader, serving for 50 years, until a stroke he suffered on a California golf course led to his death. During his half-century in the pulpit, Friedman (no relation to me) became one of the most important men in all of Colorado, not only in its Jewish community. He cut an imposing figure as he walked along Denver's 17th Street, garbed in top hat, Prince Albert coat with white piping on the vest, silver-headed cane in his firm grasp. The members of his congregation basked in their association with him. Thus, his word was law, his opinion sacrosanct; his decisions immutable, his pronouncements divine. His aura encompassed two complete generations.

The shock of Friedman's death reverberated as though it were a Richter 7. What would the congregation do? How could it get along without him?

Having had no need in any living memory to go rabbi-hunting, the members did not know where to turn. The confusion resulted in their accepting a recommendation that they hire Rabbi Abraham Feinberg, which they did, apparently without looking deeply into his background or temperament. Over the ensuing three years, arguments between Feinberg and the congregation escalated and multiplied, until it became questionable as to whether he should remain.

When I arrived at the Temple, the Feinberg situation had been festering for months. Dr. Wise had not told me about it. Either he didn't know himself, or he preferred to keep it secret, lest the news dissuade me from taking the position.

Upon arrival, I asked Feinberg if there was anything he wanted me to do at the following Friday evening's service. His curt reply was that he had no intention of appearing and that I could do whatever I wanted. The only person to whom I could turn for help and advice was the temple's executive secretary, Samuel Rose, who quickly became my confidant and mentor. He said I should simply conduct the service with no reference to Feinberg, no explanations, no apologies – just be myself.

It took some courage, but I did it, and the next Friday and the next. As we marched through July, and into August, I was still performing the services. We were only a few weeks away from the High Holy Days of September, and what was supposed to happen then? Again Sam Rose came to the rescue. He told me that I was making a powerful impact, a development that pleased him: attendance at the summer services was reaching unprecedented heights, and that was restoring the congregation's morale. Rose also said he was convinced that, even though I was very young, not yet 25, I could handle the Holy Days and the fulltime job.

So Rose went to work. In short order, I was approached by the congregation's president, who invited me to become the senior and only rabbi – Rabbi Feinberg would be leaving – and to take charge of the High Holy Days. Would I be willing?

I was naturally overwhelmed. Here I was, with the shortest tenure ever as an assistant, a mere six weeks, being offered a post ministering to more than a thousand families, just before the holidays. What about sermons? music?

readers? Torah selections? I had nothing prepared. I had never dreamed that the dénouement would come with such abruptness.

I told the president how flattered I was and then sketched the facts of my situation; I was determined to become a military chaplain, so I would remain at the temple for only one year. Further, I would not spend the year passively but would argue vigorously for my ideologies, beginning during the High Holy Days, when my audiences would be the largest. That might upset many members of the congregation, for this incarnation of Rabbi Friedman was an exact opposite of the previous one, and I would surely be guilty of lése majesté.

The temple officials' final decision came quickly and affirmatively. After that, I had no hesitation about preaching a Holy-Days series of sermons that outlined my credo. The core of the series was Jewish nationalism, and the presentation went as follows:

Of course we are a religion, but more than that, we are a culture, a civilization, a tribe of people with a history, a language, and a land. The total of those characteristics can be summed up in the word – "nation." Although we're American in nationality and citizenship, every Jew in the world has a two-faceted identity: as a citizen of the country of birth or residence; and a member of the Jewish nation, practicing its unique religion, learning its unique language, tied by memory to its most ancient heritage, bound by love and reverence to its ancestral land. In that sense, every Jew in the world is the same. Thus, a French Jew is the same as other Frenchmen in some aspects, but quite different from them in others.

This analysis poses a dilemma for American Jews who do not want to be different from other Americans in any degree. If they agree that they possess a double identity, they fear that might lead to their being accused of divided loyalty. In the 1930s and '40s, that issue was the principal argument used by those who opposed the Zionist goal. In the main, American Jews in those years, not long after their own migration and seeking desperately to become absorbed in the new world, wanted nothing more than to be considered like all others – Germans and Slavs, Italians and Scandinavians – who were struggling to sink roots and become just plain Americans. The early sociological theories spoke of a "melting pot" in which everyone homogenized into one type. Jews did not want to be told they had two identities.

So there I was, in Denver, telling members of "my" Jewish congregation something they really did not want to hear, something that William Friedman had preached against for a half-century. He told them they were not a nation, but Americans whose religion was slightly different from other religions. Aside from that, they were not different in any detail. He was against Jewish nationhood, the Hebrew language, outmoded Oriental customs such as Bar Mitzvah and wearing a head covering indoors. He believed in eliminating any practice or any train of thought that did not float in mainstream Americanism.

I was therefore an enigma to the Jews of Temple Emanuel, and although I understood their dilemma, I gave no quarter. They must be taught the new reality that the Nazi genocide and the Jewish state-to-come would impose upon them when the war was over. They must be intellectually and emotionally equipped to accommodate the future, not fight against it.

While continuing to preach and teach my fundamental principles to the Denver congregation, I built bridges and created a network of friends and contacts all over town. I was seen more and more publicly with Manuel Laderman, the city's Orthodox rabbi, and invited him to share the platform when I was installed by Dr. Wise in a magnificent ceremony attended by thousands. I think that was the first time the temple had ever had an orthodox person, wearing a *kippa* (skull cap), on its altar. I became friendly, even close, with two of Denver's prominent Protestant ministers, Paul Roberts, dean of the Episcopal Cathedral, and Jacob Trapp of the Unitarian Church. Mayor Quigg Newton, Governor Lee Knous, and the editor and publisher of the *Denver Post,* Palmer Hoyt, were among the key public figures who gave important support to Jewish causes.

My congregants liked that because it was in the mold of the former Friedman, with an important difference. I was winning over those non-Jews to the new ideas outlined above, and that helped me win over my own reluctant members. In fact, I developed a friendship with a remarkable man: Dr. Carl Hermann Voss, then of Omaha, the first executive director of the newly formed American Christian Palestine Committee. Voss was a learned Methodist minister, a Christian who took Judaism seriously as the source of his own religion, a lover of the Jewish heritage and a passionate supporter of the

Zionist idea. We remained friends for almost 50 years, until his death, seeing eye to eye on almost every issue.

As the year progressed, it became increasingly clear to me that I had to deal with a problem that my own opinions had exacerbated: an irreconcilable split in the congregation between about 100 of the oldest, most socially prominent, founding families and the large majority that had gradually embraced my point of view about Jewish nationhood.

Some analysts described it as a split between the old, aristocratic German families and the nouveaux Polish and Russian Jews who had swarmed into the membership during the past decade or so. That phenomenon was occurring in Reform congregations all over the country, and Denver was no exception. Whether the split was sociological or ideological, it made no sense to apply any social glue, for the patch would inevitably come apart.

I therefore encouraged the secession of the small group. I offered to help its members establish a new congregation and to give them a Torah scroll, and I kept emphasizing the benefits that homogeneity would bring. The new congregants could be as anti-Zionist as they wished, without feeling stifled, and they could find a rabbi with congenial ideas that would not irritate them. I, too, would have a more peaceful environment within which to continue my re-education efforts. All that came to pass, and by the time I left for the Army, at the end of my year, Denver had two Reform temples.

One other episode should be mentioned. A strongly anti-Zionist, national organization had been established by a group of Reform rabbis, and that group created a new organization called the American Council for Judaism. Its purpose was to resist Zionism by stressing the ideology that defined Judaism as a religion only. The ACJ formed chapters in many cities.

A very strong chapter had developed in my own congregation, and while most of the ACJ adherents left to join the new Reform temple, their influence in mine still remained enormous. For one thing, some old families retained memberships in both congregations.

All that came to a head one week after I left Denver, when the executive director of the ACJ, Rabbi Elmer Berger, came to my temple at the invitation of local ACJ leaders to denounce me, from my own pulpit, for the treasonable Zionist doctrines I was expounding. Berger, who resisted every effort to persuade him to enlist in the chaplaincy, had the effrontery to call me a "bad American" because I was preaching dual loyalty. He, the good American, refused to don his country's uniform; he, the true Jew, refused to join the battle against Hitler; but he found it perfectly ethical to attack me while I was en route to Army Chaplains School at Ft. Devens, Mass.

The blatant inconsistency of Berger's personal position, and that of the ACJ as a whole, was evidenced by their mutual failure to convert the great mass of Reform Jews across America to their point of view. A year or so after his appearance, when I was stationed in Germany, I received an interesting letter. It was signed by the president of Denver's ACJ chapter, a member of my congregation well known to me. He wrote in part:

> Just thought I would drop you a line and tell you we are all looking forward to your return. I am writing you this letter on the stationery of the American Council for Judaism, Inc., so as to squelch all rumors, of which I am sure there are plenty, that this organization had plans for doing away with your services on your return. As President I can assure you that this is furthest from our thoughts, and I want you to get the information first-hand. Kindest regards from everyone in Denver.
>
> Sincerely, ...

CHAPTER THREE

THE ARMY: THIS WAS MY WAR

When a civilian takes an oath and dons a military uniform, he undergoes inner confusion, loss of self, and transformation into someone new. For a newly minted officer with no previous military exposure, not even college ROTC, the disorientation is compounded by the badges of rank, and the feeling of being Alice going into the hole becomes even more intense.

Further, no one knows that the uniform is one hour old and that the warrior has been nowhere. Thus the costume suggests a thousand things as yet unborn, while underneath it, the neophyte knows he is still his virginal self. If this situation is awkward in a civilian setting of town and street, imagine what it must be in a military setting of camp and barracks.

I entered the gate at Ft. Devens to register at the Chaplain School and was immediately faced with a salute from the guard sergeant, who expected to receive one in return. Never having done that before, I didn't know whether the angle of my fingers was correct, whether I had waited too long, or whether my cap was on straight. In the next hundred yards, this embarrassment was repeated a dozen times, and instead of feeling more acclimatized, I grew more disoriented. My first lieutenant's bars established my status in everyone's eyes except mine. I, who could keep a thousand people spellbound with a stream of oratory, felt so uncertain that I could only search in desperation for the nearest building, in order to get indoors where saluting was not required.

As mystifying as the rules of behavior, stance, and bearing were the courses that composed the curriculum. During the course of six weeks, we were expected to master the following basic subjects:

- Practical Duties
- Courtesies and Customs
- Graves Registration and Military Funerals
- Map Reading and Aerial Photography
- Chemical Warfare
- Army Organization
- Military Law
- First Aid for Wounded
- Army Postal Service (and Censorship)
- Special Lectures (includes Red Cross, GI Bill, Tolerance, Command of Negro Troops, Venereal Disease Prevention, etc.)

It was impossible to learn all that – and the multitude of other topics listed in the chaplain's manual. Most of my colleagues had been through college, knew how to study, and tried their best. But only when we were posted to our assignments did we find out how small a fraction of the surface we had scratched. None of the above had anything to do with the real duties that would be required of us: easing pain; comforting young men who were frightened, homesick, or dying; explaining what the war was about and why it had to be fought; figuring out how to answer questions about God in the face of all the mud and murder, and listening, just listening, which was probably the most important contribution we could make.

Chaplains School and regular military training ended. Our uniforms were no longer costumes cloaking neophytes. We felt like real soldiers. Crowding around the bulletin board on the last day, I found myself assigned to the 69th ITR (Infantry Training Regiment) at Camp Blanding, Florida, which needed a Jewish chaplain because of its large contingent of men from Brooklyn and the Bronx. I looked forward to joining and serving them.

The camp was situated near Gainesville, then a piney-woods town about 60 miles southwest of Jacksonville, in the middle of nowhere. The commanding general greeted me warmly and escorted me to my new home, a white clapboard chapel with a tall steeple and a lovely plot of grass – a bit of Vermont in the deep south. A standard U.S. Army chapel has a small foyer and a main sanctuary, behind which are three offices and a storage room. This religious triad is a military concept reflecting the absolute equality of Catholic, Protestant, and Jew. Never mind that the three faiths encompass vastly different numbers of troops; in one of those miraculous American concepts that we take for granted, each of the three is assured religious equality. That precept extends far beyond the Army. When an American President is inaugurated, prayers are offered by a minister, a priest, and a rabbi. It is as though the Jews are considered one-third of the American population, when in reality they are less than two percent.

In our snug little chapel, we chaplains quickly developed a working relationship, helping each other in all manner of chores. Another wonderful aspect of the Army was the notion that a chaplain's basic responsibility was to *all* the men in his command; while it was understood that he had a particular responsibility to the men of his own faith, he had to be capable of transcending religious differences. Visiting men in the hospital or the stockade was a universal duty, having nothing to do with the patient's or prisoner's personal religion, so every chaplain did that. Giving a lecture on V.D. to a platoon was also non-denominational. So was conducting a bull session on some aspect of the War in Europe or the Pacific; it depended on the chaplain's knowledge of geopolitics and military events, not whether he had a cross or a Star of David on his lapel.

So it went. On Friday afternoons, the Protestant chaplain helped me take down the Christian insignia with which the chapel was decorated, put them away neatly in the storage room, and take out the Ark with Torah, candles, and *kiddush* (goblet and wine) tray for the Sabbath Eve service. Then, on Sunday morning, I helped the Catholic chaplain put up his crucifix and set out his chalice, patten, and missal. Day after day, week after week, we lived in a style of mutual respect and cooperation that was itself a lesson to the enlisted men and officers who saw us.

The camp held many training regiments, consisting of tens of thousands of troops, and they all had to negotiate the obstacle courses that were scattered over the extensive grounds and woods. The most daunting maneuver involved crawling under barbed wire stretched 15 inches above the ground, with live machine-gun fire 15 inches above that. I made it a special point to watch where my own regiment, the 69th, was scheduled to be, and whenever one of its units, no matter how small, was slated for the live-fire exercise, I was there. At first, there was an obvious unspoken question among the men; what is a chaplain doing here? Is this maneuver so dangerous that he's trying to boost our morale?

But when they saw that I was as helmeted as they were, and intended to crawl the course with them, the expressions of concern gave way to warm welcomes. The men joked and relaxed, and I was pleased to feel like a veteran whose conduct put them at ease.

The tour at Blanding also included a Rosh Hashanah service which I conducted for more than 1,000 Jewish personnel. It was held in a hangar in the city of St. Augustine, because no hall on our own base was large enough. Organizing the details seemed endless, but the reaction of the men was so positive as to make all the work worthwhile. When my Blanding stint ended, I was transferred to Camp Miles Standish, back in Massachusetts, to prepare for overseas assignment.

I spent several anxious days waiting for that assignment. Rumor had it that most of our troops would be sent to the Pacific for the final push against Japan. I wanted very much to be sent to Germany, because the themes that constituted my spiritual core would unfold in Europe and the Near East, not the Far East.

I telephoned the Chaplaincy Commission of the Jewish Welfare Board, soliciting their intervention with the War Department. The executive director, Rabbi Philip Bernstein of Rochester, N.Y., was known to me, and I begged him to use his influence. I'm certain that Bernstein did whatever he could, and I added my own earnest prayers. When my orders specified Camp Standish as the destination, I rejoiced. Standish was near Boston, which logically indicated Europe. (Of course, logic does not always determine army personnel decisions; two Japanese-speaking officers were later on board our troopship bound for France.)

We sailed from Boston on a Liberty ship, and for eight days and nights I was seasick, losing the opportunity to join one of the non-stop poker games and become a rich man. I ate only saltines and oranges, vomited frequently, and tried to concentrate on what lay ahead.

RESCUE
IN EUROPE

CHAPTER FOUR

A PRIEST WHO OUTWITTED THE GESTAPO

Landing at Le Havre, on the Normandy coast, we were trucked from the badly bombed port to a nearby replacement depot containing thousands of officers with no duties except to search the bulletin board for their destinations. The depot was so huge that it was subdivided into separate camps, each named for a different cigarette. I wound up in Philip Morris, in an eight-man tent.

During the process of drawing equipment from the quartermaster hut, signing endless papers, and simply being swept along in a tide of men, moving from medical unit, to paymaster to Post Exchange to Army Post Office, I gradually developed great respect for the military orderliness that existed in the midst of massive confusion. I am uncertain what comparison to make with civilian life. What corporation or institution is required to handle a constantly moving group of hundreds of thousands of people, keep track of their whereabouts, feed and clothe them, deliver their mail, and keep them supplied with the tools of their trade – all of that requiring a supply line thousands of miles long? While there were constant foul-ups, shortages, and mistakes, on the large scale of the millions of soldiers, sailors and airmen involved in World War II, let it be recorded to the credit of the Army that most of the time the toilet paper and Coca-Cola, as well as the ammunition, reached their destinations correctly.

We entered the camp as bewildered individuals, went through the rapid processing, and were expelled on the other end like sausages from the grinding machine, carrying a mountain of stuff, à la Boy Scouts off on an outing. We were given helmet and gas mask, canteen and flashlight, .45 Colt automatic and M-1 carbine, bedroll and field pack, K-rations and C-rations, raincoat and boots, etc., etc., all of it either draped on our bodies or shoved into the duffel bags we carried everywhere. Loaded into the workhorse GMC 1 ½-ton truck, affectionately known as a 6-by because of its six wheels, we were driven from France up into Belgium and dumped into another officers' replacement depot near the small town of Namur, there to wait until someone figured out where to send us.

In Namur, I had my first contact with Nazi persecution. The episode was on a small, human scale, easy to comprehend and feel. Later there would be macro-events, but here I was able to absorb all the nuances and possibilities, the danger and the goodness of the individual resisting. The story revolved around one good man, so the ending left you with a feeling of hope and optimism, even though the cruelty of the Nazis was enormous.

Walking down the narrow main street, I saw a Star of David hand-drawn on the dusty window of an abandoned store. The door yielded, and beyond the empty front room, I found another room containing some chairs, a small cabinet, a framed picture of a priest, and Monsieur Burauck, sitting behind a small table. The place was dim and dingy, but the smile spreading across his pinched face as he recognized the Tablets of the Law on my uniform gave a glow to what turned out to be a tiny synagogue.

M. Burauck was its caretaker, one of Namur's very few Jewish survivors. He showed me the Torah scroll in the Ark (the cabinet which held the scroll) and told me how he and the members of the congregation had hidden it from the Nazis during the long years of occupation. Pinned to the wall below the priest's picture, I noticed faded flowers and the inscription, "This man is one of the saints of the world." It was written in Flemish, an exact translation of the Hebrew phrase "*Chasidei oomot ha-olam*," which is applied to non-

Jews who, at mortal danger to themselves, have saved the lives of persecuted Jews.

In Israel today, such persons are greatly honored by the government. They're presented with a medal and asked to plant a tree at Yad Vashem, the National Holocaust Memorial Museum, on a long *Allée des Justes*. The foot of each tree bears the name and nationality of the person so honored. These Righteous Gentiles are nominated by Jews whom they actually saved. Each case is investigated as carefully as possible. As space for additional trees became unavailable, a large wall was erected on which new names are continually inscribed. The total number of Righteous Gentiles has reached, at the time of this writing, 14,706.

When I remarked that it was most unusual to find the picture of a Catholic priest on a synagogue wall, M. Burauck offered tea and told me a fabulous story. Father André was Namur's parish priest. His parish house was located in the center of town, right alongside the Hotel Horscamp. When the German armies overran Belgium in 1940, the Gestapo requisitioned the hotel and used it as a headquarters. Approximately 40 Gestapo officers lived and worked there, and many of them, professing Catholics, became friendly with the priest next door.

In an effort to win his friendship and confidence, they invited him to their quarters and in turn forced their presence on him in his refectory. Father André permitted the intrusions and accepted the invitations, because he had a well-hidden motive of his own. He was one of the leaders of the underground in that part of Belgium, and his apparent friendship with the Gestapo served as a marvelous cover for those activities.

One of the most important aspects of the underground's work was to help Jewish and other refugees escape from the Nazi murderers. Father André's parish house became a way station on that underground railroad. Under the very noses of his Gestapo neighbors, the priest gave refuge and food to the terrified victims who had been directed to the haven of his four walls.

It became his custom to shelter these fugitives in his own bedroom, often in his own bed. On one occasion, he had 22 refugees in his house, awaiting nightfall so they could move on to the next underground station. Suddenly, in the middle of the afternoon, three of the Gestapo officers entered his house without warning, seeking a bottle of cool wine. With calm courage, he stalled them at the entrance hall long enough to enable the refugees to hustle into his bedroom. The three Nazis then sat in his courtyard drinking for an hour, and he stayed with them so they would not go wandering through the house. If they had found the Jews, it would not only have meant their and Father André's deaths but also the destruction of a link in the chain of underground stations and workers who were fighting the Holocaust.

On another occasion, some 15 officers were sitting around Father André's refectory table, carousing and drinking, when a servant slipped up to him and whispered that at the back door stood five Jewish children who would have to be smuggled into the house and kept overnight. The priest excused himself from the table, brought the children through a corridor in the cellar and took them into his bedroom, where they found a few hours of rest and managed to fall asleep in spite of the drunken shouts of their sworn enemies in the next room.

When Belgium was at last liberated and the Nazis driven out, Father André could finally admit the work he had been doing. A tabulation revealed that he had harbored in his own home more than 200 Jewish refugees, most of them children under the age of 15. Shortly after the end of the War, when the priest's birthday came around, the tiny remnant of Namur's Jews gathered to decide on the most suitable birthday present for this beloved man. One sunny, morning, in a large cart, they carried it to his house – a new bed! It was, they explained, a symbol of their appreciation for the fact that for several years he had almost never slept in his own bed, giving it to others at great risk. A new one would now launch him into a new era of freedom and peace.

As a final gesture, the small group of Jews asked for Father André's photograph to enshrine in their holiest place – on the wall of the synagogue, right next to the Ark. Father André came to the synagogue the day they hung the picture, and as they tearfully thanked him for what he had done, he replied that he had simply been doing the will of the Lord in helping his neighbors.

When M. Burauck finished his story, I had tears in my own eyes – for the terrorized children, for the noble priest, and for the hope of a future in which the ideal of a genuine brotherhood of man would become universal. If only we would carry over into peacetime the kind of conduct that some people pursue under the pressure of wartime – man helping fellow man.

CHAPTER FIVE

BAVARIA: DEATH ON THE ROADS

Time: Fall, 1945 – The War ended five months ago.

Place: Southern Bavaria, a rural area extending from Munich south to the foothills of the Alps; dark, wild forests, lakes, small villages, and underground Nazi munitions factories, no longer operative.

M y purpose was to rescue wandering, homeless, traumatized Jews who had survived Hitler's horrors – gas chambers, mass shootings, incinerators – and were now seeking places of refuge. They were hungry, weary – and for good reason – frightened.

To carry out this singular rescue mission, we drove our trucks slowly along back roads, picking up survivors, 50 to a load. We then found a barn, shed, partially destroyed house, garage, stable, or any other place of shelter, and left the refugees there under the care of one of our armed men, until we could find a larger place to hold the several truck-loads we brought together for better security. Next, we supplied our "guests" with food, water and blankets, obtained from quartermaster supplies. This constituted "rescue" in the most elementary meaning of the word.

The task was dangerous and difficult because paramilitary remnants of German units, calling themselves Edelweiss, after the local flower, were hiding in the forests, trying to kill U.S. soldiers and fleeing Jews. Also on the loose were desperate Nazi civilian bureaucrats trying to avoid capture by U.S. troops. To assault my convoy of U.S. trucks, with its armed soldiers filled with the confidence of victors, the Nazi paramilitaries employed sniping tactics rather than large-scale confrontation.

Regardless of the danger, this rescue work was exactly what I wanted to do. I had been distressed for years by the failure of American Jews and Western democracies to prevent or at least reduce the great slaughter of European Jewry. At least I could now help to pick up the broken pieces. I felt fulfilled by every truckload of ravaged survivors my men and I managed to bring to safety. I don't know where God was during the Holocaust, but this work of succor was as close to godlike as anything I had done so far in life.

Our mission developed in the backwash of the destruction of Hitler's war machine. Germany was in chaos. The bombed-out cities were choked with the rubble of collapsed buildings. Piles of brick and stone reached several feet in height. Streets were impassable for vehicles. Even pedestrians could only pick their way through single-file lanes. People spent most of their time poking through the ruins for usable furniture, and tiny, impromptu markets were set up by farmers selling food, clothing, candles, and kerosene. The oncoming winter of 1945 would be frightful; there was no fuel except for broken pieces of wood scattered among the brick piles or the interiors of bombed buildings.

To top it all off, there were *ten million* refugees clogging the roads of Germany and invading the shattered cities, looking for food and shelter. They included former conquered civilians – Russians, Poles, French, Dutch, Belgians, Norwegians, and other nationalities – as well as former prisoners of war and slave laborers in German armaments factories. The U.S. Army was the only institution sufficiently strong and organized to handle this flood of liberated but desperate humanity. So the Army fed them, in America's beautiful Judeo-Christian tradition of taking care of one's fellow man.

The only lasting solution was repatriation to the countries of origin. But it would take almost a year before the Army got the refugees sorted out and sent back home. One large group – the Jews – had no country to call home. Eastern Europe, from which most Jews came, was a huge cemetery, and they refused to return to the country of Auschwitz and Treblinka, Sobibor and the Warsaw

Ghetto. Since they could not be repatriated anywhere, they accepted the only alternative – to wait in Displaced Persons (DP) camps on German and Austrian soil until they had their own nation, a development that was far from assured.

The U.S. Army was confounded by this flood of unwanted civilians, and had no training or guidance in handling it. Furthermore, battle-weary officers and troops, who wanted to be demobilized and go home themselves, resented these foreigners whose languages they could not understand and on whose account they were being delayed. The American troops were quite rough with the refugees in the summer and fall of 1945.

Because of that mood, plus some too-hasty planning, errors were made as large numbers of refugees were thrown together in makeshift camps while awaiting processing. Fights erupted in some of the camps. Czechs didn't get along with Slovaks (never mind that both had suffered from the Nazis). Lithuanians hated Russians. Poles showed their longstanding hostility to Jews, who fought back.

Gradually, the refugee populations were separated, and the long trains started to roll in all directions. At the same time, the Army realized that the Jews should be placed in their own, homogeneous camps, because without a country, they would have the longest wait of all.

At the very apex of United States Forces in the European Theater (USFET), and filtering down through Headquarters Command, the Army's attitude toward the Jewish DPs was compassionate, understanding, and patient. General Joseph T. McNarney, General Eisenhower's successor as the top commander in Europe, granted a Charter of Recognition to the Central Committee of Liberated Jews in Germany, an overall body representing a quarter of a million DPs in 64 camps. The charter established the official relationship between the Army and the Jews in the most positive terms, spelling out the rights and duties of each party. Even higher up, in Washington, the Secretary of War decided to provide the commanding general in Germany a special adviser (with the rank of major-general) to help him solve any problems that might arise with or from the Jewish DPs. I was later appointed to serve as deputy to the adviser.

In the fall of 1945, as a chaplain with the rank of first lieutenant, I was assigned to the 9th Infantry Division, part of the Third Army that had been commanded by General George Patton. Division headquarters was located in the small Bavarian town of Wasserburg-am-Inn. This was not far from Hitler's redoubt at Berchtesgaden, the famed Eagle's Nest on top of a mountain, from which he could look out for miles over Austria (his birthplace) and the Italian Alps. It was a view that nourished Hitler's megalomania, and the first time I stood in the frame of his glass-less picture window, 25 feet long and 15 feet high, in the bomb-blasted house, I could understand why it was his favorite place.

At 9th Division headquarters, I turned to the motor pool, to make the acquaintance of those whose help I would need to carry out the plan I had made to rescue wandering Jewish refugees. Sure enough, I found the one man who could provide me with the essentials – trucks, drivers, gasoline – and the paperwork to legitimize their use. He was a master sergeant from Pennsylvania, a caring Jew who listened carefully and immediately and unequivocally promised to deliver. He hated Nazis, knew enough about the recent destruction of European Jewry, and wanted to do anything he could to help the survivors.

My plan was fairly simple. I wanted a small fleet of GMC trucks, the "6-bys," to patrol the back roads of Bavaria, especially the long, deserted roads through the heavy forests and around the many lakes between Munich and Garmisch-Partenkirchen. The patrols would pick up any refugees on these roads and bring them to safety and sustenance.

That section of southern Bavaria was well known as a hiding place. Even Hitler had tried to hide here, in November 1923, on the night his attempted putsch in Munich failed. A friend, Putzi Hanfstaengel (a graduate of Harvard) drove Hitler to the family villa deep in the forest on a lake south of Munich and hid him in the attic. Two days later, the police arrived, arrested Hitler, and imprisoned him in Landsberg, where he wrote *Mein Kampf.*

American Army jeeps were usually driven with the windshield folded down onto the hood, so that the machine gun mounted between the two front seats could have a free field of fire. That left the driver and gunner exposed and prompted a deadly maneuver by the Edelweiss guerillas: stringing piano wire very tautly across the roads at the height of a seated man's neck. At 50 miles per hour, that wire hitting the Adam's apple could decapitate, and it sometimes did.

(An order was given, after several such episodes, forbidding the folding down of windshields.) But as dangerous as the Edelweiss Nazis were to American soldiers, they were far more so to unarmed refugees.

Since my scheme was not a military mission, I couldn't simply ask the division transport officer to provide vehicles and personnel. As an underground operation of sorts, it depended on that Jewish sergeant, who dug around among his friends looking for volunteer drivers, manipulated his records so that a certain number of trucks were always off the duty roster and "in repair," and always had some drums of fuel available for our little fleet.

One by one, I took the drivers out on trial runs, teaching them how to ask the ragged wanderers if they were Jewish, what concentration camps they had been in, what countries they came from originally, in what towns they were born. I also taught them some reassuring Hebrew words, especially from familiar prayers like the *Shema* or the *Kaddish*. It was all rather delicate, but had to be done, because the favorite disguise for an SS man trying to evade arrest was to assume the identity of a Jewish refugee.

As indicated above, most of the refugees were not Jewish. While concentrating on our particular search for Jewish victims, we often came across groups of non-Jews whom we transported to the large DP camps in the vicinity, such as Foehrenwald and Feldafing. That often occurred, and we were happy to be part of the general rescue operation.

In the ensuing weeks, we picked up hundreds and hundreds of Jews. Some were so gaunt, weak, and listless that they didn't care what was happening to them. We were merely uniformed men who were putting them in trucks, and for them that was all too familiar. We might be Nazis who had learned a few words of Hebrew with which to trick them. Yet they knew they could not refuse uniforms and trucks, so they climbed aboard and headed off to another unknown fate.

We also found children, as young as ten. I once encountered two of those, a boy and girl, walking slowly along a farm road, filthy, clothes in tatters, holding hands, not talking. As our truck approached, and they saw we were slowing down, they started to run, jumping off the road into a ditch, he pulling her with all his strength, which wasn't much, across a plowed field, zigging and zagging as though searching for a place to hide. I walked, rather than ran, trying to indicate by stance and gesture that I did not intend to capture them, but was a friend. Gradually the distance between us narrowed, they tired and slowed down, and I overtook them. They held hands again, as though to go together to whatever lay in store.

I told them my name and asked theirs. They did not know. Nor did they know where they were born, how old they were, what camp they had been in, or how long they had been on the road. They were completely amnesiac. Eating the bread I gave them, they followed me back to the truck, to be hugged and kissed by the burly soldier-driver who was crying because these kids reminded him of his own, who were home safe and sound.

Whether adults or children, the main problem to be solved with the refugees we found was where to put them. We placed as many as possible in established camps. But they were all filling up rapidly, because Munich, the capital of Bavaria, was the destination of choice for refugees from all over Germany and Austria. We were looking for any place with four walls and a roof; three walls would also do. The smaller towns and villages offered the best prospects because they were not so badly bombed.

A large barn would accommodate 100 people; a small hospital building, 200. I remember once coming upon a Rathaus (city hall), neither grand nor large, but intact and possessing a heating system that worked. I estimated that we could fit in 300 people if we threw out all the German clerks and their filing cabinets and turned the entire structure into a dormitory. There were two lavatories in working order, and that would do.

I strode into the mayor's room, struck an aggressive pose, drew my Colt .45, slammed the butt hard on his desk, and informed him in my best college German that this place was now requisitioned by authority of the American Army. I wanted it empty and perfectly clean by 8 o'clock the following morning. The speech ended with another slam of the Colt. Period. The ploy worked perfectly. The mayor started to protest, thought better of it, and asked meekly what he was supposed to do with his personnel and records. I answered over my shoulder, on my way out, "That's your problem, not mine." At 8 the next morning, the Rathaus staff of about 20 lined up in front of the empty, immaculately clean building – German efficiency put to good use. My crowd of about 100 ragged, unruly refugees jumped off the trucks and surged inside.

The place was thoroughly dirty before the next 8 a.m. arrived. Never mind – they were warm, fed, and safe.

As soon as possible, the rescued were transferred to larger camps, to begin the long wait for a permanent solution to their homelessness. Meanwhile, the American Army provided 2,000 calories per person daily, and the American Joint Distribution Committee (AJDC) supplemented that with an additional 1,000 calories. The Jewish Agency for Palestine, another welfare group, sent to Germany many hundreds of teachers, social workers, psychologists, rabbis, and administrators to organize life in the camps and help the residents make productive use of the time on their hands. People married, children were born. Nonetheless, theirs was a grim and essentially boring existence in a bleak environment.

CHAPTER SIX

THE HAGANAH AND ALIYAH BET

It had snowed all through the night. The small village looked like an Alpine picture postcard. I was happy to be warm under a fluffy down comforter in Bad Tölz, southern Bavaria, in the foothills of the Austrian Alps. Yesterday had been a long day of cruising the narrow roads and picking up several loads of weary and frightened refugees. At day's end I was terribly tired and did not feel like driving 100 kilometers back to base through a brewing snowstorm. So, I tucked in at an inn I knew from a previous visit, looking forward to a long sleep. I was awakened early by a summons to the telephone at the desk downstairs.

A woman's voice, low and inviting, asked if she had the right person. Was I the 9th Division chaplain who had been picking up DPs and bringing them to shelter? On whose orders had I been doing that? Who was paying the inevitable expenses? Was my commanding officer aware of what I was doing? The flood of questions threatened to continue indefinitely, so I interrupted to ask in a formal tone who was speaking, how she had found me, and what she wanted?

The woman offered no reply, so we were at a standoff. It was hers to break, and she did. She asked if I would come to meet her in Room 203 of the Royal-Monceau Hotel in Paris, at my earliest convenience. An invitation as specific as that did not require extensive deliberation, particularly since I loved Paris and could use a couple of days of leave. I told her I would come, but it would take a day to return to my HQ, and get permission and the necessary written orders. I would have to let her know the exact day of my arrival. She said she would be there, waiting for me, and her manner and tone left no doubt that an adventure was in the offing.

Three days later, I knocked on the mystery woman's door at the Royal-Monceau. She was middle-aged, plain, somewhat tough-looking, and all business, with the bearing of someone who has seen much in life. She did not immediately invite me in, but rather brusquely asked to see some identification, and when she was satisfied, beckoned me across the threshold. She took a deep breath and asked whether I would agree to work with "them." When I asked who them was, she answered in just one word: "Haganah."

The Haganah was the underground armed force of the Jews in Palestine. It defended against Arab attacks and prepared for an eventual struggle for statehood, meanwhile trying to rescue persecuted Jews in Europe and smuggle them into Palestine illegally, against the law of the British mandate. Perhaps once in a lifetime, or certainly very rarely, one might be confronted with a question containing enormous consequences, opening a path whose course was absolutely unknown.

In this instance, no data were offered with which to sift the pros and cons, yet I had to reply. The question did not permit equivocation. Delay or hesitation was tantamount to refusal. Acceptance had to be instantaneous if it were to be taken as sincere and self-confident. Not knowing what in the world I was getting into, my gut told me to say yes, and I did.

Still holding me at the threshold with a gesture, the woman crossed the salon, knocked on a door at the far end, and escorted me toward a short man with a massive shock of white hair sprouting in all directions from the sides of his large, balding head. He was wearing an old sweater, khaki trousers, and house slippers. When she told him that I would work with "them," he offered me a quick, vigorous handshake and a verbal thank-you, turned, and retired. The next time I would see him was to be more than a year later.

Now the mood changed. The woman invited me to take off my heavy coat, sit down, relax, have a coffee, and she would explain everything, including the specific details of the assignment to which I had just committed myself.

Her real name was Ruth Kluger. She had changed it to Ruth Aliav when the Palestinian Jews started taking Hebrew names in place of their Central or

Eastern European Jewish ones. Aliav was an abbreviation of the phrase *Aliyah Bet* ("b" and "v" are interchangeable in Hebrew), meaning Immigration #2 – the so-called illegal immigration of Jews who were smuggled into Palestine against British regulations, which authorized only a limited legal immigration in order to appease the Arabs. Legal immigration was called *Aliyah Aleph* (#1).

The rate of 15,000 visas per year for five years, and zero thereafter, would never empty the DP camps. Therefore, the Haganah had established a department to evade the British and bring Jews in illegally. Since Ruth had spent many years of her life working on *Aliyah Bet*, she decided to take that phrase as her very name.

Who was the little man with the white hair? His name was David Ben-Gurion, and he was chairman of the Jewish Agency. A few years later, he would announce the founding of the State of Israel and become its first prime minister.

On that occasion at the Royal-Monceau, Ben-Gurion was in the next room with Moshe Sneh, commander of the Haganah, working on operational plans. The two men were in Paris to avoid arrest by the British, who had been sending large numbers of high Jewish Agency and Haganah officials to prison camps in Rhodesia and elsewhere. The Royal-Monceau was British headquarters in Paris, and a full-sized British flag hung over the entrance. So Ben-Gurion and Sneh were pulling off a *Purloined Letter* stunt, hiding themselves (in disguise when they ventured out) right under the British noses.

The basic plan for *Aliyah Bet* involved two operations: to gather as many Jews as possible from Eastern Europe and the Soviet Union, including those places far east of the Ural Mountains, where Russia had provided refuge for many Jews; and to shepherd them all to the West, which meant the Allied Zones of Germany and Austria. There the DP camps would be established, and there the Jews would wait until some major political decision gave Palestine its independence as a Jewish state. Then they would be taken "home" immediately – no *Aleph* or *Bet*, just an open door.

The second operation involved taking some number from the camps and transporting them southward to French and Italian Mediterranean ports, from which Haganah ships would take them to the coast of Palestine. Not all the DPs were able to travel this route: it posed many hardships and required physical strength and the willingness to cross borders illegally. This second operation was more complex and dangerous than the first. But there was no sense in moving masses of people westward into Germany unless one also tried to move some number out, southward, and make a break for home across the Mediterranean.

To bring people into Germany, two routes were being set up – a northern one toward Berlin and a southern one toward Munich. The collection point for the former was the Polish border town of Stettin, about 150 miles northeast of Berlin. On trucks, wagons, trains, and their own feet, the Jews would stream from Eastern Europe toward Stettin, guided and nourished by a small band of incredibly dedicated Haganah men and women. Stettin offered holding facilities for several thousand DPs at a time, but if there were no steady stream across the border into Germany, Stettin would soon become a mess, and the blockage would affect the flow all the way back to Uzbekistan.

Thus the key to the success of the northern route was movement into Germany. But there was a hitch. Germany had been divided by the Four Allied Powers into four zones. The Russians had been given the northeastern zone, next to Poland, and Stettin sits on that border. How convenient, except that the Russians were notoriously difficult about anyone crossing their borders illegally.

That's where I came in – that is, where Ruth Kluger brought me in. The Haganah, she said, wanted me to take charge of the route from Stettin into Berlin and get it moving in a steady flow up to 10,000 persons per month. If Ben-Gurion et al. could count on that, they would be better able to organize the long chain eastward as far as Central Asia. It was an awesome request. But it was also an exciting challenge.

I would have to get myself transferred from the 9th Division to Headquarters, Berlin Command. Luckily, the chaplain currently in Berlin, Joseph Shubow of Boston, was going home. That gave me the opportunity to base my request for a transfer on the fact that Berlin could not be left without a Jewish chaplain. The city, like the country, was divided into four zones, each administered by one of the Allied powers. But only the Americans maintained a Jewish chaplain. The Russians had political commissars, not clergymen; the British had only one rabbi for their entire zone of Germany and had posted him to their own HQ in Hanover; and the French had so few Jewish chaplains in their entire army that I doubt they had stationed any in Germany. In the four commands together, there were about 2,000 Jewish personnel in Berlin and it was up to the abundantly supplied Americans, as usual, to provide the service of a Jewish chaplain to all four armies. Given that situation, it would not be difficult to arrange my transfer.

Chaplain Shubow had earlier on managed a small miracle, namely, to find in Berlin – almost totally destroyed – a house with roof intact and walls standing. It was in Dahlem, in a fine residential district in the American sector. He had requisitioned the place as the official Jewish Chaplain Center, and it continued to serve as the heart and soul of the Jewish military and tiny civilian communities for many years.

According to Ruth Kluger's plan, I would take over that house, as well as command of a dozen Jewish Brigade soldiers the Haganah would send. The brigade had fought valiantly in Italy alongside the British and was now bivouacked in Belgium; the Brits did not wish to have 30,000 well-armed, experienced Jewish fighting men return to Palestine at the very moment when the British policy clearly leaned toward the Arabs and was doing everything possible to appease them. So the brigade was twiddling its collective thumbs in Belgium, and any "dirty dozen" of them would have been delighted to get into this underground Haganah operation.

I was to arrange my house so these Jewish Brigade men could eat and sleep there; provide false DP papers for them (which we could do nicely, because we had an excellent forging operation in the second basement); hide their British uniforms and pay books, provide ragged DP clothing in exchange; and see to it that they worked at night and slept during the day so they were not on the streets, vulnerable to chance inspection. All that was possible because of a wonderful DP husband and wife team, Mr. and Mrs. Leo Bierstein (he a former furrier from Lodz), who became my housekeepers and were marvelously efficient and calm under terrific pressure.

I was to arrange for a half-dozen 6-bys to be in the backyard of the house, with enough gas tickets for unlimited mileage and a couple of good mechanics who would be at our disposal. I had learned back in Bavaria that to obtain such things simply required stealing.

Our plan was to leave Berlin around dusk with two Brigade men in each truck, taking turns driving and riding shotgun. There were several Bren and Thompson sub-machine guns in each vehicle, as well as carbines and Colts. That may sound a bit melodramatic, but we were driving about 200 kilometers northeast from Berlin to Stettin, through Russian territory, and 200 kilometers back, all in darkness. We were thus vulnerable targets, carrying a fortune in bribes every night. Anyone watching us knew that our route never varied, so it would be simple to set up ambushes.

Leaving Berlin at dusk, snaking through back streets of the city until we reached the open road, we usually arrived at the Stettin border-crossing point around midnight. The delicate negotiations at that bridge, the pay-offs, the obligatory bottle of vodka or two as a toast to seeing each other tomorrow night, and the loading of 50 people in each truck, together with the haggling about the baggage (we preferred people to those bags and bundles but understood how each bundle represented a person's entire worldly goods) – all that took an hour. Then back on the road with our precious cargo of 300 persons, wrapped in blankets, tarpaulins tightly tied around the trucks, heading back toward Berlin, where we would arrive in the French sector of Wedding just before dawn, at an apartment block we owned. Food, showers, DDT powder, and sleeping the day away was the regimen for the weary refugees, who would need many more days to unwind and begin to taste the freedom that was now theirs.

Then, for the drivers and gunners back to the Chaplain Center and the same regimen (minus the DDT). It was hard and at times harrowing. But in the course of less than a year, we pulled 90,000 people along the Stettin-Berlin route.

Two important aspects require explanation: the reference above to "a fortune in bribes" and the disposition of the DPs once they were safely in Berlin. The currency of choice all over Europe at that time was cigarettes. Under the arches of the Brandenburg Gate, in the heart of Berlin, the black market flourished and established trading values. A pack of 20 cigarettes was stable at $15, or $150 per carton of ten packs. At the army Post Exchange (PX), a carton cost 70 cents, and GIs were allowed one carton per week. A soldier who did not smoke could buy his carton, sell it, take the $149.30 profit to the Army post office, buy a money order, and mail it home to his wife or mother, who could surrender it for cash at the local post office.

After doing that for a year, a soldier would have made $7,500, about 20 times as much as his base pay for the same period. The price for admitting one Jew at the Stettin border crossing was $150, one carton of cigarettes. At the rate of 300 persons per night, we were talking about $45,000! The task of gathering that many cigarettes for daily trade strained every brain and nerve. Some dedicated soldiers helped, soliciting their comrades for cigarettes and bringing in hundreds of packs every day. The soldiers who contributed out of their weekly ration were among the most generous benefactors the Jewish people has ever had. My father was collecting among his friends back home, and I was receiving many mail sacks full every week. I was also receiving visits from Army postal inspectors asking about these hundreds of thousands of dollars worth of "gifts from home." The inspectors were perplexed because I was neither selling on the black market nor buying money orders. My father, bless him, was reading all the stories about the black market. He wrote to me about it only once, saying that he was not going to ask me what I was doing with the cigarettes because he was certain I was not violating any laws, civil or religious.

But in spite of all the efforts, including collections within the DP population itself, there was no way we could keep abreast of the daily need. The Haganah gave me huge amounts of cash, and I would sometimes go into the black market to buy our medium of exchange. The situation eased only when Antwerp became the first port in Europe to re-open after the war, and shiploads of supplies began coming in. The JDC, also called the "Joint," was able to send all the cigarettes we needed, and I began to receive freight-car loads.

As for the second matter, we were under constant pressure to move as many DPs out of Berlin as we brought in there. Berlin had two camps: one in the southwestern part of the city, a large German former prisoner-of-war facility called Schlachtensee, housing about 7,000; and a second on the edge of Tempelhof Airfield, in city center, housing about 3,000. Thus we could hold roughly 10,000 DPs in the city at any one time. Once that number was reached, every load of 300 we brought in at dawn had to be matched by 300 sent out by nightfall. At least twice a week, we had to send a convoy of 1,000 people, by truck or train, southwest out of Berlin to the American zone.

Berlin, after all, was an island in the middle of the Russian zone. To leave the city in any direction, one had to pass a Russian control point. We had to pass one at Helmstedt, and there, unlike the one across from Stettin, bribes did not do the trick. Paperwork was needed. Most of the papers were forged in the Chaplain Center in Dahlem, and many convoys were turned back for a variety of reasons. But by the middle of 1946, following a decision by President Truman under dramatic circumstances I'll describe later, problems of entering the American zone ceased. Once in, the DPs were taken by Haganah and Jewish Agency personnel to an established camp, where they could be squeezed in, or more often to a new camp being opened to accommodate either them or compatriots arriving in Munich through the southern route via Czechoslovakia and Austria. At the peak of the Aliyah Bet operation, the camps numbered 64, containing a quarter of a million Jews.

Additional room became available in the American zone as groups were organized there and transported down south to French and Italian ports, where the Haganah ships came in to pick them up for the run to Palestine. Far more often, it was a run toward Palestine, and a heart-breaking one. Of the 65 Haganah vessels, 57 were captured by the British and the refugees taken to a camp set up on the island of Cyprus; at its peak, the camp held more than 60,000 men, women, and children. Only the tide of history could compensate their suffering and mental and physical despair. When the state of Israel was declared on May 14, 1948, the first ship to arrive, the following evening, came from Cyprus.

CHAPTER SEVEN

TRIUMPHANT SEDER, TRAGIC RIOT

Aside from the palpable sense of changing history by aiding the migration of a whole people across continents, I shared many other episodes and events that were the realizations of earlier dreams. Later, when I thought back to those years in which I had a hand in the destiny of my people, I felt blessed and fulfilled by my activities. I knew other chaplains who complained of boredom stemming from the performance of routine duties. Yet when offered the challenge of joining in the adventure of shaping a nation – for I felt that was exactly what we were doing – they demurred out of fear or lack of imagination.

The inability to think in grand sweeps connotes mediocrity and ordinariness. Some people are perfectly satisfied being ordinary. But when one is *dis*satisfied and bored, relief lies in joining great enterprises outside of oneself. So many things were happening to me almost every day that the pace left me breathless, yet even more energized and motivated.

I remember preparing for the 1946 Passover Seder – the first Seder after liberation, celebrating freedom from the Hitlerian madness. His "Thousand-Year Reich" had lasted exactly 12 years, and the human race – at least the portion he had enslaved – was free again. My mind played with the magic of the Jewish tradition, which was so tribal and particularistic on the one hand, yet so universal in its message on the other. I thought that every person in every nation who ever felt the lash of tyranny must now feel like a Jew escaping from

Egypt, and I thought that this first Seder in Berlin should be a tremendous affair, open to the whole human race. Since that might not be practical, at least we should take the biggest hall we could find and see how many it would hold.

The Schöneberg Rathaus was the place. It was the municipal hall of Berlin's largest borough. Almost two decades later, President Kennedy would speak to a vast crowd in the square below from the balcony of this same building. Its main dining hall could hold well over 2,000 people. Since there were that many Jewish military personnel alone, we hoped that some would not attend, leaving room to invite DPs, German Jewish survivors who had returned to their home city, non-Jewish military, and the very few German Christians who were clearly known to have been anti-Nazi and to have helped Jews by hiding them.

It was a gala dinner. The huge hall was decorated with the four Allied flags and the Jewish flag of the unborn state, as well as flowers and banners, and it resonated with enthusiastic singing even before the Passover ceremony began. We were overflowing with supplies, for I had received permission to take several trucks and men down to the main American warehouse in Mannheim and load up with whatever they had available. The Army quartermaster-general had thought of <u>everything</u>. We brought home to Berlin kosher wine from Algeria, *matzot* from Palestine, gefilte fish in tins from the U.S., salami from Hebrew National, kosher chicken from the Jewish Welfare Board. And our mess sergeant produced the most wonderful meal anyone had eaten in a long time. We had enough *Haggadot* (books telling the Exodus story) to go around, and almost 2,000 participants read and sang loudly. Hebrew was heard in many accents. The Russian Jewish troops were the most boisterous, shouting and pounding on the tables. I learned later that, for many, this was the first Seder in their entire lives, perfectly understandable when one thinks of the suppression of religion by their government.

The uninhibited joy of the Russians was perhaps due to another fact altogether. I had invited all four commanding generals, by letter and then on a personal visit. I had also invited each to read a section of the *Haggadah*, and to make a short speech on any subject of his choice. All four had accepted. The head table was arranged with four special arm chairs and four full-sized, national flags hung as backdrops. Three chairs were occupied, and the three commanders made wonderful presentations. Major General Kotikov was absent, his chair empty, but his countrymen sang loudly. Freedom reigned.

★ ★ ★

At the other end of the postwar emotional spectrum, in the DP camp at Landsberg, an unusual, but not entirely unexpected event occurred in May 1946. The camp was located in buildings that once constituted a prison (Hitler himself was incarcerated there in 1924-25, during which time he wrote *Mein Kampf*), and later a German Army barracks. The Jews living in Landsberg had a well-organized existence, for the director of United Nations Relief and Rehabilitation Administration (UNRRA) was sympathetic to them, the JDC and Jewish Agency for Palestine (JAFP) teams were cooperating well, and the schools and internal camp police consisting of DPs themselves occupied the energies of a large number of people. Yet something in the air of the place, with its memories of Hitler's presence, seemed to keep the people's nerves on edge. One day a rumor swept through the camp, like a prairie fire out of control, to the effect that a 12 year old boy had somehow been spirited out of the camp into the nearby woods and killed by Germans. Rage and pent-up hatred exploded in a furious attack by hundreds of Jews who burst through the camp gates, poured into the small town, broke windows, overturned buses, started fires, and beat up Germans on the street. The *Bürgermeister* called on the American Army for help, since it was the Army's responsibility to maintain law and order, and American soldiers slowly forced the DPs back inside the camp gates.

But that didn't extinguish the emotional flames. Back and forth went the pushing and shoving: the Jews trying to break out and attack Germans, and the soldiers trying to keep them penned in; the Jews by now in the thousands, and the army calling in tanks and setting up some machine guns on tripods. The DPs started shouting such insults as "American SS," "Nazis," and "Gestapo," chanting rhythmically and in increasing volume. The soldiers were fingering their rifles. A far more murderous riot could have erupted, killing dozens on both sides.

The Jews made one more surge to break out. The soldiers surged in and scooped up 30 or 40 people in the front ranks, cut them off from the mob, hustled them into trucks, slammed and locked the gates, and announced over bull horns that a thorough investigation would immediately be made to determine if, indeed, any child had been abducted or murdered.

As the crowd quieted down, still milling around the central camp square, and the Army removed its weapons, the DP camp police began their own quiet search to determine what had really started the rumor. It soon located a family whose young son had slipped out of school, which caused the boy's teacher to send a messenger to the family's room to inquire after him. The mother became hysterical and started to scream that her boy was missing. In fact, he had left the camp through a hole in the fence and gone into the woods – he later explained – "to be alone for a little while." In fact, while the rioting was going on at the front gate of the camp, a small search party went looking through the woods behind the camp, found the boy, and brought him back. But that did not become known until an hour or two later. By the end of the day, the camp population, nervous and exhausted, bedded down early, except for the families of those arrested and taken away by the Army.

The Americans now had a two-fold problem on their hands: a nasty PR situation vis-a-vis the Jews, and a real maintenance-of-order and financial situation vis-a-vis the German townspeople who had been assaulted and lost property. The latter issue was turned over to the Army's G-5 section and quietly settled through compensation. The former was much stickier. The Jewish DPs had rioted. They had made defamatory remarks against American troops and damaged civilian property and several among those arrested were carrying knives, pipes, and sharp sticks, all defined as weapons. There was no way to dismiss those facts without subjecting the Army to criticism. So it was decided to indict the 19 young men who were considered the most inflammatory and dangerous and to release the others. The famous Landsberg Trial began.

A media storm broke in the Jewish community papers in the U.S. Headlines blared: **NAZIS KILL JEWISH CHILD; JEWISH DPs RIOT AGAINST U.S. TROOPS; AMERICANS ARREST 19 JEWS; MILITARY COURT-MARTIAL BEGINS IN LANDSBERG.**

A Jewish Congressman, Adolph Joachim Sabath of Illinois, an important member of the Armed Services Committee, wrote to the War Department demanding that it insure a fair trial, or he personally would fly to Germany and oversee the proceedings. Other politicians took up the cry. The Army knew it had a hot potato on its plate, and pressure from Washington descended on the headquarters of U.S. Forces in the European Theater (USFET) in Frankfurt.

The commander of the theater, General Joseph T. McNarney, was intelligent, perceptive, fair, direct, and straight. He had at his disposal a civilian Advisor on Jewish Affairs, with the simulated rank of major-general, sufficient status to deal with equally high-ranking Army officers. As a nominee of the five leading American Jewish national organizations, the advisor had the confidence of the Jewish establishment; and as appointee of the Secretary of War, of the military establishment. It was a carefully devised and successful mechanism for handling the delicate issues that arose constantly between the Army and the DPs.

The newly appointed advisor was the same Rabbi Philip S. Bernstein of Rochester who had previously served as director of the Chaplaincy Commission. He was a warm, outgoing person, astute in defusing crises – in all, one of the best civil servants the Jewish people could have put forward at that historic period. The Army's top brass liked Bernstein, as did everyone else who dealt with him. He was a superb diplomat, and was to figure prominently in the events of the next couple of years.

When General McNarney turned to him for advice on the Landsberg trial, Bernstein said the Army should take two steps: send a chaplain to oversee the proceedings, with authority to implement any procedure that, in his judgment, would emphasize the Army's fairness; and provide its best lawyer to serve as defense attorney for the 19 Jewish defendants. Bernstein suggested that I be intimately involved in both undertakings: as the overseeing chaplain and as the person who would search the adjutant-general's office for the best defense lawyer. McNarney agreed, and those arrangements were released to the press in Washington, dampening anger and anxiety. Rep. Sabath said he would take a wait-and-see attitude.

Conducting the prosecution before the seven-officer court was a nice Jewish fellow from Denver, Capt. Herman Gulkin; the defense attorney was

Capt. Abraham Hyman, the best lawyer the Army had in Germany. His task had been to review every death sentence passed by any military court in the entire theater to make certain that it was proper and legal; Hyman was a meticulously careful lawyer.

The weeks I spent on this episode might be considered an excessive output of time and energy, but it actually was not. A very sensitive political and human situation, conflict between Jews and Army, required careful handling lest it escalate into a serious and explosive issue. General McNarney understood that when he sent me to the scene as his plenipotentiary. I channeled my effort into several areas of attention: the camp; the Adjutant General's office; the courtroom; the press; the attorneys for prosecution and defense; the incarceration process; and McNarney's office.

My first duty at the camp was to provide moral support to the families of the 19 prisoners. Next, the general population of the camp required daily attention in order to lower the level of hostility, which was best done by providing the camp committee and the DP police with information they could circulate.

The search through the adjutant general's office for just the right defense lawyer required days of interviews and phone calls throughout the entire American zone. Finally, the preferred recommendee, Capt. Hyman, had to be persuaded to accept the assignment. He was about to be demobilized and didn't want to get involved in this DP business. His intuition told him that long years would pass before the fate of the Jewish refugees would finally be settled and, once involved, he would not be able to extricate himself, but would have to remain on active duty until the end. It took me many hours of discussion with Hyman, during which I discovered the depth of his conscience – and exploited it mercilessly to a "successful" conclusion. He soon became a devoted advocate of the DP cause. Abe Hyman and I remained friends until his death in Israel 50 years later.

The trial lasted about ten days, and I developed friendships with the prosecutor and the full colonel who presided over the court. That gave me the opportunity to meet them *outside* the courtroom, where I provided them with background information about the psychology of the DPs in the wake of their inhuman experiences. That effort on my part proved most valuable, for it gave key court officials a sense of the outrage that actually caused the riot.

The press – German, foreign, and *Stars and Stripes* – reported on the trial daily. Various reporters came to me frequently for comment, seeking background explanations about the Jews and their attitude to the Army. I was happy to be available, to provide balance that helped keep sensationalism out of the reportage.

One of the top leaders of the Central Committee of Liberated Jews in Germany, Samuel Gringaus, a former judge in Lithuania, offered his legal services to Hyman and sat at the defense table. I asked him to serve as a channel to the entire DP population, for this trial was known throughout Germany, and it was vital that a steady flow of information be disseminated to all 64 camps. Riots in other places would surely break out if a widespread conviction developed that the Landsberg 19 were being unfairly treated. A daily briefing with Gringaus was a crucial link in maintaining a quiet atmosphere.

As the trial proceeded, I began to discuss the end-game strategy with Hyman and Gringaus, and we decided to push for separate incarceration. Hyman brilliantly argued the case for it, and the court agreed.

My daily reporting to him kept General McNarney informed of all aspects and kept him in the position of reassuring all questioners that the matter was under control and proceeding peacefully.

The defendants were found guilty only of carrying concealed weapons; additional charges involving intent to harm were dismissed. They were sentenced to three months in prison, and Hyman pleaded cogently (according to our earlier tactical decision) that they be placed neither in a military stockade, with soldiers who might remember and resent the epithets shouted during the fracas, nor for obvious reasons in a civilian prison among Germans, but incarcerated separately in a building that the Army controlled and could secure.

The court agreed and consigned the convicted men to a large, run-down manor-house near Bayreuth, and granted permission for their relatives to visit them. A small military detachment was placed in charge of the house; four MPs in shifts and a KP unit. It was all very relaxed. Long before the prescribed three months passed, a Haganah group of a few men in British uniforms arrived one day in a truck, with orders (forged) to release the 19 prisoners whom they then spirited away to Genoa. From there, an illegal ship took them toward Palestine. I have a photo album with a picture of all 19, inscribed to me in Hebrew with thanks for the care I gave them. I look at it occasionally and smile at the happy ending to a difficult and potentially dangerous interlude.

CHAPTER EIGHT

VENGEANCE AND SURVIVAL: THREE STRIKING STORIES

In order to comprehend the suspicion, rage, and frustration that produced the Landsberg riot, it is necessary to reflect on the recent experiences of the DP-camp inmates. Anyone who had not suffered and endured the Hitler years, could barely understand what was festering in the memories and nervous systems of those who had lived through the hell. We outsiders tried to empathize, but our efforts were feeble, and we were shocked every time we heard the sentiment expressed, by someone who had survived Auschwitz, that he or she couldn't handle life and would really rather have perished with the others. All of our work to help re-establish strength, health, and the physical aspects of life mattered less in the long run than the recovery of spirit, hope, and will to start anew.

The mood that festered among the DPs – capricious conduct, excitable excesses, melodramatic solutions, and a general sense of nervousness – produced dozens of violent episodes. Three will illustrate the bizarre quality of Jewish existence in postwar Europe: the lynching of a Kapo; the failed attempt of a Russian GI to desert; and the literal saving of a life with Torah scrolls.

The first: One morning, while I slept late after the night ride back from Stettin, some DPs burst into my room with the news that a lynching was about to occur in the camp at Schlachtensee. Someone had recognized a person there as having been a Kapo in a Nazi labor camp. There was no term of greater opprobrium among Jews. Kapo is an abbreviation of *Konzentrationslager Polizei* – concentration camp police – and refers to Jews who did the masters' bidding, controlling and often brutalizing other prisoners.

A Kapo was often required to beat other Jews. A kitchen Kapo, who ladled out the daily soup ration to the line of prisoners, could scoop from the top of the pot, where the gruel was thin, or from the bottom, where he might draw a piece of vegetable or meat. He could thus show favoritism to one person or another, for which he would later be rewarded in some way. Some Kapos were actually sadists, selected for their work by the Nazis because of that very characteristic. All Kapos lived longer than other prisoners, and some made it until liberation.

Camp inmates therefore hated the Kapos even more than they hated the Nazi guards, if that were possible. So when someone occasionally recognized a former Kapo amid the thousands in a DP camp, a lynch mob would form in a matter of seconds to obtain bloody revenge. Neither UNRRA nor military officials favored this mob rule, because the hatred that fueled it could easily get out of control and seek other targets, once the Kapo's blood had whetted its appetite.

I understood that because I had once witnessed such an event at a DP movie show. The shout "Kapo, Kapo" arose in the middle of the screening, followed by "Here's the bastard…!," and hundreds promptly charged toward that spot, climbing over the seats, and pounded to death the alleged criminal. Within a few minutes, it was revealed that they had killed the wrong man.

Even with the blood lust unleashed in Schlachtensee, some saner head must have prevailed, for the alleged ex-Kapo had been rescued and taken to the camp director's office, and I had been sent for. To avoid the over-heated atmosphere of the camp, I shifted the "venue" to my house and set up a semblance of a trial. It did not take long. Many witnesses appeared, so there was no question of mistaken identity; many others recited the Kapo's deeds and conduct over a long period, which were sufficient to condemn.

The only remaining question was whether to turn him over to the U.S. Army for punishment, as I had suggested, or to let a committee of his peers execute judgment. In almost all matters that concerned them and me, the DPs would heed my judgment, for they counted me as a friend and benefactor. In this case, they listened politely to my suggestion and unanimously shook their heads in the negative. Silently they took him away, and within the hour one of them returned to me to report his death by hanging. That night at supper in the mess hall, the announcement was made, and the crowd started to chant "Hallelujah – the traitor is dead."

★   ★   ★

Another episode, of a different sort but typical in its own way, involved a soldier in the Red Army, Mark Shapiro, born in Kiev. As I noted earlier, since I was the only Jewish chaplain in Berlin, soldiers in Russian, British, and French uniforms, as well as American, came and went from my house at all hours. We held Friday night services there because the central reception rooms could accommodate about 150 seats. We also held a Friday night buffet supper after services, and beginning early Friday afternoon lots of soldiers came around to help with the setting up. Many vehicles were parked nearby in lots made vacant by bombing. There were, of course, Military Police of all armies, for with this much activity, there might be problems that only MPs could settle. After a while, however, the MP surveillance became so routine that those good fellows joined everyone inside. They had become curious to see what a Jewish Sabbath service was like and what kind of food these Jews ate.

I stress the naturalness of the mood, because my housekeeping staff and I used the crowds, the singing, the milling around the tables as a cover for the clandestine, basement operations that never ceased: forging papers, making up travel manifests for the DPs being shipped out, sorting DP mail, providing food and lodging for Haganah agents on the move – and rendering assistance to Soviet soldiers who wanted to desert.

The last activity led to the incident with Sergeant Shapiro. It began innocently enough in the huge Reichschancellery, Hitler's former headquarters and a symbol, in its massiveness and luxuriousness, of the Führer's vainglorious regime. The building lay mostly in ruins when I arrived in Berlin. But because of its importance and style, it was the first place I visited.

After sitting amid the rubble for a long time, pondering what Hitler had done to the world and the Jews and his own Germany, I started to wander through other parts of the building and came to a broad, circular staircase leading downward, with no end in sight. As I descended ever deeper, the stairway grew darker and finally pitch black, and I began to feel eerily alone in a silent Nazi hell, from which retreat began to seem like a good idea. Suddenly a deep voice shouted *"Stoi"* – "halt" in Russian – and a bright light flashed right in my face, pinning me to the spot.

The man behind the light turned out to be Sergeant Shapiro. He was as nervous as I, for he had heard me walking around upstairs and taken me for one of the multitude of lost and hungry men who wandered through the broken city looking for food or somebody to rob.

Shapiro was the Russian non-commissioned officer in charge of this building. He had been here since his unit first entered the city and had made himself a comfortable billet way down in the former shelter of General Wilhelm Keitel, chief of the German general staff. To this remarkable place he now invited me, and it was a fairyland of bunker luxury: tiled floors and carpeted walls, electricity and running water, real beds and a stocked refrigerator. We had vodka and tea and more vodka and tea, sufficient to encourage an exchange of confidences and presents. We spoke in our only common language – broken Yiddish. He gave me a piece of Hitler's marble map table, which I have to this day, and I gave him my American Colt .45, which, as you will soon learn, he did not keep very long.

Shapiro started to come to the Chaplain Center. First he came on Fridays, then he added Saturday mornings, and as he sat through the service, memory began to feed his mood. In our many subsequent conversations, he would talk about his grandparents and about their stories of what Jewish life was like before the Bolshevik Revolution of 1917 outlawed religious education and practice. Being surrounded by so many Jewish soldiers of all nationalities, he developed a sense of Jewish identity, which he admitted never having felt before. And then one day he said he wanted to come to America. He knew that would be impossible to do by any legal means; therefore he had decided to desert, and he asked if there was any way I could help.

His was neither the first nor the last such request I received. I had worked out a system to help many people, not only soldiers, who needed a new identity. The best way was to mix them in with the mass of DPs in either of our two camps, giving them refugee clothing and a set of DP papers that would stand up under any scrutiny.

I explained that to Mark, of whom I had become quite fond, and told him exactly how to pull it off. He was to come to the Chaplain Center, *in uniform*, on a weekend day, when the crowd of visitors was large, and disappear into our cellar. He would emerge some days later as a DP, whenever we had a crowd of DPs in the house for some occasion or other, and then leave with them on their truck; nobody would ever be able to find him among the thousands in the camp.

Mark agreed, but then disobeyed – an act for which he paid with his life. He left his barracks one Friday night, but not to come to the center. Instead, he went to his German girl friend's house for what he knew would be their final evening together. He was followed there surreptitiously by Russian Army Intelligence. He proceeded to lose track of the time, and just before dawn, realizing there would be no crowds at my house at that hour, he panicked, donned some old civilian clothes his girl friend gave him, and told her he was going to my house. When he walked out, the Russian agents seized him and hustled him away in a car. The girl friend got to my place several hours later and told me the story through her tears.

I found out two days later that Mark had been taken to a Russian military prison in Potsdam, charged with being a spy, because he was out of uniform, and being a potential deserter. He was shot. His photo is in my scrapbook.

★ ★ ★

A third strange episode had a happier ending. A man named Martin Riessenburger had been the cantor at the Pestalozzi Strasse synagogue, and, during the war, he had eluded the Nazis through various means and helpers. By 1943, he was hiding deep underground in a mausoleum in Weissensee, a Jewish cemetery in East Berlin. He kept alive by coming out in the pre-dawn hour and scavenging for garbage; but he knew, as he later related to me, that the cold down in the tomb would soon kill him.

One night, just before Riessenburger thought he would perish, a miracle happened. As he was about to set forth on a foraging expedition, he heard a truck approach the cemetery gate, dump a load of something, and run back and forth over it several times. He imagined the something to be bodies. But when he ventured up top to investigate, he found instead a load of Torah Scrolls, some still clothed in their velvet covers. It was such a surrealistic sight that he thought he was hallucinating. Then he realized that it was simply another Nazi insult and degradation of the Jewish people and their religion.

In a flash, Riessenburger saw his salvation. Torah scrolls are written on animal skins, which can fend off cold. Therefore, they could keep him alive. Feverishly he began to pull the Torahs down into his hiding place. He managed to get scores of them underground before dawn broke, which was important because the next day the remainder up on the street would disappear. What he had salvaged would have to last until the war was over.

And so they did. Wrapped in the skins, shaping pieces of them to cover his arms and feet, and tearing strips to tie the pieces around his trunk and limbs, he lived through the frightful winters of 1943 and 1944. The war ended in May 1945, and Martin Riessenburger emerged alive, having literally been saved by the Torah.

When he told me this story in 1946, he took me into his second room, where several scrolls lay intact. He gave me two, one for the weekly Torah reading and one for the *Haftorahs* (a supplementary passage, usually from the Prophets). From a strictly Orthodox point of view, those two scrolls are probably considered "not kosher" because they were defiled. But I have conducted services with them for the past 40 years and consider them the most holy ritual objects I own.

Martin Riessenburger is gone, and so are the congregations from which the scrolls came, but the story embodied in them lives on. As long as someone possesses the scrolls, and is possessed by them, they are eternal.

I am not sure whether those three stories possess a common thread or fit comfortably into a single picture frame. What do they really signify? Do they reveal anything about the deepest meaning of life? Having thought of them often, I offer two suggestions that at least satisfy my own yearning for an interpretation:

A. **Achieve fulfillment in life**

1. Revenge (against the Kapo) is not enough. After the purge that accompanied a blood-letting, what are you left with? Nothing but a let-down feeling. You don't feel good. The bad memories remain with you. You have not found peace.

2. Escape (Shapiro to the United States) into a better world is easily thwarted – by error, fate, design, diversion – and is not a valuable, secure route to permanent inner happiness.

3. Hope and persistence (Riessenberger in Torah skins) are the genuine characteristics that can help you overcome evil and danger and carry you into a better existence throughout your life.

B. **When opportunity knocks, answer the door**

1. If destiny puts the former Kapo in your hand, you cannot let him go. That does not necessarily mean lynching, but you must bring him to justice.

2. If escape is possible (Shapiro), don't tamper with it. Follow the rules, fast and straight.

3. If the enemy makes an error (defiles Torahs), and unwittingly gives you an advantage, you must recognize it quickly and exercise it to the maximum extent possible.

Reading the Haggadah at the first Passover Seder in Berlin after the liberation.
To my right is Joseph Shubow, the outgoing chaplain, and to his right the American,
British, and French commanders.

General Joseph T. McNarney signing the Charter of Recognition to the Central Committee of Liberated Jews in Germany, 1946. To his left: Dr. Samuel Gringaus, chairman of the Central Committee. The three other men in front row are DP officers of the Central Committee. Back row, left to right: Rabbi Philip Bernstein, General Huebner, Major Hyman, Colonel Scithers, and myself.

Escorting David Ben-Gurion into troubled DP camp Babenhausen in 1946.
His words and presence brought them hope.

Rabbi Stephen S. Wise led a delegation of U.S. Jewish leaders to visit the DP camps in Germany in 1946. Purpose: to raise morale among DPs.
Front row, left to right: Rabbi Samuel Snieg, chief rabbi of DP community; Nahum Goldmann, WZO; Rabbi Stephen S. Wise, World Jewish Congress; Jacob Blaustein, American Jewish Committee; Dr. Samuel Gringaus.
Back row, left to right: Captain (Chaplain) Herbert Friedman and Major Abraham Hyman; I.L. Kenen, founder of AIPAC; Rabbi Philip S. Bernstein; Judge Philip Forman, JDC; Leon Retter, member of DP Executive Committee; two unknown.

My debut on the American Jewish national stage in June 1947, accompanied by
Bill Rosenwald, and to his left, Henry Morgenthau.

When we invited President Eisenhower to open the special conference celebrating the 10th anniversary of V-E day, he invited us to bring a delegation to the White House. There Bill Rosenwald presented him a 2000-year-old clay lamp excavated in Israel.

Over the years a warm personal relationship developed
between Ben-Gurion and myself.

Paula Ben-Gurion and I never discussed affairs of state.

Following the 1956 Suez-Sinai Campaign, Egypt expelled her Jews.
Terrified, they arrived in Naples.

CHAPTER NINE

THE KIELCE POGROM

In post-war Poland, even though three million Jews had been exterminated and only some thousands remained, a murderous anti-semitism also remained. Incredibly, it began immediately after the defeat of Hitler and claimed over 1,000 lives in 15 months. The climactic event was a pogrom in the town of Kielce on the Fourth of July, 1946, which left 42 Jewish bodies neatly stacked like firewood around the fountain in the central square.

It was a shock of such magnitude, as word spread throughout Eastern Europe, that the normal wave of displaced persons fleeing to the safety of the West rapidly expanded within days. The course of history was clearly changing before our eyes.

The pogrom and its possible aftermath held serious implications for the U.S. Army in Germany, which would receive the brunt of a mass flight. Rabbi Bernstein and I, the Army's advisory team on Jewish affairs, therefore flew to Warsaw one week after the Kielce pogrom. General McNarney wanted a detailed report; what might the Army be called upon to handle?

We found Poland's small Jewish communities in a state of near-hysteria. People were leaving their shabby homes without even attempting to take belongings, deserting their little shops or stores without locking the doors – just running. We estimated that 60,000 Jews might be in flight from Eastern European countries within the next 90 days and that the U.S. zone of Germany should expect to receive that number. A longer-term forecast would increase the total to 100,000, even 150,000, within the next twelve months, involving Jews fleeing from central Russia.

The chronology of our investigation in Poland brought us first to the American ambassador, Arthur Bliss Lane, with whom we had two conversations, at the beginning and end of our trip. Warsaw was pitiful and pathetic in the nakedness of its destruction. Even Berlin was not so totally flattened. There was only one usable hotel in the city, the Polonia, and it was overflowing. Bernstein's rank had gotten us two beds there; the ambassador's rank plus the muscle of the U.S. Government had gotten him two whole rooms.

Ambassador Lane suffered from painful gout, and he received us with his foot propped up on a hassock, his face in a grimace. He was helpful in briefing us on the background of events but utterly unhelpful in terms of what the United States could and would do to press the Polish Government to control the murder of Jews that was sweeping the country.

Lane explained that the Polish authorities could not control their citizens; they were blaming the Jews for having brought communism to Poland and every other Eastern European country. It was, of course, a false and outrageous pretext for non-Jewish Poles to take out their frustrations on the most convenient – and traditional – scapegoat. Yet the manner in which Lane developed this thesis, as well as his choice of words, tone of voice, and various nuances, gave Bernstein and me the distinct impression that he understood and was sympathetic to what he called "the sense of outrage" of the Polish population.

In addition, he followed that with a shrug and a reference to Poland's "historic anti-semitism." He thus did not say a word that could lay him open to criticism. It was a polished, diplomatic presentation that left us terribly uneasy, for it was clear that Lane did not intend to make any official protest or effort. In short, he was implying that pogroms were not the business of the United States.

At the end of our trip, when we again visited the ambassador to summarize the conclusions and recommendations we would make to General McNarney, we tried once more to enlist the American diplomat's support in putting out the fire. Our argument this time was based on the difficulties the U.S. Army would face, and we suggested, none too subtly, that the diplomatic branch should try to help the military branch. Lane replied simply that he would not like to be in the general's shoes right now. Translation; an internal problem in a foreign country – at least this problem in this country – was not the concern of the U.S. Department of State.

Our second appointment was with the Polish prime minister, Edward Osobka-Morawska, and several of his officials. He was polite, urbane, and impressed with the fact that an American general in Germany worried about the situation of Poland's Jews and had dispatched us to investigate. But he regretted that he could not add much to what we had already learned from Ambassador Lane. The prime minister explained that a large, underground movement sought to overthrow his government, and the movement was using Jew-baiting in the same manner that Hitler had done when he sought to take control of Germany. This underground coalition consisted of Fascists, Russia-haters, and similar groups. According to their propaganda, the Jews were running the present communist government; the great majority of the people hated the government; therefore, murdering the Jews would help overthrow it. He was saying essentially the same thing as Lane – with the added twist that the fascists who were killing Jews were also his enemies, for they wanted his head also.

The PM's argument continued in circles. He could not stamp out the fascists because, he admitted, they had substantial popular support. Of course, their propaganda was all lies, because how could the Jews be said to be running the government when there were only three Jewish ministers out of a total of 70? And so it was clear that no assistance could be counted on from the Polish government side. Its officials seemed unhappy but were essentially paralyzed, that is, self-paralyzed.

In a solidly Catholic country like Poland, the reigning cardinal may be the most influential man in the nation. Thinking that Augustus Cardinal Hlond might therefore be able to defuse the situation, we asked for and received an audience. It was not necessary to brief him in detail, for he was quite familiar with the facts and mood. After learning of the concern felt by the U.S. Army, he replied to our request for help in the negative. Our entire interview, held in his chancery, was conducted standing up. It was short, decisive, and entirely unresponsive to our needs.

The tall, heavy-set, bull-necked man showed no sympathy, nor did he attempt to mitigate the harshness of his refusals by word or facial expression. No, he would not call in the leaders of the right-wing groups and ask them to instruct their followers to stop their murderous activities. No, he would not issue a pastoral letter to the clergy instructing them to condemn the pogroms. No, he would not invoke the Papal Bull issued by Pius XII condemning anti-semitism as being anti-Christian.

When we asked for some explanation of that very hard-line position, he said that the Jews had brought this situation on themselves by imposing godless communism on a God-fearing nation, so they deserved whatever punishment the Polish people were currently visiting upon them. He did not go so far as to say that Jews should be eliminated, but he approached that position very closely. The interview was over. We left deeply offended and depressed, but determined not to accept the cardinal's attitude.

We therefore followed up, two months later, with a visit to the Pope's summer residence in Castel Gondolfo, south of Rome. Rabbi Bernstein and I were received warmly, graciously, and sympathetically on a sunny afternoon by the same Pius XII who had issued the Papal Bull we had asked Cardinal Hlond to invoke. The Pope listened carefully, without interrupting except for an occasional murmur of distress when we described something bloody or horrible. When we finished, he asked many questions, seeking to penetrate to the core of the matter: what had the people said whom we had interviewed? Why was the U.S. Army willing to look after all those Jews for an unknown number of years? and so forth until he was finished.

Saving Hlond for last, he said simply that the cardinal's conduct was unsatisfactory. Therefore, he, the Pope himself, would go over the cardinal's head and issue the pastoral letter we had asked for. He would address every parish priest in Poland, giving the moral instruction, and would require that his letter be read in all their churches on the same Sunday three weeks hence. That way, every church-going Pole would hear at the same moment his Pontiff's edict forbidding pogroms against Jews. He commented on the shame –

obvious enough to anyone with moral bearings – inherent in such public behavior occurring only a year after the world was rid of Hitler.

Then the Pope ushered us through French doors opening onto a balcony. Below us, on a beautiful green hillside, we saw scores of children playing. He told us, with visible pride, that these were all Jewish children he and other priests had hidden and saved from death at the Nazi's hands. He was housing them in his own palace until their future would be determined.

Another dramatic moment developed some weeks later. When the pastoral letter was read, it was as though a blanket had been thrown over a fire. The murdering ceased, and although Jews continued to flee Poland, at an accelerated rate, their blood was no longer spilled.

During our investigation in Poland, we held one more curious interview worth recounting. We went to see Yaacov Berman, the leader of the Communist Party (whose office, ironically, was in the most lavish baroque palace I have ever seen). Berman had spent the war years in Moscow, together with other communist leaders-to-be: Rudolf Slansky of Czechoslovakia; Anna Pauker of Rumania; Matyas Rakosi of Hungary; all of them were learning the trade of communist leadership that would become their vocation. And here he was, ensconced in his.

Our talk with Berman, conducted in Yiddish, did not involve putting out the murderous fire. We asked for technical assistance for the Jews in flight. He knew that the Haganah was managing the logistics and that its finances and other facilities were limited. We thought that our conversation, Jew to Jew, in one of our own languages, would surely reach into his heart, and that he would offer concrete help if possible.

Instead, we got a blistering tirade of pure communist ideology: these Jews must consider Poland their motherland and must not desert her; they should remain to help build a strong and successful socialist state; and if they continued to flee, he would do everything possible to stop them, to the extent that he would make sure they left *nacket und borvess*, naked and barefoot.

And that's the way most of the scores of thousands did arrive in Germany, figuratively if not literally naked, escaping from the murdering fascists, the communist boss, the indifferent ambassador, the powerless prime minister, and the hating cardinal. Shepherded by the devoted Haganah leaders across barriers and borders, welcomed by the humanitarian Americans, they came in wave after wave, sometimes a thousand a day by train and hundreds a day by truck, ever westward to safety, even though to an ill-defined future.

Before returning to Germany, we wanted to see the rescue mission in operation. So we flew to a town called Nachod on the Polish-Czech border. During one long night, we witnessed hundreds of refugees, harassed and hounded, survivors of long years of terror or of wartime slave labor in freezing lumber camps in Siberia, boarding trucks, hunkering down under the tarpaulins, without baggage, without papers, parents holding their hands over the mouths of children so that no accidental cry would escape, fear and fever in all of their eyes.

A few encouraging words were whispered by the Haganah men, who went from truck to truck, checking drivers, weapons, jerricans of fuel. The bribes were paid, the old and tired engines coughed into life, and the convoy lumbered across the border and toward Germany. It was heart-breaking and nerve-wracking to witness the indignities. Those people, who had suffered so much and come through alive, were once again assuming the role of the ever-wandering Jew. Germany would be safe, but only a way station. When the wandering would truly end, no one could prophesy. But we all knew that this flight was a gathering of people whose will for a permanent solution in their own country could not forever be frustrated.

After the trucks crossed at Nachod, trains took the people west to Prague, southeast to Bratislava in Slovakia, west again to Vienna, and thence to the final stop in Munich, which became the center of a large Jewish population. By the time the whole operation wound down, in mid-1947, we had a quarter-million Jews living in 64 camps in Germany and Austria. That represented a seven-fold increase over the 35,000 who had been on German soil two years earlier. It was a major migration, and it foreshadowed all the later waves into Israel when that state was finally established.

We flew back to Germany, wrote the final report, which received General McNarney's immediate approval, and found that one more flight was required. McNarney was already mobilizing manpower and supplies to absorb the flood of refugees. He felt, however, that he needed higher political approval to keep the German border open. Therefore he suggested that Rabbi Bernstein fly to Washington, see President Truman and get the green light. Within a week Bernstein was back in Frankfurt carrying Truman's letter of approval. A frenzy of activity followed. It centered on a search for new camp locations – which had to be cleaned out, fitted with cots and kitchens and toilets – and on the thousand details necessary to make life there decent and clean.

After Rabbi Bernstein returned from Washington, he asked if I would come to Frankfurt HQ to serve as his aide, since the officer doing that job, Chaplain Emanuel Rackman, was being demobilized. (He would later become the President and Chancellor of Bar-Ilan University in Israel.) I agreed, of course, honored to work with Bernstein at the very highest Army level.

It was not easy to leave Berlin, to which I had become very attached, or to leave the DPs and camp personnel and Haganah "boys" and JDC team. We had become a well-knit unit, managing two large camps and a steady flow of refugees from Stettin. One consolation was that my successor would be Chaplain Meir Abramowitz, with whom I had shipped overseas; I knew his spirit, enthusiasm, and ability to be first rate. Meir (Mike) later became a Joint Distribution Committee (JDC) officer in a camp in Italy, married a lovely DP there, and wound up in Miami, where he has recently retired after a long and successful rabbinical career.

From my vantage point as Bernstein's aide, I could view the whole picture. Policy involving Jewish DPs throughout the European Theater was set in our office. Following the Landsberg trial, Major Abe Hyman, who had handled the trial so skillfully, accepted an invitation to join our staff, even though he predicted (correctly) that this decision would keep him in Germany five more years. (He closed the office as the last advisor in 1950.)

We worked with the major Jewish organizations from the United States and Palestine; mobilized a dozen new chaplains to ride the trains every day, offering comfort and security to the refugees; visited the camps constantly to determine problems and solve them; and coordinated our efforts with the Central Committee, whose scope had expanded from Bavaria to encompass the entire American zone. It was a rich experience, filled with enormous satisfaction.

Especially enriching was the spirit of the DPs. They had a strength and a measure of courage I had never seen before. They sang songs fiercely and proudly, as though to remind the world that they were alive and vibrant and therefore entitled to a solution to their homelessness; and as though to remind themselves that they would not be forgotten but would eventually gain that solution. The DPs were simply inspiring, and no matter how much any of us gave them in the way of material good and our own efforts, we received ten times as much in return. I have always been grateful for their example of determination, confidence, faith in self, belief in man, and, above all, the courage to avoid permanent despair and always to hope.

CHAPTER TEN

BABENHAUSEN'S DESPERATE DPS

The office of Advisor on Jewish Affairs to the Commanding General of the European Theater consisted of the Advisor, Rabbi Bernstein, a most tactful yet powerful man; Major Hyman, a skilled and effective lawyer, and myself, recently promoted to captain. We were physically located in the I.G. Farben Building in Frankfurt, a massive complex belonging to one of Germany's largest industrial corporations, which had not been hit by a single bomb during the entire war. Half the city of Frankfurt was rubble. Yet this complex was absolutely intact, for a specific reason: It had been pre-selected as the future American Headquarters and was therefore not to be damaged.

Our set of offices immediately adjoined those of the commander himself, the four-star General McNarney. The status and condition of the Jewish DPs was not only sensitive enough to warrant the appointment of a special advisor to assist the Army, but it was also to keep the advisor instantly on hand in the event of trouble.

Rabbi Bernstein's simulated rank of major general entitled him to a large villa in the neighboring suburb of Bad Homburg, a lovely, wooded section in the foothills of the Taunus mountains. The house belonged to a general in the German Wehrmacht, who at that moment was in prison. I had a room in the house. Bernstein skillfully used the residence, and his large liquor ration, as a hospitality center, constantly entertaining senior staff officers during evenings that included relaxed discussions about Jews, what they were like, what the religion stood for; their hopes for a homeland in Palestine; what the basic notion of peoplehood meant.

Those low-key conversations, buttressed with cigars and drinks and aided by Bernstein's endless supply of stories and jokes, did more to explain to those officers the psychology and yearnings of the DP population than any number of ordinary briefings that usually left listeners half asleep. His approach reduced resistance, engendered support and sympathy, and made our fundamental job of interpreting the needs and wants of the DPs to the Army infinitely easier.

The larger picture of the DPs' future remained unclear. President Truman proposed that 100,000 Jewish DPs be transferred from the camps in Germany to Palestine as a humanitarian gesture, without prejudicing an ultimate political solution. His suggestion quickly became bogged down in diplomatic controversy with the British Government. Thus the future looked bleak, and the major Jewish organizations in the United States understood that. They were particularly sensitive to the mood of despondency in the camps. Anxious to do something impressive to show support for the DPs, they organized the most prestigious American-Jewish mission ever assembled and sent it to Germany. Heading the delegation was Rabbi Stephen S. Wise, the top religious and organizational leader of U.S. Jewry. Other members representing major institutions were: Dr. Nahum Goldmann, Zionist Organization and Jewish Agency; Jacob Blaustein, American Jewish Committee; Judge Philip Forman, Joint Distribution Committee; Isaiah L. Kenen, American Jewish Conference and America-Israel Public Affairs Committee (AIPAC).

The stature of the delegation was intended to send a message to the DPs; that American Jewry stood solidly behind them and would do its best to achieve what they wanted so badly – an independent homeland in Palestine to which they could go openly, legally as a birthright. The delegation also brought a message of heartfelt appreciation to the U.S. Army. At its highest levels, that institution had become sincerely and deeply involved in the effort to make camp life bearable and had become frustrated with the political stalemate that prevented a permanent solution.

The Army was showing the very best side of American humanitarianism in its handling of a civilian refugee situation, a task for which it was not trained. A high point of the delegation's visit was a splendid dinner given by General McNarney at headquarters. Rabbi Wise addressed the wearers of the glittering array of stars and medals at that table, thanking them, complimenting their understanding and sympathy, stressing the morality of their conduct – without striking a single false note of flattery.

The delegation returned to the United States and stated emphatically in its report that everything possible must be done to aid the DPs. The report coincided with the Jewish community's growing consciousness, as expressed in the rapidly accelerating campaign of the United Jewish Appeal. During the previous year, 1945, with the War still on and amid deep gloom, the campaign had produced $15 million. (Although Allied victory was at hand, it was obvious that money could not help save the lives of Europe's Jews.)

Both the attitude and the fundraising goals changed dramatically once the war ended. For 1946, under the leadership of Executive Vice-Chairman Henry Montor, and former Secretary of the Treasury Henry Morgenthau Jr., the UJA proposed a campaign goal of $100 million – almost seven times the amount raised a year earlier! American Jews met the challenge with great enthusiasm. Lay leaders rallied; effective plans and good organization were created; pace-setting gifts were solicited; and the goal was *surpassed* by $2 million.

To go from $15 million to $102 million in one year demonstrated that action had replaced frustration, determination had replaced impotent rage; and feelings of solidarity and peoplehood overwhelmed an American Jewry that had been separated by oceans of space and a half-century of time from its European roots. In the decades ahead, the growth in Jewish fundraising would be astonishing, and I would be an integral part of it.

Another significant result of the delegation's visit to Germany took place just a few weeks after its members returned home. On September 7, in the war room of the I.G. Farben Building in Frankfurt, General McNarney and Dr. Samuel Gringaus signed an historic document that recognized the Central Committee of Liberated Jews in Germany as the legal representative – the acting government, so to speak – of the quarter-million Jews in the camps. This Charter of Recognition stated expressly that the refugees, although at present homeless, were indeed a political entity, and their recognition as such was the first step toward the inevitable conclusion of providing them with a homeland. The ceremony that day foreshadowed one 14 months later, on November 29th, 1947, when the United Nations would confirm the partition of Palestine into Arab and Jewish states. Thus is history usually made – in small steps, one leading to another.

In Frankfurt, the signatories to the Charter were invited into the general's dining room, the same one in which the American delegation had been feted a few weeks earlier. This time, the half-dozen refugees present were treated with the same respect and dignity as had been extended to their famous American predecessors. The Central Committee members, all well-educated men (Chairman Gringaus had been a judge in Lithuania), all sophisticated, all tempered in the fire of the previous years, all experienced leaders (even though the youngest was only twenty-five), made strong impressions on the military brass. That was important, for the Army had decided to issue identity documents to the committee members, entitling them to use Army transportation, enter areas controlled by the Army, enjoy currency privileges, and receive many other forms of logistical support that would enable them to travel freely throughout the American zone in pursuit of their now-legal activities. A liaison officer of the G-5 Section, a full colonel named Scithers, was placed at the Central Committee's disposal.

I expended a great deal of effort behind the scenes to supplement Phil Bernstein's discussion evenings. Field-grade officers – majors and colonels – would be the ones to carry out the orders of their superiors, without the benefit of the psychological and factual explanations offered in the living room at Bad Homburg. So I made my rounds again and again through the G-5 section and Colonel Scithers' staff to explain the logic of maintaining the morale of these innocent victims.

The Central Committee members were like the cabinet of a government-to-be. In their visits to the 64 camps, they brought hope and information, listened to complaints, and ironed out bureaucratic hassles with the Army, as it was now their new official right to do. I felt myself and my constant interventions akin to an oil can enabling a balky engine to run more smoothly. Gradually everything worked well, up and down the line.

Through this Charter of Recognition, the U.S. Army was saying something that no other arm of any Allied government was yet willing to say – that the Jewish DPs must be recognized as different. All other DPs could be repatriated to a homeland; only the Jews were without one. That difference could be remedied by a political decision beyond the Army's capability. But in the meantime, the Army would declare, in effect, that Palestine had to be recognized someday as the DPs' homeland. Thus, the most important military arm of the United States was accepting the basic premises of the Zionist movement. How remarkable!

I maintained a high level of involvement in DP affairs. Chaplain Abramowitz in Berlin kept the refugee flow coming from Stettin in the north, while the numbers moving along the southern route to Munich increased daily.

Soon the rate reached one trainload – with about 1,000 passengers – entering Munich every day. The first-stage truck and subsequent trains crossed four national borders, starting in Czechoslovakia, touching Hungary, then Austria, and finally Germany. The journey took several days and offered no comforts whatever: no beds, not enough seats, frequently no food except the parcel each person carried; and very often the cars were the same freight wagons that had carried other Jews to their deaths in Treblinka or Auschwitz. There was every opportunity for trouble: at borders; with babies and pregnant mothers; with traumatized individuals who desperately sought freedom but could not stand the shock of re-boarding those "death" wagons.

Escort personnel from the JDC or Jewish Agency, or even plain-clothes Haganah men dressed like refugees, almost always traveled on the trains. But Abe Hyman and I wanted an additional layer of support in the person of a uniformed U.S. Army officer, carrying travel orders for the train, who could deal officially with border-crossing difficulties. Although such an officer could be requisitioned through the Army's G-5, we preferred someone we knew would be knowledgeable about and sympathetic to the state of mind and nerves of the passengers, as well as able to communicate with them in Hebrew or Yiddish. The solution was to have a Jewish military chaplain on board every train every day. But by this time, more than a year after the European War had ended, few Jewish chaplains remained on active duty in Germany; most had been transferred to the Pacific theater or demobilized.

Rabbi Bernstein quickly agreed to persuade the Army to requisition a dozen Jewish chaplains for temporary duty. The call went out. Some demobilized men re-enlisted; some new ones volunteered. In a surprisingly short time, every train rolling in to Munich's Central Station had a chaplain on board. Distribution of the passengers to other destinations throughout Germany also took place at the Munich station, so that refugees arrived at their camps before the day was out. The tremendous flow continued with hardly an incident – save one.

On the morning of October 1, I stood at a railroad siding at Babenhausen, near Frankfurt, facing a silent rebellion. Peering fearfully and questioningly from the boxcars of the international train were 1,200 DPs from Poland. I was attempting to persuade them to detrain and enter the camp that lay before their eyes. It was a former prisoner of war facility in which the Nazis had held Russians and other captives, a rough-hewn, dirty place; concrete floors strewn with rodent-infested straw, a few outhouses, some three-tiered bunks, watchtowers every 50 meters, and endless coils of barbed wire. The passengers balked at entering such a place.

Travel-weary, hoping for a better life, viewing Babenhausen with foreboding, they did the only thing they could do – strike. They refused to get out. Their eyes, staring stonily above grimly set mouths, eloquently expressed arguments I was to hear constantly for the next 48 hours: "The Nazis packed us in boxcars and brought us to barbed wire camps. The Poles wouldn't let us live. We're sick of being ordered about by men in uniform, tired of being kicked around. How can our children and pregnant women live in this place? Did we flee for our lives to come to this?"

It was the kind of deeply ingrained distrust and bitterness and weariness that could lead to a riot. Nobody wanted that. The Army would not and could not get tough with these recalcitrant victims of history. And the DPs, for their part, instinctively felt the Army's good will. They heard officers criticizing other officers for not having dismantled the barbed wire earlier. They heard the explanation that the Army was opening camps at an exhausting rate, so sometimes something slipped – like the wire inadvertently left in place.

Nevertheless, having been the victims of outrage for so long, they would not now submit to more, even from the Americans.

In this delicate crosspatch of emotions, my positions as a Jew and an American officer chafed one against the other. I could not seem to be throwing my uniformed weight around to force the DPs to disembark, but neither could I let them stay on the trains. I had to make clear my sympathetic understanding for their plight, without reinforcing their stubbornness.

Although the situation was obviously explosive, I was sure it was not hopeless. A heartening precedent had been set only the day before, when a previous trainload of refugees had also refused to disembark at Babenhausen. Abe Hyman of our office and two Third Army chaplains, one a Catholic, had intervened persuasively. A long line of GIs had gone up and down the train distributing food and drink. Gradually, people jumped down from the cars, and by nightfall all but a handful had entered the camp.

But today's bunch was tougher. I made the round of the boxcars, talking to hundreds of people, both individually and collectively with a microphone. I argued that, while the accommodations at Babenhausen were far from perfect, the Army was providing a haven for them. It would now do all in its power to improve conditions as quickly as possible.

The faces before me remained impassive for the most part. When my listeners spoke, it was to voice their litany of bitterness or to ask when they would be able to leave the camp and proceed to Palestine. By the end of the day, we had convinced only 120 people to enter the camp. More than 1,000 remained on the train. I slept fitfully in the camp that night.

If melodrama were to dictate this account, I could report that the back of the resistance was broken by some *deus ex machina* – a momentous event, a single bold stroke. Actually, I arranged a series of actions that together succeeded in emptying the train and filling the camp. First, early the following morning, I organized a group of the previous arrivals to board the boxcars and persuade their new comrades that the place could be made livable. GIs could already be seen dismantling the hateful barbed wire. The DPs already inside took several hundred of the newcomers back with them.

Later in the morning, Rabbi Schechter, of the orthodox *Vaad Hatzalah* (Rescue Committee), persuaded another hundred or two to make the move.

And in mid-afternoon, Lieutenant-General Keyes, commander of the Third Army, arrived and took the microphone. As I translated his words into Yiddish, the DPs were quiet and more attentive than they had been all day. When he finished, he jumped into a jeep, took the wheel himself, shouted for them to follow him, and drove slowly into the camp. Behind him trudged most of the remaining refugees.

That was the end of the DP rebellion at Babenhausen. By nightfall, all but 105 were in the camp, and most of the laggards entered the next day.

Army and JDC personnel fed, registered, billeted, and cared for the sick among them. Morale soared, as the bustling sounds of hope replaced the grim stillness of the previous 48 hours. When I left, at 10 that night, everyone had a cot and blankets, everyone had been fed and had cleaned themselves up; new clothing was being issued; and the camp was quiet. This time it was a near-calmness, not the heavy silence of disillusion and latent hysteria. The situation seemed stabilized.

Stabilized, but not resolved. As the days and weeks passed, word spread about what had happened. No matter which camp in Germany I visited, I kept hearing the name Babenhausen. It became a symbol for restlessness, for the huge problem of being stuck in camps without a solution for the future. The question grew more persistent: "When will we get to Palestine?"

About two months later, I was able to help supply an answer. David Ben-Gurion, chairman of the Jewish Agency, was in Paris, en route to Switzerland to attend the first World Zionist Congress to be held since 1939. He wanted to visit a refugee camp – not a model operation, but one in which he could see the true, rough fiber of DP life. I obtained permits for him and his companion-bodyguard, Mordechai Surkis, to enter the American zone, and I took them to Babenhausen.

We were joined there by Abe Hyman and Dr. Chaim Hoffman (later Yahil), head of all the Jewish Agency personnel working in Germany. Hoffman was a gentle, soft-spoken, educated European who personified the best type of immigrant who had gone to Palestine in the 1930s. He was now applying his talents and communicating his optimism by working among the DPs. I was certain that the visit by this prestigious group would raise morale and further improve the mood in the camps.

We therefore publicized throughout Babenhausen the time and place of Ben-Gurion's appearance. He was the clear and undisputed leader of the Jewish population of Palestine (about 600,000 at that time) and the leader of world Jewry's thrust toward a sovereign state. He was a fighter – the small, cocky, bantam rooster – the charismatic, world-famous symbol of the Zionist force. A visit from him would be incandescent.

For the occasion, we utilized the camp's largest stable, with a small stage at one end and standing room for thousands of people. Ben-Gurion's presence did indeed produce an electric wave of excitement. So many DPs crowded in that it seemed almost all of the camp's 5,000 residents were pressed into that area. They knew that this dynamic, white-haired man was their link with a history they thought had forgotten them.

For the first time, there were smiles inside the gates of Babenhausen. And then came the inevitable question – poignant, pleading, uncertain, wavering, but persistent: "When, Mr. Ben-Gurion? When will we get to Palestine?"

As Ben-Gurion listened to those questions, he began to weep, the only time in my long relationship with him I saw that happen. The tears fell slowly. He spoke through them, quietly but firmly. I remember his words almost exactly:

"I come to you with empty pockets. I have no British [entrance] certificates to give you. I can only tell you that you are not abandoned, you are not alone, you will not live endlessly in camps like this. All of you who want to come to Palestine will be brought there as soon as is humanly possible. I bring you no certificates – only hope. Let us sing our national anthem – *Hatikvah* (Hope)."

With that, this great leader of the Jewish people and future prime minister of the state-to-be turned to those of us standing on the platform with him for help with the song. Alas, there wasn't a good voice among us. The mass of people carried the tune.

In that way, the people of Babenhausen understood that their unloved camp was not the end of the line but a way station on the road to freedom. The distrust and bitterness I had faced on the railroad tracks in October finally gave way to patient hope in December. Post-war Jewish history was proceeding once more along its troubled but true course.

CHAPTER ELEVEN

THE ARMY TALMUD

So much of the DP story seems to concentrate on the purely material aspects of life – trucks and trains, bed and breakfast, medicines and clothing – that it is important to add some insights on the spiritual side. After the apparent absence of God during the maniacal years of their torment, the survivors were not strong in religious faith. But they were fierce in their ethnicity; they clung to each other desperately and were loyal to their peoplehood. Their self-definitions did include some religious holidays, a few ritual artifacts, and books of traditional significance.

In the camps, although religious services were not overwhelmingly attended, Passover and Chanukah involved massive preparations and major excitement. In the same vein, when a project was proposed that contained the essence of Judaism but skirted the problem of belief in God, it met with wide approval. One such idea began to surface toward the end of 1946, and even though it took several years to come to final fruition, both the continuous discussion about it and the progress reports concerning its development were part of the spiritual balance I spoke of earlier.

The chief rabbi of the Central Committee (and thus of all the Jews in the camps), Samuel Snieg, and his assistant, Rabbi Samuel Rose, were obsessed with the notion of printing in Germany an edition of the Talmud – a 19-volume collection of laws, commentaries, dialogues, legends, and moral aphorisms recorded over more than a half-millenium by hundreds of rabbis and scholars.

It seemed to them that this compendium was exactly the correct symbol for marking the end of the Nazi period. Reprinting the Talmud on German soil would be the example par excellence of Jewish indestructibility in the face of the most vicious attack ever launched on a people or culture. We were still walking the stage of history, and reprinting the Talmud would prove it. The idea of a DP edition, produced in the land of book-and-people burning, contained a touch of genius.

The Snieg-Rose theme captured the imagination of Rabbi Bernstein, who sold it to General Lucius D. Clay, soon to succeed General McNarney as commander of the entire European Theater. The practical difficulties were immense, however. To print 19 large, folio volumes required the use of a major printing plant over a number of months, perhaps years – hard to find in post-war Germany – as well as mountains of scarce paper and large sums of money.

The JDC quickly guaranteed to underwrite part of the expense, and the Army guaranteed that the German economy would contribute the balance – up to a quarter-million marks. By 1947, part of the paper was available – brought in from Sweden, as I recall – and a printing firm in Stuttgart began making the plates. Rabbis Snieg and Rose commuted from Munich to supervise and correct the proof sheets. The first volumes were bound in 1949. Seven hundred and fifty sets of 19 volumes each were completed, dedicated to the U.S. Army of Occupation, and, in 1951, shipped to notable individuals and the great libraries of the United States, Israel, Europe, and Canada.

The title page contains drawings of a Nazi labor camp and a sandy beach in Israel, together with these words:

> Published through the Rabbinical Association
> in the American Zone of Germany
> With the help of the American Military Command
> and the Joint Distribution Committee, in Germany

The dedication page contains this paragraph in English:

> This edition of the Talmud is dedicated to the United States Army. The Army played a major role in the rescue of the Jewish people from total annihilation, and after the defeat of Hitler bore the major burden of sustaining the DPs of the Jewish faith. This special edition of the Talmud, published in the very land where, but a short time ago, everything Jewish and of Jewish inspiration was anathema, will remain a symbol of the indestructibility of the Torah. The Jewish DPs will never forget the generous impulses and the unprecedented humanitarianism of the American forces, to whom they owe so much.

> In the name of the Rabbinical Organization
Rabbi Samuel A. Snieg
Chief Rabbi of the U.S. Zone

In the Hebrew Introduction, there is a paragraph specifically devoted to Rabbi Bernstein. It reads:

> As time passed we longed to produce the complete Talmud but it was beyond our capacity to do so. Therefore we turned to the authority of the American Army in Germany that they should enable us to produce the Talmud. This wish succeeded, thanks to the help of the Advisor on Jewish Affairs to the Army, Dr. Rabbi Philip S. Bernstein, and our request was fulfilled, with the help of God. And this day is a day of good news in Israel.

A set of the Army Talmud sits on my bookshelf. And while my efforts to study it are still fraught with difficulty, my appreciation of the work as the symbol it was intended to be grows deeper with each passing year.

CHAPTER TWELVE

ACROSS THE ALPS ON FOOT

Any account of the Jewish DP experience, during the frenetic period 1945-1948, must deal with three basic phases: the *gathering* of the ragged element of survivors into camps as the havens where the American flag represented safety and sustenance; the *waiting* in those camps during the long years when hope for a homeland in Palestine was thwarted by the political considerations of the British; and the *flight* from the camps by a minority of the DPs in a dangerous effort to reach the Promised Land. Tales of the first two phases have been told, in some measure, earlier in this memoir and elsewhere. But the third is largely untold, except for the single, most famous episode of the S.S. Exodus.

The flight out was generally directed southward to the French and Italian coasts, for the voyage to Palestine could be made only by ship. Neither railway nor roadway was practical for the long journey, since crossing the borders of many countries en route would require a tangle of identification papers, visas, bribes, and accompanying support personnel. Nor was there an air option, because of cost and – in that early era of commercial aviation – insufficient equipment.

The convoys out of Germany, usually 50 trucks or more, crossed the Rhine via a long bridge at Kehl that brought them to French soil in Strasbourg. Escorting in the lead of the long line of vehicles were a couple of jeeps, flying the Stars and Stripes and manned by a few Haganah operatives in the hybrid khaki uniforms that could be taken for American, waving sheets of paper stamped with large red seals and ribbons. (A chaplain, Max Braude, once told me that he possessed a certificate of a Kentucky Colonel. That title was a standing joke in the United States, but it impressed the red-ribbon-loving border guards.)

The British knew as well as the Haganah the only feasible route for the DPs bound "illegally" for Palestine. So British agents kept the Kehl bridge under surveillance, calculating that 2,000 or so Jews would wind up in the Marseilles area within a day or two after crossing it. The Brits also examined the small ports nearby for tramp steamers that might be lurking to pick up a large human cargo.

The Italian ports provided a different story. Austria is contiguous to Italy, so crossings could be made at many points. Because the British could not watch them all, the Haganah preferred to use the Austrian-Italian route more often. One large obstacle stood in the way: the Austrian Alps.

In Austria, south of Berchtesgaden, in the Alpine town where Hitler had his "Eagle's Nest," was a DP camp called Saalfelden. This camp had a very special significance: it provided a staging area from which groups of refugees who were willing to take the risk attempted to enter Italy by walking across and around one of the highest mountains in the Alps. That mountain, called Gross Glockner, reaches 12,500 feet into the sky. Snow piled up on it most of the year; the air was quite thin, and it was invariably very cold and windy. Yet many DPs, after years of warding off death at the hands of the Nazis and additional years of waiting for a homeland, seized this perilous escape opportunity.

From Austria, there was no possibility of organizing lengthy truck convoys. Small groups, 40 or so persons, had to circumvent the Alps on foot and then re-assemble on the Italian side into shipload size, to be sent by truck and train to the ports of La Spezia or Genoa. I marched with one such group, so that I could literally know and feel what they experienced, and I have never forgotten it.

My participation in this journey was not illegal from the U.S. Army's viewpoint. I was in full uniform and fulfilling one of my functions, namely familiarizing myself with all aspects of DP life. Nor did laws and regulations inhibit the group's movement. There was no Army regulation against DPs crossing borders in an attempt to reach a port, nor interest on the part of UNRRA officials in preventing Jews from leaving the camps. And the Italian border police were notably lax, even friendly, for they knew the DP destinations and understood that the travelers were not planning to remain as a burden on Italian soil.

I went to Saalfelden, to watch the procedure. The slow, painstaking process of selecting the group focused on each individual's health and strength, because the journey was enormously difficult from a purely physical point of view. Nevertheless, old people were smuggled into the column – at the last moment, in the dark of night – by their adult children who did not want to leave them behind. Babies were also smuggled in, hidden in knapsacks carried on their parents' backs. Everybody in the group received warm clothing provided by the JDC. It added weight and made climbing more difficult, but without it many would freeze: When fatigue overtook them, and the column halted for rest, hikers often simply fell into the soft snow and went to sleep. It was therefore easy to drift into death, and some did, especially those who were feeble or not warmly dressed.

The preparations continued. Each person received food and a large canteen of water. They added still more weight, but the total journey ahead could easily be 72 or more hours, and the nourishment was essential. In addition to a full pack on the back, some hikers carried a small case holding precious things they could not discard: a photo album of loved ones, now mostly dead; notebooks with accounts of what had happened to them during the Holocaust years; a good-luck item.

Thus garbed and burdened, they set forth, silently, in the night, for sound carried far in the high Tyrolean Alps, and they must, if possible, go unnoticed. The Haganah escorts and guards, additionally loaded down with strong torches, weapons, ice axes, and long staves to help pull weary people up slippery slopes, marched on both sides of the column and to its front and rear, like sheep dogs watching their flock as it moved slowly along.

Although the Haganah guards did carry personal weapons – side arms and carbines – I was told that so far there had been no need for them. Many small groups had proceeded ours without incident. They did not use paved roads, and there were no bands of ex-Nazis nor highwaymen in the wooded, mountainous terrain. Patrols of Austrian border police were irregular and infrequent. Nature, not human enemies, took a toll.

The journey on foot was truly arduous. Struggling through hip-high snow, sinking in and pulling out, falling, tripping, calling for help, sometimes panicking; crossing bare, stony ridges; picking a wind-swept path between large boulders; traveling a circuitous route through forests, ravines, and valleys – always vulnerable to the bitter wind. It was a miracle that the column was not cut to pieces and thoroughly decimated.

But the Haganah escorts were skilled and the refugees' willpower massive, so slowly, slowly they all inched toward either of two destination points. One was Merano, Italy, and there were two ways to reach it: through Lienz, in Austria, where Haganah trucks picked them up, bribed their way across the Italian border, and drove to Merano; or via the preferable route, if an unguarded point could be found, on foot across the border toward the Italian village of Brunico, where they could be driven to Merano. There they boarded trains and headed for the Mediterranean coast. Genoa and La Spezia were the favored ports, as well as nearby coves and bays for small vessels.

Once the group with which I traveled reached Genoa and assembled with others, its members boarded the Haganah vessel, and I left them to return to Frankfurt. But I knew what would happen next. When the ship was at sea, in international waters, the British were free to follow it. And at a time and place of their choosing, usually close to the Palestine coast, their naval vessel would pull alongside the refugee ship, and British marines would literally jump across on board. Sometimes there were brief scuffles between the DPs and marines; sometimes injuries, infrequently deaths, mostly silent acquiescence.

The British escorted the DP vessel into Haifa harbor, herded the people across the dock to another ship, which took them to the island of Cyprus. There they were put in a prison camp. As the numbers I cited earlier testify, the British were all too tenacious and successful in tracking and intercepting the refugee ships.

One point about the whole Aliya Bet movement in general, and the flight from DP camps in particular, must be understood. Whether from Austria to Italy, or from Germany down to the French Riviera, the British always knew that the Jews were coming, and the Jews always knew that they had only one chance in nine of not getting caught. The Jews also knew that, if apprehended, they would wind up prisoners on Cyprus.

But as a Mediterranean island, only about eight hours from Palestine, Cyprus was <u>almost</u> home and thus a worthy goal. Out of 66 vessels sent forth by the Haganah, 57 were caught, and approximately 60,000 passengers were taken to Cyprus. That was a great victory, and the fact that the Haganah viewed it as such, and continued the operation, infuriated the British. It also made the brutal climb across the Gross Glockner well worth the effort and danger.

CHAPTER THIRTEEN

THE STOLEN BOOKS OF OFFENBACH

Hitler's regime, under the direction of its philosopher, Alfred Rosenberg, planned to accumulate a vast library of Judaica. The perverted purpose: to enable Nazi "scholars" to search the literature for quotations that would serve to condemn the Jews and their religion in the eyes of the world, thus validating the charge that this whole people endangered mankind and must be exterminated. Jews, the exercise aimed to prove, worshipped money, extorted it from the Christians they despised, were sexually unclean and promiscuous, believed in communism, spat at churches, possessed a secret government that plotted to take over the whole world; and there were many other similarly poisonous accusations.

The most insidious aspect was to prove all that by using the Jews' own words, taken from their own documents. To that end, the Nazis commandeered a large warehouse in Offenbach, just across the Main River from Frankfurt, as a repository for Jewish books, manuscripts, other documents, and incunabula from all the countries in Europe under German domination. Over the years, the pilfered collection grew to more than three million items, and knowledge of its existence spread through the Jewish world.

After the War, Allied inventories of Nazi government buildings turned up the collection. It ultimately came under the authority of the Fine Arts Section of the American military government. A professor at the Hebrew University in

Jerusalem, the famed Gershom Scholem, applied through the Jewish Agency for permission to examine the materials. The military government granted permission on two conditions: that the scholar remain in Germany no longer than 90 days; and that he not remove a single item. Scholem accepted the conditions, arrived, paid his respects at our office, and went to work in Offenbach. Our office heard nothing from him until a distraught call brought me to the warehouse.

There, Scholem explained the problem. In his diligent search through the enormous pile of materials, he had identified and set aside 1,100 pieces, mostly hand-written manuscripts of incalculable value, each one unique, all looted from museums, synagogues, private collections, and all absolutely irreplaceable. He was so nervous about the treasured items that, loath to see them thrown once more into the anonymous pile or stolen for sale on the black market then flourishing in Germany, he kept them segregated in five large, wooden crates. He had marked each with his name and address, but without a description of contents.

Scholem then asked the Fine Arts Section to reconsider its previous requirement and allow him to take the five crates to Jerusalem, where they would be carefully kept in the Rare Book Vault of the Hebrew University Library. The American authorities refused, explaining that the Jewish Theological Seminary (JTS) in the United States had put in a bid for at least part of the Offenbach corpus, and the Army did not want to get in the middle of an argument between Palestinian and American Jewish academic institutions. Therefore, the materials would remain under military jurisdiction in Germany until final disposition was decided.

Scholem was beside himself with fear that if the crates were left in the Offenbach depot, word of their value would leak, and they would be stolen. The threat of theft had not existed before he arrived because a vast collection of three million undifferentiated items was not tempting, and their existence was known to only a select few individuals. But now that a small collection of most precious items had been chosen and conveniently gathered in five crates, gossips or leaks created a dangerous situation.

Single pages of Beethoven or Mozart manuscripts, including those of the most dubious origin, were commanding $10,000 on the black market. Even at much lower prices, the parchment manuscripts in all those crates would fetch several millions. Scholem was also enraged that the JTS had intervened, preventing the material from going to Jerusalem, which he regarded as its rightful home. When he finished telling me the story, he actually broke down from fatigue, strain, and worry.

I came up with an instant solution: I would steal the boxes and see that they reached safekeeping in Jerusalem. I made that rash and risky declaration without consulting anyone and without having a plan in my head; my response came straight from the heart.

I told Scholem not to worry and to spend the last few days of his visit touring the city of his birth, Berlin, where I had friends who would care for him. I would inform him before long how and when the crates would reach him, and assured him that I had the most remarkable reputation for keeping promises. I wanted very much to comfort him. Slowly his face relaxed, and as we parted, he said carefully that he was inclined to believe me.

The following scheme soon evolved: I would tell Captain Jacob Benkowitz, the officer in charge of the Offenbach depot, of my intention to remove the crates of books (of whose real contents he was unaware) for distribution to the many DP camp libraries. That was permitted by Fine Arts and had already occurred many times. I would "borrow" a Joint Distribution Committee ambulance, just the right-sized windowless vehicle. On New Year's Eve, a few days hence, I would pull the ambulance up to the rear loading dock around midnight, when the personnel on duty would presumably be somewhat less than sharply alert. If not too drunk, they would see only a khaki-colored vehicle, with Army plates and an officer in uniform behind the wheel. I would ask one or two to help me load, then drive the ambulance to a locked garage, where it would sit until I could secure orders from my headquarters for a few days leave-time in Paris. Thence the final step was to load the ambulance and myself into a freight car bound for Paris, and deliver the crates to Jewish Agency officials.

Everything went smoothly, and January 15 found me at 135 Avenue Wagram, Paris, in the Jewish Agency office, with the ambulance parked on that elegant street. I was somewhat less elegant, having slept in the freight car alongside my precious vehicle. The Agency agreed to send a message to

Professor Scholem that I had the books, but also insisted that it would not compromise its status in Germany by trafficking in stolen U.S. Army goods. Illegal immigration against the British was one thing, but entering a conspiracy against the Americans was another.

Agency officials did, however, give me some helpful advice. They told me that Dr. Chaim Weizmann's library in England was being packed and shipped to Palestine, on a vessel leaving from Antwerp in a few days. Integrating my five crates with dozens of his would be the easiest way to smuggle the goods in to Palestine and Scholem. So it turned out to be. I drove the ambulance to Antwerp, got my cargo on board, informed Scholem how and when it was due to arrive, and considered the matter closed.

One morning, a few weeks later, I found two Criminal Investigation Department (CID) men waiting for me. They quietly and calmly charged me with grand larceny, laid out their evidence, and indicated they were submitting it to the Judge Advocate General, who would convene a general court martial. They had done a very thorough job and had me dead to rights: the license number of the ambulance, the number of the freight car, the names of the Jewish Agency man in Paris, and the vessel at Antwerp, even the receipt I had signed to get the boxes out of the Offenbach depot. I had signed the name of Koppel Pinson, the JDC education officer who was authorized to draw books of no particular value for distribution in the camps. The fact that he had left Germany months before hadn't bothered me, although I did put my initials under his name.

I denied everything, simply to stall for a short time, until I could plan a strategy. The best course, I decided, was to tell the whole story to Rabbi Bernstein. His reaction was wonderful. At first he was worried that I would have to endure some serious punishment; then he chuckled over the complexity of the adventure, and wound up praising me for the idealism of the deed. That last thought gave him a vital clue as to how to proceed.

He suggested that he would pave the way for me immediately to see General Lucius D. Clay, the new Commander of U.S. Forces in the European Theater, to throw myself on his mercy by stressing the idealistic motives that impelled me. In other words, I should readily admit to the crime and ask for clemency. That's exactly what I did.

Clay was a quiet, firm, very intelligent man, a four-star general who was as much an administrator as a warrior. He listened, asked questions, and at the end clearly understood the circumstances and the motivation behind my action. He thought for several moments, then called the head of the CID, to inform him that charges against me were to be dropped. No court martial would be convened. He, General Clay, would personally handle the matter.

He then turned to me, gave me a short lecture on the dangers of excessive zeal, and said he would recall the crates from Jerusalem. Following that, I would be ordered back to the United States for an honorable discharge from the Army.

From Clay's point of view, it was a just and humane solution. I accepted the second point – there really was no choice – but decided instantly that I would push my luck and seek to change his mind on the first. I pleaded with him not to submit the crates and their precious contents to another journey. Luckily, nothing had happened so far. I suggested that Professor Scholem be ordered not to open the boxes except in the presence of some U.S. authority in Jerusalem, so that an inventory could be taken and an affidavit prepared stipulating that nothing was missing. Then the crates could safely be left in Jerusalem under the joint custody of Scholem and the U.S. Army's representative until final disposition was agreed upon.

Clay listened carefully, said that made sense, and ordered an aide to carry out such a plan. I breathed a sigh of relief, expressed my gratitude for his broad-mindedness, and left in wonderment that the difficult and risky thing I had done had ended with such success. I was also struck at the historic proportions of the episode. These manuscripts, remnants of our people's past, at risk of destruction in the present, had been saved for the future, and I had been privileged to play a pivotal role in the adventure.

My relief at the deal involving the materials proved to be short lived. The crates were stored in the library of the Hebrew University on Mount Scopus in Jerusalem. But 18 months later, during the War of Independence in Israel, Scopus fell into Jordanian hands. What tricks fate plays!

Once again, however, patience and ingenuity solved the situation. A clause in the armistice agreement with Jordan permitted Israel to station 25 or so of her soldiers on Jordanian territory – in reality, a 100-meter trench on Scopus –

as a symbolic gesture of supervision over the Hadassah Hospital and the few university buildings. This group of men rotated every two weeks The Israeli officer in charge knew that the Scholem material lay in a nearby Hebrew University building. He succeeded in bringing small numbers of manuscripts to the trench and hiding them, one at a time, under his soldiers' shirts.

When the rotating group descended from Scopus to Israeli territory in U.N. vehicles, there was no body search, and the hidden cargo returned to Israeli hands. The relieving group was taken up, and two weeks later, when they came down, another batch came with them. This process was repeated – over the course of <u>several years</u> – until all the manuscripts had been brought down and carefully gathered by Scholem, with no loss whatsoever.

And so, in the end, the story does conclude happily. Rescued from the Nazi trap, brought to British Palestine, carried through the fire of the birth of Israel, caught in Jordan's hands, and free at last, the manuscripts seemed like living beings, their course paralleling that of the Jewish people itself.

★ ★ ★

I have often reflected on the significance of the three dramatic episodes I've recounted in this memoir: Martin Riessenburger's survival by the grace of animal skin Torah scrolls; the Army-JDC creation of a unique edition of the Talmud; and the five cases of Professor Scholem's manuscripts. Although ostensibly isolated, they are, I believe, linked in a very fundamental sense.

The linkage goes to the heart of the secret of Jewish existence: the inner, profound meaning of what has kept this people alive throughout the millennia without any physical defense (until Israel's birth), economic security, political muscle, or other vital elements of a normal nature.

Jewish people have lived everywhere with a memory of an ancient epiphany at the foot of a mountain in the desert; a yearning for a social order based on justice and morality; a belief that the future will provide such an order for all mankind, not just the Jews; and a prayer that their national existence could eventually be realized in an independent, sovereign state. Where are these beliefs to be found in tangible form?

All are in the sacred books that have been the singular baggage this people has carried with it in every land and every century of its wandering.

Books! They form the soul of the Jewish people, the sustaining strength of its stubborn refusal to die out. The very core of its mysterious immortality lies in the books it has read and cherished and re-read as its essential nourishment. The Bible, completed probably in the fifth or fourth century BCE (Before the Common Era); the Talmud, completed a thousand years later; the Prayer Book, compiled in the 10th century CE (Common Era); medieval poetry; Biblical commentaries throughout the Middle Ages; modern philosophy in the 20th century. Saving those books amounts to saving the People of the Book, for the intellectual and spiritual messages they contain are the best guarantee of the people's continued physical existence.

The last time I saw Professor Scholem, shortly before he died, he told me that occasionally he looked into the rare book vault of the Hebrew University National Library and smiled contentedly. So did I.

CHAPTER FOURTEEN

ERNEST BEVIN'S UGLY TIRADE

In December 1946, the Zionist Congress decided not to attend any more London conferences with the British or the Arabs. Progress on the "Palestine question" had reached a dead end, at least for the time being.

The U.S. Army, in an effort to be practical and to ease the large burden of supporting a quarter-million displaced persons, revived President Truman's suggestion of transferring 100,000 refugees to Palestine as a humanitarian gesture, without reference to eventual political solutions. To push that idea once again, General Clay suggested that Rabbi Bernstein take to London a letter from Clay to Ernest Bevin, the foreign secretary, asking Britain to agree to this move. Bernstein took me along, and off we went, expecting a negative reply – but not the severe rebuff we received.

It was the end of January 1947, the second winter after the War, and England was freezing, still short of fuel as well as food. Both weather and mood were very grey. We entered Bevin's office in Whitehall to find this most senior officer of His Majesty's Government huddled in an overcoat behind his desk, a small heater at his feet, scowling and barely civil. He read Clay's letter, wasted no time in thinking about it, and immediately launched a vulgar, profane, anti-semitic attack.

A staunch Labourite, Bevin had started his working life as a stevedore, was proud of his working-man's origins and his career as a trade union official, and was known at times to adopt as a negotiating stance the posture he was now displaying. But he also had experienced years of dealing with people in the highest stations, and he knew perfectly well how to act in a refined manner. In our case, he had apparently decided to be rough. He pounced so quickly that it was clear he had made his decision in advance and was simply waiting for us to appear so he could lay into us.

I cannot – and would not – repeat his tirade, for too many words were of the four-letter variety. He particularly favored the use of a certain adjective beginning with "f," which preceded the noun "Jews" in every instance. He started in a general fashion, talking about the war: Britain had won, but was now suffering as much as if she had lost. Perhaps it would have been better if she *had* lost, for then the Americans would have offered the relief they were now giving the German aggressors.

It was a sour and bitter approach. After further bemoaning, Bevin's main point emerged: Britain could no longer afford to honor certain obligations. They weighed too heavily, and he had decided simply to dump them. Then the profane secretary really unloaded:

> Never mind the 100,000 f–ing Jews. Why should they always come first? Let's talk about the 100,000 British troops in India. They are costing us a fortune. If the wogs want their independence, let them have it. We are going to pull out. We cannot maintain this pretense of an empire upon which the sun never sets. It is a 19th-century concept we can no longer sustain.
>
> And what about another 100,000 troops in Palestine? Why should we carry a world problem on our backs? We were saddled with it after World War I, when we were appointed as mandatory power, but this has gone on too long. Let the bloody Arabs and the f–ing Jews kill each other if they want, but we British should get out of the expensive role of trying to stand between them.
>
> (Bevin continued with an attack against the Jews for the manner in which they were exploiting the Nazi terror by giving the whole world a guilty conscience): Is it England's fault that the Nazis killed Jews? Why should we have to pay for it? If the Jews want a homeland that belongs to

someone else, let them fight for it, but we do not have to stay in the middle. It's absurd. And if there are Jews clogged up in some dirty camps in Germany, why should England be concerned? If we agree to allow another big bunch of Jews into Palestine, the Arabs will make our life hell, and we'll never be able to pull out; we will only get mired deeper.

I am sick and tired of the constant whining and moaning of the Jews. I cannot help the Americans with their proposal – we have already said no to Truman on this matter, and I am now saying no to General Clay. Let him find a different solution. If he loves the Jews so much, let him take them to America. As far as I am concerned, I say the hell with the Jews.

I have not put all that in quotation marks, because there is no way to reconstruct Bevin's exact words, except the profane ones. But I have given the essence, the tone, and the line of logic – as well as at least one exact quote: "the hell with the Jews." Aside from the vicious hatred he was expressing, and the indifference to the fate of the DPs, he was stating larger matters of British policy. He was actually hinting that England intended to pull in her horns, to withdraw from two of the world's major trouble spots, India and Palestine, thus contracting her spheres of interest. That was really the beginning of a new role for England as a minor power.

In the "conversation" with Ernest Bevin, there was absolutely nothing further to be said. Bernstein and I were dazed, shocked beyond speech. It was all too reminiscent of the reactions we had received in Poland a half-year earlier, when the authorities there had refused even to try at least to ameliorate the perilous situation in which the Jews lived and had instead blamed the victims themselves.

We returned to General Clay with the important political intelligence that Britain probably would soon reveal her intentions on Palestine. And a few weeks later, in February, the British announced that they were turning the Palestine problem over to the United Nations for solution. The matter took from February to November, and it was quickly clear to the U.S. Army that there would be no relief; instead, we would all pursue a holding pattern. Finally, on November 29, the UN voted to partition Palestine into two states,

Arab and Jewish; and the British announced that they would withdraw their administration and their troops by May 15, 1948.

The Jewish Agency accepted the partition plan, while the Arabs rejected it with an attitude of all or nothing. Guerilla warfare started the next day and continued for six months, until five Arab states turned it into full-scale war against the newly declared Jewish state.

For me, the few months following the Bevin tirade consisted of almost constant travel, as I went from camp to camp throughout the American zones in Germany and Austria. My goals were to build morale, create projects to keep people busy, and talk about the future in order to combat the hopelessness of the present. It was a very tough period. Because the DPs were both aware and cynical, they grasped the basic facts: political deadlock, which would keep them stuck in the camps; a foundation of support that would assure no hunger, disease, or danger; make-work projects that would keep them busy. But their children were missing years of education, and adults were not creating an economic base for themselves. Further, cynicism was rampant among them; the world powers' alleged concern did not exist; nobody really cared except the Jewish welfare organizations. The mood was depressed, and even hard work by all those groups and our office failed to lift it. But we had to keep trying.

I went to Munich many times to consult with the Central Committee. Purim was coming, and we worked out a major program in all the camps to create a festival spirit. Lots of wine was poured, troupes of singers and dancers traveled from camp to camp before and after the holiday; ingredients were found (in Army commissaries) for baking mountains of *Hamantaschen* (the special Purim pastry); balloons and toys for the kids were bought on the German market; khaki cloth was procured to make uniforms for the effigies of Hitler, the most popular candidate for the role of Haman, the villain of Purim. The committee, blessed with official backing, did a marvelous job in a short time. At least for the week of rejoicing, the mood in the camps lightened.

The Passover holiday followed immediately, and it became the basis for an even-more-complex operation, involving thousands of DPs in the preparations. The previous year, I had simply taken a few trucks to the main quartermaster depot to draw the supplies. Now we needed a large distribution network – dozens of trucks, hundreds of loaders – as well as drivers, accountants, cooks, et al.; rabbis, cantors, choral groups, local dignitaries, et al.; books, flags, new clothes, white tablecloths, flowers, etc.

Since there would be no physical freedom this Passover, we tried to achieve mental and spiritual freedom, a release from despair. And once again it worked.

The experience of the two holidays gave me an insight into the manner in which Jews must have lived during all the trying centuries of oppression on various continents. If the outer circumstances of their lives were inhospitable and gloomy, they turned inward and lived an inner life based on the calendar, rituals and holidays. There they found a peace, a lifting of hopelessness in the practices and beliefs of Judaism. That happened before my eyes, not in an 18th-century shtetl or 16th-century ghetto.

Our people were maintaining their religion, which in turn was maintaining them. Peoplehood, ethnicity, nationality, all revolving around a specific homeland, together with a sense of God-given, messiah-driven mission and purpose, composed the elements of a strong will to survive. At that point in history, such feeling was as important as bread.

CHAPTER FIFTEEN

ARMING ISRAEL ... WITH MESSERSCHMITTS!

In 1947, we did not have a political solution for Europe's Jewish refugees, but we did have money to spend on their welfare. That year, in fact, the Joint Distribution Committee got a larger share of the United Jewish Appeal's national campaign receipts than did the Jewish Agency for Palestine. (I think that made the year unique in the more than half-century existence of the UJA.) Even the Agency understood that, although Palestine would eventually receive the horde of homeless survivors, the organizations that cared for them in Europe required maximum support in the meantime.

With money not in question, ameliorating the refugee problem demanded ingenuity for its solution. We brainstormed and tried to think a year ahead. What would do the most good: more doctors and health workers? more luxuries like cigarettes? more visits by delegations of American lay leaders to show them they were not forgotten? more books (the JDC was already involved in the Talmud project)? more entertainers? more subsidies for Organization for Rehabilitation through Training (ORT) to open more vocational schools in the camps? Some ideas were accepted, a consensus gradually developed, and more pieces were added to the foundation of support. Thus, the quality of life in the camps improved.

I wish it were possible to pay adequate tribute to the organizations and personnel that sustained the *Shearit ha-Pletah* (the saved remnant – DPs). Time has blurred many names and programs. But the U.S. Army stands uppermost, by the measure of dollars spent, energy devoted at the very top, and numbers of people employed up and down the line. The JDC and Jewish Agency, working with UJA money, formed the two strong bulwarks of support coming from the international Jewish community. I cannot imagine what life would have been like in those hard years without them. Their people were sincerely devoted and worked with compassion and skill.

Among the other important organizations that worked on the refugees' behalf were:

- ORT, founded more than 100 years earlier in Russia, on the principle of teaching trades so that people could become independent wage-earners. ORT operated schools all over the world and set up a network in the camps, envisioning a time when mastery of a skill would enable a refugee to start a family and a new life. The organization introduced machinery and instructors, and the latter brought with them a wave of optimism that camp life was not to be forever.
- The Hebrew Immigrant Aid Society (HIAS) assisted those who had the opportunity to apply for admission to the United States. At work shortly after World War II ended, HIAS helped thousands navigate the bureaucratic maze and survive the blizzard of paper work.
- The *Vaad haHatzalah* (Rescue Committee), organized through the orthodox community in the United States and England, served the unique function of caring for the special needs of the Orthodox DPs, a task that sometimes required intervening with or interpreting for the largely non-Jewish UNRRA directors of the camps. Whether they needed a kosher supervisor or a *mikveh* (ritual bath), camp inmates knew they could turn to an organization that had an accepted status in the welfare establishment.

As effective and loyal as those groups were, another merits even greater praise – the Haganah. The men and women involved in its many branch operations – in Europe and Asia – quite literally risked their lives, which was not required of the people working in any of the other organizations. Two of its sections – Bricha (flight) and Aliyah Bet (illegal immigration) – demanded courage and often heroism. Crossing borders or climbing mountains, traveling on false papers, working in strange countries with only the flimsiest knowledge of the language, leading a convoy of nervous refugees whose single outcry might cause disaster, or brashly offering a border official a bribe (the refusal of which could mean prison or worse) – almost every act during the course of almost every day brought Haganah agents face to face with danger.

The group's Palestinian Jews were beautiful in their fearlessness, devotion, modesty, and love for their people and land. In a dark century, they shone brightly. Every new generation should read of their exploits, which ranged in scope as far east as Uzbekistan and as far west as Belgium. At its peak, the Haganah spanned a quarter of the globe, herding and shepherding a quarter-million wandering Jews, watching over them in the night, urging them forward, nursing and caring, slowly bringing them to the edge of final freedom. Theirs is a unique story.

In addition to the Bricha and Aliyah Bet people, the Haganah possessed an elite corps called Palmach (Commandos). Israel's legendary generals, Dayan, Allon, and Rabin, were all officers in the Palmach and helped to create its traditions and reputation. A small section of the Palmach, called Palyam, devoted itself to the sea. They manned the scores of illegal ships, recruiting some Jews from the Diaspora to help, but relying mainly on their own numbers. The ships they operated were mostly decrepit, tired, ill-fitted, technically inadequate, uncomfortable for the passengers, and even more important, not always seaworthy. They were essentially tramp steamers that had been rusting in obscure Mediterranean ports until some Haganah scout found them and made a deal with each captain.

The deal usually included a specific sum for the captain, deposited in a bank account whose name and number would be known only to the recipient and the Haganah. The money would be waiting for the captain when he emerged from prison. He knew the odds: The British were intercepting almost every ship, confiscating the vessel and jailing its master.

So in setting the price, the captain calculated the worth of his ship as well as a lost year of his life. Palyam's young lions of the sea accepted such vessels without fear, sailed them into sometimes unfriendly ports, loaded the eager exiles bound for home, and sailed out, waiting for the British patrol plane that inevitably spotted them. Then the race was on, even though Palyam and DPs both knew how it would end. These were gallant sailors who sought neither gold nor new lands, neither silver nor slaves, only the privilege of carrying a cargo of weary survivors home. When Israel became a state, the Palyam formed the core of the Israeli Navy.

The final Haganah project I want to describe was known as *Rechesh*, which translates broadly as "gathering or accumulating weapons." Only a small number of people were included in the inner circle of the project, for its affairs were highly sensitive and delicate. Although history has credited various individuals with *Rechesh* leadership roles, the fact is that Ben-Gurion himself was the leader of the operation who involved himself in both its policy making and implementation. Because he believed in trying to find a common path with the Arabs, he was always prepared to compromise on the question of land, accepting every suggestion made in favor of partition, and maintaining this consistent position during the long decades of Zionist struggle before and after 1948.

But in his heart, Ben-Gurion believed that the Arabs would never agree and that independence would come only through war. Weapons in Jewish hands were in very, very short supply, however; so this genius of a leader concentrated with utter singleness of purpose on the task of building an army and supplying it adequately. He left many matters to others, having no head for economics nor much interest in the daily husbandry of government. Preparation for war he dealt with himself, in great detail.

There were two sources for arms: the United States and Europe. Ben-Gurion believed he would find in the former sympathetic friends who would take his long shopping lists containing thousands of items and, using a network of devoted Jews to organize the search, produce a cornucopia of surplus American military equipment. That indeed came to pass. In 1945, he found a man, Rudolph Sonneborn, in whose New York home the network was formed through the skill and broad knowledge of Henry Montor, the then executive director of the UJA. It was called the Sonneborn Institute, quite an academic name for an undertaking whose product was to be uniforms, tents, flashlights, entrenching tools, revolvers, rifles, ammunition, boots, sleeping bags, and endless other paraphernalia.

What began with that "soft" materiel expanded later to much heavier stuff, but some details of that development must await another chapter. Stockpiling through the Sonneborn Institute continued for more than two years, and it still proved insufficient when war broke out. Where would Israel have stood without Ben-Gurion's forethought and execution? The Jewish political figures, some inside Palestine and some in the Diaspora, who counseled against declaring the Israeli state in 1948, would probably have prevailed had the military preparedness not been started when it was.

Europe contained many huge munitions dumps. (Every army sold surplus material rather than taking the trouble of crating and shipping it back to the States or England or wherever.) The Haganah's *Rechesh* operation took on the task of penetrating the dumps in order to carry off – through purchase, bribery, or "liberation" – the items considered most critical. (Liberation was a U.S. Army slang euphemism for stealing a desired object or getting it very cheaply. If one GI asked another whether he had yet liberated a Leica camera, the answer was either that it had simply been taken, i.e., stolen from some luckless German, or that it had been acquired for a pack of cigarettes.)

The *Rechesh* operatives were quite flexible. They were prepared to pay a reasonable price to the quartermaster officers in charge of the dumps. When such a purchase could not be made, for whatever reason, the Haganah usually attempted to find a sergeant, in the right position of access, who was willing to be less rigid and to pocket the bribe. That method could produce small quantities, which were welcome and useful, but could not satisfy the larger needs.

Liberation, therefore, came to be the method of choice, for once access could be gained, by bribe or break-in, very large quantities were available. All it took was a big enough fleet of trucks and a pre-arranged hiding place. The most useful items were Bren and Sten guns, .50-caliber machine guns, light and heavy mortars, automatic rifles, carbines, Thompson submachine (Tommy) guns, grenades, and millions of rounds of ammunition.

Once stolen, driven away, and hidden, the items had to await an available ship. Crates, boxes, and bales containing all those goodies were then loaded, and the DPs were loaded on top of them, providing a bit of camouflage in case the ship was boarded by British marines. Actually, the British seemed less interested in the weaponry than in the refugees. Currying favor with the Arabs, the Brits were intent on proving their ability to stop the flow of the Jewish population. And as a result, after they carted people off to Cyprus and docked the ship at Haifa, British Marines often ignored it, giving the Haganah a fine opportunity to remove the weapons.

I became personally involved in one particularly memorable piece of *Rechesh* derring-do. A remarkable *Rechesh* officer named Ehud Avriel, a member of kibbutz *Neot Mordechai* in the Galilee, was poking around Czechoslovakia's huge Skoda military-industry plant in 1947. One of the items the Germans manufactured there during the War was the famous Messerschmitt ME-109, considered one of the best warplanes of WWII. While meandering through the semi-abandoned plant, Avriel discovered a hangar containing 11 brand-new ME-109s! It was an incredible find, one that could give the Haganah an element of strength it did not possess and had no way of acquiring legitimately.

The challenge lay in getting the aircraft from Prague to Lod (now Ben-Gurion) Airport in Palestine. It was simply too complicated to try to fly them: Several refueling stops would be necessary, each of which would require landing permits in the five or six countries en route. Nor was there any possibility of sending the planes by ship because the Haganah had neither ships with the requisite open-deck space nor cranes to lift them. Ehud asked me for help – ideas and the assistance needed to implement them.

I won't reveal all the technical details, because many other people were involved, but a solution did emerge. We acquired three large transport planes, American C-54s that could land and take off from the Skoda works' private airstrip. We located mechanics who could detach the wings of the Messerschmitts; ground crews who could load the fuselages inside the c-54s and lay the wings alongside; and pilots who could fly the transports from

Prague to a friendly military airfield near Rome, refuel, and continue nonstop to Israel.

One accident resulted in the loss of pilot (a Canadian non-Jewish volunteer), transport plane, and cargo. Everything else went smoothly, and the new state of Israel found herself with a small fleet of fighter planes with which to fight off the Egyptian Spitfires supplied by England. In 1948, in the War of Independence, the Israelis did just that. Consider the irony of that air-combat situation! Eight years earlier, in 1940, when the pivotal Battle of Britain was fought in the skies over England, the Spitfires shot down so many Nazi Messerschmitts that Hitler had to abandon his projected invasion across the English Channel.

That change of events saved Western Europe. Now, over the skies of the Middle East, these very same aircraft were once again in battle, and this time the Israeli Messerschmitts beat back the Egyptian Spitfires. There must be a moral here. Does success have to do less with planes than with pilots and their defense of homeland against aggressors? Ehud Avriel, later in his life Ambassador to Italy, has entered modern Jewish history as one of the saviors of his country. I felt gratified and honored to have been able to help him.

MAKING WAVES IN
THE UNITED STATES

CHAPTER SIXTEEN

HENRY MORGENTHAU
AND THE STOCKADE

In June 1947, I flew back to the U.S., via commercial aircraft at my own expense, with orders to report to Camp Kilmer, New Jersey, to be processed for discharge. I simply could not contemplate another bout of seasickness on another troopship, preferring the non-pressurized DC-4, which made five stops and took almost 24 hours to get to New York.

I do not recall why I stopped at the UJA office, but fate was certainly directing my steps, for the UJA people were looking for me as I walked in the door. An emergency conference of Jewish leaders from every community in America had been convened at this midpoint of the annual fundraising campaign in order to re-energize the key workers. The main theme of the conference was the condition of the Jews in the DP camps. The main speaker was to have been General McNarney, but he had been compelled to cancel at the last moment. And the UJA fastened on me, as an authentic witness and participant just arrived from Germany, still in uniform, to take McNarney's place and read the speech he had prepared.

I agreed and proceeded to Galen Hall in Wernersville, Pennsylvania. I didn't know much about the UJA, but I did know a lot about the DPs and how vital it was to help them.

The conference chairman was Henry Morgenthau, former Secretary of the Treasury, under President Roosevelt. Although I had no inkling of it at the outset, Morgenthau was about to enter my life in an important way.

The conference was droning along, moving through a pre-arranged agenda in an unexciting fashion, when a short man at a front table jumped to his feet in an obviously agitated mood. Why, he demanded, had he been dragged from Los Angeles clear across the country to listen to this drivel? The national office should think twice before summoning people to an "emergency" conference that had no emergency tone or feeling about it. What was the emergency? What was he supposed to convey to his people back home to stimulate them to greater efforts? He himself had come here hoping to hear something new, something that could inspire him as the chairman of the second largest Jewish community in America, and he had heard nothing at all new.

During his tirade I had grown increasingly angry, starting to squirm in my seat, muttering, leaning forward to listen, then turning away in disgust. I couldn't understand what he was driving at. I knew nothing about the psychology of advertising or sloganeering, but it seemed to me that was not the way to raise money for this particular campaign. Or was it? I was conflicted, wanting on the one hand to shout back at him that this was history in the making, not new slogans, but afraid that I might do harm because there was probably something about the fundraising business that I simply did not understand.

Henry Morgenthau was watching my restlessness, and when Mr. Los Angeles finished and sat down, Morgenthau rose and barked an order to me, almost as though he were my commanding officer, that I should get up and reply.

The way in which Morgenthau did that, without any introduction, released my pent-up frustration, and I started to tear into the unfortunate man sitting there in front of me. It was as though there was no one else in the huge room. Everything I felt poured over him in a torrent. What kind of a person was he? What new things did he want? The fires in the ovens had been banked now for two years. Did he want them re-lit, so he could report some scoop he had heard at this conference? Had he already forgotten what that must have sounded like? Were his people out in tinsel-land so jaded that they needed blood to run again from bullet holes in a million bodies? I could not bring him news of blood, thank God, but I could give him plenty of mud.

I tried to draw a verbal picture of what life was like in an ordinary DP camp. How each day stretched endlessly, hopelessly. How the dream of a some-day homeland gave way to grey, monotonous barracks, with no indication to their inmates that any power in the world was working toward a solution. Children were born, and just washing their diapers was a major problem, for thousands lived in a place with only a few laundry tubs. Old folks died, and just burying them was also a major problem, for their relatives did not want to leave them behind in German soil. Every single act of life, every minute of every day, was a problem. Nothing "new" ever happened, and that was the greatest problem of all, for the inmates were marking time while history worked out a destiny that lay completely out of their control. I hurried on in this vein:

> How would you like to be not in control of *your* life, Mr. Los Angeles? The only messages to bring back to your community are these: the survivors are waiting to be rescued; the DPs must be patient and you free Jews *im*patient, straining to help; the struggle for independence in Palestine is the only ultimate solution, and all energy must be directed there; the final victory over Hitler will come when the camps are empty and their survivors living free and normal lives in their own land.
>
> Don't look for sensations, stories of dying Jews, pogroms. Hope instead for the same thing you want in your own life – that when someone asks you what's new, you can answer, "Everything's OK." That is what you should want for the people in Europe. Be strong, be steady, increase your support, and always remember that money buys material things; but more important, it builds morale. Sustain the morale of the DPs while they wait for history to decide their fate. That's not new – that's an old Jewish story.

I sat down, wringing wet, purged. The man from Los Angeles stood up and slowly applauded, and others did the same. Then the whole room rose to its feet in a stunning signal of support for those on whose behalf I had pleaded. The conference passed its resolutions, assigned quotas for increases, did all the necessary business and adjourned successfully.

Mr. Los Angeles, it turned out, was Max Firestein, the head of Max Factor cosmetics and the most important Jewish leader in that city. We became great friends, and I saw him many times in the decades ahead. His support of Israel and endangered Jews the world over was solid, sincere, and generous. When I apologized for lashing into him, he told me how grateful he was to me for responding as I had. He had deliberately offered himself as a target, hoping that someone would galvanize the whole audience by shooting at him.

Henry Morgenthau asked me to come to his office the next day. He said I could be enormously useful to the fundraising campaign and wondered whether I could accompany him on a national barnstorming tour for the next three weeks. He had chartered a DC-3 and wanted to visit as many as four or five cities every day. I explained that I had orders to report to Camp Kilmer for separation from the Army, and when he asked what he could do about those orders, I suggested that he call the staff sergeant at the separation center and explain what he wanted. A patrician accustomed to dealing at the highest levels of government, Morgenthau replied that he did not know how to negotiate with a sergeant but did know how to talk to his former cabinet colleague, Robert Patterson, the Secretary of War.

Lifting the phone, he got through immediately and explained to "Bob" that he had a chaplain whom he wanted to remain in uniform another month and be assigned to duty with him. Would Bob please arrange it? During the conversation I was signaling frantically, trying to tell my new patron that he should ask for written orders from the War Department. The Army worked solely through paper, and I knew I would be in trouble without new orders. Morgenthau paid no attention. As far as he was concerned, his friend, the Secretary of War, had approved this, and what better authority could I want? I said meekly that I wanted a piece of paper, but he was no longer listening; he'd turned his attention to our itinerary.

We started in Tulsa, stayed a few hours, went on to Oklahoma City, stayed a few hours, went on to Salt Lake City, and on and on, as day blurred into day. The Jewish leaders in each city were most obliging, usually meeting us at the airport and arranging for a room to be placed at our disposal, whatever time of day or night we arrived. For some reason, that was usually two in the morning or eleven at night or an equally inconvenient hour. Nevertheless, our top contacts and potential donors all seemed to understand the seriousness of our mission, and they cooperated handsomely.

I had requested one stop in Denver, having agreed while still in Germany that if I got back to the States by June 17, I would appear at the community mass rally on behalf of the campaign. Morgenthau not only accepted that but also wired and telephoned the president of my congregation, Louis C. Isaacson, asking that he and it "lend" their rabbi (me) "to the nation until July 1st."

We landed in Denver to a welcome fit for a victorious football team: band, balloons, banners, and a large cheering crowd. I was acutely embarrassed, but Morgenthau was delighted. So were the campaign officials and the two largest local contributors, Jesse Schwayder and Adolph Kiesler, for this augured well for the success of the fundraising. An audience of 2,000 sat and stood in the East High School auditorium to lend their support to the cause. It was a fine, soul-satisfying day in every way. (The following year, I served as chairman of the Denver campaign and brought Golda Meir there to address a similar mass rally. I have a photograph of her sitting on a couch – between the same Messrs. Schwayder and Kiesler.)

When the tour was complete, I reported to Camp Kilmer for my discharge processing and was promptly arrested at the gate for being AWOL (absent without leave)! In a scathing reprimand, the commanding officer pointed out that never in his Army career had he seen a *clergyman* guilty of this violation. Where had I been all these weeks? He would have to appoint an investigative team to make certain there were not more serious crimes to be unearthed. I kept interrupting to explain, but every time I mentioned the names of Secretary Morgenthau or Secretary Patterson, he became livid, shouting that this was the craziest excuse he had ever heard. Did I think he was some kind of fool to swallow such a story?

Finally, the commander ordered me to the post stockade so I could cool my heels while he tried to cool his wrath. That took two days, during which he sarcastically told me that if I could produce written orders to substantiate my story, he would apologize; if I could not, he was going to court-martial me. After more verbal tussles, we finally made a deal: he would allow me one phone call, and if that produced nothing, I would agree to his starting legal proceedings against me.

With heart in mouth, I called Mr. Morgenthau. Luckily, I reached him and got to explain my plight, and he promised an immediate resolution. Within a half-hour, an official telex arrived from Washington:

BY DIRECT ORDER OF SECRETARY OF WAR ABOVE-NAMED CHAPLAIN WAS PLACED ON SPECIAL DUTY FOR ONE MONTH AFTER RETURNING TO ZONE OF INTERIOR (U.S.), WITH FORMER SECRETARY OF TREASURY, HENRY MORGENTHAU, FOR PURPOSE OF EXPLAINING DISPLACED PERSONS PROBLEMS IN EUROPE.

When the commanding officer strode into the guard-house with that telex in one hand and a cigar in the other, I felt the crisis was over. He invited me to his office, offered a whiskey to go with the cigar, and begged me to understand that he was only a lowly colonel, never dealt with cabinet secretaries, thought I had concocted a most unlikely story, and had decided not to be gulled by it.

I assured him that I understood his predicament and I held nothing against him, but would appreciate his cutting through all the red tape of demobilization as quickly as possible. He got me through in one hour. There was only a single hitch. In my "201" file there was a note to the effect that, upon separation from active duty, I was *not to be invited* to serve in the Army Reserve Corps, which was the usual offer made to every officer being honorably discharged. The commander looked at me quizzically, shaking his head but not daring to ask what *that* was all about, for fear of receiving another outlandish explanation. And I did not offer one, but the thought crossed my mind that this was probably part of a deal that General Clay had made with the CID months ago, in the matter of the Offenbach books.

I walked out of Kilmer, took a bus to New York, bought a civilian suit at Brooks Brothers, and flew home to Denver.

CHAPTER SEVENTEEN

DYNAMITE BRICKS AND A MEXICAN SHIP

I may have become a civilian in the eyes of the U.S. Army, but not in the calculations of the Haganah. Its commander in the United States was Teddy Kollek, aide to Ben-Gurion, later director-general of the prime minister's office, ultimately world-famous mayor of Jerusalem. Teddy was headquartered in the Hotel 14, next door to the Copacabana night club on East 60th St. in Manhattan. Some said that the Hotel 14 served as the location where the Copa's showgirls plied a trade in addition to their dance routines on the nightclub stage. Whatever the case, there always seemed to be a steady flow of male visitors to the hotel, and all the traffic headed for Teddy's suite of rooms was buried anonymously in the general stream.

Although I had not been a "soldier" in any significant sense, and in any case considered myself happily free from military life, Kollek's Haganah that year enlisted me in the service of two quasi-military operations. One skirted the law; the other was plain illegal. But both of them, the Haganah felt and I agreed, were important to the establishment of a Jewish state and – in the meantime – the survival of the Palestinian Jews who would be creating it.

The projects involved the acquisition and then shipment of munitions to Eretz Israel (the Hebrew name for Palestine). The acquisition part encompassed many co-conspirators, complicated logistics, the fending off of investigators – and a risk of imprisonment. The shipment involved breaking the law, which embargoed sending arms to the Middle East. Yet I undertook the task without hesitation because I was convinced that it was not a quixotic adventure but a matter of life and death for the state-to-be.

Jews couldn't establish a state without a "war of independence." But we had almost no heavy arms and thus could very well lose that war. Such an outcome would shatter not only a centuries-old dream but also, and for me far more tangibly, the hopes of displaced Jews waiting in camps in Germany and the island of Cyprus. Waves of suicides were also waiting to happen. Anything I was asked to do to strengthen the Palestinian-Jewish population's fighting capacity was therefore legitimate, even if the laws of the United States said otherwise. So when Teddy outlined the munitions project to me, I started straightaway to plan its implementation.

As I will detail later in this chapter, the Jews suffered from a serious shortage of heavy artillery. In response, the Haganah's experts came up with something called a satchel charge. It consisted of assembling two stacks of dynamite bricks, three bricks to a stack, wired together, attached to a detonator cord of the desired length, and tucked inside a standard knapsack. One soldier could easily carry a knapsack of six bricks in each hand. Placed against a stone wall, an iron gate, or any other obstacle, these bundles could blow a hole large enough for troops to move through. They were much more powerful than ordinary land mines but – like a mine – could also be buried in a path when enemy tanks were expected.

The satchel charge was therefore a versatile weapon, cleverly improvised, very functional, easily assembled. There was only one problem: obtaining the dynamite in brick form. The best bricks were manufactured in Wilmington, Delaware, at the Dupont plant, and their export to the Middle East was forbidden under the terms of the U.S. Government's embargo against sending weapons to that inflamed area of the world. Although President Truman was extremely sympathetic to the Zionist movement and the idea of a Jewish state (which he ultimately recognized minutes after its birth), strong forces in the State Department and Congress preferred that the United States remain neutral in the impending armed conflict. An embargo on arms signified neutrality.

In 1947, embargo or not, dynamite bricks and many other embargoed items had to be obtained and shipped, whatever the cost or risk. So Teddy Kollek's plan, after discussion and tinkering, went forward.

I was to set up in Denver a mining company carefully documented with appropriate permits, quit-claim deeds, a full set of journals and ledgers, balance sheets, profit and loss statements, tax payments on profits. Reading through all that paper work, one could well be satisfied that it described a real, operating company. The documents were executed by two skillful lawyers, selected by me for their discretion and loyalty to the cause as well as their technical expertise. The set of books was kept in a locked safe in my office at Temple Emanuel, where I served as rabbi.

My company then started ordering dynamite bricks from Dupont for shipment to its office in Boulder, Colorado. A vigorous search, plus a lucky tip, had uncovered a perfect storage place a couple of miles outside Boulder; an abandoned mine shaft with tracks and ore cars still intact, running about a half-mile into a mountain.

The Dupont shipments arrived by freight car. A wonderful man, Sam Sterling, with his gang of local Jewish War Veterans as stevedores, unloaded the crates in the railroad yard, trucked them to the mine shaft, and rolled them deep into the mountain on the ore cars. Sam was devoted and efficient; he loved the idea of what we were doing, and his men loved him.

During all the months of the operation, there was only one mishap. Because of an error in the Dupont shipping department, several of my orders got backed up, and instead of being sent in the small quantity that each order called for, many orders were bunched together. One day the sheriff of Boulder County bellowed over my phone that 33 freight cars full of dynamite were in the railroad yard, enough to blow the city of Boulder off the map, and if I didn't get them unloaded by nightfall, he was declaring an emergency that would give him the right to send them back to Delaware or turn them over to the nearby U.S. Rocky Mountain Arsenal.

Within minutes, Sam Sterling was rounding up his crew, and I was canceling my confirmation class and all other appointments. Believe it or not, working through the afternoon and all night long under lanterns, we got the stuff tucked away. At daybreak, I brought the sheriff over to the freight yards to show him the empty cars. Luckily, he asked no questions about where the cargo had gone or what it was for.

To me, the whole incident was a replay of the Stettin-Berlin situation. There, once we had the DPs in, we had to get them out. Here, once the bricks were safely stored, we had to get them out – to make room for more. The basic plan was to ship them to the port of Tampico, Mexico. Before we even started ordering from Dupont, I had decided that the best way to transport south was to create another "commercial" operation.

We formed an export company for the selling and shipping of canned fruit to the Far East. After measuring various cardboard cartons, we discovered that our bricks fit exactly into Del Monte fruit cartons, with no space left over so that nothing would be loose and shifting inside. But how could we get thousands of cartons? Only one way suggested itself: go to California and steal them. We did exactly that. A single foray yielded enough cartons.

The final step, repacking the dynamite so that it appeared to be peaches or fruit salad, required a sizable working space. We couldn't do it outside the mine on the open ground. But fortunately, a solution lay right at hand. The president of the congregation, Philip Milstein, owned a bonded warehouse. He would not unlock it for us, nor did we ask him to do so. We needed only his large yard, to bring in our trucks, and the loading dock, to unpack crates of bricks and repack cartons of fruit. The loading dock even had an overhang, so that a rainy night would not disrupt the process. It was perfect.

Phil was a friendly, jovial fellow. A former Army officer, he had the breadth of vision to understand what was at stake if I revealed our purpose to him. As a result of his social standing in town and his long-time family connections, as well as those of his wife, he had a natural linkage with those congregation members who opposed Zionism and statehood. Yet, with his logical mind, sense of fairness, and awareness of the DPs' plight (which I had told him in great detail), Phil's opinion was swinging away from that of his social peers. I gave him great credit for that and felt comfortable taking him into my confidence.

Nevertheless, that was risky. If I were wrong in my assessment of Phil, it could mean serious trouble for Operation Bricks, and for me. He was president of the temple, and I was breaking the embargo law of the United States. Once he knew what I was doing, could he permit it? If he couldn't, and told the authorities, my arrest would cause a public scandal that would besmirch the congregation's name. He would have the right, at the very least, to ask me to dissociate myself from the temple immediately, so that any risk or scandal would be mine personally.

In the end, I decided to be straightforward with Phil because I had innate faith in his intelligence and basic Jewish loyalty, as well as in our friendship. His answer was simple and swift. He agreed on one condition; that I inform him immediately if any crisis loomed, otherwise, he wanted to observe the "need to know" rule. That is, he needed – and wanted – to know none of the details of the operation.

And thus it went. The dynamite came in, the "peaches" went out. Periodically, I traveled to the Hotel 14 in New York, got a whopping amount of cash, deposited it to the special account in my Denver bank, and paid taxes on the theoretical profits of my two companies.

There is one footnote. Two clean-cut gentlemen in white shirts began to visit me in my temple office. I have no idea where they picked up the trail – perhaps from Dupont, the Boulder sheriff, or someone who happened to be wandering past the freight yards. I received the visitors courteously, answered the questions I chose to answer, dodged others, and kept repeating my quiet request to know what they were looking for.

They dodged that one, for they had no hard evidence. They never charged me with anything, but kept coming back. I insisted that they take my books for inspection, which they finally did – in a rather resigned fashion, knowing they would show a genuine industrial operation. The books were returned on the very next visit. Sometimes the visitors would veer off on an apparently unconnected line of questioning, such as their curiosity regarding a clergyman's being so heavily involved in a big mining operation. Did the Jewish religion permit this? Then *I* would veer off – on the Talmudic line of reasoning that no one is supposed to make a living from the Torah, that every rabbi should have a legitimate occupation, the famous Rabbi Akiba was a shoemaker, etc., etc.

We were toe-dancing around each other, and eventually they desisted. I am certain they had the feeling something was wrong, but they could not put a finger on any fact, and so they had to give up. I did not tell Phil Milstein about it, because he lacked the requisite "need to know," until years later. At that point, he responded with a gentle smile, a pat on the back, and the words "Well done."

The success of the acquisition plan led to the urgent need for the second part, namely, securing a ship that could transport the "goods" to Palestine. An American vessel could not be used. But the Haganah was nothing if not imaginative. An alternative was found. Teddy Kollek telephoned me in Denver one day with an order to proceed to Mexico City on a special mission and quickly outlined what had to be done.

It seems that the Haganah had taken an option to purchase a tramp steamer in the port of Tampico and had four days left in which to exercise the option, at a cost of $400,000, or lose the deposit and the ship. The vessel was to be used to transport to Palestine the military equipment and supplies then being accumulated throughout the United States via the Sonneborn Institute.

I was given the address of another Haganah operative already in Mexico City, a certain Avram Fein, a carpenter from kibbutz Ein Hashofet (named for Justice Louis Brandeis). Avram and I were supposed to perform a blitz fundraising miracle in the time allotted, whereupon he would take the money to Tampico to complete the purchase of the vessel. Teddy also gave me the names of two of Mexico City's prominent Jewish leaders who were willing to help: Elias Sourasky, a banker; and Arturo Wolfowitz, the Pepsi Cola distributor.

As Avram and I entered the lobby of Sourasky's office building, we saw a stunning sight. Embedded in the center of the marble floor was a huge swastika, a mosaic of colored stone, set in a black circle. What weird symbolism was this for a proudly Jewish banker? He was quick to explain. The building had housed the Mexico City office of the Nazi central bank, and after war broke out, the Mexican Government expropriated it as enemy property. Sourasky had bought it from the government because he wanted to walk into his building every day and wipe his feet on the swastika. Psychological revenge, when no other kind was possible? Who knows? It gave him great satisfaction, and he refused to remove the hated symbol.

Sourasky called Wolfowitz and some other men. We went to work very quickly to canvass the city's roughly two dozen Sephardic synagogues. My colleagues knew from experience that it was impossible to get them all together because of ancient rivalries, petty personality squabbles, national-origin animosities, etc.; Syrian Jews wouldn't associate with Lebanese Jews, for example. Therefore, we had to convince each group that it held the fate of Palestine exclusively in its hands, that if its members failed to raise their quota (which was assigned to them on the spot), doom would result, and they would be cursed in this life and for eternity.

Four of us raced from synagogue to synagogue, after another team had set up each meeting. We kept going far into every night and started as early as possible next morning. We asked for cash, not pledges or promises. In some cases, where a person known to Sourasky had a temporary cash shortage, he would offer to advance money from his own bank account. By noon of the fourth day, the requisite $400,000 was in an attache case, handcuffed to Avram, who flew off to Tampico to buy the ship. Mission accomplished.

It was a remarkable display of national Jewish solidarity, combined with local communal pride. The city's Jews were proud that a Mexican ship would carry ammunition to fight for Jewish independence and that they alone had been chosen to finance it. This was not an international campaign in which they played a small part. They had the sole responsibility and were determined to succeed. (Elias Sourasky later became a major contributor to many projects in Israel that bear his name, particularly at Tel Aviv University and a Tel Aviv hospital.)

I have always found that Diaspora Jews respond well to challenges if some careful thought is given to their local psychology and the approach is based on what their local leaders recommend. A challenge from Israel herself is acceptable, even welcome, but implementation cannot be dictated from abroad. Any official from afar, who would also be conversant with local customs, would be very helpful because of the combination of Israeli moral authority blending in with local conditions. When Avram and I met in his kibbutz many years later, we reminisced with pleasure over that Mexican episode.

Was I operating under a code of the ends justifying the means? Perhaps. I was involved in a period of history when cataclysmic events had wiped out millions of innocent people, leaving a pitiable remnant in limbo. Its rescue could come only from the establishment of a state whose birth would hinge on a war for independence that required assistance in obtaining vital armaments.

When I recall the judgments I had to make involving the requirements of the law versus the requirements of necessary action, I find that I acted quickly, in conformity with my personality and the basic principles of my credo as elaborated in the preface to this volume.

There were three such instances: the Haganah work on the Berlin-Stettin road; the cases of manuscripts sorted out by Professor Scholem; and the dynamite bricks. In each of those instances, as a colleague said, I played the role of "facilitator, funnel, ferryman of precious cargo that was homeward bound." Whether it was Jewish people, Jewish books, or Jewish weaponry, those actions were aimed to restore life possibility and life equilibrium through the creation of a new instrument of power, the Jewish state, to balance the previous powerlessness that had led to the destruction of one-third of the world's Jewish population.

I don't think any issue of ethics or morals was involved in those decisions. It was an elemental desire to see Israel survive as a nation and a religion. The only possible rebuttal to the Nazi gas and ovens would be the rise of the Third Jewish Commonwealth.

One American Jew who started his work in the pre-state period, and remained connected with the defense establishment for the next 40 years, was Al Schwimmer. A great feat of his resulted in three B-17s, the bombers known as Flying Fortresses, being flown in stages from Tinker Field in Oklahoma to Israel – without adequate navigation aids or radio equipment. Some observers thought B-17s were worth more in building Israeli confidence and causing Arab fear than in actual military operations. Be that as it may, getting them over there was a great demonstration of the ingenuity, daring, and "long arm" attitude that was to mark so much of future Israel Defense Force (IDF) methodology.

Schwimmer organized and built the entire Israeli aircraft industry during his lifetime of work. That even included production of a supersonic jet fighter plane, the Lavi. The project was later scratched because of economic considerations, but it was important to know that such technical and industrial capacity existed in the young nation.

Another element of the Haganah operation started less happily, though it ended well. A young daredevil from Las Vegas, Hank Greenspun, "liberated" a boatload of .50-caliber machine guns from a U.S. Navy warehouse on Treasure Island, off the coast of San Diego. Hank headed the boat for Mexico – to rendezvous with our newly purchased Mexican ship. But he was caught red-handed by the U.S. Coast Guard. There was simply no way to wiggle out; the goods were stolen, the embargo violated. Hank was sentenced on a felony charge to a year and a day in penitentiary and fined $10,000. The jail time was suspended and the fine paid by the Haganah, but Hank's American citizenship was revoked. In 1961, Congress, at President Kennedy's direct request, restored that citizenship, after Hank had lived in limbo for 13 years without it. He died not long ago, having achieved prominence as a newspaper publisher and public figure, fighting for many liberal causes in general, and for Israeli defense causes in particular.

Joining Greenspun and Schwimmer were hundreds of others – anonymous collectors, packers, and shippers who took risks, yet look back with pride and nostalgia to those hectic months as a high moment when they felt connected to a cause greater than self. To them, we owe a salute of gratitude for bravery and idealism.

A little known but fascinating postcript to my munitions and ship-buying ventures. In April 1948, six weeks before the new state's Declaration of Independence, the armament issue suddenly loomed in Palestine in a way that is humorous now but was dead-serious then.

After the United Nations reached its historic decision on November 29, 1947, to partition Palestine into two sovereign states, one Jewish and one Arab, the Jewish institutions agreed, but the Arabs refused. Deciding instead to attack, the latter organized a guerilla operation under the command of an Iraqi general named Fawzi Bey el Kaukji, who invaded Palestine north of the Lake of Galilee. The British forces were to remain in Palestine until their withdrawal on May 15, 1948. But they had no intention of becoming actively engaged in this dangerous fighting.

Ben-Gurion was determined to declare the establishment of the Jewish state the day before the British flag came down. That meant six months of fighting against Kaukji's troops, who were much better armed. U.S. General

George Marshall warned Ben-Gurion that Jewish forces could not defeat the Arabs and urged that a Declaration of Independence for Israel be postponed. Ben-Gurion's number two man, Moshe Sharett, concurred. But Ben-Gurion decided to continue with his plan and started mobilizing military resistance to the invading Arab forces.

Months of skirmishing ensued, during which the Arabs had reached the southern end of the lake, where several kibbutzim were clustered. If they were conquered, Jewish morale would drop precipitously.

On April 1, 1948, a decisive parley of war took place on the question of how much manpower and weaponry should be deployed in order to stop Kaukji in his tracks. The major question was the disposition of the only artillery the Jews possessed – four French 75-millimeter cannon dating from the Franco-Prussian War of 1870-71! Should all four be committed to the defensive line across the bottom of the lake in hopes that their fire would force an Arab withdrawal?

The Haganah chief of operations, General Yigael Yadin, years later the famous archeologist of Masada as well as a deputy prime minister, said yes. To have any chance of beating back the Arabs, Yadin declared, he needed all four guns – antiques though they were – and their small supply of ammunition right in front of the most important kibbutz, Degania.

Yadin knew his Bible and quoted Jeremiah, chapter 50, verse 3: "For out of the north there cometh a nation against [Judah], which shall make her land desolate, and none shall dwell therein." Jeremiah was referring to the attack by the King of Babylon, who destroyed Jerusalem and the Temple in 586 BCE. "The north" had long been a phrase of sinister import and a colloquialism to describe the invasion route a foreign enemy would take.

Kaukji had invaded from the north, Yadin pointed out, and must be stopped at the kibbutzim or the whole country might fall. He insisted, as the Jewish military leader, that he must have the guns for that vital defense.

Ben-Gurion argued in rebuttal that the heart and spiritual center of the country was Jerusalem, founded by Kings David and Solomon, that it symbolized Israel's sovereignty, and that Jerusalem's capture could not be risked because it would utterly destroy the morale of the entire population. The four guns therefore had to be placed in a position to defend the Holy City.

There was no comparison between losing Galilee and losing the capital – if it had to be one or the other, the choice was clear.

The two men debated that day for eight hours. The debate raged back and forth, involving more than a dozen other military men and political leaders. Several of them told me the story in later years. The conclusion reached was typical of the Jewish personality that characterizes hundreds of solutions in the Talmud – compromise.

Two guns were to be left at the southern end of the lake, and two guns were to be taken up to Jerusalem. The shells were carefully counted out and divided.

The outcome: Kaukji was stopped. To this day, the symbol of his defeat is a small rusty Syrian tank on the front lawn of Degania kibbutz. The two guns to defend Jerusalem were not really needed, because the Arab guerilla force never got near the capital city.

Six weeks later, on May 14, right on schedule, Ben-Gurion read out the Declaration of Independence. Next day, Sir Alan Cunningham led the departing British forces to their warships in Haifa harbor. And the following day, the regular armies of five Arab states attacked from all directions. They were defeated after a year and a half of fighting.

CHAPTER EIGHTEEN

"BAG MAN" FOR TRUMAN

President Harry Truman took a wonderful attitude toward the Zionist thrust for statehood in Palestine. He understood the passions, motivations, and, above all, humanitarian needs behind the movement. His understanding stemmed simply from his natural instinct to veer toward what he considered, in an uncomplicated way, to be right.

In the delicate period between November 29, 1947, when the United Nations passed its resolution approving partition, and May 15, 1948, when the British planned to terminate their mandate and the new Arab and Jewish states were to be declared, the President faced many critical moments requiring calm judgment. One involved Chaim Weizmann, the foremost Zionist leader, who was soon to become the first president of the new Jewish state.

Weizmann was in the United States undergoing treatment for a condition that threatened him with blindness. Problematic negotiations were continuing around such delicate questions as to whether the Negev desert in the south should be included in the territory allotted to the Jews. Weizmann felt he had to talk with Truman directly to convince him to intervene with Warren Austin, the U.S. delegate to the United Nations, who was being influenced by the pro-Arabists in the State Department. That group was in favor of including the Negev in the proposed Arab state – because of their predisposition to give the

Arab states a larger share of the land and because the Negev adjoins the Sinai Desert, which belonged to Egypt

Truman was refusing to see Weizmann on the ground that fairness would require him then to see the heads of the Arab delegations, and he had been refusing them because he did not want to make any concessions in their direction. Weizmann's desperation overrode his understanding of Truman's political position, so he pushed for an appointment.

The key contact in all that was a Kansas City gentleman named Eddie Jacobson. He and Truman had been partners in a haberdashery store they set up after Captain Truman returned home from World War I. The business went bankrupt. When Truman ran for a local judgeship (which he won), Jacobson stayed with the store and worked it out of debt. The two men remained life-long friends, and when Truman was President, his door was always open to Jacobson. Word of their relationship was passed on to Weizmann, who mobilized several people, myself included, to importune Jacobson to obtain the appointment with Truman.

Eddie called Harry to say he was coming for breakfast two mornings hence. Although that delighted the President, he was canny enough to interject a warning that they could talk about anything under the sun except Weizmann. Jacobson didn't argue the point over the phone. After breakfast, the two men sat in the Oval Office, and Eddie made his pitch. Truman gave his reasons for refusal. It seemed like an impasse. Jacobson's eye caught a glimpse of a bronze bust of Andrew "Stonewall" Jackson on Truman's desk and turned the conversation to that subject. Truman explained that he greatly admired Jackson's personality, ideals, manner, and politics.

That gave Jacobson the opportunity he needed. He said that Weizmann was *his* hero; that this tired, old, almost blind man had struggled all his life toward a goal that was now in sight but that, in its final weeks, needed a helping hand from the sympathetic American President. The plea was warm, personal, and irrefutable. Truman surrendered, saying, Jacobson told me years later: "Okay, you bald son-of-a-bitch, you win. Tell Weizmann I'll see him."

Shortly thereafter, a famous photograph was taken on the White House porch, showing Weizmann presenting a Torah scroll to Truman. The Negev remained within Israel, and the Torah remains in the Truman Library in Independence, Missouri.

In 1948, both Truman and Israel faced survival tests – one through an election and the other through a war. Truman's election was a high priority for the American Jewish community, not only because of internal American domestic considerations, but also because of his foreign policies in relation to Israel. Conventional wisdom gave him no chance of winning, however. The very popular Republican candidate, Thomas Dewey, former district attorney and governor of New York, was the odds-on choice. The only cabinet member who offered to help in Truman's campaign was Charles Brannan, Secretary of Agriculture, a Mormon from Denver, devoted and loyal to Truman. He was not a money man, nor did he move in political-funding circles, but he did ride the campaign train with Truman right down to election day.

The plan was to start in Kansas City in September, proceed to the West Coast, then traverse the entire country en route to Washington, D.C., arriving on the eve of election. Several whistle stops every day would place Truman – on the back platform – amid multitudes of voters and would give him the chance to make short speeches and answer questions. At the end, the statistics were amazing: on board for 35 days; 356 speeches to audiences totaling 12 to 15 million people. The election result validated the strategy of going directly to the electorate.

The problem was to keep the train running, and Jewish community leaders mobilized every resource to that end. Henry Montor, director of the UJA, asked me if I could assist. Abraham Feinberg, a top Democratic politico, requested specifically that I work towns along the train route, raising cash and bringing it to the train each day.

The high stakes were clear. If Harry Truman were elected, Israel could count on major financial support; talk of a possible $100-million loan was in the air. I quickly agreed to help. My first assignment was to go to Kansas City a few days before the train was due there, visit a carefully selected list of people, explain the purpose of the project, and ask for campaign contributions. It was not the usual system of soliciting a pledge, with the check to follow sometime later. This would be cash in a brown paper bag.

That initial foray produced about $25,000, a substantial amount of money in those days. I boarded the train with my paper bag, feeling very proud but not especially nervous; muggings of ordinary-looking citizens were not common at the time. The first person to greet me was Secretary Brannan, whom I knew from Denver. He took the bag. I felt relieved and went over to meet the President. Our first conversation was brief, but friendly. No mention was made about money.

In the course of the next few weeks, as the cash-in-the-bag delivery was repeated each day, I grew comfortably into the role of member of the Truman campaign team. I would listen to a speech, talk to a reporter to obtain reactions as to how the campaign was going, jump off, hasten by car to the next town on our list, do my collecting for a day or two, and climb back aboard with the bag. I covered several cities, collecting in all many tens of thousands of dollars for the campaign.

I gradually developed an easy relationship with Truman. We had many conversations – about Germany, the Marshall Plan for European recovery, the Nazi genocide, the rebirth of Israel, his hopes for strengthening the American economy, and the new nuclear sword hanging over mankind.

Only one Jewish action or attitude made Truman angry; the assassination of Count Folke Bernadotte by the Stern Gang, an underground Jewish group. He couldn't understand the reason for such an act. He wanted the Jews to live up to the high moral standard their religion promulgates. He talked freely about a U.S. loan to Israel, saying that if he were elected, he would be in position to execute it. We also spoke frankly about the fact that this Jewish effort to keep the train going from town to town was about the only serious fundraising taking place on his behalf. He was not embarrassed to say how much he appreciated it.

And so it went – through Denver and Salt Lake City to California and up the West Coast to Seattle, then eastward across the continent. Others in our little group of fundraisers got on and off the train, each contributing as much time as possible, finally reaching that climactic day when the *Chicago Tribune* printed its huge and famous **DEWEY WINS** headline, which was so neatly contradicted by the next day's tally.

In his memoir, *Years of Trial and Hope*, Truman has included a letter, dated November 29, 1948, he wrote to Chaim Weizmann, responding to the latter's message of congratulation on the election. The letter sums up Truman's personal feelings and attitudes toward the plight of the Jews and the emergence of the new state. Here are some excerpts:

Today – the first anniversary of the UN Partition Resolution....

I was struck by the common experience you and I have recently shared. We had both been abandoned by the so-called realistic experts to our supposedly forlorn lost cause. Yet we both kept pressing for what we were sure was right – and we were both proven to be right. My feeling of elation on the morning of November 3rd must have approximated your own feelings one year ago today, and on May 14th (Proclamation of Israeli Statehood) and on several occasions since then.

I remember well our conversations about the Negev, to which you referred in your letter [of Nov. 5]. I agree fully with your estimate of the importance of the area to Israel, and I deplore any attempt to take it away from Israel. I had thought that my position would have been clear to all the world, particularly in the light of the specific wording of the Democratic Party platform....

Since your letter was written, we have announced in the [U.N.] General Assembly our firm intention to oppose any territorial changes in the November 29th Resolution which are not acceptable to the State of Israel. I am confident that the General Assembly will support us in this basic position.

We have already expressed our willingness to help develop the new State through financial and economic measures. As you know, the Export-Import Bank is actively considering a substantial long-term loan to Israel on a project basis. I understand that your Government is now in process of preparing the details of such projects for submission to the Bank. Personally, I would like to go even further, by expanding such financial and economic assistance on a large scale to the entire Middle East, contingent upon effective mutual cooperation.

In closing, I want to tell you how happy and impressed I have been at the remarkable progress made by the new State of Israel. What you have received at the hands of the world has been far less than was your due. But you have more than made the most of what you have received, and I admire you for it. I trust that the present uncertainty, with its terribly burdensome consequences, will soon be eliminated. We will do all we can to help by encouraging direct negotiations between the parties, looking toward a prompt peace settlement.

CHAPTER NINETEEN

FIGHTING MCCARTHY IN MILWAUKEE

From my base in Denver I traveled widely, making fundraising speeches on behalf of the United Jewish Appeal. One of the people who heard me speak several times was a UJA leader from Milwaukee, Benjamin Saltzstein, who also was president of Temple Emanu-El B'ne Jeshurun, a large, influential, and classically Reform congregation in the city. Saltzstein approached me with an offer to become the rabbi of his congregation. He said he had observed from afar how I was succeeding in changing the nature of the Denver congregation, and that was exactly the medicine his temple needed in Milwaukee. He felt it was necessary to re-orient his congregation along the lines I espoused, and since he enthusiastically subscribed to them, I grew increasingly interested in the proposal.

I loved Denver: the horseback riding in Estes Park; the phenomenon of bright sunshine almost every day in the year, particularly when there was snow on the ground; the symphony concerts in Red Rocks Park; the powerful influence of nature in daily life. All of that made it very hard to contemplate leaving. On the personal side, our children Judith and Daniel were born there, and our family took roots in a circle of friends. I knew it would be painful to leave the key people who had supported me in all the changes I had introduced. Yet there was an undeniable pull to work in another city, to "save" another congregation for Zionism and a richer Judaism.

Saltzstein started to talk about drawing up a contract. That, I explained, would not be necessary. I do not believe in employment contracts and have never had one in my entire life. I felt they were meaningless, especially as between rabbi and employer.

The most important condition in the world is freedom, and in my opinion, contracts restrict freedom in interpreting the mandate of the rabbinate. My interpretation on various issues might run counter to the feelings and opinions of officers or members of the congregation. If they opposed what I proposed, and if I could not persuade them otherwise, why should I remain? Conversely, in order to avoid giving offense and getting fired, why should I muzzle myself? Craven rabbi is a contradiction in terms.

In short, relationship between the rabbi and congregation should be simple; if either becomes alienated from the other, they should quietly and simply separate, without the enormous trauma of a congregational fight. I also had, and still have, an unconventional view regarding salary negotiation; pay me what you think is fair and what you think I'm worth. Accordingly, I found out what my Milwaukee salary would be when I received my first paycheck. It was quite fair, and so was the temporary house the congregation offered while building us a modern brick-and-glass structure, on staid old Lake Shore Drive, according to the plans of the Denver house we had loved so much. The birth of our daughter Joan was the joyous climax to a new home in a new city. Our family of five settled in happily.

We moved to a city so fundamentally different from Denver as to seem like another country. Milwaukee was conservative, almost Central European in its German-Polish characteristics, yet possessing a socialist mayor. There was a tremendous liberal tradition in the heritage of Senator Robert LaFollette, an early Progressive, but an even-more-powerful conservative tradition that had sent its then junior senator, Joseph McCarthy, to Washington.

We arrived in 1952, during the height of McCarthy's re-election campaign, as well as his national witch hunt to root out "subversives." I was drawn immediately into those events, for this man and his tactics represented to me the highest form of danger to American democracy. Samuel Eliot Morison, in his *Oxford History of the American People*, labeled McCarthy "one of the most colossal liars in our history." He was creating a mood of fear through broadside condemnation. He hurled accusations of communism and treason against individuals without evidence or documentation other than a sheet of paper he would wave in the air, claiming it to be a list of 203 or 120 or 6 or whatever his imaginary number of purported traitors.

No target was beyond McCarthy's reach. He would attack teachers, for example, by flourishing a paper for the television camera and announcing in a nasal tone his dreadful formula: "I'm holding in my hand a list of members of the teachers' union who are teaching communism in their classrooms...." No one ever saw the list, no names were ever made public, but a pall of fear began to spread among teachers, and slowly they began to immobilize themselves. They watched their every word, lest it be misinterpreted; they thought carefully about every book brought into the classroom, lest it be scrutinized by some McCarthyite parent; they ceased to pursue intellectual analysis, usually enriched by examining both sides of a question, because one of the sides might be considered disloyal.

The basic constitutional premise of innocence was being turned on its head, and a national mood developed that caused people to fear being judged guilty and then having to struggle to prove their innocence, which could be agonizingly difficult. The very air of freedom was poisoned by the corruption that typified McCarthy's form of attack.

He went after the theater and film industries with special viciousness, destroying the careers of hundreds of talented people with nothing more than innuendo as his major weapon. The senator and his staff would pursue particular individuals with bulldog tenacity, digging into their personal lives to uncover memberships in organizations or sexual conduct or financial irregularities that could be exposed publicly and thus ruin the reputations, even the livelihoods, of the person involved. This was terrorism, plain and simple.

Among the first of McCarthy's targets was the Department of State itself. He accused it of being soft on communism, with "known" communists in its ranks. After intensive investigation, not one of the hundreds of employees named by McCarthy was found to be a card-carrying communist. One of his most outrageous targets was General George Marshall, the choicest of America's soldiers and diplomats, the man who appointed Eisenhower as commander-in-chief, the man who fashioned the post-war plan for the reconstruction of the destroyed European continent. What were people to think if an individual as exalted as Marshall could come under attack, with neither proof nor defense, for President Eisenhower did not yet speak up on behalf of his mentor, let alone condemn McCarthy. It seemed that America was being cowed into silence and submission. A fog, a miasma of suspicion and fear spread over the landscape.

When McCarthy finally went over the edge by actually accusing the U.S. Army of being communist-infiltrated, a Boston lawyer, Joseph Welch, defended the Army in a manner reminiscent of the sounds of freedom in the Massachusetts of two centuries ago – that is, with arguments drawn from the bedrock principles of democracy. And when the "Army-McCarthy" hearings went on the air, the news commentator Edward R. Murrow bravely and brilliantly explained to the American public what a dangerous criminal this senator was and urged resistance to his campaign of terror.

Fortunately for Wisconsin, it had a heroic journalist: William T. Evjue, the editor of the *Madison Capital-Times*. Evjue was circulating petitions calling for McCarthy's recall. He was pretty much alone in that effort. The state's major newspaper, *The Milwaukee Journal*, although anti-McCarthy, did not join in actually collecting signatures.

I enlisted with Evjue in this struggle, raising my voice in public, constantly seeking opportunities to explain why McCarthy was evil and why we should stand up to him. I used my own pulpit for the widest possible dissemination of my views. Whenever I would announce a sermon about McCarthy, the Friday evening audience would fill the 1,500 seats, and the Saturday morning newspapers would carry the story on their front pages. The headline I loved the best read like this: RABBI CALLS McCARTHY STORM TROOPER! I still have a copy in my scrapbook.

We collected about 100,000 signatures. One day I was visited in the temple office by three friends of the senator's, who offered "friendly" advice that I should desist from these attacks, or I would be unhappy with some consequences that might unfortunately occur. I wrote down the names and official positions of my visitors, and indicated to them that there were still laws in this country protecting citizens against such threats, and if they ever dared to annoy me again, I would seek their arrest.

What I deemed a more serious problem arose from another quarter. An officer of the temple came to warn me of unhappiness among certain board members with my "mixing religion and politics." They were displeased with such headlines as the one I cited above; with such a visible position on the part of their rabbi; with a possible inference that all Jews were anti-McCarthy, thus possibly provoking a wave of anti-semitism from the state's German-American farmers who supported the man. Some of my board, the officer confided, wanted me to withdraw to a quieter posture.

Those vague rumblings became louder during a visit from the treasurer of the congregation, who informed me that several members had resigned in disagreement with my stance. I responded that my position came directly from the biblical prophets who inveighed against falsehood and immorality, who thundered for justice and truth. I quoted the sacred Holiness Code in Chapter 19 of Leviticus, which lays down the moral basis of Judaism and says in verse 16: "Do not go about as a tale-bearer among your fellows." McCarthy's entire approach was based on gossip, rumor, and innuendo – exactly what Leviticus was condemning.

On the other hand, I acknowledged, it was not fair for me to cause financial loss to the congregation. Therefore I offered to make up any such loss by obtaining enough new members to compensate for those who left. I told the treasurer to supply me each month with the dollar value of all defections and to give me 30 days in which to replace it. The arrangement lasted until the November election. I worked hard, silently, approaching liberal friends who approved of my stance, asking for their help in nominating other friends who might join our temple and pay the requisite dues, thus redeeming my pledge.

In all, as I recall, about 20 members resigned over the several months, and I had little difficulty obtaining the same number of replacements. Soliciting was soliciting – whether the dollars were for the UJA or Temple Emanu-El B'ne Jeshurun or any other worthy cause – and I had certainly learned by then how to solicit.

In return for this obligation on my part, I declared that I never wanted to hear another word from a board member concerning this or any future public position I would take on an issue that I felt was against the high moral and ethical standards of our religion. Fire me, if you don't like what I am doing, I said, but don't attempt to subvert my freedom to fight evil.

McCarthy's goons returned once more, demanding that we give them the rolls of signatures on our recall petitions, so they could check whether all the signatories were really voters and not just false names and addresses. We rejected that, of course, but considered the request as fair warning that they would seek to steal or destroy the documents. Next day, we took them across the state line and placed them in a safe deposit box in a Chicago bank. Soon attorney Welch, broadcaster Murrow, and President Eisenhower finished off McCarthy. Samuel Morison concluded his account in these words: "When McCarthy demanded that he be allowed to fish in FBI files for the names of new victims, Eisenhower denounced him as one who tried 'to set himself above the laws of our land' and 'to override orders of the President.'"

Although McCarthy won re-election, the Senate then censured him with an emphatic vote. America slowly returned to normalcy and democratic safety, having learned, one hopes, how close a single individual can come to destroying freedom, and how vigorously the nation must fight to prevent demagoguery that can so easily lead to fascism.

★   ★   ★

In the course of trying to reinvigorate the spirit of the Milwaukee Jewish leaders toward the local UJA campaign, I met a wonderful person, Albert Adelman. Although he himself was American-born and lost no family members to the Nazis, he carried the pain of the Holocaust. He also carried a sense of joy that there was now a sovereign Jewish state that could provide strength, pride, and protection. Adelman's boundless energy and enthusiasm carried him to the very top of the national lay leadership. In the late 1960's, he was directly in line to become the general chairman of the national United Jewish Appeal, when an unexpected financial situation triggered his resignation.

For the UJA as well as for Adelman, it was a tragic turn of events. He was one of the handful of American Jewish lay persons, who held the fate of Israel's future in their hands. His wife, Edie, a strong, intelligent woman, comforted him at the moment when he voluntarily surrendered the opportunity to become chairman. Knowing how much he loved his UJA work, she encouraged him to continue working in the ranks for additional decades to come. He did just that, continuing to travel to other cities; joining missions to Israel, appearing at all national conferences where he was welcomed at top level strategy meetings; serving as a loyal officer who accepted his assignments with grace.

The efforts I kept making, in the ideological realm, to bring the congregation around to accept my doctrines and concepts, slowly began to bear fruit. I could feel a gradual understanding dawn on an ever-increasing number of members. That was an enormous satisfaction, a repayment for the energy I was investing to explain nationalism, peoplehood, pluralism, ritual, language, and liberalism. That energy was being taken away from other areas of my life and work – from family, friends, correspondence, studying, recreation time, and wider communal projects. Yet I was getting the feeling that it was all worthwhile, when an episode occurred – trivial in itself – symbolizing the struggle I was waging.

A disagreement arose in the congregation over the date of Confirmation, which was a sacred event for religious school students in the calendar of the early Reform movement. I had no objection to the ceremony of Confirmation. Even though it had no religious basis, it did serve to keep the kids in religious school until age 15 or 16.

Since confirmation was held at the end of the school year, usually late May or early June, it fell reasonably close to the festival of Shavuot, the holiday memorializing the giving of the Ten Commandments on Mt. Sinai or, as tradition says, the whole Torah. In Temple Emanu-El B'ne Jeshurun of Milwaukee, Wisconsin, for many decades, Confirmation had always been held on a Sunday, with no particular relationship to Shavuot. Sunday was convenient, and attendance could fill the Temple. Confirmation was a huge social occasion with parties, presents, new clothes, all of which really marked the beginning of the summer social season, as well as a tribute to the children.

I insisted, however, that the ceremony be linked to Shavuot and be held on the very same day, whatever day of the week that happened to be. Would anyone dream of observing Yom Kippur on the nearest Sunday? In pursuing my point of view, I stressed all the arguments for the belief system I had been trying to inculcate: pride in Judaism; the open practice of our religious tradition (nothing "peculiar" about hundreds of people coming to Temple on a weekday morning); joining with other Jews all over the world doing the same thing on the same day, celebrating the birth of the Jewish nation in the ancient desert, as well as the graduation of our own children into adult Jewish responsibilities; and many similar arguments.

The fight raged for months. Majority opinion began to coalesce around scheduling Confirmation "on the correct date." A small minority disagreed. They had their rights also, which meant that they could split off from Temple Emanu-El B'ne Jeshurun, form their own congregation, and keep whatever customs they wished. That is what happened, and a second Milwaukee Reform congregation was born. It has grown and flourished over the decades. Begun in dissent, it has prospered in conformity. It is today strong in its Jewish identity and practices, observing its Confirmation on Shavuot. I have served only two congregations in my career, but have given birth to two more. Even though the extra two were born of conflict, not many rabbis can beat that record.

★   ★   ★

In late 1952, after I had been in Milwaukee less than six months, two of the most esteemed leaders in the American Jewish community, William Rosenwald and Edward M. M. Warburg, offered me the highest post in the nation's Jewish "civil service": Executive Vice-Chairman and CEO of the national United Jewish Appeal.

I was overcome. On one hand, I knew that for the past five years I had been one of the most effective speakers in the country on behalf of the UJA. I knew hundreds of the key players, both lay and professional, in dozens of communities nationwide. And I was steeped in the two major themes of the campaign: the Holocaust and its aftermath, the DP period, as well as the birth of the new State of Israel. On the other hand, I had expressed my doubts about the impropriety of leaving the congregation so quickly.

Rosenwald and Warburg pressed on, to explain that Dr. Joseph Schwartz, who currently held the position, was desperate to leave because he did not feel temperamentally suited for the job. Schwartz was a remarkable man in many ways: a former Orthodox rabbi, scholar, and social worker; the former European head of the American Joint Distribution Committee (the JDC, or "Joint"), the legendary organization that had been distributing relief to Jews and Jewish communities all over the world throughout most of the 20th century.

Schwartz's office had been in Paris, and when the Nazis occupied France in 1940, he escaped one step ahead of them and established the JDC headquarters in neutral Lisbon. For five years during the war, he discovered and created opportunities to bring help to beleaguered Jewish communities. He helped rescue individuals, set up contacts behind enemy lines, and supported links with Jews in the Soviet Union through agents from Palestine who infiltrated even into Soviet Gulags in Siberia. His achievements were heroic and epic.

When the Israel Bond Organization was established in 1950, the incumbent CEO of the UJA, Henry Montor, left that post to take over the new operation. Someone had to take over the UJA quickly, and Joseph Schwartz was selected. Everyone knew and admired him, but, in retrospect, it should have been apparent that this was not a job for him.

The UJA's top job required a fighter, on many fronts simultaneously. Schwartz was introspective, quiet, sometimes shy. He was deeply intellectual, contemplative, careful in thought, slow to act. As hard as he tried, he simply could not confront the constant battles of a UJA campaign. The arguments between the UJA and the individual communities regarding the division of the funds raised were sometimes exhausting. If the UJA chief executive had no stomach for the fray, millions could be, and were, lost. Schwartz was a good soldier and would stay until a replacement could be found, but he begged that this be done quickly. Such was the argument of Warburg and Rosenwald.

After careful thought, I declined. My reasons were based purely on the local situation in Milwaukee. I, of course, did not put that single congregation on the same plane as the UJA's worldwide service. But good manners, civility, and common courtesy made it impossible for me to leave abruptly. I had arrived only a few months before, and already the congregation was building a house for our family according to our specifications. The officers were making every effort to embrace the new ideas and demands I was throwing at them: hiring a cantor, unheard of in most Reform congregations of the time; changing the Confirmation date as described above; my freedom to be away on UJA business whenever that organization called; a tolerant attitude toward my anti-McCarthy activities; and on and on. It would not be fair of me to leave them so quickly and suddenly, when all the activity in the congregation was filled with such promise for the future. Temple Emanu-El B'ne Jeshurun had hired me to create just such excitement and instill just such values. That was happening, and it would surely deflate if I left before all the new practices were firmly locked in place and the congregation had become acclimated.

Take the matter of the cantor, for example. I wanted to introduce the richness of traditional music to the service, and Hebrew songs into the school curriculum, and Bar Mitzvah ceremonies, and all the added dimensions that music represented. To many in the congregation, those additions represented a return to orthodoxy; to others they were most welcome. I pushed and prodded. The Board finally agreed, and we obtained a jolly, chubby tenor named Sol Altschuler, who quickly endeared himself to adults and children alike. He was a wonderful addition to our congregational life. The longer I stayed, the more permanent a fixture the cantor would become.

I felt in my heart that in declining the UJA offer, I was making the correct decision. I am not certain that Rosenwald and Warburg bought my explanation. But they were seasoned campaigners and – what's more – gracious exemplars of old German-origin, "aristocratic" Jewish families. We parted with the same sense of mutual respect as before. We were to meet again, two years later, when they returned with reinforcements and achieved quite a different outcome.

CHAPTER TWENTY

ISRAEL BONDS:
A NEW FINANCIAL INSTRUMENT

I n the late spring of 1950, Israel faced a major problem from the confluence of several events: *massive immigration*, at the rate of 30,000 or more per month – almost a thousand refugees every day – coming from the displaced persons (DP) camps in Germany, as well as from Yemen, Iraq, Iran, Rumania, and other European countries; a *precipitous drop* in income from the United Jewish Appeal; and a *shortage of food* in Israel that led to rationing. Top Israeli officials concluded that they must search for additional methods of financing. The officials, particularly Finance Minister Eliezer Kaplan, were overwhelmed by the magnitude of the challenges, demands, and pressures, all of which thirsted for enormous sums of money.

The crisis was hardly surprising. The state of Israel had been born only two years earlier. She had been fighting against five Arab enemy states during most of that time since her birth, had lost 6,000 war dead (1% of the population), and had nevertheless managed, by a powerful act of will and sense of destiny, to admit and settle a staggering number of refugees – doubling the pre-war population to 1.2 million. Some observers, both inside and outside the country, described the open-door policy as suicidal; others defined it as a noble expression of the very purpose for which the War of Independence had been fought. Such elemental matters had consumed all the intellectual and physical energy of the small cadre of leadership, with little left over for items such as finance.

When the Israeli leaders did start to think about monetary needs, their attention turned naturally to the worldwide Diaspora, particularly to the affluent and pro-Zionist American Jewish community. The UJA had provided increasing sums from 1945 through 1948, which peaked during the War of Independence, and then started to decline. Once that war was over, Jews in the far-off United States relaxed and reduced their contributions. Apparently they possessed neither the insight nor the foresight to understand that the newly minted country would continue its sacred mission of welcoming refugee and immigrant Jews and would therefore need continuous support until it could achieve economic as well as political and military independence.

After lengthy debate within the cabinet and the Jewish Agency, it was decided that Prime Minister David Ben-Gurion and Finance Minister Kaplan should convene a Jerusalem conference to determine a strategy for meeting Israel's financial needs. Invitations went out to 50 persons, with special emphasis on the UJA's top leaders, key Zionists, and select supporters from Great Britain and South Africa.

The date was set for September 3 through 7, 1950. The meeting was held in the King David Hotel, in a room facing the crenellated wall of the Old City, 400 yards distant. On its parapets could be seen Jordanian soldiers with rifles aimed at the steel shutters of the meeting room.

Ben-Gurion chaired the session for two full days. At his side were Kaplan, Minister of Labor Moshe Sharett, Prime Minister-to-be Golda Meyerson (later Meir), and Berl Locker, chairman of the Jewish Agency. The American delegation included UJA officers Henry Montor, chief executive, and Sam Rothberg, Abe Feinberg, Joseph Meyerhoff, and myself; Stanley Myers, president of the Council of Jewish Federations; Rose Halprin, president of Hadassah; Nahum Goldmann, president of the World Zionist Organization; and a leading economist, Robert Nathan, former assistant to President Roosevelt.

The meeting hung heavy with a sense of impending fate, but also with a sense that the invitees were willing and able to confront the future. History was to be made in that room by people who loved Israel and wanted only the best for her.

A month before the Jerusalem caucus, in New York, the American invitees met in a preparatory session to exchange ideas and establish preliminary positions. This meeting was chaired by Rudolph Sonneborn, a business man, who had established himself by undertaking the leadership of the U.S. Haganah five years earlier.

Henry Montor opened the meeting by declaring that the UJA was a failure and could not meet Israel's needs. This judgment was bizarre, coming from the very leader who had brought the UJA campaign to increasing heights during 1946 to 1948. In a way, however, it might have been expected, for Montor was fiercely intense and persistent. Once an idea seized him, it consumed him, and he convinced others through his fanatical concentration that he was right. That characteristic would prove his genius and his downfall. For now, he focused on a single *idée fixe*: the UJA was doomed, and a new financial tool was needed. Montor listed these reasons:

- Local community needs were taking a greater share of the funds raised, and almost no one was fighting hard to preserve a sizable UJA share.
- The Zionist groups – Zionist Organization of America (ZOA), Hadassah, and Histadrut – hampered the UJA. They had their own aims and campaigns, which were more important to them than the larger cause.
- The ZOA had failed to inspire the average American Jew to commit to a strong relationship with Israel.
- Criticism from various organizations that Israel was too socialistic, too theocratic, or – paradoxically – too irreligious, hurt the cause.
- No channel existed for direct contact between American Jews and Israel.

Montor presented statistics to support his thesis. In 1949, the UJA had received $79 million. In 1950, it had received $60 million by July 31, but little more was expected. Dividing that total between the Joint Distribution Committee (JDC) and the Jewish Agency could leave Israel with as little as $25 million, and if that turned out to be the case, then 1951 could result in *zero* for Israel. It was a startling conclusion.

Having laid his groundwork, Montor proposed that the state of Israel issue government bonds, just as the United States and many other governments did, to finance its operations. Rumors had been circulating that the finance ministry in Jerusalem was considering such a move. But this talk at the Sonneborn meeting was the first indication that it was being considered by UJA officials.

★ ★ ★

A bit more financial grounding may be helpful. There is a basic difference between a UJA dollar and an Israeli bond dollar. The former is a gift, a charitable, tax-deductible contribution, since the funds are used for the underprivileged, the needy, the elderly, the new immigrants, and provide social assistance in the fields of health, education, and welfare. The latter is a loan, to be repaid, with a competitive interest rate, on a specific date. When a government issues bonds, laws and regulations govern the use of the funds it receives. Bond purchases are not tax deductible to the buyer, and the interest earned is sometimes taxable as income. In loaning money to a governmental body in order to earn the interest, the buyer feels that such a transaction is a safe investment.

Israel had been receiving outright gifts through the UJA and other sources as contributions to immigration, hospitals, universities, museums, etc. But those would not build an infrastructure for an economy that required huge investments in industry, agriculture, transportation, energy, and technology. So Israel began to think of asking American Jews and those in some other countries to loan her money.

One would have expected the UJA to oppose violently such powerful competition. Yet here was chief executive Montor suggesting that his organization was about to fail and that government bonds offered the only feasible substitute. Feverish discussion ensued. The Sonneborn meeting ended with the decision that, since the Israeli Government was inviting a cross-section of American Jewish leaders to consult on financial problems, those of us receiving invitations should certainly accept and should bring with us the following tentative opinions:

1. The UJA should remain in partnerships with the local community campaigns.

2. The UJA should make vigorous educational efforts to secure a better understanding of Israel's needs and better percentage of the local American campaigns.

3. If Israel decided to float a large bond issue, all pro-Israel organizations should lend their support.

4. If Israel decided to seek financial aid from the U.S. Government, the same forces should lend their support in the political arena.

★   ★   ★

From our perspective today, Israel bonds have been a tremendous success. Consider the major and vital projects they have funded: a national water-carrier system that brings water from the Lake of Galilee in the north to the far southern Negev desert and distributes it for personal use as well as irrigation for agricultural self-sufficiency; oil pipelines, highways, and railroads; harbors and ports; airfields, telephone networks, electric power plants, computer research and development facilities; and similar undertakings all intended to increase exports and earn dollars abroad. The Israeli economic miracle of the 1990s stems from the investments in infrastructure that began in the 1950s, and those, in turn, stemmed from bond dollars.

So Israel has clearly benefited from having the use of both kinds of money – the free and the borrowed – from the UJA and from Israel bonds. But in 1950, at the moment of decision, no one could prove that the flow of both could be sustained. Perhaps the free dollar would dry up; perhaps the bond dollar would never grow; perhaps the competition between them would cause both to falter. Those were the concerns in the minds of invitees to the Jerusalem conference.

David Ben-Gurion's opening speech was a tour-de-force. He told of war and armaments, war and independence, war and the British; talked about the Arabs fleeing Palestine and the flood of Jewish refugees entering Israel; detailed the plans for new agricultural settlements and new housing in the coming three years; and spoke of the reservoirs of future immigration and the scenarios of future wars. It was B.G. at his best. White plumes of hair streamed from his large head in all directions; his short arms chopped the air in deadly emphasis. He used it all to mesmerize, seduce, overwhelm the audience. Here is the final passage:

> We are placing before you not an easy task. We here in Israel fear that we are facing a supreme test. We are willing to do so; and it is my belief that every Jew in the world is facing the same test....We built and fought and were not disappointed in our belief that the best way to help the Jews was to tell them to help themselves. We believe that every one of them, even the most miserable Jews in Yemen or Morocco, who were oppressed for centuries and who were devoid of any material or intellectual means, are capable of being partners in the great work of self-emancipation, of building a new life for ourselves....
>
> We are free to build a new country, to shape a new life, to become a free, independent people and a moral factor in the world. To become a people who will enhance the name of the Jews throughout the world. We believed, and we did it, and there were two forces behind it.
>
> The first was dire need, and the other was vision. The need by itself could do nothing. Misery alone, privation and degradation alone, can only engender more of same. Just as vision alone can do nothing. When vision is not rooted in reality, it can become a mere chimera, an idle fantasy, just words. But when you join the dire need and suffering of a people with a great vision of self-help, they can change the face of the world. This is the secret of our victory. We fought with our backs to the wall but we fought for a great thing and we had to win.

We did it, but it is not yet finished. The task we are asking you to participate in seemed almost impossible, but it was done. I tell you in this great hour in our history, in this hour of our triumph and supreme tests, we must not fail.

Dr. Nahum Goldmann, the veteran Zionist leader, spoke on the morality of the situation. He said: "....American Jewry has not risen to the occasion of the last two years. I must say that Israel has done a colossal job, and we Jews outside have done a very far from splendid job. This period can end either with success or tragedy. We Jews outside want all the pride and joy and happiness and enthusiasm, but take very little of the anxiety and worry....The time may come when Israel may be forced not to admit Jews. This will be a moral breakdown for the Jews of Israel, and for the Jews of the world as well....I am convinced that this conference will be a success if the 50 Jews around this table, with all their devotion and intelligence and loyalty, will make up their minds to do the right thing. The Jewish people will follow good leadership."

After a day of travel, to show the invitees the Army, the new settlements, and the like, everyone reconvened for two days of soul-searching discussion. We all recognized this as a dead-serious occasion, one that might determine Israel's existence, or at least the *raison d'être* for that existence – an open-door immigration policy. If that policy were not maintained, much of the luster surrounding the nation's birth would be diminished.

Dialogue among the delegates was sometimes quiet and reflective, sometimes loud and recriminatory. Henry Montor, usually ice-cold and tightly reined-in, exploded at one point in the discussion, railing at those who feared a bond drive and were hiding that fear behind a pious concern for the health of the UJA. No one, Montor declared, should put local needs before Israel's needs. American Jewry must be prepared for the same austerity in its communities as Israel was in hers. His listeners should shed no crocodile tears for the UJA, which was being raped and raided by a diminishing share of the communal campaign. A new way must be found to bring in money.

Economist Robert Nathan had assisted FDR on the War Production Board and now headed his own consulting firm. He had been invited to this conference principally because of his professional skills, but also because he was a caring Jew and a passionate supporter of Israel. He offered a calm analysis at a critical moment in the debate. Nathan explained that the normal method of developing a country and its economy to benefit a growing population was to utilize the inhabitants' savings by investing them in new projects. But the pre-state population of Israel could not save enough to develop the economy <u>and</u> absorb the immigrants.

Calculating on the basis of 600,000 immigrants arriving during the next three years, at an average cost of $2,500 per person for their absorption, Israel needed to allocate $1.5 billion to that purpose. Ben-Gurion had said in his opening speech that Israel would provide $500 million. Could she do that? Yes, Nathan said, with more austerity and a lowering of the standard of living. Would it be feasible to raise the remaining $1 billion in the United States through a four-point program: contributions to the UJA; an Israeli Government bond issue; private investments; U.S. Government aid?

Further, could Israel repay if she borrowed? Yes, Nathan continued, if she has enough working capital to produce and earn enough through increased domestic consumption plus exports. He foresaw a prosperous Israeli economy. With a daring immigration policy, one must have a daring financial policy. A continuous flow of capital would produce new wealth, and bonds could be redeemed. The real question would be whether American Jewry would display faith and confidence in the future of Israel.

A new orientation was needed: not charity alone, but constructive development out of increased capital. "We need vision," Nathan declared. "The question is not can we do it, but are we willing to do it?"

Julian Venetsky, one of the UJA leaders, made two suggestions: establish a single campaign for Israel, embracing all the other pro-Israel causes; and then separate it from the local Federation campaign in every city. The arguments over how to divide up a campaign between two different needs, Israeli vs. local, would no longer exist. Each cause would be supported separately – the appeal to each contributor would be crystal clear.

Moses Leavitt of the JDC suggested a restriction of immigration. He felt that the state of Israel was more important than the lives of another 100,000 or so Jews. Harry Sachar of London, who had been Chaim Weizmann's secretary, also questioned an unrestricted immigration policy. Perhaps it should be moderated or the flow controlled. Joseph Schwartz, who a year later would become the UJA's chief executive, disagreed strongly. He said that open immigration could not be stopped unless the Israeli Government were actually willing to turn back ships and planes bringing Jews to the homeland.

Fascinating insights arose from a dialogue between Nathan and Stanley Myers of the Council of Jewish Federations and Welfare Funds (CJFWF):

> SM – What will be the impact of a popular loan (i.e., bond drive) on intergovernmental borrowing?
>
> RN – That depends on political, not financial, considerations. A popular loan will not interfere if political relations between Israel and the United States are good. A military aid program could be obtained from the U.S. without reference to a popular bond sale. More money could also be obtained from the Export-Import Bank.
>
> SM – What will be the impact of a bond issue on philanthropy?
>
> RN – Adverse. (Author's note – Nathan was wrong in this judgment, as was Montor, who held the same opinion.)
>
> SM – How successful will the bond issue be?
>
> RN – Some people say it will produce only $50 million annually. I disagree. It will produce much more.
>
> SM – How secure will these bonds be from the standpoint of redemption?
>
> RN – They can be repaid on time, and new ones floated continuously, if Israel uses wisely the money it takes in.

Abraham Feinberg had been one of Israel's strongest supporters over a long period of time, a man of firm convictions, yet moderate in thought and speech; a man who personally practiced his own four-point program through generosity in his UJA gift, purchase of bonds, private investment (in Israel's Coca-Cola plant), and political influence in the Democratic Party for U.S.

Government aid. He seemed to express a widely held consensus when he made these arguments:

1. Unrestricted immigration must remain the policy. We cannot promulgate an American Jewish White Paper of 1950. (That referred to Great Britain's 1939 White Paper, which limited immigration to Palestine. Countless Jews murdered by Hitler could have been saved if the door to Palestine had been fully open.)

2. We must recommend the issuance of Israel Government bonds on the international market, and float them in the United States with the cooperation of all Jewish organizations.

3. We must seek financial help from the U.S. Government and increased charitable dollars through the UJA.

I had been invited to this Conference as a result of my three years of extensive public speaking on behalf of the UJA. Since Henry Montor, Sam Rothberg, Julian Venetsky, and a group of others were making a powerful case for abandoning the UJA, it was necessary for the more moderate advocates like myself, who supported the new bond proposal but not closing the UJA, to support that position. I did that and also lobbied privately to win over key individuals.

I wound up working furiously during the conference and speaking vigorously for my point of view. I was in favor of a bond sale but emphasized that it was clear to me, based on my fundraising visits to scores of communities, that the UJA could command much more energy and achieve better results. I could not accept Montor's predictions of zero results next year nor fathom the motivation behind his argument. I thought it would be wasteful to close down the UJA operation altogether.

Most of the conference participants agreed with me, favored trying the bond approach, and strengthening the UJA. Both efforts could be undertaken. Total dollars coming into Israel would increase. I was happy to see that become the conclusion of the conferees.

At the closing session, prior to passage of the resolution, Golda Meyerson vigorously rejected any suggestion for the restriction or "regulation" of immigration. She compared the present economic and absorption problem with the military problem in 1948: If we recognize today, as we did two and a half years ago, that we have no alternative, she said, the situation will be resolved. Expressing the conviction that Israel would achieve prosperity and repay any loans, she urged the adoption of a bond issue – but called also for the continuation of the UJA.

On September 6, the conference adopted a three-point program to obtain $1 billion in the United States to support the immigration of hundreds of thousands of Jews and help make Israel economically self-sufficient in the next three years. An abridged text of the resolution reads as follows:

> MEETING IN THE HOLY CITY OF JERUSALEM in the free and democratic State of Israel which has triumphed against all dangers and difficulties in establishing its independence, we, the members of the delegation from the United States, have been privileged to meet with the Prime Minister and other members of the Government to consider the economic situation of Israel.
>
> After a comprehensive and frank discussion, we have arrived at the following conclusions: Israel will require $1.5 billion for the next three years. The people of Israel are ready to make the utmost sacrifice to assume their share of this responsibility. But $1 billion must come from the United States. Requirements of such scope cannot be provided in full through voluntary contributions alone, and consequently additional channels must be found to discharge this obligation.
>
> Therefore we believe:
>
> A. That the United Jewish Appeal must be continued on an enlarged scale to elicit the widest possible response.
>
> B. That should the Government of Israel decide to float a public loan in the United States as a means of obtaining funds for the financing of constructive programs, American Jewry will extend its fullest

support and we pledge ourselves to render maximum service in the
attainment of this objective.

C. That there are many opportunities for private investment in Israel
in productive and profitable projects. To realize the potentials in the
field of private investment, more intensive efforts should be
undertaken, both in the United States and Israel.

Once the die was cast, events moved very swiftly. Henry Montor left the
UJA to organize the new campaign for Israel Bonds. Joseph Schwartz was
persuaded to leave the JDC and take on the onerous task of revitalizing the
UJA. Registration of the bond issue with the U.S. regulatory commissions
was completed with record speed. Offices were opened, people were
hired, advertisements were written, and an organization emerged, all within
weeks.

In May 1951, nine months after the Jerusalem conference, David Ben-
Gurion came to the United States and kicked off the Israel Bond Campaign in
Chicago, with a rally of 100,000 people at Soldier's Field and a ticker-tape
parade down State Street. First-year sales brought in $52 million.

As of year-end 1998, the 46th anniversary of The Bond Drive, a total of
$19 billion had been sold, of which $15 billion had been repaid to purchasers
who submitted their bonds for redemption. Even the most visionary thinker at
that 1950 meeting would not have predicted such an outcome. What was
launched in a combined mood of desperation and conviction resulted in the
proud performance of a people galvanized by the desire to turn an evil century
into a huge rescue of its sons and daughters and the rebirth of its sovereignty.

Incidentally, the gloomy prediction 40 years ago of the demise of the UJA
was wrong. At this writing, about $700 million is being raised in the annual
campaign, of which about $300 million goes to Israel and other overseas needs.
An additional $1-billion campaign, called Operation Exodus, run entirely to
help Israel absorb the current wave of immigration from the Soviet Union, was
successfully completed between 1990 and 1995.

Another special campaign begun in 1965 by the UJA for the construction of
schools in Israel, produced an additional $250 million; and two emergency

campaigns, after major wars in 1967 and 1973, yielded additional hundreds of millions of dollars.

Because many capable and dedicated leaders have been responsible for the twin miracles described above, it may be unfair to single out one. Nevertheless, great sweeps of history are often best understood when viewed through the actions of an individual. So I will quote the words of Joseph Meyerhoff of Baltimore at the conclusion of the Jerusalem conference. He said essentially this:

> Why are we fussing around about conflict and competition between UJA and Israel Bonds? The leaders have to do both, and if we do, the people will follow. I am one of the top UJA leaders in Baltimore. I will take the chairmanship of the first bond drive in my city, and then I will take the chair of the very next local UJA campaign. That will demonstrate our double responsibility. It's very clear and very simple.

Meyerhoff went home, did what he said he would do, and succeeded at both tasks. His example set a tone for almost all of American Jewry.

It set a tone for me as well. I had always felt that our best leaders would assume the double responsibility, and I tried to encourage that attitude by my own conduct. Between 1952, when the bond campaign started in earnest, and 1955, when I took the helm of the UJA, I accepted as many speaking engagements for the bond drive as I could possibly manage. I was running around the country as the national chairman of the UJA speakers' bureau and a well-known advocate for UJA fundraising. Yet I knew that whenever I made a bond drive speech, I set an example for other lay leaders and helped to build a sense of unity.

As the CEO of the UJA, I continued to support the Israel bond effort in many significant ways. I mediated in local communities when conflicts arose over dates of big-gift functions; persuaded UJA-minded leaders to accept the chairmanship of bond meetings in their communities; helped to acquire speakers from Israel for bond meetings, especially if I had a personal relationship with the particular Israeli star whom the local chairman wanted;

and performed any other task that would underscore the basic principle that we American Jews should serve Israel in every possible capacity.

I never forgot the most important truth: that both kinds of dollars were helping to build the country.

RESCUE
AND THE UJA

CHAPTER TWENTY-ONE

GRAND ANNIVERSARY, CHALLENGING JOB

O n the weekend of June 3-5, 1955, an extraordinary national conference of the UJA took place in Washington, D.C. Its purpose was to commemorate the 10th anniversary of liberation from Nazi tyranny and to celebrate a decade (1945-1955) of unprecedented humanitarian victories. The organization's top leadership gathered from across the nation, and a unique array of America's wartime military leaders accepted the invitation to be present – the first time ever that a group of three- and four-star generals had been presented to an American Jewish audience.

Also present were the six civilians who had been appointed as advisers on Jewish affairs to the commanding generals of the European Theater. So were the two former DPs who had been chairmen of the Central Committee of Liberated Jews in Germany and the man who had been director-general of the UNRRA. Israel was represented by its ambassador and its minister plenipotentiary to the United States.

This marked the first and perhaps last occasion on which such a powerful and comprehensive assemblage will have sat at one dais. Their speeches will be preserved for posterity in the appendix to this volume. Their words embrace all the emotions of that historic decade, from horror at the memory of what they had seen to elation at the victory of the human spirit in the subsequent renaissance of the Jewish people and the Israeli state.

THE PROGRAM PARTICIPANTS

General John H. Hilldring – Assistant Secretary of State, 1946-47.

General Joseph T. McNarney – Commanding General, U.S. Forces in Europe, 1945-46; Military Governor, U.S. Occupied Zone, Germany.

General Lucius D. Clay – Commanding General, U.S. Forces in Europe, 1947-49; Military Governor, U.S. Occupied Zone, Germany.

General Mark W. Clark – Commander-in-Chief, U.S. Forces of Occupation in Austria, and U.S. High Commissioner for Austria, 1945-47.

General Clarence R. Huebner – Acting Commander-in-Chief, European Command 1949; Acting Military Governor, U.S. Occupied Zone, Germany, 1949.

★ ★ ★

Herbert H. Lehman – Governor, State of New York; U.S. Senator, State of New York; Director-General, UNRRA, 1943-46.

★ ★ ★

Advisors on Jewish Affairs

Judge Simon H. Rifkind, 1945-46.

Rabbi Philip S. Bernstein, 1946-47.

Judge Louis E. Levinthal, 1947-48.

Dr. William Haber, 1948.

Harry Greenstein, 1949.

Major Abraham S. Hyman, 1949-50.

★ ★ ★

Dr. Zalman Grinberg and Judge Samuel Gringaus – Former Chairmen,
Central Committee of Liberated Jews in U.S. Occupied Zone,
Germany.

★ ★ ★

Abba S. Eban – Ambassador of Israel to the United States.

Reuven Shiloah – Minister Plenipotentiary of Israel to the United
States.

★ ★ ★

Rose L. Halprin – Acting Chairwoman, American Branch of Jewish
Agency for Palestine.

★ ★ ★

William Rosenwald – General Chairman, United Jewish Appeal.

Mrs. Hal Horne – Chairwoman, National Women's Division, UJA.

National Chairmen, UJA

Morris Berinstein

Samuel H. Daroff

Joseph Holtzman

Sol Luckman

Jack Weiler

★ ★ ★

Joseph J. Schwartz – Retiring Executive Vice-Chairman, UJA.

Rabbi Herbert A. Friedman – Incoming Executive
Vice-Chairman, UJA.

The weekend program began with an historic ceremony in the White House Rose Garden. Receiving a delegation of UJA officers, President Eisenhower reminisced about his personal experiences in visiting liberated concentration camps, especially his shock and horror in seeing the few survivors and the heaps of corpses. Those visits, he said, determined his attitude toward the postwar role of the U.S. Army in providing relief and succor to the swelling DP population.

Eisenhower recalled his decision to appoint an Army chaplain, Major Judah Nadich, a Conservative rabbi from New York, to advise him on the needs of this surviving remnant. That led to a series of six advisers serving the commanding generals during the ensuing five years. Such action by a battle-hardened army, which accepted the responsibility of caring for camp survivors for the next several years, is magnificent testimony to the American tradition of decency, fair play, tolerance, and kindness.

At the conclusion of the ceremony, William Rosenwald presented the President a glass bell jar covering a small, clay oil lamp. An inscription read:

> To Dwight D. Eisenhower
>
> President of the United States of America
>
> who has kept the Lamp of Freedom burning
>
> –
>
> Presented in deepest gratitude by
>
> the United Jewish Appeal for his
>
> distinguished humanitarian service
>
> to victims of Nazi tyranny.
>
> –
>
> This antique lamp from the Land of
>
> the Bible, dating from approximately
>
> 50 C.E., symbolizes 20 centuries of
>
> Jewish history in which each generation
>
> renewed its devotion to freedom's ideals.

One of the purposes of this weekend conference was to note the retirement of Joseph J. Schwartz as UJA executive vice-chairman and to install me in that position. In an address, Rabbi Bernstein said some kind things about both of us and concluded with these words: "Tonight we reaffirm our faith in the future of mankind. If a little decimated people such as we encountered just ten years ago could rebuild its life, could so quickly establish something out of the ashes of the old, could so soon bring a functioning democracy into existence, why should we despair of the future of mankind? Why should we despair of the future of peace and freedom? Israel points the way; Israel holds out – not to Jews alone, but to all mankind – the beacon and the promise and the hope of what men can be. Yes – hope."

General McNarney, visibly moved by Phil Bernstein's oratory, rose in his usual quiet way, shaking his head slowly, remembering those days a decade past, and told his audience:

> As I recall it, I was on my way to address a UJA conference in Wernersville, Pennsylvania, when the weather closed in and my plane was grounded.... You called on a young man who used to do some work for Phil and myself in Germany and who had also just arrived from there, to say a few words in my stead. He made such a remarkable impression on you then – and has continued to do so for the past several years – that you have just elected him to be executive vice-chairman of your great humanitarian organization. I refer to my friend and former associate in Germany, former chaplain and captain in the United States Army, assistant to the adviser on Jewish affairs, Rabbi Herbert Friedman. Along with all of you here, I want to express to Rabbi Friedman my heartiest congratulations on his new assignment and to wish him that full success which I know he will attain.

McNarney went on to make a remarkable speech, sensitive, understanding of the Jewish spirit, and so deeply spiritual that it revealed the true nature of the American-Israeli nexus as based on religious and moral themes. He noted that the Bible played a major role in the upbringing of Presidents Truman and Eisenhower, and created an atmosphere of understanding on their parts. The speech, crafted by a military man, seemed surprising, until the realization dawned that the men who rise to the very top of that profession must be thoughtful, even philosophical, must believe it possible for humankind to transcend its more primitive destructive instincts. If they did not believe that, they would be brutes, and they are not.

Following the War, General Hilldring had become, successively, Assistant Secretary of State in Charge of Occupied Areas; alternate delegate to the United Nations (when the vote on partitioning Palestine came up); and a special assistant on Palestine affairs. In all of these posts, he was one of the strongest supporters of emigration to Palestine and the rebuilding of a sovereign Jewish state. His words expressed his convictions.

The next person called to the podium was Ambassador Abba Eban, whose oratorical genius had earned him the sobriquet "The Voice of Israel." No speaker in any language matched his ability to express the glory and the grandeur of Israel's rebirth:

> This decade has been the story of a spasm in the life of a people which counts its generations in thousands of years. Never will it find any period which can compete with this, in the poignancy of its suffering or in the sublime heights of its exaltation.
>
> The United Jewish Appeal has not been an idle spectator at these great events. It has attended all of these turbulent changes with its vigilance, its sustenance, and its love. It has mourned the dead, consoled the bereaved, lifted up the fallen, healed the sick, sustained and revived the ancient pride of the Jewish people, laid the foundations of a homeland, guided and reinforced its infant steps. It has brought the Jewish people from the threat of its total extinction into the absolute certainty of a proud and sovereign survival, amidst the dignity of statehood and the youthful exuberance of its newly won freedom....

The evening concluded with the presentation by Senator Lehman to the assembled generals and advisers of 2,000-year-old oil lamps similar to the one that had been given to President Eisenhower the day before. Lehman then told a story about the President and UNRRA.

The long, emotionally exhausting evening was rich in its evocations, moving in the memories stirred, and authentic in the assemblage of honorees. Everyone in the audience knew he or she had witnessed a unique spectacle of the makers of history laying bare the living bones of a momentous era, which thereafter would only be pages in a history book.

The conference resumed the following morning in a more prosaic mood, with a long line of delegates at the microphone proffering their fundraising checks and their reports on the progress of the annual UJA campaign in their communities. After the emotions of the evening before, money matters made a welcome change. But not for long. A new mood was created by the introduction of two individuals who were living reminders of the dead. These two, each an outstanding leader, each a former chairman of the quarter-million Jews in the DP camps, offered his personal story and his own fears and hopes, and extended thanks for what had been done a decade earlier to bring him and his companions back from the edge of the abyss.

The first to speak was Dr. Zalman Grinberg, a physician, who had been elected first chairman of the DP Central Committee and gone on to become director of the Beilinson Hospital, then the largest in Israel:

> My friends, I come to you as a living witness. It is not difficult to recall the hour of liberation, when the dedicated forces of the American Army broke open the notorious Dachau concentration camp.... The noise of the oncoming American troops visibly disturbed our German guards. As the noise grew louder, the 'master race' tightened up with fear. They couldn't decide on a course of action. Finally, in a frenzy, they started to flee, but opened a last, reckless burst of machine-gun fire, and in the very last minute before the Americans crashed in, there were 136 more Jewish victims of German bullets.
>
> A group of us, physicians, started to give first aid to the prisoners still living. We gathered the sickest and wounded and carried them off to a nearby monastery, St. Ottilien, where there was a German military hospital. We turned this into the first Jewish DP hospital, with a capacity of 1600 beds.

The second representative of the DPs and survivors was Samuel Gringaus, a former judge in his native Lithuania, who signed the charter of recognition with General McNarney. Since then, he had taken up residence in the United States. An author, lecturer, intellectual, Gringaus spoke of the ideology of the DPs, the "*shearit ha-pleitah*" (the surviving remnant):

> I personally had the privilege of working continually with Rabbi Philip Bernstein and his wonderful team of Abe Hyman, now director of the World Jewish Congress, and Rabbi Herbert Friedman, now your executive vice-chairman. The names of Bernstein, Hyman, and Friedman are connected with the greatest achievement in the field of refugee policy: the opening of the gates of the American Zone of Germany to the infiltrees. By this act, about a quarter-million Jews were saved.... In this connection, I deem it appropriate to mention the splendid work accomplished by the field workers of the JDC. Their work in the years after the War adds a glorious page to the history of this humanitarian organization....

I'm sure the audience felt as I did; that we were listening to the civilized intellectual, the man of reason, and of belief in the rule of law, the quintessential Jew – yet the man who would urge resistance and uprising and war once implacable evil showed its face on earth. Gringaus was a powerful example of the dynamic required when a man of thought must become a man of action: no paralysis in the transition.

Two final items remained on the conference agenda: Joseph Schwartz' parting words and my own incoming ones. Schwartz spoke of fleeing the Nazis, setting up shop in Lisbon, returning to Paris after the War, aiding the DPs. He concluded with a passionate, prayerful coda about the meaning of the new state of Israel.

William Rosenwald retained for himself what he called the "honor" of introducing me, and did so in his usual style of starting with a joke. He told the story of a high government official who was asked why a particular man was applying for a certain position. The answer was, "I think he needs the money, and I don't think he knows what he is getting into." That line enabled him to say that neither condition applied to me. He described me, at age 37, as "one of the most sought-after young rabbis in this country" and a person intimately familiar with the work of the UJA – after serving as a volunteer for eight years following three years in the chaplaincy working with the Holocaust survivors and the Haganah in Europe.

I thought it a good idea to respond to Rosenwalds's opening joke with a feeble attempt of my own: "Mr. Chairman, ladies and gentlemen, when Mr. Rosenwald said I knew what I was getting into, he was wrong. In the course of only six days in office, I have apparently put a whole year on my life. But in truth, I am still 36." Then I said, in part:

> I am glad to be getting into the UJA and especially to being installed there by Mr. Rosenwald's hands. The general chairman of the UJA is a person who sits at the summit of Jewish life in America, and for us to know that we have one such as he is reassuring. To know that he is possessed of the strength and conviction which are his gives us the firm feeling that we are under the captaincy of a man who can excellently lead the major enterprise of American Jewish philanthropy. To have been inducted into office by him is something which I shall not forget.

So ended the memorable Washington conference of 1955, celebrating ten years of freedom and rehabilitation, repair and reconstruction, and inaugurating what no one dreamed of at the time: decades and decades of the most devoted efforts, whose end is nowhere in sight. The constancy of those efforts means that American Jews have developed the mature understanding, patience, and staying power to see the terrible yet majestic 20th Century to its end – and if necessary beyond, until peace and stability descend upon the people and the land, both called Israel.

CHAPTER TWENTY-TWO

MOROCCO I: SPECIAL NEEDS

People tend to forget that Jews are scattered around the world. Someone had labeled those in the Moslem world of North Africa and western Asia "the Forgotten Million." The largest and one of the neediest concentrations resided in Morocco. My attention was drawn to them, and I decided to see their situation firsthand, so that I could begin to sensitize my audiences to their plight. That was a far-sighted attitude in 1953. Morocco then was under the control of the French, and almost no one imagined that within 20 months the French would be replaced by an independent Arab government, with obvious implications for the safety of the Jews living there. I could foresee the upcoming departure of the French, and I wanted to throw a spotlight on that part of the globe. I made the trip in November 1953 and subsequently delivered the following report to the UJA:

THE JEWS OF FRENCH MOROCCO

Tucked away in the northwest corner of Africa is the neediest Jewish community in the world today. In a strange and far-off place called French Morocco, remote from the traveled highways of the world, there exists a community of more than one-third of a million Jews living among eight million Moslems, Arabs, and Berbers. They are spread across a territory from the Atlantic Ocean to the Sahara Desert. They live in crowded, filthy quarters in the large cities, as well as in distant villages in the Atlas Mountains.

They are mainly the descendants of the Sephardic Jews who were expelled from Spain in 1492 and found their troubled way from Gibraltar across to North Africa. In the city of Marrakesh, far to the south, an exotic place of strange flowers and huge walls, where Winston Churchill often went to paint, we calculated the Hebrew dates on the cemetery stones and found the oldest to be 1559, although local legend has it that there are others still older.

The basis of the problem in Morocco stems from a triangular situation – French, Arab, and Jewish. Casablanca today is a bustling, modern port city of almost a million people, well-known because of the meeting held there, in 1943, between Roosevelt, Churchill, and de Gaulle. But 40 years ago, Casablanca was a primitive, walled town of 50,000 ragged inhabitants. The transformation occurred in the four decades since France established a protectorate. The French arrived in 1912 and started to develop and exploit. They brought much to Morocco, and while it is true that the area has served as a source of great wealth for France, the local population has benefited greatly from the introduction of schools, hospitals, roads, and factories.

At any rate, colonial empires are being broken up all over the world today, and Morocco is no exception. The Arabs want their independence from the French and are pressing hard for it in the United Nations. It is inevitable, given the precedents of India, Indonesia, Egypt, and other areas in the past few years, that they will achieve it, at least in some measure. But the struggle is bitter and difficult.

The Arab nationalist party is called *Istiqlal*, and its members fight the French with terror as well as political pressure. There are shootings and incidents daily. The Jews are caught right in the middle. There is little question that the fate of the Jews is tied to the fate of the French. While the French are in power, the Jews feel more-or-less secure. Hatred between Jew and Arab in the Moslem world is a matter of long tradition. The antagonisms are old and deep. Let me give you an example:

In the old bazaar of Marrakesh, one section consists of Jewish artisans who make copper trays by hand, hammering out really beautiful patterns. They bend over the anvils in little cubby-holes for 15 hours daily, sitting on mud floors, their youngest children already learning the craft. We witnessed a scene in which an Arab was bargaining with a Jew over the purchase of a platter. The conversation went something like this –

Arab: I love this beautiful tea tray, made by your unworthy Jewish hands. How much must I pay to free this lovely thing from your dirty grasp?

Jew: It saddens me to let this object of my labor pass into your lecherous fingers for any price.

Arab: Don't be so moral. You would sell your mother for money.

Jew: Give me your filthy money – and may the beautiful tray be soiled by your filthy use.

This was not merely Oriental bargaining – although it was undoubtedly partly that – but a symbolic representation of underlying tension and bad blood.

How do these masses of Jews live? Of 80,000 in Casablanca, 50,000 reside in what is called the *mellah*. This is a ghetto worse than anything I have ever seen. The DP camps of Germany and Austria after the War are very familiar to me. The tent encampments in Israel of three years ago are equally familiar. I have seen the meanest slums in American and European cities. Absolutely nothing can be compared to a *mellah*.

It has crooked little alleys, often no more than a yard wide, containing low doors through which one crouches to emerge into a courtyard surrounded by dozens of little openings that are literally holes in the wall. In each hole or room, which has no lights, water, or air, unbelievably large numbers of people live. Families are huge – birth control is unknown. Usually there is one bed, on, under, and around which sleep six to ten people. There are often no chairs or table. Cooking is done on the floor, as is eating. There is no question of sanitation. Water in the *mellah* is obtained by buying it from water sellers.

It is fantastic to realize that people go out through the *mellah* gates each day, work outside, see life outside, and then return to this festering, stinking place to sleep each night. We saw pretty young women, dressed in presentable Western clothing, going out to work in shops and offices, and coming back at the end of the day. We saw others, who, having made the break, swore they would never return, and found a room on the outside, although that meant separation from family. There is a social ferment going on at the moment that will eventually lead to the dissolution of the *mellah*, unless there is a forced emigration first.

The ferment is due partly to the expanding horizons of the younger generation and partly to the extensive program of health, education, and welfare that is being supported by outside agencies such as our own JDC. When you bring those elements to people, you make them dissatisfied with the cubby hole. Let us not go into the question of whether we do them any favor or not. There are those who would say, leave them in the cubby hole, they know no better. But I think few would subscribe to that. Progress means irritation, agitation, excitement, advancement in the face of all kinds of difficulties. And I, for one, feel it is right and proper to teach them to be dissatisfied with what they have, so that they may strive for better.

Let me give you a few examples of the kind of JDC programs and projects that will increase the rate of dissolution of the old pattern. We saw a large polyclinic of four stories. The place was a beehive of mothers and children. One of the nasty diseases of Morocco is "parch" (favus, tinia). It invades the scalp of children and causes sores running with pus. At the clinic, a mass attack is being made on this scrofulous disease.

A battery of X-ray machines has been brought in. The child's head is placed under X-ray, and after several exposures, the hair falls out. In the next room are about 25 nurses, locally trained (which was no small task), plucking individual, subcutaneous hairs with tweezers, to get every single follicle. The skulls are swabbed in many successive treatments with a thick greasy paste containing various medicaments. Bandaged heads or egg-bald heads of children are a most common sight in the Jewish parts of the *mellah*. Gradually, the hair grows back, free of the parasites, and the clean, curly locks are matched only by the smiles on the faces of the emancipated boys and girls.

In this same clinic, there are departments for many other things, such as care of new-born babies – how to wrap, feed, take their temperature, all matters commonplace to us but a real revolution to people bereft of such benefits until four years ago. In the basement of the clinic is a modern, sanitary milk plant under the supervision of a young Dutchman. Machinery has been brought in to sterilize the bottles, fill them automatically, seal them hermetically, and then, of all miracles, pasteurize them. Every mother, bringing a baby or child to the clinic for any kind of treatment, gets four pint bottles at each visit. Medical care and milk are free. As an aside, let me say that it was quite a thrill to see, in the large mixing room, containers of powdered milk, with the stencilled emblem – "Donation of the U.S. State Department," from the depot at Eau Claire, Wisconsin.

You have all heard of the dreaded eye disease called trachoma. In Africa and Asia, millions are blinded by it. It is most common to see blind beggars sitting in the hot sun, their eye sockets crawling with flies, while they cry out for a pittance. An experimental clinic has been set up by the JDC right inside the *mellah* for the cure of trachoma. In one area of two square blocks, 2,200 people were tested. Of those, 1,600 had some form of trachoma. The results of treatment were startling. More than 400 were completely cured, and another 400 showed improvement; the last half were too far gone for any change.

There are many schools, all subsidized in one way or another by the JDC. There are the schools of the Alliance Israelite, where thousands of children receive secular and religious education in both French and Hebrew. An organization called Otzar-ha-Torah operates a school for

800 boys. There is even a normal school, under the direction of a French rabbi (an army chaplain), where teachers are prepared to staff the expanding Jewish school system all over Morocco. There are many kindergartens where the children are taught to drink milk (which they disliked intensely at first, never having had any) and to play constructively. One such kindergarten was being operated by a young woman who had been sent to Switzerland to get her own education and training.

At all the schools, a free lunch is given the children – the only hot meal they receive during the day. At Marrakesh, we stumbled across quite a scene. A young woman, who turned out to be 22, was literally fighting with the principal at the entrance to the school. She was the mother of five children. She was trying to register her 4-year old boy. The principal was trying to explain that the boy was too young for the school. The mother was shrieking that she wanted him enrolled so that he could eat. It was pitiful – and at the same time indicative of the very real help being offered by the school and lunch program.

The third aspect of the JDC program is economic rehabilitation. If people can be trained or encouraged or helped to improve themselves economically, they can hope to make a break from the *mellah*, for no law keeps them inside except the law of poverty. With a specific trade or skill at their command, young men and women could always find work in an expanding labor market. The fixed job is the key to freedom.

The Organization for Rehabilitation through Training (ORT) has a large and wonderful vocational training school in Casablanca. Four hundred boys board there. A large workshop teaches metalworking, welding, woodworking, motor mechanics, and other special skills. There are dormitories for sleeping, classrooms for study, dining hall for meals. The lunch we saw consisted of fish, vegetables, beans, and zucchini, with dates for dessert.

What is the ultimate solution for these third-of-a-million Jews in Morocco (and, incidentally, their brethren nearby in French-ruled Tunisia, whose situation is identical)? What can and should be done? What conclusions did we reach?

It seems to me that the picture is clear – perhaps, I admit, because our visit was short. Had we stayed longer, the answers might have grown more complex. But we talked to lots of people and got answers that seemed to fall into neat categories. Three major conclusions emerged:

1. The future of Morocco's Jews will be difficult, if not impossible, as the Arabs continue to win more and more independence from the French.

2. The Jews' immediate emigration is also difficult, if not impossible, for Israel cannot take them now except in the event of actual pogroms. I shall explain this in detail when I report on Israel in two weeks time.

3. It is therefore obvious that we must use this interim period, however long or short it should be – (it actually took only two years until the first pogrom occurred) – to continue to improve health, education, and economic conditions with an eye toward ultimate emigration. Life itself will thus become more bearable inside Morocco, and Israel will ultimately receive a population whose health and educational standards will be considerably higher than at present.

One last matter. At the JDC International Conference in Paris, which we were fortunate to attend, someone asked why the UJA should be concerned about these Moroccan Jews. Haven't they always lived in squalor and poverty? How far can we go to rescue every remote remnant of the Jewish people in the world? The questioner went on in this vein, apparently expressing the misgivings of many American Jews who wonder why their UJA money should be used for this particular group.

My answer comes from the heart. I am convinced that these Moroccan Jews are good human material. They have been ground down under brutal poverty and ruthless Arab oppression for centuries. We have found them now in this condition. Miracles have been wrought in the four short years that organized help has been given to them. They constitute a small replacement for the six million murdered in Europe. If we have found this reservoir, let us not be dismayed at the temporary burden it represents but rather rejoice that here are some Jews who can be gathered in to enlarge the fold. Why should we be concerned about them? Simply because they are ours – our brothers and sisters.

In one of the villages near the Sahara, in the foothills of the Atlas Mountains, far from Warsaw and Berlin and New York and Jerusalem, a car with American visitors stopped. The visitors talked to two young Jewish boys, and asked, with love and kindness: "What do you need? What can we send you?" Out of the poverty and the want and the fear came the strong, simple answer: "Please send us a few Hebrew books."

Across many centuries and wide, wide spaces, Jew was speaking to Jew.

★   ★   ★

I spent many months travelling around the United States, telling the story of Moroccan and other North African Jewries. Because this was all new and involved giving much historical background, I needed to sensitize the American-Jewish, basically Ashkenazic audience to the phenomenon of a relatively large Sephardic population of brethren in need. Although the audience was cautious, and fairly slow to react, I could sense it gradually accepting responsibility. The process involved, in effect, adding a new layer to the already accepted themes of Holocaust and Israel. It was important to accomplish this familiarization process before some real, dire problem exploded, which in fact occurred even sooner than I had anticipated.

The French had just lost the battle of Dien Bien Phu in Vietnam. It seemed incredible that a powerful, modern European nation had been defeated by lightly armed jungle guerillas. But it had happened. And as the French prepared to withdraw from Southeast Asia, I could see them, in my mind's eye, withdrawing from North Africa as well. Should that occur, Arab rule would be established in Morocco and other countries. I could therefore envision a period in which a huge migration of Jews would flow to Israel, from the Atlantic to the Nile. That, in turn, would have tremendous repercussions in Israel, for war was again looming there.

Back in Milwaukee, after much travel recounting the story of Moroccan Jewry, I was faced once more by the chief officers of the UJA, William Rosenwald and Edward Warburg. Their first appearance had been in 1952, asking me to assume the executive leadership of the national organization. It was relatively easy to demur, for I had just taken the rabbinical position. But here they were again in mid-1954 with the same request. They had been searching continuously during the past two years, but had found no one who possessed the qualifications needed, and they remained convinced that I was the person for the job. My work in Germany with the DPs and the several years thereafter of constant appearances on UJA platforms throughout the United States represented a combination of experiences which impressed them. Their arguments were very strong and resonated with greater urgency this time. My head was filled with the North African Jewish problem and with the danger to Israel of another Arab attack.

I talked the matter over with Ben Saltzstein and Ed Prince, the two men who had brought me there. They made clear they were sorry to lose me but agreed that they should not stand in my way. I was – and still am – impressed by their broad-mindedness. One seldom finds lay leaders capable of putting their own projects aside for a larger, communal good. Of course, that quality is exactly what attracted me to Ben and Ed in the first instance.

So I accepted the UJA offer effective one year hence, i.e., in June 1955, giving me time to complete my current confirmation class, the synagogue time to conclude its calendar of other activities, and a search committee the opportunity to choose my successor.

Sadly, conditions in North Africa continued to deteriorate, and the immigrant-absorption process in Israel was showing increasing strain. A report given to the UJA National Conference in December 1954 included the following:

> On August 3, 1954, in the Moroccan town of Petitjean, there was a flare-up of mob violence... six Jews were dead. There has been no recurrence since

then, thanks to the vigilance of the French authorities. However, the memory of it cannot be erased. The vast majority of Jews live on the thin margin of a crumbling economy. In a depression, such as the one currently plaguing Morocco, the Jews are pushed to the very edge of starvation and despair. Thus emigration becomes a compelling necessity.

Israel has made forward strides at great cost in personal sacrifice, belt-tightening, and hard grueling work. American Jews have helped make possible these advances by tremendous contributions of resources and energies. Today's immigrants, unlike three years ago, will avoid the discomforts and degradations of reception center and camp living. Instead, within five hours of their arrival, newcomers will find themselves in a ship-to-settlement operation that transfers them quickly to homes and jobs in new settlements. Of those who entered the country in the final months of 1954, some 44 percent went directly to agricultural settlements, 52 percent found employment as manual laborers in rural areas, and only four percent went into reception centers. David Levy, a former foreign minister of Israel, came as a young boy with his family in this wave.

It must be realized that the decision to receive a minimum of 30,000 North African newcomers in 1955, plus a minimum of 5,000 immigrants from other areas, was based on a calculated risk. As Dr. Giora Josephthal, treasurer of the Jewish Agency, has said: "We will take them in. This is our *raison d'être*... but this immigration can wreck the whole achievement of the last three years." Whether it does or not, will depend to a great extent on the Jews of the United States and the funds they provide.

After reading that prognosis, with its dire closing paragraph, I sat back and started to think, in very graphic images and for the first time, about the UJA job to which I had committed myself. Up to now, I reflected, my thoughts had been conditioned by abstractions and ideology. Suddenly, a great wave of anxiety almost drowned me. I was facing not abstract concepts like "nationhood" and "peoplehood," but the reality of the living land of Israel, needing roads and water and guns, and at the same time taking in sick children coming from places of fear to this place of safety. They needed a house, not a tent, and a house cost lots of money.

I now had to lead the effort to get that money. Suppose I failed? Suppose I didn't know how? Suppose I got some, but not enough? Suppose a war broke out in the first year of my watch, and tons and tons of money were needed? My God, what had I let myself in for?

CHAPTER TWENTY-THREE

MOROCCO II: SPECIAL FUND

French colonial rule in Morocco came to an end in July 1955, and as the French flags came down, the fate of the Jews drifted into a danger zone. Sultan Mohammed V returned to Casablanca from his exile in Madagascar in a white DC-3, that also contained 20 ladies of His Majesty's Royal Harem. On that same day, the flag of the Moslem Istiqlal (Independence) Party went up, and rioting started against the Jews.

The Sultan tried to discourage such excesses, but the political and religious passions of the celebrating Moslem nationalists overcame his plea for moderation. The crowd sought Jewish blood and found it. More than a thousand wounded were brought from the *mellah* to the more secure courtyard of the Talmud Torah school, where doctors and nurses gathered to help.

I spent the first two weeks of July in Morocco and traveled to many cities where the same violent story was being repeated. I talked to scores of staff members of the main organizations: JDC, ORT, Lubavitch, Alliance Française, and the Jewish Agency. The Agency's people were functioning here clandestinely, and their young men from Israel began to form small groups of local Jewish youth to receive training in self-defense with the long staves so effective in the Asiatic martial arts.

All those kind, caring outsiders, who were devoting their lives to improving the well-being of the Moroccan Jews, came to a similar conclusion: The future safety and security of this community lay only in migration. Moslem nationalism of the Istiqlal Party was incompatible with a large Jewish presence in Morocco. That lesson became obvious to me, brought home through my own first-hand observations and interviews with scores of Jews at every level – including the thin layer of wealthy, socially assimilated families. Many of them admitted to feeling more at home with French culture, language, and citizenship than with Israeli; they considered their options to be relocating in Paris or remaining in Morocco – if they felt close enough to the royal family to receive protection. But they agreed that the solution for the masses, who held to traditional Judaism, was to be found in the new Jewish state.

I returned to New York convinced that we must work immediately toward that solution. Further Jewish casualties would be unconscionable.

It was clear that we would have to prepare for the migration of hundreds of thousands of poor Jews. Such a migration would cost heavy millions. How could we raise the money?

I thought of the idea of calling for a special fund, that is, one whose proceeds would not be shared with the local communities. Sharing was the established pattern in the UJA's annual campaign, so I would be seeking a drastic exception. I knew in the back of my mind that future occasions might require a similar exception; this first effort, therefore, had to be an acknowledged success. For the present, I had a large-enough concern; would the local Federations, our partners, agree to participate in a campaign in which they would not share? All of those thoughts swirled through my head as I visited Moroccan hospitals and schools, talked to the wounded about their fears, to the mothers in the child-care clinics, to the Israeli teachers, to the French military, to the American Embassy officers. Out of that melange of impressions, a sense of order emerged, and I saw the steps to be taken, one by one.

A few months later, I convened a one-day national conference in New York on the subject. About 400 local UJA leaders from across the entire country attended. Senator Herbert Lehman of New York was in the chair. The Israeli foreign minister, Moshe Sharett, made a special trip to add weight to the occasion and stress its seriousness. His words were brief but telling: "The Israeli Government had been planning to step up our appropriation on behalf of the North African immigration. We now find ourselves utterly unable to cope with that increase...because of the second emergency into which we were flung...when Egypt found itself assured by the Soviet Union of a vast, overwhelming superiority of arms." He left his listeners in a stark and somber mood.

The meeting hinged on two presentations – one by Edward M. M. Warburg, president of the JDC, and the other by myself – followed by questions and discussion from the floor, culminating in a vote concerning the establishment of a special fund that would go to the national UJA and be earmarked entirely for Moroccan Jewry. An extra gift was to be solicited from each donor. The fund's national goal would be $25 million – more than half the amount sought for the *regular* UJA campaign that year!

People outside of fundraising would consider that a very bold move. But if I had learned one thing about the art of raising money, it was that a definite relationship exists between the amount sought and the amount obtained: the larger the amount being asked for, the larger the ultimate contribution. One could not act wildly, of course. The amount sought had to relate to the donor's previous record, financial capability, emotional identification with the cause, and other factors. It is an interesting fact that, in 1955, the number of big givers – those who contributed $10,000 or more a year – totaled only 400 in the entire nation. (Over the succeeding decades, that number has increased to more than 7,000.)

In order to create some excitement, interject some controversy, and present our case in an unusual format, Warburg and I decided to concoct a role reversal. He was publicly known as the JDC president who strongly advocated support for Jews in need in many countries around the globe. He would have been wholly expected to speak on behalf of Morocco's Jews. I was known publicly as the fiery Zionist, the pro-Israel advocate, the one who should have declared that the effort to divert funds to Morocco must not occur at the expense of Israel. Instead, each of us assumed the other's position – and succeeded in keeping our listeners alert and interested.

Warburg launched his attack by asking why we were deliberating on raising large sums for Morocco when Israel was in such deep trouble and needed money much more desperately. Fedayeen (terrorist guerrillas) attacks occurred as daily fare on Israel borders. Kibbutzim were forced to divert manpower for guard duty. Casualties occurred every night. (All of that, in fact, would culminate in war a year later.) A convincing speaker, coming from that segment of the German-Jewish community whose general position had not been pro-Zionist, Warburg made a striking impression and really shook the audience.

In my response, I agreed that Israel was worthy of support. But I argued emotionally about Jews in danger of pogroms, whom I had just seen a few weeks earlier and whose bloody plight could be avoided only by getting them out of a place in which they had no future and an unsafe present. I talked about babies who needed milk and children whose scalps were crawling with parasites.

Warburg countered that he worried more about the nation of Israel than a population of Jews in trouble in any one country; I rebutted that an immediate danger took priority, and back and forth we went. The escalation of argument found us almost shouting at each other.

The effect of the dialogue was startling. It became obvious to everyone in the audience that both positions were correct, and that a "normal" campaign that year would not satisfy both sets of needs. An extraordinary approach was required, and that was exactly what we were proposing in the special fund. The audience approved it – perhaps without realizing that they had just introduced a new method into the course of major Jewish fundraising in America.

To complete this part of the story, let me report that the UJA's regular campaign for 1956 raised more than the previous year, and the Special Fund for Morocco raised about $14 million extra. We didn't reach the full goal, but the new venture was clearly successful.

Two other new and valuable ideas emerged from the special fund effort. I introduced a department at the UJA a department that had never existed before – PCB, pre-campaign budgeting. The procedure involved sending a team of UJA lay and professional people to meet in each city with a similar team of local Federation people in advance of the next year's campaign, to establish what the division of funds would be. Some of these meetings were cordial and simple, with the locals not attempting to exaggerate their needs and the UJA not seeking to fight over every last percentage point in the split of proceeds. But others were bitter, even to the extent of threatening a divorce – separate campaigns for separate purposes.

I remember such brinkmanship occurring in Chicago and Los Angeles for many years. I was perfectly willing to go my own way in both cities. I firmly believed that the largest contributors favored the needs of Israel and world Jewry and that a campaign pegged exclusively to those causes would raise more than the amount the UJA was currently receiving from a joint campaign that included local needs.

Fortunately, that prospect never materialized. National lay leaders and local leaders alike always hesitated at the brink and settled on a formula that both sides accepted on the basis of compromise.

The PCB meetings took place in 30 or 40 of the major communities in the country during a hectic period in October-November, in preparation for the next year's campaign. They required an extraordinary amount of work, mobilizing lay leaders to do the traveling, teaching them how to make that year's case, and arranging the logistics. But the results were worth the effort. After several years, we brought the UJA share of the national campaign back up to 55 percent, with every percentage point translating into millions of dollars. The whole process emerged from the special fund concept.

The second, and closely linked, idea was ideological – a definition of priorities. In simplest terms, the question at every PCB meeting was, whose needs are more important, Israel's or your local Jewish community's? That question was thrashed out over and again, in city after city, year after year. The issue, seemingly centered on money, really revolved around philosophy and belief, and it led hundreds of our top leaders to define what they thought and felt about the historic demands of the times through which we were living.

That was precisely my goal. My whole purpose was to educate a lay leadership in an understanding of Jewish history. The only successful way to raise money is to *raise people* who are thoroughly and passionately convinced that they are serving the destiny of the Jewish nation. And to bring them to such an understanding and conviction, I felt it my responsibility to utilize every possible occasion to teach, interpret, explain, convince.

I placed the entire matter on the highest level, the historical level. I explained that I was not fighting for UJA organizational prestige, which is a petty motive; nor seeking to score points as in a debate. I readily admitted I was trying to get them to understand that by building and strengthening Israel, as well as gathering in the beleaguered Jews of Africa, Asia, hopefully the Soviet Union, and wherever else necessary, they would be guaranteeing their own survival here in the United States. Why? Because in the process, they would become linked to a transcendent cause, a cause so much larger than themselves that they would draw strength from it. If we lost overseas, whether in Morocco or Israel, and were left alone here, we would be small, diminished, depleted, disgusted with ourselves, lacking pride to transmit to our children, so that in a very few generations, we would probably dwindle to a tiny sect.

But if we won on the larger stage of Jewish destiny and historical survival, we would flourish here, filled with a sense of self-worth and a strong determination to build our own American-Jewish community into a fully creative structure that could struggle successfully against the threat of mindless assimilation. The more money we poured into Israel and world Jewry, the more we would also contribute to our local needs. Giving more each year becomes easier and easier as people grow increasingly accustomed to the *mitzvah* of philanthropy.

Temporary changes in national and personal economic conditions always affect fundraising adversely, but it increases again. Judging in terms of decades, as I always did, one sees only growth. The history of American-Jewish fundraising, while I was directing it and after I left it, attests to the accuracy of that appraisal.

CHAPTER TWENTY-FOUR

A FRESH FLOOD OF REFUGEES

At dawn, we walked down to the river bank. Across the frozen fields of Hungary we saw Jews coming – running, staggering, falling, running again. They came empty-handed, for knapsacks had grown too heavy and suitcases had long ago been thrown aside while crossing the 20-odd kilometers of plowed and muddy terrain to reach the Austrian border. Their clothing was ice-encrusted, their eyes red with weariness, and some groups had suffered casualties.

I was with Moses Leavitt, executive director of the JDC, on the Austro-Hungarian border, in late November 1956, trying to figure out how to give effective aid to the Jews fleeing the aftermath of Soviet brutality against the Hungarian Revolution. We talked to one man whose wife had been shot by drunken Russian soldiers. We talked to another who had been forced to leave his two children, 8 and 2, in a hospital, suffering from frostbite. It was a choice between leaving them, perhaps forever, or dragging them along, perhaps to their death. He elected to give them life, albeit as orphans, under Soviet control. He cried bitterly.

There was much shooting to be heard along the length of the river, which marked the frontier. The Hungarian soldiers, not 50 meters away, shot at us as we turned and walked away.

Earlier, a JDC worker in Vienna had told us that approximately 10 percent of those fleeing were Jews. Thus our relief efforts, after administering first aid in the border tents to people distributed among the various Jewish and Catholic agencies, would encompass around 17,000 persons. Now, standing at that spot on the river, swirling with fog and mist, heavy with danger, lonesome in the bleakness of winter, we saw the ineradicable human spirit in those trying to escape the tyranny of armed communist might.

Could we even think of deserting them, the twice-persecuted, the Jews with Auschwitz numbers on their arms who were now running a second time to save life itself? None of our lay leaders and professionals would walk away from this problem. In a manner that Jewish tradition demands, we were obligated to feed and clothe, house and nourish, heal and counsel, and finally resettle these 17,000 and others who kept coming through the frozen nights.

In the closing months of 1956, events were moving with dizzying speed. Egypt was expelling Jews in the aftermath of the recent war with Israel. Hungary was in revolt, with scores of thousands fleeing. Poland was seething with a suddenly renewed anti-semitism, so Jews were fleeing there, too. Rumania was permitting emigration. Morocco, as I have just related in detail, was proving unable to stem the constant Jewish outflow, despite orders to close air and sea ports.

A vast area appeared to be deep in the midst of a new refugee period involving more than 100,000 Jews from many lands, one of the largest streams since the first two years of statehood. Many of us felt we had been thrust back a decade in time, to the end of the Hitler period, when the roads of Europe were filled with refugees seeking haven.

At a hastily assembled meeting of American-Jewish leaders on November 30, 1956, the facts and the speculation were laid out in detail. The group decided to continue the special fund approach by calling for an emergency rescue fund of $100 million above and beyond the regular, annual UJA campaign. There was no disagreement. The picture, as 1957 dawned, was quite clearly one of flight, terror, deportees, escapees. Everywhere people were running toward freedom. Some would wind up in the U.S. and elsewhere, but Israel would take most, because an ever-open door was the very premise of her existence.

American Jews would also play their role, holding aloft a banner, writ large for all to see, containing the pledge of their hearts, souls, and treasure to the task of rescuing and transplanting fellow Jews. At the end of that meeting, I knew the pledge would be kept again.

On the last day of the year, I left again for another look at the European picture – at the Hungarian border and in Vienna, Marseilles, Naples, and Paris. I was accompanied by Leavitt, one of the most experienced professionals in the field of refugee relief operations and the man who made the basic recommendations as to how much money should be spent, where, and on what. Acerbic, quick, impatient with mediocrity and social chit-chat, he was just the right companion in the fast-moving scene we were entering. Leavitt would analyze a situation, make suggestions for handling problems, perhaps solicit advice from his staff of field directors, and do it all with a self-confidence that commanded respect.

On January 6, 1957, we stood on the dock in Naples and watched the arrival of the vessel *S.S. MISR*, an Egyptian ship whose very name recalled the Hebrew word for Egypt – Mitzraim. Normally, the *MISR* carried Moslem pilgrims to Mecca. This time, her cargo was 1,000 Jews being expelled from Egypt. The ship had been chartered by the International Red Cross as a mercy vessel to bring to freedom Jews who had been jailed in Egypt during the Suez War. The pain and shock, the anger and bewilderment felt by those Jews poured out in a torrent of relief when they found sympathetic people waiting to welcome them. They did not know we would be there. Then they saw the large group of friendly JDC workers; officials of HIAS (Hebrew Immigrant Aid Society), who would help process documents; Jewish leaders of the Italian community; Jewish Agency personnel, who would arrange transportation to Israel; non-Jewish Italians from the Ministry of Labor, who offered temporary shelter in an emigrant center; and Jews from far-off America. Seeing all those people, they cried for joy, knowing they were not forgotten. And then they poured out their stories in an emotional outburst.

The narrations followed a similar pattern, with only minor variations. The terror usually began with a knock on the door in the dead of night, with a police officer, sometimes in uniform, sometimes in mufti, delivering an order for expulsion or prison. For those imprisoned, there was a day spent on paperwork in the Cairo Citadel; then transfer to the Abassich (a community-owned Jewish school that had been requisitioned and converted into a prison) for two months; then transfer to Alexandria's official prison for one day (the train ride made in handcuffs); and finally onto the expulsion ship, where the deportee signed a statement that he was leaving Egypt of his own free will! Two months-plus in prison, often hungry, often enduring police brutality, always taunted and mocked, fearing for the safety of other family members now separated and scattered – that was the fate of thousands.

Those not imprisoned but simply expelled had to scurry frantically for boat and plane tickets, to sell their furniture and personal possessions to scrape together a few dollars, and to bribe officials to obtain the necessary papers. Bank accounts were blocked, jobs lost, businesses confiscated, in a calculated program of robbing the Jews and pouring their wealth into dictator Nasser's coffers.

At that point, more than 8,000 Egyptian Jews had already been expelled – some with European passports that had been in their family for generations, but most stateless, stripped of their Egyptian nationality. Those on the *MISR* with whom we spoke voiced their conviction that Egypt would expel its entire Jewish population – 45,000 to 55,000 people – within a few months. The officials of the Jewish Agency in Jerusalem were frantically preparing to receive such a flood.

Other vessels were scheduled to unload their passengers at Naples and Athens in the weeks ahead. We left with the feeling that the plans for temporary settlement in those two cities were in order and that the staffs of the various relief organizations were motivated to provide as much physical and psychological support as possible. We left feeling, too, that we were well equipped to convince our followers back home of the urgent need for relieving the misery we had seen.

From Naples and Rome, we went on to Vienna. This city in the center of Europe, through which all roads and rumors pass, always offered the latest gossip about what was happening to Jews anywhere on the continent – and sometimes anywhere in the world. Information could always be obtained from a journalist, government official, professional spy, or businessman passing through.

In Vienna, we caught the first serious whispers of the new wave of anti-semitism developing in Poland. Oddly, it had nothing to do with the Jews themselves: anti-semitism had become a weapon in the struggle for power that was continuing between communists and nationalists on one hand, and between Stalinists and Gomulka, leader of the Polish Communist Party, on the other. The issue was the question of who is a true anti-semite. The Revolutionary Student Council of Wroclaw (Breslau) University demanded the expulsion of all Jewish students from the university. Gomulka refused to accede to this demand. He was then charged with being soft on Jews.

Two young men, presumably from the student council, had recently walked into a crowded restaurant in the center of Warsaw shouting that they wanted to kill a Jew. They attacked a man who appeared to be a Jew, although he in fact was not, and beat him unconscious, as most patrons watched in silence. The story appeared in *The New York Times* of January 8. Our informant said that a low-level panic was setting in and that many Polish Jews were migrating to other countries. The total Jewish population in Poland numbered between 45,000 and 70,000; it was impossible to estimate the number who would leave if permitted to do so.

We picked up a second rumor; legal migration might soon be starting again from Rumania. In that country, the exit of Jews was usually on-again, off-again, with no one quite sure how to predict the next move. But one thing was usually reliable in Vienna; smoke means fire. And sure enough, as we continued to poke around, we found people who had been keeping watch at the South Station and seen bedraggled Jews disembarking from the Bucharest train. At first just a handful, but now a handful almost every day. It looked as though something big was developing.

We drove eastward, through the Austrian province of Burgenland, to the Hungarian border. Two months earlier, on November 4, the Russians had sent their tanks right into the center of Budapest to crush the revolt the people were attempting to mount. The Hungarians were the first, before the East Germans or the Czechs, to try to ameliorate the harshness of Russian domination. The Soviets understood what was at stake and crushed the freedom movement with utter brutality.

Street fighting in Budapest was intense; hundreds killed, severe reprisals, all resulting in a mass flight. During December alone, an estimated 150,000 Hungarians fled their homes and belongings, risking their very lives because border guards were ordered to shoot to kill. They fled primarily westward, toward the Austrian border, for that at least was a neutral country where they could feel safe. All along the Burgenland border, there were Hungarian watchtowers, manned often by Russians, on one side, and emigrant reception centers on the other. Winter there is very cold and snowy, and the area contains many small rivers. The Austrians therefore set up their receiving points as close to the border as possible, in large tents containing gas heaters. When the refugees staggered in, freezing wet, they were immediately treated to hot drinks and warm blankets. Gradually the panic and adrenalin that sustained them during the final spurt to safety – as they avoided bullets and icy water – would recede, leaving them flat and exhausted.

★　★　★

Returning to Vienna, we watched the reception process accorded to the refugees. Great acts of heroism were performed by the small corps of JDC and HIAS social workers, who were working 16 hours daily. Thousands of people passed before them, nervously asking questions, and their eager and pathetic queries about visas to various countries were answered with tact and patience. Sometimes I was not sure who was more tired, the refugees themselves or those sitting at the little wooden desks trying to help them. The care and maintenance of this caseload constituted a tremendous financial burden – and toting it was my responsibility. I would go home and try to raise the necessary money.

I made a quick stop in Marseilles to inspect a holding area where Moroccan-Jewish immigrants waited en route to Israel. The area, maintained by the JDC, was a vital link, known to the French authorities, who resisted all protests from Rabat. Conditions in the camp were very good, and the inhabitants had no complaints. At the moment, there were about 3,500 residents, and all the programs to keep them occupied were functioning nicely. I stayed overnight, talked with the camp leaders, the teachers, and their pupils, and left with a warm feeling. For once, there was no crisis, no danger, no emergency; everything was under control.

Our trip ended in Paris. Officials from the Jewish Agency flew in from Israel and Geneva to discuss the entire problem. Now we could begin to see overall numbers, estimates, costs, timetables. It was clear that a calculation of 100,000 Jewish refugees entering Israel in 1957 might well be an underestimate. It was also clear that Israel's housing program would have to be drastically revised and accelerated. Careful social engineering was required to disperse these new groups of immigrants throughout the country. Since there were large numbers of children in the Egyptian and Polish groups, there would have to be schools in the areas designated for them. In short, brain power and money would be needed immediately.

Ben-Gurion realized all that intuitively, before he had the statistical results of our survey. On January 3, at a meeting of the central committee of the Mapai party, he made a major policy speech that included these urgent words:

> One of the important results of the Suez campaign is that we have assured ourselves of a lull on the military front....Hence the priority must be given once again to the needs of immigration and economic independence....This year we may expect from sixty to one hundred thousand immigrants. This is a heavy burden, but it is a sacred and precious burden, and it must now have first priority.

I returned to New York in time to report on a closed-circuit TV network. Modern technology had made it possible to set up movie-sized screens in a synagogue social hall or a community center auditorium, where thousands of people could gather. The UJA had rented one hour of time on the coaxial cable and had arranged to place the screens in some 30 large communities. I gave a detailed, emotional report, covering the period from the Suez-Sinai War to the present, designating these 75 days as among the most eventful in our recent history, and ended with these words:

> Our campaign is beginning to mount in pace and intensity. People realize this is an extraordinary moment. Already gifts are being made beyond the

previous highest level of many individuals' giving history. Every man and woman who is counted in the leadership group of the American Jewish community must now step forward and make a maximum personal gift to the Emergency Rescue Fund, in addition to his or her normal annual gift. This is now the moment for heroic and noble action.

During that hectic year, the only relief possible would come during a quiet two weeks in August when I would recharge my batteries with swimming, resting, and reading. It was exactly during that period that tragedy struck. One fine August morning, a phone call came from brother Sam in New Haven: our mother had died in her sleep. She had been at my family's house just a week earlier, sitting on the deck, enjoying the children at play on the grass below, chatting with my father and me, seemingly in sound basic health despite several ailments.

I was overwhelmed by both guilt and sadness. The tempo of my life had left little enough time for my wife and children, but almost none for my parents. I was flooded with guilt that I had given my mother so little of myself over the years. Yet I knew that she understood, for she had told me how pleased she was by what I was doing for Israel and Jews. These two causes were extremely important to her as well, which had made it easy for her to be so forgiving.

CHAPTER TWENTY-FIVE

JAILED IN RUMANIA

In early and then late summer of 1958, I moved to address two other segments of world Jewry that were also cut off from, and largely unfamiliar to, American Jews. This time the locales were Iran and Rumania, two very different cultures under two very different political regimes.

Iran was home to a population claiming a heritage of 2,500 years of continuous existence since the destruction of the First Temple in Jerusalem. The territory known today as Iraq and Iran was called Babylonia in ancient times. When the Babylonians conquered Judea and destroyed the temple in 586 B.C.E. (Before Common Era), they enslaved the greater part of the Hebrew population. Only 50 years later, the Babylonians themselves were conquered by the Persians, whose ruler permitted the Hebrews to return to the land of Judea. Only a small number took advantage of this noble amnesty. The great majority remained in the hospitable environment of the Tigris-Euphrates Valley, and the present Jewish inhabitants are proud to call themselves direct descendants of the original Judeans.

When the state of Israel came into existence, a steady flow of Iranian Jewish immigration developed, and it has continued to this very day. Although there were no formal diplomatic relations between Iran and Israel, there were consular links up to 1979, when the Shah was deposed. The Israeli presence in Teheran took the form of consular, trade, and technical aid missions. There was a simple explanation for that anomaly: Iran had received enormous assistance of all sorts from Israel, and reciprocated by permitting a constant emigration to continue.

Among the Jews remaining in Iran, however, living conditions were desperately hard and unsanitary. In 1958, I went to Teheran to see the situation at first hand. On July 11, back in Jerusalem, I wrote to my mailing list:

> There is an Air France flight non-stop from Tel-Aviv to Teheran, and I made the trip a few weeks ago. There are about 83,000 Jews now in that country, of whom 80% are so poverty-stricken that daily bread is a real problem.
>
> The people need every kind of help – food, clothing, bathing, medicine, sanitation, schools, jobs, money, and a whole range of medical care. The ghettos are horrible – hundreds of people living in crowded courtyards. Sanitation and hygiene are the major problems. One toilet for 50 people becomes a main cause of disease. Public baths must be built. People must be taught to keep their hands clean. All water is infected, and to teach the women to boil water raises the question of the few pennies needed to buy fuel for the fire. Health and utter poverty are interconnected.
>
> The Joint Distribution Committee is doing a *terrific* job. There are only eight foreign staff members (American, British, etc.) who must train local personnel, administer the whole network of programs, and simultaneously provide guidance and inspiration. I had the feeling that this was a tiny band of true heroes, working selflessly in a far outpost. I saw wonderful progress among children. The Joint has a young American expert in child care. She has taught several score of local girls to be kindergarten teachers. They receive $18 per month. Two kindergartens have been organized, taking care of 1,000 children. They are fed at the school, receive new clothing twice yearly, a bath once weekly, a haircut when needed, and have the services of a nurse at all times. This is paradise, compared to the situation a few short years ago.
>
> Our duty in Iran is clear. Through hospital, clinics, and personal training, we must help eliminate disease. Through issuing supplies, we

must help combat hunger and nakedness. Through schools, we must make educated humans out of ghetto urchins. Through emigration, we must help those who wish to go to Israel. All this can be done and is being done. To sum it up, here is another section of world Jewry, not very large but terribly in need, toward whom we must stretch our hands in the task we have set ourselves – to relieve the want of every Jew we can reach.

That letter was written more than one-third of a century ago, and the situation described then has been completely changed. The Jewish population in Iran today has shrunk substantially. The small middle class of that time has completely emigrated to Israel and other lands; the poorer class has become today's middle class; and there are no longer any totally helpless poor. While the Jews' economic condition has improved, however, their political condition – like that of most Iranians – has declined since the downfall of the Shah. If one were thus to predict the future of Iranian Jewry, the picture would include a steady emigration down to a zero base.

★ ★ ★

In September, an alarming situation developed in Rumania. Because that poor country had been low on Hitler's list, the Nazis did not occupy it until the last year of the War. At that time, the Jewish population totaled approximately 800,000. In only one year of their devilish work, the Nazis managed to murder half the total. A large migration to Israel started immediately on the establishment of the new state, but it was cut off after one year by the communist government's decree.

From 1949-58, almost no one was allowed to leave Rumania. Chief Rabbi Moses Rosen, an enigmatic personality, worked extremely hard to maintain morale among the Jewish communities scattered around the country. He kept a spirit alive through establishing kosher kitchens for the needy and schools for the children, and by exercising a very public role as a member of the Rumanian Parliament. Some derogate his importance by hinting that he collaborated with the oppressive regime, thereby obtaining various favors for his flock, and that the collaboration consisted of political and financial support in the West for

Rumanian officials, including the prime minister himself. Others say that Rosen was an authentic hero who disregarded his personal safety while seeking to protect the Jews solely through the authority of his office. He made strong representations to the highest officials of the land, demanding help for his needy people.

There is no evidence to support the allegation that Rosen collaborated with the regime. He did enjoy seemingly extraordinary privileges: the right to travel freely to Israel, Western Europe, and the U.S.; become an officer of the World Jewish Congress; maintain an apartment in Jerusalem; and retain contact with the JDC. Yet the proper conclusion appears to be that he was completely legitimate in all his dealings with the Rumanian government and guilty of no sordid political chicanery.

I have always thought of Rosen as a remarkable person who conducted himself as a symbol of Jewish pride, practicing his stewardship, remaining with his people while migration reduced their post-Hitler population from 400,000 to the present 20,000. His was a unique leadership. His famous Chorale Synagogue in Bucharest played host over the decades to thousands of Jewish visitors who came to witness the phenomenon of a Jewish community in a steady state of migration, while at the same time the dwindling numbers maintained their dignity as a fully functioning entity. And so they will continue to do, until the last Jew to leave turns off the lights in the synagogue. Rabbi Rosen died in 1996. His name and achievements will live prominently in Rumanian Jewish history.

In 1958, after nine years of no migration, Jews from Rumania suddenly began to appear unexpectedly on trains arriving in Vienna. A hastily devised system provided assistance, and further transport to Israel was organized. The people were of all ages and came from all provinces, carrying the smallest hand luggage and almost no money. Their numbers mounted rapidly to hundreds per week, then thousands. If such a heavy influx continued, a much more elaborate infrastructure of support would have to be established.

In October, I went to Geneva to meet with Charles Jordan, European Director of the JDC, and Eran Laor, European head of the Jewish Agency, to confirm the operational and financial plans needed to manage this welcome flow. I would also have to visit Rumania as soon as possible. That turned out to be January 1959, because November and December were completely devoted to organizing and preparing for the 1959 UJA campaign. During those two months, the emigration tempo from Rumania increased. New routes were opened through Athens and Belgrade.

In Geneva, I was re-asserting to all the parties interested in Rumania that the Jewish organizations would continue to pay $1,200 for every Jew permitted to leave. That price had been agreed to months ago, without any haggling. It was the price the Rumanian authorities had fixed because it was the highest they could imagine – equal to the price of a good horse, the most highly esteemed living object.

The real hero of those most delicate and difficult dealings was Shaike Dan, chief negotiator for the Mossad. Tall and thin, relentless in his pursuit in country after country of every opportunity to enable endangered Jews to emigrate, Dan has been the unsung champion of legal or illegal escapees for the past 40 years. Nowadays, over the age of 80, he still boards planes at Ben-Gurion Airport for distant destinations to work out sticky problems. The Jewish people and the state of Israel owe much of their new-found strength to this dauntless and modest man.

I read recently that Shaike Dan put the Rumanian price for ransoming Jews at the equivalent of $3,000 per head. I willingly yield to his recollection on that detail. In any case, it was he, not I, who negotiated with Prime Minister Ceaucescu (whose family probably pocketed most of the ransom money). My role was to ratify the sums Dan had agreed to pay, and to ensure that the arrangements were in order for the transportation of the emigrants. And so I did.

The purpose of my Rumanian visit was to make certain that emigration would continue, that the arrangements previously made regarding payments to various government officials were secure, that bribes were given to new, low-level functionaries in key positions at the visa offices, the railroad stations, and the like. There had been stops and starts in the past few months, and we were eager to make the flow smooth and continuous. The machinery had to be greased so that it would not creak.

I finally departed for Bucharest the first week in January in possession of a tourist visa. I stated my occupation – Jewish philanthropic official – clearly on the visa application. The Rumanian secret police nonetheless later charged me with hiding my true double identity as a CIA agent and Zionist spy behind a false "tourist identity."

I suspected from the very start of the trip that there might be trouble. At the Rumanian Embassy in Washington, officials indicated a "preference" that I fly via their airline, TAROM, which I would board in East Berlin. Since those were days of very cold Cold War, I was not pleased at that prospect. But "preference," in professional diplomatic language, meant command, and I didn't want to risk forfeiting a visa.

When I boarded the TAROM DC-3 in East Berlin, bound for Bucharest, I was the only passenger. And so I remained the entire day, as we droned through the communist circuit, stopping at Warsaw, Budapest, Belgrade, Sofia, Tirana, and finally Bucharest. It was an eerie feeling to sit all alone, never being allowed to disembark, speaking to no one; the silence and solitude created a mood in which all kinds of scenarios flashed through my overly excited mind.

As I disembarked at Bucharest airport, two men were waiting at the bottom of the steps. They introduced themselves as TAROM agents. But their long, belted leather coats and polished boots, as well as the practiced manner in which they placed me between them, with each one sliding an arm through mine, said secret police or army intelligence; my intuition said the former.

Before leaving Washington, I had arranged to be received by the American ambassador, in case I needed his good offices for any reason. And, of course, there were similar arrangements with the resident Israeli ambassador. As the two agents and I entered the cavernous but empty airport terminal, I saw a small group of men standing some distance away, looking at me and my companions. One shook his head slightly, which I took to mean that they would not approach me. I heard one of them say in Hebrew that he had no idea where I was staying. I asked my escorts in German (our only common language) the name of the hotel to which I was going, and when one answered, I repeated it very loudly so that my friends were sure to hear, whereupon they immediately left the terminal.

The TAROM men drove me to the hotel, arranged the formalities at the desk and tramped right up to my room with me. When I entered the bathroom, one accompanied me. That signaled the kind of problem I'd be having for the next two weeks.

With cold politeness, I asked if I might make a phone call to "my old friend," the American ambassador (whom I had never met). Equally politely, the security man said he knew the number and would place the call for me. In a great gush of simulated old-school enthusiasm, I explained to the ambassador that I had just dropped into town and wanted to come over for a drink to reminisce about old times. After a suitable pause, I thanked him and said I'd be right over. I stalled a bit with the unpacking, hoping the two goons would disappear, but they simply made themselves comfortable in a matter-of-fact manner, sending me a message that I had better get used to them. When I explained that I was going to the American Embassy, they shrugged and said they would take me there.

Upon arrival, they attempted to drive right through the gate and up to the front door, but the Marine guard refused them entry. He passed me through the gate and locked it behind us. When I emerged several hours later, the agents were still in their car waiting. They again took me to the hotel, where they placed two chairs in the hall outside my door and made it clear that they'd see me in the morning.

Inside the ambassador's living room, I had felt safe and comfortable for the first time that long day, not simply because of the familiar furnishings and cheery fireplace but also because I knew that the inhabitants would be concerned for my safety. The ambassador was a State Department professional named Clifford R. Wharton who was calm, seasoned and confident; his Israeli counterpart, Deputy Chief of Mission Aryeh Harel, had been hastily invited to join us. Each had an aide or two with him. Chatting over drinks, I relaxed, only to be brought back to the reality of the time and place by the host's whispered instructions that Harel and I should enter the bathroom. There we would have two or three minutes alone in which to make the necessary arrangements concerning times and places to meet in the days ahead. Telephones were not safe, nor were conventional verbal codes, nor even the Hebrew language, and it was assumed that all the rooms were bugged.

All that seemed to me melodramatic, yet the circumstances mandated such precautions. Harel and I settled on alternative cafes whose locations I would have to memorize. A sharp rap on the door indicated that our planning session was finished.

At dinner, the radio in the center of the embassy dining table was turned up to full volume, and we whispered to each other. Our host and his staff were completely sympathetic to the emigration of the local Jews and offered assistance where possible, the only caveat being that they could not jeopardize the status of the United States Embassy by violating any Rumanian laws. I therefore felt perfectly at ease with my companions, talking freely about obstacles I would have to overcome in order to achieve the purpose of my visit.

The main obstacle was to get rid of the two alter egos who had attached themselves to me. I could not permit myself to be tailed every day and night. We discussed that for some time, getting nowhere, when one of the Israelis suggested a simple solution: I would slip out of the hotel unnoticed and not return for as many days as were needed to finish the most crucial operations on my agenda. He assured me that the agents would be furious at having lost me but would wait patiently for my return. Why? Because when they forced entry into my room and saw all my clothes, they'd assume that I would be coming back.

And that's how it worked out. But first I decided to waste two days playing tourist. The agents followed me everywhere, bored and tired.

At one point during that interval, I managed to lose them for a few hours, giving myself enough time to reconnoiter the exits from the hotel. The easiest was a fire-escape ladder outside my bathroom window. So early one morning I left via that route and made my get-away without incident.

One night, I slept on a bench in a small synagogue; another night, I curled up in a blanket on the ground under a vegetable wagon in the market in the Jewish quarter; the third, I didn't sleep at all; and the fourth was spent on the couch of the man to whom I gave the $5,000 in gold I had brought with me.

I had accomplished my mission, and had a head full of impressions and stories. I felt empowered by my experiences to argue forcefully for maximum support and pressure on behalf of the migration of Rumanian Jews to Israel. I saw that the people were tense, nervous, fearful, distraught. How could they be otherwise? When they registered to emigrate, they lost jobs immediately. That was a terrible thing in a controlled economy with no free labor market, where one could not go out and look for other work. The breadwinner in a household had the great worry of maintaining the family until departure, which might be a matter of months. Money represented a real problem. The cost of all the departure documents for a family often ran more than a full year's salary. International Jewish organizations sent food and clothing parcels as well as financial assistance, but basically, there was only one thing to do: sell one's private possessions. And the market, flooded with such merchandise, was poor. Prices were ridiculously low.

As I walked through the streets of Bucharest's Jewish quarter, I saw on the front of buildings lists offering for sale furniture, bedding, radios, lamps, clothing. At places called consignment stores, sellers left their property in the hope that it would be sold. I stood before the windows of the largest such shop in Bucharest, and as I looked at the chinaware, glassware, paintings, and flatware, I thought of all the family meals represented by these objects, and how wrenching it must have been to give up such familiar but personal and memory-laden possessions. Yet their owners had no choice: the sentimental objects of the past had to be sacrificed to pay for the future that beckoned. Property not sold would be left behind in any case, for there was a limitation on outgoing baggage. A person could take 40 or 70 kilograms (88 or 154 pounds), depending on the work category to which he or she was assigned.

On the Friday night during my "escape" period, I went to the great Chorale Synagogue, where Rabbi Rosen presided. The main area was packed with hundreds of men, and women filled the balconies all around. I could not be sure whether they came primarily to worship or to enjoy the tight, communal feeling. In any case, they pressed together, and as the choir sang mightily (by far the best synagogue music I had ever heard in my life) you could almost literally feel these Jews unite with one another in a physical and psychological mass.

The members of the Israeli legation arrived, and as a path to the front pew was cleaved for them, the reaction of the crowd was fantastic. People reached out to touch the Israelis, buzzing and whispering and staring at these few young men as though they were the forerunners of the Messiah.

I left the synagogue in the Israelis' company, and as we walked in the dark and icy streets, we heard behind us voices asking when permits would come, how long would emigres have to wait – questions followed by blessings being bestowed on the diplomats and Israel itself. The Israelis heard but did not respond or even turn around. Rumanians were not allowed contact with the Israeli legation. But out of the darkness continued to come the whispered voices of Jewish people seeking to be united with the land these young men represented.

On Saturday afternoon, I went to a small synagogue where some Jews had gathered in a *Chevrat Shas*, a Talmud study group. It grew dark, and when they finished, we broke a meager crust of bread in the symbolic third meal of the Sabbath. They gave me jam made from an *etrog* (a lemon-like citrus fruit) they had received from Israel the past *Sukkot* (fall harvest festival). The room exuded love and warmth, even though our physical surroundings were dark and dirty, and so cold that we huddled together.

The man next to me asked about the city of Beersheba, in southern Israel. He was worried because, as a 55-year-old radiologist, he was going there without equipment or books – nothing but his clothing. Could he find a job? I gave him the answer he already knew; that the Israelis would welcome him and try to find a workplace for him, and that although his adjustment would be difficult, he would find what he wanted most – freedom and peace.

My listeners sighed. This was the deepest dream of all, to be at home, among Jews, in a place where they could not be hurt again. From Nazism to Communism represented almost 20 years of no freedom. At last there was a chance of finding it. Was it any wonder that these Rumanians were registering to leave, despite the extreme difficulties and the risks that lay ahead?

I returned to the hotel, exhausted but exhilarated, after four days. Although my work was finished and I was ready to leave the country, my two friends, the secret policemen, were not so inclined. They were angry, frustrated, and determined to take some revenge. When they learned that I was back in my room, they pounded their way in at 6 a.m. to inform me that, since I had declared myself to be a "tourist," we would all go touring to beautiful Lake Snagov, where the delightful winter sport of ice-fishing awaited us. I protested vigorously, but there was no way out of it.

Some hours later, the three of us stood far out on the solid ice covering the lake, the agents properly dressed and shod, I hopelessly inadequate in thin-soled Oxfords, as they showed me how to cut a hole in the ice with a circular saw. Seated on the blocks of hewn ice, we dropped our lines and patiently waited. I *im*patiently began to freeze, obviously in misery, to their great delight. Every attempt to bring this torture to an end was rebuffed, and they kept me there until they saw that the limit had been reached. Depositing me back in the hotel, they grinned and said they would have an equally interesting day of "tourism" planned for the morrow.

Next day, I was taken to a cellar room in what was probably the agents' headquarters building and interrogated for hours – standing, rarely sitting, under bright lights – concerning my "real" identity as a Zionist spy and CIA agent. I do not recall how fearful I felt. I do recall that I kept trying to reassure myself that nothing serious could happen, that I should not be melodramatic, that this situation would work itself out to some normal conclusion. While calming myself with such bromides, I heard another voice saying down deep that crazy things did happen in real life in this Cold War period. It was a fearsome day, and when they kept me overnight, I did lapse into despair. They would not permit a call to the American Embassy.

Next morning, the questioning resumed, more threatening in tone, until a uniformed officer suddenly interrupted. He hustled me outside and into a vehicle, where I saw my suitcase, drove me to the airport, and escorted me onto a Sabena flight bound for Brussels. He waited in the plane's cabin until just before the door was closed and then departed, all without a single word of explanation.

After I reported the entire episode to the American Embassy in Brussels and they made inquiries in Bucharest, an official explanation emerged: I had been deported because of currency irregularities involving gold. The only serious repercussion was the registration of my name in the black book of undesirable visitors to Rumania.

I discovered several years later that the list had been passed on to the Soviet Union. My request for a visa to that nation was refused. Why? I asked. The Soviet vice-consul in Washington offered me the polite and friendly advice to forget it: I was obviously considered some sort of security risk. As a result, I never made it to the Soviet Union, despite my natural eagerness to go during the great Jewish emigration of the 1970s.

The important fact is that Jewish emigration from Rumania proceeded beautifully from 1958 onward. The Rumanian S.S. Transylvania left Constanza, a port on the Black Sea, every Sunday, with 2,000 Jews aboard, arriving in Haifa three days later. In one year, that vessel brought 100,000 people to freedom and a new life. Thus, almost the entire post-Hitler population of 400,000 Jews was transplanted to the Jewish state.

CHAPTER TWENTY-SIX

"I AM JOSEPH, YOUR BROTHER"

In October 1960, the annual UJA mission to Israel was assembled, with a planned stop in Rome en route. There, an extraordinary event made front-page news. It was not anticipated, and came as a complete surprise to everyone present except the central figure in the drama.

What *was* anticipated was exciting enough. On October 17, the first large delegation of American Jews ever to be received by a Pope was to meet with John XXIII in the Vatican. The audience had been arranged through a trio of friends: Benjamin Swig of San Francisco, Francis Cardinal Spellman of New York, and James Zellerbach, the American ambassador in Rome. The meeting had taken a half-year to organize, was important as a breakthrough, might be more important as a precedent for future encounters, possessed significant theological and political possibilities, and was filled with great expectations.

The delegation consisted of 130 top-level, mostly Jewish men and women. Research had discovered that this Pope, when he was papal nuncio in Turkey in 1942, had performed a truly great act of humanity. The Aliyah Bet, working underground in Eastern Europe, had rescued 700 Jewish orphan children from under the very noses of the Nazis, brought them to a port on the Black Sea, acquired two vessels, and set out for Palestine. In order to reach the Mediterranean, they had to pass through the Strait of Dardanelles, controlled by Turkey, which was a German ally. The papal nuncio, with great courage, had intervened strenuously with the Gestapo in Ankara and obtained permission for these two vessels to pass. He literally saved the lives of the children, and we wanted to thank him, in the name of the Jewish people, for his deed of 18 years earlier. Cardinal Spellman successfully urged the Vatican bureaucracy to grant our request for an audience.

Although an agreement was reached in principle, the technical details and arrangements took months to settle. I had suggested that we employ classical languages: I would address the Holy Father in Hebrew, and he would respond in Latin. Vatican officials hesitated. They feared that the use of Hebrew in this setting might imply recognition of the state of Israel, whose official language Hebrew obviously was. (And they were not altogether wrong about the motive behind my suggestion.) Their decision was that we should speak in our respective vernaculars – I in English and he in Italian.

The texts covering arrangements flowed back and forth across the ocean and were finally settled. We prepared a hand-written parchment scroll expressing our gratitude. Hoping the scroll would reside in the Vatican museum, we encased it in beautifully crafted olive wood from Jerusalem. The Vatican officials at first demurred, for it seemed too much like a Torah scroll, but we finally convinced them that even a Torah scroll would have been quite familiar to their Lord.

On the morning of the audience, everything went smoothly, exactly according to the script and choreography. The Pope was seated on a white throne, garbed in white, and our delegation stood in a semi-circle around him. The Vatican had opted for an intimate environment rather than a large, formal chamber, where everyone could have been seated, but at a distance from the Pope. Speeches were exchanged, gifts given, photographs taken. The mood was very relaxed, and the deed looked as though it were done. I gave the signal for our group to turn and leave, when suddenly, and with no word of warning, the unexpected happened.

In a 180-degree about-face from the previous stylized performance, the Pope rose, lifted his hand in a friendly gesture to recapture our attention, beckoned for us to crowd closer, and started to speak extemporaneously. The atmosphere began to crackle with a kind of electricity. A sense of expectation created a sort of nervous tension.

Monsignor Paul Marcinkus, a Vatican official originally from Chicago, stepped into the breach as translator. According to the doctrine of Papal Infallibility, every word of the Pope is sacred. He was now speaking "*ex cathedra*," but without a text. The editor of *Il Osservatore Romano*, the official Vatican newspaper, standing nearby, began to write furiously. All the Church dignitaries looked anxious – they had no idea what was coming.

Only the Pontiff knew what he had in mind, as well as the hint he was about to give. He began by saying that all of us understood the set-piece nature of the previous ceremony and its mandatory character. But now that we had gone through that, he wanted to say something personal, intimate, and meaningful. He had been thinking of his own private name, Angelo Giuseppi Roncalli. Giuseppi translates as Joseph. That had brought to his mind the Biblical Joseph sitting on a throne as vice-premier of Egypt, dealing out food to all the petitioners from the neighboring, drought-stricken countries, including Canaan. Then Joseph's 11 brothers – the very ones who had sold him into slavery and thought he was long since dead – entered the hall. The Bible tells us that Joseph recognized them at once, although they did not recognize him. After some conversation, he decided to reveal himself to them, stretched forth his hand, and said to their amazement, "I am Joseph, your brother!"

After telling the Biblical story, with its dramatic closing line, the Pope animatedly, almost excitedly, said to us, his audience, "I am revealing myself to you. I am Joseph, your brother." There was an explosion of breath, deep inhaling, wonderment from his listeners. He went on: he felt that Jews and Christians were truly brothers and should act that way toward one another. He felt that we had to cross bridges toward each other and overcome centuries of hatred, bloodshed, and misunderstanding. In closing, he said that he had a plan in mind to achieve such a goal.

None of us had any idea that he was hinting at a Vatican Council, which he was soon to convene and which, a few years later, would reverse the Church's pernicious doctrines of contempt toward the Jews. All we knew at that moment was that this friendly, jovial, almost simple man was offering his hand in brotherhood and friendship, revealing his inner feelings about Jews.

The air was charged with excitement. It was an incredible moment. Everyone was still, motionless. Then, ever so slowly, one person jostled against another, and the crowd began gently to dissolve into clusters, finally flowing slowly from the room.

When the document, *Nostra Aetate* (In Our Time), issued by a Council of 2,000 bishops in 1965, finally appeared, the Church had turned its face toward the Jews. The charge of deicide was repealed; the doctrine that the Jews had been rejected by God was eliminated; the replacement of the Jews as the chosen people by Christians was discarded.

Since then, Catholic theologians have agreed that serious progress has been made toward eliminating those negative teachings, and there is significant willingness by Catholic leaders to implement *Nostra Aetate*. The process of bridge building and understanding must continue.

The 25th anniversary of the issuance of *Nostra Aetate* included a two-day seminar in New York, organized under the joint auspices of Fordham University (Catholic) and the American Jewish Committee. I attended the seminar. The hall was full. A representative of the Vatican, Father Fumagalli, spoke. He had studied for years in Jerusalem and warned the audience that he would be more easily understood in Hebrew than in English. (His listeners nonetheless chose the latter.) Father Fumagalli made several cogent points:

1. The Jewish people has a unique role in God's design for human salvation.

2. The Church must dialogue with the Jews.

3. God will reveal Himself to the Jews in a mysterious way.

4. The persecutions suffered by Jews have finally opened many hearts.

5. The Church admits that medieval Christianity contributed to anti-semitism, which the Church today condemns as a sin.

6. The Church must prepare a document on the Holocaust.

7. In the past 25 years, the Church has issued 29 documents on anti-semitism. These doctrines against prejudice must be taught in all seminaries and included in all school curricula.

The extraordinary session with the UJA leaders, culminating in John XXIII's historic pronouncement, "I am Joseph, your brother" and leading to *Nostra*

Aetate, followed by decades of dialogue and exploration, represented a crucial turning point in the collective life of the Jewish people. It is fitting to pay tribute to the memory of Pope John XXIII, who started the march down the path of reconciliation. Not long ago, Pope John Paul II, going beyond the earlier statement, visited the synagogue in Rome, as the first Pope ever to do so, termed the Jews "our elder brothers," held a memorial concert in the Vatican for victims of the Holocaust, and established diplomatic relations with the State of Israel. There is still much ground to cover, but the air is filled with hope for further and constant progress over time, so that one by one the issues that have separated the two faiths will be replaced by ties that bind.

Major-General Ezer Weizman, Commander of the Israel Air Force, charmed a UJA Young Leadership Mission, July, 1962.

In October 1963, two of my oldest friends, Eddie Ginsberg, destined to become UJA General Chairman, and Shimon Peres, destined to become Prime Minister and father of the Oslo Accord, spoke to the same UJA study mission.

Ambassador Yitzhak Rabin and Prime Minister Golda Meir consulting in September 1970 at New York's Hilton Hotel about President Nixon's telephoned request for Israel to aid King Hussein by interdicting a Syrian invasion of Jordan.

President Kennedy received an interfaith committee of clergymen.
The Catholic and Protestant clerics chose me, the only rabbi,
as group spokesman. Joseph Meyerhoff stands in the center.

President Truman and I were friends from the time I worked
with him on the 1948 campaign train.

At the 20th anniversary of V-E day, 1965, a festive dinner brought together (from left to right) General Pierre Koenig, French commander in WWII; Baron Guy de Rothschild, head of the French-Jewish community and Edward M.M. Warburg, president of the JDC and UJA.

Due to Yale's alphabetized seating policy, Henry Ford II and Herbert Friedman sat next to each other in class, just as we do here at a UJA conference in Chicago in 1966. Max Fisher, Ford's close friend, sits to his left.

Lieutenant-General Yitzhak Rabin, chief of staff of Israel's Defense Forces, giving the low-down to a UJA mission in July 1966.

Dr. Joseph Schwartz, my predecessor at the UJA, reminiscing in 1968
with Prime Minister Levi Eshkol.

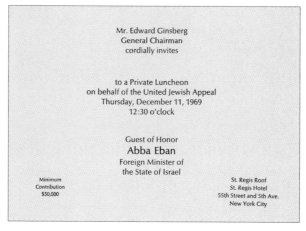

Mr. Edward Ginsberg
General Chairman
cordially invites

to a Private Luncheon
on behalf of the United Jewish Appeal
Thursday, December 11, 1969
12:30 o'clock

Guest of Honor
Abba Eban
Foreign Minister of
the State of Israel

Minimum
Contribution
$50,000

St. Regis Roof
St. Regis Hotel
55th Street and 5th Ave.
New York City

This invitation to a private fund-raising luncheon stated the minimum
amount to be contributed. The highest luncheon-level we ever
conducted was $250,000. One year later we ran two successful
dinners at the million-dollar level per contributor.

In March 1969, Ruth Aliav (Kluger), who had recruited
me into the Haganah Aliyah Bet section in 1946, presented
me with the "Aleh" medal for pre-statehood services in
underground operations.

Dedication of the Denmark High School in Jerusalem; October 22, 1968; The cast
(from left to right): my wife Francine and I; Philip Zinman; Larry Schacht;
Mayor Teddy Kollek; my in-laws, Charles Bensley (president of the Israel Education
Fund and founder of the school) and his wife Hilda; Ralph Goldman, executive director
of the IEF; and a Jerusalem cleric.

Moshe Dayan at the Suez Canal

Golda Meir below the Golan Heights

Abba Eban at the Western Wall

In January, 1970, I pieced together the segments of a film that would show the
geo-political condition in Israel during the War of Attrition. The film was telecast
on a closed circuit from coast-to-coast in dozens of Jewish communities.

CHAPTER TWENTY-SEVEN

MOLDING YOUNG LEADERS

An idea that appears correct in concept, and therefore worth trying, sometimes turns into a blockbuster of historic worth. The Young Leadership idea was one such triumph. Indeed, many in the top ranks of the Jewish world describe it as the most significant achievement of all the decades of my efforts on behalf of the Jewish people.

The praise has often been embarrassing. Yet on reflection, it seems to me there are several reasons for such a judgment: the success in converting an abstract idea into a concrete institution; the length of life of that institution – now almost 40 years old, a complete generation; the number of people – nearly 3,000 – who passed through the process; their influence on others in multiples reaching to the tens of thousands; the effect on the campaigns in their communities across the entire country; and the replication of the program in every other national and local organization in America, as well as international and Israeli organizations. A few simple ingredients led to this success: the articulation of an ideology, the creation of an elite *esprit de corps*, and the development of a sense of duty and obligation.

The Young Leadership idea grew from a feeling I had at the end of the 1950s that a new generation of leaders would have to be created to replace those I had first met more than a decade earlier. Remember that I had been appalled at the end of the 30s by the apathy, weakness, absence of organized protest, and even fear on the part of the American Jewish community. It was only in the second half of the 40s, when the war was over, the full facts of the Holocaust began to make an impact, and comprehension spread that an independent Jewish state was the only solution, that I met for the first time a set of determined, zealous, capable lay leaders who were almost fanatical in their compulsion to solve all the problems.

I encountered such a group in Berlin in 1946, and was smitten by their devotion. They had come to see the displaced persons in Germany, gone on to Poland to soak up the sights and smells of that massive cemetery, and returned to the United States to awaken their fellow Jews. I fell in love with their activism, and on returning to America in 1948, threw my lot in with them for years to come.

The professional director of this UJA group of dedicated leaders was Henry Montor, a former rabbinical student at the Hebrew Union College, the seminary of the Reform movement. As executive director of the United Palestine Appeal, he had become a passionate advocate for the creation of a Jewish state. His leadership style consisted of swift decisions that demanded swift action from his followers. He was a charismatic genius with a fierce will. When he became the CEO of the United Jewish Appeal, his firm demands became law for those lay leaders loyal to him.

And Montor did perform miracles. The 1945 annual UJA campaign raised $15 million. He insisted that the 1946 goal be $100 million, for the War was over and now there was an opportunity to assist and heal the wounded survivors of Hitler's madness. His demands and charisma prevailed. Energy poured from the American Jewish communities. The goal was exceeded. And 1947 produced $125 million, with 1948 shooting up to $148 million.

The flaws in the man consisted of a dictatorial style, mercurial volatility, self-confidence to a fault, and inability to compromise. He expected his demands to be met, and largely they were, to the advantage of the fragile displaced persons in the European camps, in the immediate post-war years. Montor strongly influenced the lay leader of the group, Sam Rothberg, a person of incredible energy who remained on fire for four decades, first as an officer of the UJA, later as chief officer of the Israel Bonds organization, then as the chairman of the Hebrew University – an entire lifetime spent in the volunteer service of Israel. I never met another like him.

Scores followed Rothberg with utter loyalty, and these men put life into the American Jewish community in the late 40s. That is, they awakened the zeal and created the modalities for action. The positive 1948 reaction to the birth of Israel, when American Jews finally began to lend their strength, sprang from the agitation of these few score men, whose passion was contagious and who rushed from city to city with an almost messianic sense of mission.

I say that with profound respect for their role and deep love for their comradeship; I worked productively with them for years. I say it, too, as a backdrop to my intuitive feeling that, even as these men provided the leadership that was immediately needed in the 1950s, they could not provide it in the 60s. Why? Because they were people of raw emotion. Intellect, logic, rationality played no part in either their personalities or their value systems. They felt no need to "explain." Either you understood them or you didn't.

Whether they were actually born in Eastern Europe (as many were) or not, that generation of leaders carried the memory of Minsk and Lodz and Vilna deep within their souls, and the cries that came from their hearts on behalf of murdered or stateless Jews were so genuine as to be demeaned by any complicated explanations. The ghetto and the shtetl were speaking. What more was needed? The evocation of memory was basically an emotional approach, and for a certain audience it produced the desired Pavlovian reflex. That first generation did its job magnificently by obtaining an automatic, gut reaction. Would that hold for the _next_ generation as well?

I thought not. The next generation lacked the necessary historic memory. It possessed, instead, a university degree. And its leaders would have to possess one, too, plus an appreciation of the emotional component which was gradually diminishing with the passage of time. The emotion would have to be created by visiting sites of the destruction in Europe, making excursions to the new state, listening to powerful and passionate speakers.

Out of those assessments and convictions, a plan began to form in my mind. I would seek to accumulate a list of younger men (this was long before the feminist revolution) who possessed leadership characteristics. When I had a large enough pool, I would convene a national conference and determine whether it would be possible to start some sort of national program of education and inspiration. If this all sounds tentative and exploratory, it was exactly that. Thus, what was to become the now-renowned Young Leadership Cabinet began as a quiet, unheralded process, with a thought in my head and a notebook in my pocket.

Beginning in the fall of 1959, I adopted the practice of jotting down in that notebook the name of every American-Jewish young man who caught my attention in some way. I traveled constantly throughout the communities and at each meeting I attended, I watched carefully for the young men who stood above the level of the crowd. One might have an especially keen mind and the ability to express himself with crisp precision, another a strong speaking voice and a commanding presence. Still another might announce a particularly large donation for a person of his age. A fourth might take exception to the majority view and possess the self-confidence to stand against it, while a fifth might come up to me quietly after the meeting to state an impressive opinion or ask a penetrating question. Those and other indications marked the person as someone to be remembered. After a full season of traveling, my notebook contained approximately 400 names.

It was time to mobilize them and test the waters. I decided to convene the national conference one weekend in November, 1960. I wrote to the executive directors of the Jewish community federations across the country, telling them I was going to try to form a group which we would teach, train, and inspire to assume leadership roles. I told them of the pool of potential candidates I had assembled, urged them to add members of their own communities who fit the profile, and asked their opinion of the idea in general.

I still have the replies, which were remarkable in their opposition. Many insisted that this was not the job of the national UJA but should be left to the local Federations themselves, or to their national council. I wasn't very surprised at the reaction. It represented the usual narrow-minded turf protection rather than a broader concern for what might promote larger national and international goals. I had encountered the same type of opposition from within the Zionist ranks, several of whose leaders suggested that my job was to raise money and not to get involved in "educational work," which should be left to X, Y, or Z organization.

Under the stimulus of such bureaucratic thinking, I began to formulate the simple principle that henceforth motivated my entire professional approach: IN ORDER TO RAISE MONEY, ONE MUST FIRST RAISE PEOPLE.

Whenever in my life I was asked to explain the art or science of fundraising, I always replied with that one sentence. Here is the sequence: instill in people the facts of the case you wish them to make; add an ideology to the factual base; provide the inspirational component necessary to build conviction. When you have raised such advocates, they will go forth and raise the money. It is generated fundamentally by one person asking another to give it.

Peripheral support systems – brochures, advertising, films, videotapes, large public meetings with famous speakers, and similar devices – certainly help. But the root of it all is one dedicated person exerting influence on a friend, peer, even a stranger. If the cause to be served has galvanized an army of capable and devoted people, it will enjoy the financial fruits it is seeking. And by extension, if my job as CEO of the UJA was to raise money, then the only possible route to success was to concentrate on raising people. At the UJA and ever since, that is exactly what I have spent my life doing.

Despite the nay-saying and hesitating I've described, the call to that national conference in November 1960 produced 250 attendees, all of whom came at their own expense. In numbers, quality, and enthusiasm, the meeting resulted in a spectacular success. The battery of speakers we presented for that weekend was impressive:

- Hon. Michael Comay – Israeli ambassador to the U.N.
- Maj. Gen. Meir Amit – later head of the Mossad (Israel Intelligence)
- Chet Huntley – NBC Correspondent
- Philip Klutznick – incoming general chairman, UJA
- Moses Leavitt – executive vice-chairman, JDC

Never had such an array of personalities been assembled for an audience of unknowns – young, untested, not large contributors. And the audience understood, intuitively if no other way, that an investment was being made in them; they were being treated as though they were important to the future, and when people are so treated, they react in kind. The total impact of the program was powerful.

I took a personal gamble in the form of a four-hour lecture entitled "One Hundred Years of Jewish History: 1880 to 1980." If my premise was correct – namely, that we had to lay an educational foundation, fill in the knowledge the young men lacked, and only then add the overlay of emotion – the topic I selected was also correct, for it dealt with events in the lives of their fathers and grandfathers with which I was attempting to connect them. If neither the topic nor the educational approach succeeded in capturing them, then the gamble would fail. I was nervous, because I sensed how much of the future was at stake. Yet I distinctly recall my feeling, from the moment the weekend started, that it would be a great success.

I picked 1880 because that was the watershed year, the beginning of the huge Jewish migration to America from Eastern Europe. This is essentially the story I related:

After the assassination of the liberal Russian monarch Alexander II, the reactionary Czar Alexander III took over. His prime minister, Pobedonostsev, suggested that the Jewish problem in Russia could be solved by a simple arithmetic formula: one-third of the Jews should be killed, one-third forcibly converted to the Greek Orthodox Church, and one-third expelled.

Those decrees, announced in May 1881, came to be known as the "May Laws." They triggered a massive movement westward – in wagons, on trains, by foot – to the ports of Hamburg and Liverpool, where tickets to the United States in steerage (the bowels of the ship) cost $25. By the time World War I interrupted the shipping schedules, 2.5 million Jews had tumbled into New York, Baltimore, and Galveston. "Your grandfathers and grandmothers came then, clutching their meager belongings."

At the same time, tiny numbers of pioneers, inspired by the new Zionist movement, trekked from Europe to Palestine and started the first farms and kibbutzim. The American and Palestinian Jewish communities grew in tandem, not knowing that they were marching toward a joint destiny a half-century later. Between 1900 and 1910, sure signs of Jewish strength were already manifest in the New World; and these very same years produced the famous Second Aliyah crop of leaders who would one day take Palestine into sovereignty and statehood.

For six years World War II raged, and as the fires burned, the ashes of millions of Jews darkened the sky. The souls, if not the bodies, of American Jewry were seared in those fires, tempering a new strength, a sharp determination to find the path toward retributive action.

The opportunity came almost immediately, as the push for an independent Jewish state exploded into its climactic period. The next 36 months, from 1945 to 1948, gave Jews all over the world the chance to ventilate, to let the adrenaline rush take command, to act to gain control over their own fate. "Your fathers and mothers came alive with a roar, gathered the money, raised their own political consciousness and that of non-Jews around them. They sang and danced their way through the night of May 14, 1948, after the British flag came down and the Star of Israel rose to a new glory in a miraculous turn-around of history."

The things I said in that lecture summed up a period my listeners hardly knew and whetted their appetite to learn more. In addition, I was consciously trying to create the kind of pride I was certain they had not felt before. I wanted those young people to be proud of being Jews and of being connected to Israel. They should feel simultaneously the sense of responsibility that accompanies the possession of something as precious as freedom.

That new sense of independence and pride required a Praetorian guard to protect, strengthen, and nourish it, so it would yield ever more fruits. "Each of you has to become a guardian," I told them. "I am very firm on that point. No one has the right to share in the joy who does not also share in the work. If you want to be part of this great cause, you must enlist as a soldier for the rest of your life. If you don't want to take part, good-bye."

I also told them the Biblical story of the commander Gideon, who separated his men into those who wanted to fight and those who didn't, and sent the latter home. I told them my own story, from the formation of an ideology while still a teenager; through the war chaplaincy, working with DPs, and serving secretly with the Haganah, through joining the UJA, first as a volunteer, then as the chief professional. I outlined the bare bones of the ideology that motivated and sustained me, and urged them to accept it: respect for the people of Israel, love for the land of Israel, faith that Israel's message benefits all mankind, and is worth preserving. This rubric combined intellectual and emotional elements, which, as with fundraising, I have always felt to be the successful formula.

Many years later, when a researcher from the Hebrew University was interviewing me regarding the start-up of the Young Leadership movement, he asked, "Is it really just the intellectual involvement that is important? Don't you have to add a certain emotional involvement? Intellectual involvement by itself is nothing. You can get people intellectually involved with the Chinese or the Hottentots."

I agreed, and reminded him that I had said this all along. On the other hand, I pointed out, if you depend on the emotions alone, you will lose this generation because its members don't have the background with which to appreciate the emotion in question. Their grandfathers had the necessary apperceptive mass. All you had to say to the old generation, was one word – like "Cossack." Indeed, the first story Golda Meir told in her autobiography occurred when she was six years old and frightened by Cossacks riding into town on their big horses, swinging curved swords. After moving to America, she saw a Milwaukee policeman on a big horse and felt the same fear, until someone explained to her that in America the policemen are not there to hurt people but to help them.

The reaction of the present generation is not automatic. First you have to teach them what a shtetl in Russia was and what a Cossack was, and only then can you get down to the bedrock of what their emotional reaction as free Jews must be, should they ever be summoned to help fellow Jews in danger of today's version of Cossacks.

The first National Young Leadership Conference ended on a high note of resolution. I asked for a vote on the question of organizing an inaugural mission to Israel during the coming summer of 1961. I reminded them that those who voted affirmatively were expected to be on board when the flight departed. I wanted to establish from the very beginning that a vote on any issue was not a matter of raising one's hand, but of making a commitment that absolutely had to be honored. If one voted for an issue, one had to perform; otherwise, vote negative or abstain. Just over 100 hands went up, and when the flight took off seven months later, it had 104 passengers. They came from 49 communities, and their average age was 32.

In addition to the mission, a fuller program evolved from many suggestions made during the floor discussions. A book was to be sent to every member every month on some subject relating to Judaism or Israel. Members were expected to participate in three major events each year: a national retreat or regional conference; their own local Federation-UJA campaign; and a mission to Israel.

After a three-year process of winnowing and adding, I felt the time had come to formalize the group, which had been reduced to a core of 33 first-class individuals who were somewhat educated in the Jewish tradition and experienced in community work. We named that group the Young Leadership Cabinet, decided to unveil it publicly at the large annual UJA conference in December 1963, and asked New York's Senator Lehman to dedicate it. Each year subsequently, the Lehman Award has been given to the outgoing chairman.

The members of that initial group are considered the founding fathers, and, hopefully, their names will exist a century from now in the UJA archives. Today's cabinet has 350 members – much too large a group, in my opinion – and a separate Women's Cabinet has been formed, with its own 150 members. Despite ongoing attempts to merge the two groups, a mutually satisfactory (if socially unfashionable) agreement has kept them separate. In my view, each doing its own work will contribute more to the communal welfare – in funds raised, projects completed, new talent recruited, and general enthusiasm.

A wider development has also taken place over the years. The Jewish communities quickly saw the movement as a valuable new instrument and began to create local leadership training courses. Thus my thesis – an increase in knowledge would produce a better performance on the part of community volunteers – was validated in city after city. The Federations organized all sorts of educational/social devices, bringing young leaders together for a nine-month course in Judaism, a six-month course in familiarization with the major communal agencies, or a one-day visit to Washington to learn about national and international problems.

There was no limit to the ingenuity communities displayed in creating curricula, and most efforts produced enthusiastic new recruits. I myself visited scores of communities, taking part in the local Federation programs, lecturing, leading discussions, answering questions, urging the formation of missions overseas to concentration camp sites and on to Israel.

So often in the field of communal service, people work very hard without seeing the immediate or even long-term results of their efforts. I have had the unusual gratification of witnessing, over one-third of a century, the expansion of this Young Leadership concept into a permanent feature of Jewish life on the local, national, and international stages. The concept and its systems have a long and promising future. In today's pragmatic America, people ask, What are the practical results of the Young Leadership Movement over the decades of its existence? The question is fair. Yet the movement is so widespread geographically, and involves so many thousands of current members plus alumni (membership terminates at age 40), that it is impossible to calculate the hours of work contributed, the number of dollars donated by the activists and raised from others, the new ideas conceived, or the volume of enthusiasm generated.

During the interview in 1975 with the Hebrew University researcher, I was asked whether I could quantify the results of the Young Leadership program. I gave him one statistic. In 1975, 68 Jewish communities in the U.S. raised more that $1 million in their annual campaign. In 57 of those cities, the chairman of the campaign was someone who had graduated out of the Young Leadership Cabinet.

Speaking of individual conduct, there are hundreds of other examples to be given, and I am selecting three. All the others, whose work I cannot cite because of space constraints, will not resent their omission, for they all have a sense of pride in what they achieved, and they know that I recognize their value.

Alan Rudy of Houston, a real-estate developer, chairman of the cabinet in 1975-6, conceived the notion of organizing a mission of Young Leadership types from across the entire U.S. and set the number at 1,000. Never had the national UJA nor any individual Federated community aspired to a battalion of such size. He named it *Koach* (strength), portraying what that march of

American Jews through the streets of Jerusalem would symbolize as a morale-builder for the Israeli population. He phoned, wrote, flew, and drove to round up his flock. Rudy's tireless efforts produced the *Koach* mission. It was a splendid achievement. In later years, the big cities of Miami, Philadelphia, and New York were encouraged to follow that one man's example.

Irwin Field of Los Angeles, a manufacturer, served in the cabinet, performed well in his soft-spoken way, and was then called to higher duty as general chairman of the national UJA campaign – the first Young Leader to rise to the very top. In so doing, he made the vision concrete. That is, he gave flesh and life to the notion that a second generation of leaders could be trained, educated, and inspired to head the largest Jewish philanthropy in the U.S. (and the fourth largest in the entire nation). When finished with the national job, Field later accepted the task of chairman of the local L.A. campaign. That was a good soldier at work.

Gordon Zacks of Columbus, Ohio, also a former Y.L. Cabinet chairman, rose to the rank of deputy general chairman of the National UJA, then veered off into a behind-the-scenes role as adviser on Jewish affairs to an aspiring politician named George Bush. When Bush became Vice President and later President, Zacks stood at his side for 12 years as informal, unpaid, untitled private adviser, explaining Jewish and Israeli personalities and problems, offering suggestions and solutions, smoothing over many a rough diplomatic patch. And it was Zacks who instituted the process of widening the horizon of Young Leadership thinking, taking it beyond fundraising to the political arena. He did so by stressing the importance of AIPAC (American-Israel Public Affairs Committee), journalistically described as the "Israeli lobby" in Washington. Zacks convinced his contemporaries that political work, explaining Israel's positions to congressmen and Senators, was as important to strengthening Israel as raising money in her behalf. Year after year, he preached that message to each new class of cabinet members. The young leaders supported it with such energy that a rousing assembly (3,000 strong) is held in Washington bi-annually. So important has that gathering become that the President of the United States and prime minister of Israel, along with scores of congressmen and their staff members, are happy to respond to invitations and to attend.

Raising people by strengthening their individual Jewish identities, linking their hearts and souls to the land of Israel and the worldwide people of Israel, influencing their children's attitudes in the same direction, is the central purpose of the Young Leadership Cabinet. As the work continues, and if yet another generation is raised with these same values, the effort to preserve the Jewish future in America will be considerably fortified. As I will emphasize at the end of this memoir, that future is imperiled by present trends of assimilation and large-scale ignorance of Judaism. Ominous predictions of self-diminishment are surfacing. It is therefore all the more necessary that the Young Leadership Movement be strengthened to produce ever-more effective cadres to perform its redemptive work.

AIDING ISRAEL'S STRUGGLE

CHAPTER TWENTY-EIGHT

SINAI VICTORY AND NUCLEAR MIGHT

66 I have just returned to the hotel from a long visit with David Ben-Gurion.

There had been another murder last night by Arab infiltrators, and his eyes were red from sleeplessness. He spoke about the wonderful morale of the people of Israel under this ceaseless harassment; then asked about the morale of Jews in the United States. 'I believe they are with us,' he said; and I assured him we were."

So I wrote in mid-July of 1956. That was a memorable year for international crises. Events of major historic importance followed one another relentlessly, and one was simply carried along, with not much time to think or plan. There was the Suez Canal War in October, followed by the Hungarian Revolution in November, capped in early December by the flight of Hungarian refugees. The year ended with Egyptian passenger liners dropping tens of thousands of Jewish refugees in Athens and Naples.

In July, all of those events were still to come. But I was already privy to the mounting concern among top Israeli officials regarding Egyptian intentions and to some of the discussions they were having as to what preparations to make.

Back in New York, despite my premonitions about war in the near future, we went ahead with plans for a UJA study mission to Israel in October. We knew the value of the mission technique, and we were learning how to mobilize people in many communities so that we could call ours a continental mission. Its results in money and enthusiasm were substantially greater each successive year, and we could honestly talk about missions as representing a new national instrument for fundraising.

We held a large inaugural conference for the 1956 regular campaign and Moroccan special fund and invited Dr. Giora Josephthal, head of Israel's immigration department and treasurer of the Jewish Agency, who had a special talent for inspiring people with his simplicity and sincerity. He spoke about war. "The Arabs will not occupy our country. We will fight for every dunam [quarter-acre], for every inch of our precious water pipeline. The Arabs may bomb us in sneak, hit-and-run attacks, but they cannot invade Israel....We are not panic-stricken; far from it. But there is a feeling of loneliness. Except for you, we are quite on our own. We turn to the Jews of the world who wanted Israel, just as we wanted Israel, and we are sure there will be a response."

He went on to outline a five-point preparedness plan being put into operation in case war broke out. Total cost of this program exceeded $50 million. The five points were:

1. Accumulation of a six-month reserve of fuel, wheat, and raw material – in case the country is cut off from the outside world.

2. Construction of storage facilities for these reserves throughout Israel, so that various localities could be self-sufficient, in case the country is cut apart.

3. Construction and dispersal of electric power stations, in case the two main stations at Haifa and Tel Aviv are destroyed. Electricity is necessary not only for industrial and civilian use but also for water distribution. Many small power plants must operate in all parts of the country.

4. Building of air-raid shelters and slit trenches: at least minimal protection must be provided against aerial bombardment.

5. Increased production of Israeli-made weapons.

He closed with words that sank into every heart: "In 1948, I doubt whether you really believed that we could beat the Arabs; 650,000 Jews against 40 million Arabs. It seemed fantastic at the time. Nevertheless, you gave us the benefit of the doubt. You stood with us and we were victorious. You must give us this chance again."

The situation in Israel was heating up. Small bands of Arab guerillas were constantly harassing kibbutzim and moshavim (collective farms) along the borders and inland, so that no farm or village felt itself to be completely beyond the range of suicidal attackers. Isolated bus routes were vulnerable; small development townlets posted guards around their perimeters; watch towers were erected, especially along the edge of the Gaza Strip; farmers never went to their fields unarmed. Because the big cities were beyond the reach of the fedayeen (guerilla) bands, urban dwellers felt only a momentary *frisson* when they read the newspaper. The rural people carried the actual burden, not only the psychological one. Wedding celebrations were invaded; casualties mounted; sentry duty at night became an additional chore for tired farmers who had worked all day.

The program Josephthal had described went forward. The Israeli media did its best to show the world what was happening. Ben-Gurion himself, as well as General Moshe Dayan, the chief of staff, and other government and Army officials, spent a whole day at a border settlement strengthening the defenses. Newsreel cameras all over the world showed Ben-Gurion stringing barbed wire for a village defense system.

I wrote to the national leadership and the top local officers: "We must raise as much money as we humanly can. Money can mean the reduction of suffering; the maintenance of new villages on the border; the quicker absorption of immigrants. Money can prevent breakdown and can sustain courage.

"We have made a good start, yet we cannot relax for a single instant. We have not attained anywhere near our maximum effort. More work, more attendance at meetings, more solicitations, more contributions must be the order of the day for the leadership. The people will follow, I am confident, if the leadership is vigorous, assertive, demanding. Let us never forget that Israel's very life may depend upon the events of the next few weeks."

In the midst of this stress and danger, a new emergency developed. On June 11, the Moroccan authorities ordered the Jewish Agency, which operated under the name Kadima ("forward march") in Morocco, to suspend all its activities, close both its offices and its staging camp outside Casablanca, and destroy its files. Further, the Moroccan internal security office refused to renew the visas of 20 Israeli personnel who were running the immigration. The pressure for that decision came from the Arab League, which did not want large streams of Jews going to Israel to strengthen "the Jewish enemy." The Moroccans said they would permit individual emigration, but each person would have to process his paperwork himself. That was tantamount to reducing the emigration to a trickle.

The day before, June 10, Moroccan police ordered a French ship that had sailed with 1,100 Jews to return to port. Since the vessel was already outside Moroccan territorial waters, the French captain ignored the orders and continued toward Marseilles where there was a Jewish Agency camp that could receive the emigrants. The Moroccans were furious and issued orders to police at all ports and airfields forbidding any further mass departures, with instructions to turn back all Jews who tried to leave the country.

The scene at the processing camp near Casablanca, which contained more than 7,000 people, therefore bordered on panic. People did not know whether to remain sleeping on the ground or to try returning to the *mellahs* (ghettos) and villages from which they had come. In addition, they worried about getting food and water – a concern reminiscent of the DP camps in Germany ten years earlier.

But the solution in Morocco would involve the same techniques as we had used earlier. Whenever Aliya Aleph becomes impossible, then Aliyah Bet must be pressed into service. And so it was.

In a July 14 letter from the King David Hotel to my constituents in the U.S., I described the situation of that day, the French national holiday commemorating the revolution of 1789. The French had been delivering Mirage aircraft to Israel, and we celebrated the day in honor of France by visiting an air base. I wrote:

"I saw the new French jets in operation, talked with the Israeli pilots and ground crews, saw how hard they were working to master this equipment. The intensity of effort was remarkable and thrilling. Then came the paradox of watching a pilot who had just climbed out of this electronic marvel of a plane, stripped off his G-suit, and turned in his automatic film of the mission, walk out to the main road to hitchhike into town, because there were no jeeps on the base for use by the personnel. This sleek jet pilot became just another anonymous hitchhiker without any frills or privilege.

"I revisited Lachish in the northern Negev – having been there a year ago when the first immigrants were brought in. At that time they were housed in wooden huts. Today the huts are for tools and chickens. The people now live in two-and-a-half-room concrete houses, have learned some Hebrew, and send their daughters to school. Frankly, I cannot believe my eyes. There is water, grass, and electricity; cotton, gladioli, and sorghum; schools, synagogues, and workshops. Here, too, a victory is being won – against unemployment, fear, newness. Settlement and integration are proceeding at a wonderfully satisfying pace."

As for our October study mission to Israel, we set a $10,000 minimum as a criterion for participation, and despite the fact that there were fewer than 500 contributors at that level in the entire country, we sought a mission membership of 100. It was a bold target. As the departure date approached, we achieved the goal, and enthusiasm mounted.

Other events that summer had gathered an ominous momentum:

> June 4 – Gamal Abdul Nasser announced there would be no renewal of the Suez Canal Company (British) concession after its expiration.

> June 13 – The last British troops left their Suez Canal base.

July 20 – United States and Great Britain cancelled their offer to put up $270 million to build the Aswan dam, because Egypt had made a secret deal with Czechoslovakia through Russian collusion for war materiel.

July 26 – Nasser nationalized the canal, outlawed the Suez Canal Company, and promised that the tolls Egypt would collect in the next five years would build the Aswan Dam.

August 2 – British and French nationals left Egypt.

August 16 – Nasser boycotted the London Conference, called to negotiate the Suez crisis.

September 10 – Nasser rejected the 18-nation proposals.

September 23 – Britain and France submitted the Suez dispute to the UN Security Council.

Behind the scenes, in the greatest secrecy, other moves were being made. One of the most experienced and reliable Israeli agents, Asher Ben-Natan, whose code name in the Aliyah Bet was Artur, and with whom I had worked many years ago in Austria, was called to the Defense Ministry in Tel Aviv for a new assignment. The young director-general of the ministry, 33-year old Shimon Peres, a favorite of Ben-Gurion, and a life-long friend of mine, gave Ben-Natan instructions to leave for Paris immediately to serve as a special representative of the defense ministry for all of Europe. Peres explained to Ben-Natan that his mission would soon become clear.

On October 22, a secret meeting took place, under the tightest security precautions imaginable, in a private villa in the Paris suburb of Sèvres. Around a large wooden table sat about a dozen men, including Ben-Gurion and General Moshe Dayan for Israel; Prime Minister Guy Mollet, Defense Minister Bourges-Manoury, and Foreign Minister Christian Pineau for France; Foreign Secretary Selwyn Lloyd for Britain. These men were planning a war. It would be known in Israel as the Sinai Operation and worldwide as the Suez Campaign.

The objectives of the three allies differed, but they had in common the goal of breaking Nasser. In their book *Every Spy a Prince*, Dan Raviv and Yossi Melman offer a tightly condensed summary:

> Israel's aims in the war were to destroy Egypt's Soviet-equipped army, while breaking President Nasser's declared blockade of the Red Sea route to Eilat. There was also the publicly stated aim of stopping Palestinian terrorist attacks on Negev villages, emanating from Egypt's Gaza Strip.
>
> Britain's prime minister, Anthony Eden, motivated by his visceral hatred for Nasser, hoped to restore British control over the canal, which the Egyptian leader had nationalized. Eden expected that the humiliation would topple Nasser, who was riding a wave of Middle East radicalism directed against Western interests.
>
> France was primarily concerned with stopping 'Nasserism' because it provided inspiration to the FLN – the National Liberation Front in Algeria, which was fighting to dislodge the French occupying forces and to declare Arab independence.
>
> Even before the Sèvres conference, France had begun to arm Israel for the war to come. From April, French cargo planes and ships arrived in the darkness of night and unloaded an abundance of weaponry: tanks, fighter planes, cannon, and ammunition.

The Sèvres meeting was drama on the highest level, and we in the United States knew nothing about it at the time. While the three allies were meeting in the Paris suburb, our UJA mission was flying to Israel and starting its itinerary, which was to culminate with a state dinner hosted by Ben-Gurion himself on October 25.

The mission itself proved most rewarding. Because the Iron Curtain was opening a crack, we saw 65 immigrants, mostly Polish and some Rumanian Jews, alight in their new country. A relative would shout when he saw the long-awaited family deplaning; then the surge of reunion, the kissing and hugging and crying. Our mission members, never immune, cried also. Another day we went to an agricultural school where hundreds of children performed, some in chorus, others in ballet; some with flute and timbrel, others distributing flowers. Again, our heartfelt identification. And so it went for most of the week: the general atmosphere replete with rumors of war; the immediate environment of the mission members replete with emotional homecomings and immigrant absorption. We headed toward the climax of the week, the state dinner.

The King David Hotel dining room was resplendent. The management and staff had performed to the maximum of the young country's ability: searching everywhere for crystal vases to fill with the gorgeous flowers that the Israeli sun produces; starching the table linen and polishing the silver, which had been borrowed from a dozen of the richest private homes; dressing and rehearsing the staff so that it resembled an experienced Swiss cadre. Our people were equally resplendent: the women in all their jewelry, the men in three-piece suits and brilliant ties. A sense of excitement was in the air. How often, after all, does one dine with a prime minister?

The presiding officer for the evening, Zalman Shazar, chairman of the Jewish Agency and later president of Israel, tried to get the group seated, for protocol required that all be seated and all movement cease before the prime minister and his party entered the room. But before Ben-Gurion could enter the room, he first had to re-enter the country, and as the UJA people were gathering in the hotel dining room, his plane from France was landing.

His mind was crowded with worries about the impending war; the opening moves could be planned, but not the subsequent ones, nor how it would end. His emotions were aroused as well, for he knew how fragile his young state was and how he was about to endanger its very existence. In addition, he was suffering from a high fever. Common sense would have taken him home to bed and the doctor. His duty sense took him straight to the King David Hotel.

Entering the room with a rapid stride, Ben-Gurion seated himself at the head table between Zalman Shazar and me, nodded perfunctorily to one or two of his colleagues, and immediately ordered Shazar to start the meal. The absence of a *beracha* (blessing) over bread; the abruptness of behavior; the obvious preoccupation with something other than the present moment left the onlookers slightly bewildered. Lifting spoon to soup, he growled to Shazar and myself that we were to ask him no questions, discuss no politics, and if we were compelled to talk, then confine ourselves to philosophy or something equally abstract. His mood was so detached, his face so flushed, that we sensed something very serious in the wind.

The meal was eaten hastily, and tension rose in the room, as everyone gradually realized that something was wrong. When Shazar arose and began an elaborate introduction of B-G, the latter tugged at his coat and curtly ordered him to finish. The prime minister's long-awaited speech to the mission consisted of one full sentence, in which he stated that the visitors should note well the condition of the nation at this moment, should have confidence that the people of Israel would rise to their duty and perform it heroically, and they – because they had come here with love – should return home immediately and do their duty with equivalent fervor. Once again tugging at Shazar, he commanded him to start the singing of the national anthem.

None of us three – Shazar, Ben-Gurion, nor I – was capable of carrying a tune properly. But as our first, wavering notes emerged, the audience rose and *"Hatikvah"* swelled mightily through the large room. Almost before it was finished, expecting no applause and not receiving any, the prime minister strode from the room, surrounded by aides and guards, leaving behind a totally bewildered audience. They had no idea of what he had so elliptically attempted to warn them. They moved out into the hotel lobby, excitedly asking each other, and those of us in authority, what his words and appearance meant. We could offer no explanations. Bewilderment turned into resentment among small numbers of people, and an evening that had begun with high expectations ended with a certain annoyance and disappointment. Our staff made the requisite announcements concerning luggage and next morning departure for the airport. The crowd slowly dispersed to the bar or to bed.

Around midnight I received a telephone call from Levi Eshkol, the finance minister, suggesting we meet immediately. He told me what was happening, explained Ben-Gurion's behavior, and urged me in the strongest terms to make absolutely certain that all the American visitors leave the country next day (Friday), for on Saturday – *Shabbat* – there were no flights, and Sunday might be too late: War might start on Monday. The government did not want to worry about the fate of this important group of American Jews, and it was my responsibility to make sure they were transported out of the country to safety.

Once I knew what was happening, I acted swiftly. The great majority did leave Friday morning. A few stragglers were tracked down and urged to depart. I found the last mission member, Ike Schine of Bridgeport, Connecticut, at the Technion Institute in Haifa, on Sunday morning, and peremptorily escorted him and his family to Lod Airport, promising him faithfully that by the next day he would understand. He was very annoyed, but a week later, when I was back in New York, and the shooting was all over, he called to apologize for his anger.

Few observers realize that linked to the Israeli-French collusion in planning the Suez War was a matter of transcendental significance: the emergence of Israel as a potential atomic power. I have never seen evidence as to which country initiated the nuclear collusion, France or Israel. Each had her own motive for doing so, but in all probability the idea came from the fertile brain of Shimon Peres, the golden boy of Ben-Gurion's entourage. Peres knew that his mentor's fondest hope was to obtain nuclear capability for the fledgling state. Ben-Gurion had fashioned Israel's army out of the conglomeration of pre-state underground forces. He had broken the individual militias, including his own Haganah, and harnessed them under one command. With that he had won the War of Independence.

But no one knew better than Ben-Gurion that the future would bring many more wars, cruelly testing the strength of the little country, and it was not automatically guaranteed that she would survive them all. The magic weapon and ultimate deterrent was the atomic bomb. Ben-Gurion's preoccupation with obtaining the bomb for Israel obsessed him even in the midst of the War of Independence. He met in December 1948 with a Russian Jewish chemist, Maurice Surdin, then living in France and working with the French Atomic Energy Commission. The talks came to nothing, but they indicate how early B-G started on the track down the atomic path.

Two other key people supported Ben-Gurion in this pursuit. Moshe Dayan was extremely enthusiastic. He also foresaw future wars and feared that Israel might come to require a large standing army, which could bankrupt the economically struggling state. While the acquisition of atomic power was also frightfully expensive, in the long run, once the initial investment had been made, it would cost less than a permanent army. And it would be a much stronger deterrent, and thus a better defense. Also urging Ben-Gurion on was one of Israel's greatest scientists, German-born Ernst Bergman, chairman of the Israeli Atomic Energy Commission, established in 1952.

The window of opportunity suddenly opened in 1955, when President Eisenhower announced his "Atoms for Peace" program, an idealistic American effort, like the earlier Marshall Plan, to assist developing non-Communist countries in the form of cheaper energy. Under that program, the United States provided Israel with a small five-megawatt research reactor, located on the sea where the Sorek brook entered the Mediterranean, a few miles from the Weizmann Institute. Now Israel could begin training technicians in the intricate new science of mastering the atom.

Shimon Peres immediately started pursuing the French for a larger reactor. He exploited the fact that Guy Mollet, the head of the socialist government then in power, had become a friend through their common membership in the Socialist International, whose meetings Shimon attended faithfully. The sympathetic Mollet introduced Peres to the various layers of the French bureaucracy. Shimon himself told me later that he had pushed and pushed, to such an extent that many French officials began to think of him as Israel's foreign minister. That brought him into direct conflict with the actual foreign minister, Golda Meir, who took a serious dislike to him and protested his conduct vigorously to Ben-Gurion. In addition, Golda passionately opposed Israel going atomic. Her reasons were based not on morality but on economic and geopolitical considerations. Peres, however, had Ben-Gurion's unqualified backing and continued building support in France for the project throughout the year 1956.

Israel's atomic objective and the British-French collusive planning for the Sinai Campaign finally came together. It is not clear who suggested that Israel join the attack. The French and British had been discussing it between themselves. Suddenly the Israelis were in the picture, probably because they could provide a powerful addition: a strong ground-and-air attack southwestward across the desert, enabling the French and British to make their thrust from the north, and hitting Egypt from three directions at once.

Israel thus became a most attractive partner. And as an added inducement for her to join the conspiracy, Defense Minister Bourges-Manoury offered on

September 21 to give Israel a large reactor. On October 3, just a few weeks before the invasion, Bourges-Manoury, elevated in the interim to the prime ministership, and new Foreign Minister, Christian Pineau, signed a top-secret agreement to supply a large, 24-megawatt reactor, plus the necessary technicians, know-how, and 35 kilograms of enriched uranium.

The war came and went. The combination of the British Navy, French aircraft, and Israeli infantry liberated the canal. It was all over in 100 hours. Construction of a "textile factory" started near Dimona, a Negev immigrant town that had several genuine textile factories. The work took three years, and rumors swirled everywhere; but it was not until 1960 that concrete evidence became available. A high-flying American U-2 reconnaissance plane eluded Israeli radar and took photographs proving that the factory was indeed a reactor. The pictures were published worldwide, and the U.S. Government demanded the whole truth from the Israelis.

Much more annoyed was Charles de Gaulle, who had become president of France two years earlier. He had been attempting reconciliation with the Arabs, even offering independence to Algeria. The fact that France had provided Israel with atomic capability did not endear the French to the Arab world. Further, de Gaulle loathed the idea of any other country possessing a *force de frappe*. He therefore threatened not to supply additional uranium, which would mean shutting down the reactor when its present fuel rods were exhausted.

In June, Ben-Gurion went to Paris to attempt to reason with de Gaulle. When asked bluntly why Israel even needed a reactor, B-G replied that it was only for peaceful purposes and that no facility would be built at Dimona for producing weapons-grade plutonium. In December 1960, Ben-Gurion announced publicly in the Knesset that Israel was building a second atomic research reactor – for peaceful purposes. That mollified de Gaulle, who agreed to supply the final parts required to complete the installation, but no additional uranium.

Later, François Perrin, the scientific head of the French Atomic Energy Commission, indicated that a reprocessing plant capable of extracting plutonium from spent fuel rods was part of the original agreement signed back in 1957 by the then-prime minister, Bourges-Manoury. Since de Gaulle had refused to honor that agreement, Perrin's board permitted a private French company, St. Gobain, to sell its technology and plans to the Dimona project.

Israel had became an atomic power. The next eleven years, until 1967, passed without war.

CHAPTER TWENTY-NINE

THE ISRAEL EDUCATION FUND

Whenever the steady beat of fundraising and administrating offered a day or even an hour free of the incessant demands made by telephones, airplanes, meetings, or speeches, I would retreat into my favorite occupation; long-range thinking. The trick was to catch that fleeting opportunity, to sit alone with a favorite idea, toy with its pros and cons and feasibility, and calculate how to coax it into birth and nourish it into full growth. Many ideas quickly died, but a few felt important, seminal, capable of bearing permanent fruit, and on those I concentrated.

I always believed that my responsibility as the UJA's CEO obligated me to think and act on many different levels – providing inspiration, controlling administration, managing relations with the local communities, soliciting large gifts, setting financial targets, and above all, creating new methods for achieving the organization's goals.

The 1950s were filled with frantic waves of immigrants – hundreds of thousands of people flooding into Israel, needing food and shelter at a time when the economy there was often in recession, the military expenditure prodigious, and the thin layer of top leadership stretched almost beyond human limit. We in the United States worked frantically to mobilize the necessary support. Nevertheless, one had to find moments of quiet in which to think ahead, not just for the next day's work, but for the long-term future as well.

I always returned to the basic question: What is the character of the state we are helping to build? Rescuing people and dealing with their physical needs was the easier task, because it dealt with tangible ingredients such as houses, farms, jobs, and villages. But the real strength of the Israeli nation would depend on its economy – and morale – and on a much more complicated "tangible," the Army.

Those broad areas demanded a well-educated and highly motivated population. If we were to create an Israel that could be a beacon unto its own citizens and even – in the traditional Biblical sense – unto all nations, we would have to solve social challenges more complicated than physical needs. Education was the indispensable force. It would elevate the economy, protect the state, and drive the nation to greatness.

If one analyzed carefully the educational system in the Israel of 1960, the gap between ideal and reality was tremendous. Overcrowded classes; short supply of qualified teachers; many pupils coping with the new language of Hebrew; brief school day due to lack of funds; no pre-schools; education finishing at grade 8 – all those and many other debilitating conditions resulted in a school system seriously insufficient for a young country aspiring to higher standards. The inadequacies could not be overcome by the most dedicated efforts of teachers and administrators. Major remedial action was desperately needed. But first, the Israeli public and its American supporters had to realize that enhancing the level of education was as important as acquiring the next level of fighter aircraft. I came to the conclusion that the UJA should undertake a separate, special fund to raise educational standards and achievements in Israel.

On June 15, 1961, I wrote a letter that was probably the earliest formulation of thoughts on that subject: "In the face of larger immigration, principally from Rumania into Israel, plus Soviet MIG-19's coming into Egyptian hands, Israel is constantly struggling. These are the two main financial burdens. But there are many other serious problems, not the least among them being education. I have long hoped that there might be a time when the UJA could begin to contribute to education in Israel, which is not free beyond the 8th grade. With the traditional Jewish emphasis on higher education, Israel should be a land where everyone could receive university training. This is a beautiful dream, and we are today far from it."

I had many conversations with the successive ministers of education, Zalman Aranne and Abba Eban, concerning the future of education in the country. The weightiest problem was money. The goal of free, universal, secondary education was impossible for Israel to attain, and the law limited it to grade 8 and below. In addition, the school day was shorter than it should be, extra-curricular opportunities – including sports – were minimal, and many teachers were unlicensed.

I very much wanted the UJA to find some way to assist in this area and began to delineate the specific problems to be solved. First and foremost was the legal question of the tax-deductibility of the contributions we would be soliciting. Education was an Israeli Government responsibility, and according to IRS limits on deductibility, philanthropic funds could not be applied to any program that was a basic government responsibility. Therefore, we could do nothing to assist grades 1 through 8. The government had no legal obligation to provide services in pre-kindergarten, kindergarten, and high school, however; so those would be the areas in which we could work.

Pre-kindergarten was as appealing as high school because the results of Operation Head Start in the United States had already demonstrated the benefit of acquiring early reading skills. Strong reading ability undergirded success in later schooling; put another way, drop-out rates years later were directly related to inadequate reading skill.

Next came the challenge of working out a set of rules that would satisfy both the government in Israel and our own federated communities, where we would be raising the considerable sums required to build schools. We and the government needed to agree on the distinction between operating budgets and capital fund budgets. I wanted the UJA to be responsible for raising the multi-millions for construction and the ministry of education to undertake the operating budget.

My reasoning stemmed from the fundraising we would have to do in the communities. Potential donors to an education fund would have to make unusually large contributions and at the same time maintain or even increase their annual gifts to the regular campaign – an overall commitment that would take them several years to pay off. Therefore, we could hardly expect to obtain still more money for a school operating budget. Further, the Israel government's taxing power could be expected to increase, as the population and the economy expanded, so the education ministry should be able to handle those budgets.

For the UJA, there was also a delicate political problem: getting each local federation to approve our raising large sums in its community without sharing with the local federation. We needed an approach that would allay the understandable fears. The best one, I decided, would be to offer the strongest possible guarantees right from the start, rather than to negotiate and compromise my way through the usual process that marks most communal decisions. I therefore wrote a stringent set of regulations designed to protect the interest of the local federation and simply published them as the operating rules for the soon-to-be established Israel Education Fund (IEF).

The rules were as follows:

1. The minimum gift to the IEF would be $100,000.

2. Before the donor could make a gift to the IEF, he or she would have to increase the amount he or she was contributing to the local annual campaign.

3. Every prospect for an IEF gift would have to be cleared by the local federation with regard to the amount and timing of the solicitation.

4. Schools built with IEF contributions would carry the name of donors, if they desired – as distinct from annual gifts, which were anonymous.

5. Dedications of the buildings in Israel would be public events to which donors would be invited.

Carrying out this campaign would require a strong lay and professional leadership, and I did not want to divert any of the top UJA lay leaders from their work in the annual campaign. Furthermore, I wanted someone with qualifications in the field of education, someone whose experience would lend weight to the presentations and solicitations required. By a happy coincidence, I found the perfect lay leader right in my own family. After having been divorced, I married Francine Bensley in 1963. We had been introduced earlier in Rome, when she came there to join some family friends who were on a UJA mission. My new father-in-law, Charles Bensley, was eminently suited to head the Israel Education Fund.

Charles J. Bensley, Esq., had been on the Board of Education of the City of New York for 13 years. As chairman of the board's Building and Sites Committee, he had built more than 300 schools at a cost of several hundred million dollars. He had just the right background of knowledge, contacts, and visions we needed, and he agreed to be the founding president of the IEF. This was a lucky break that augured well for the new venture.

Charlie immediately addressed the question of gathering the research that would validate the need for this new campaign. To gather the comprehensive data, he assembled a high-quality team to accompany him to Israel. The three experts were: Dr. Harold B. Gores, president of the Educational Facilities Laboratories of the Ford Foundation; Dr. William Jansen, former superintendent of schools of the City of New York; and Dr. Harold Wilson, dean of the School of Education of the University of California at Los Angeles. I secured the services of Abraham S. Hyman, my valuable colleague during the post-war years in Germany, to do the staff work.

The indefatigable Charlie led his colleagues on a three-week trip throughout the entire country of Israel, visiting dozens of schools, interviewing scores of teachers and principals, meeting with all the relevant politicians and finance ministry officials; and concluding with the top ministers themselves. Abe Hyman then wrote a 218-page document entitled *Survey of Education in Israel*, which summarized the data and the team's conclusions. The group returned to the United States highly enthusiastic about the improvements our project could bring to Israel's education system.

I broached the matter publicly at the regular quarterly meeting of the Council of Jewish Federations and Welfare Funds in March 1964. Augmenting our team were Joseph Meyerhoff, of Baltimore, who was just finishing a four-year term as general chairman of the national UJA and would become the second president of the Israel Education Fund; Philip Zinman of New Jersey,

later the third president; and Ralph Goldman, a veteran officer of the Joint
Distribution Committee who was joining as executive director of the IEF.

It was an excellent meeting. I posed the basic question – why do we need
this new fund? – and proceeded to answer it from five points of view –
economy, defense, politics, Jewish tradition, and the making of a nation. I made
these points:

The Economy

In order to develop a highly skilled and technologically advanced
society, such as exists in the smaller countries of Western Europe, Israel
has to make major improvements in the general educational level of its
population, especially in scientific, engineering, computer, and other
hi-tech skills. Without an education system that can propel a constant
advance in technology and science, the economy will struggle
desperately to grow. (Those sentences, spoken one-third of a century
ago, sound almost prophetic in view of the impressive progress made by
Israel's economy in today's industrialized world.)

Defense

Modern defense requires a high degree of training and skills for the
handling of sophisticated armor, artillery, aircraft, and missile systems. I
have often summed up this very complex matter in one short sentence:
A small nation can lose a war in its classrooms. More than ever before,
the science of war now begins, with knowledge of mathematics and
computer technology. For example, long-range artillery is aimed and
fired from computers located in trailers that often sit a half-mile from
the guns themselves.

Any analysis of Israel's defense problems assumes that her forces
will never match those of her combined enemies from a quantitative
standpoint but *must* be able to surpass them qualitatively. This
superiority in quality depends on two factors: weapons and manpower.
Concerning weapons, she must always obtain the most advanced in the
world, through a combination of purchases from the United States and

research in her own production facilities. There must be no compromise on this subject. Concerning manpower, quality refers to the standard of training, in the classroom and in the field, of officers, tank commanders, pilots, and all other critical personnel. We are not speaking of morale and fighting spirit but of sheer technical skill, which must be studied and absorbed. From a purely military point of view, Israel's existence depends on continuously improving educational standards.

Politics

Democracy rests on stability, which in turn rests on rational attitudes of the citizenry toward the imperfections of government. If people believe there is discrimination in the system, a street mob – uneducated, fed by hysteria and/or demagoguery – can explode into violence. It is a fact, and we are all proud of it, that Israel enjoys the most solid, stable democracy in the entire Middle East. But we must never forget the Wadi Salib episode, which occurred in Haifa some years ago. It involved mainly North African Jews, recent immigrants, relatively uneducated, living in slums at a barely subsistence level. Large numbers of them took to the streets, burning and looting, in an uncontrollable tirade that took many hours to subside.

The root cause was a feeling on the part of these Sephardic citizens that they were being unfairly treated in a society dominated by Ashkenazic (European) Jews, who controlled all the levers of power. A sense of discrimination is a social evil that cannot be dissipated over night yet must be dealt with to avoid a constant plague of similar outbreaks. The worst symptoms of social inequality are found in the job market, where the illiterate or semi-educated citizen will always be at an economic disadvantage.

If nothing is done about that situation, if it is accepted as a natural social condition, the very foundations of democracy may erode. Personally, I am deeply convinced that Israel's political stability and the democratic future will depend directly on a higher level of education for *all* groups.

Jewish Tradition

We are the People of the Book, and should therefore be ashamed if the standard of learning in Israel remains lower than our highest expectations.

The country has a highly educated elite, stemming from continental Europe, America, and the kibbutz. Almost every kibbutz, or group of kibbutzim, has created its own high school. The elite runs the country in all key sectors: government, army, industry, universities, social services. But social conditions never remain frozen. What we consider today a high level of secondary education, fit to produce a ruling elite, may by tomorrow's standards be considered inadequate.

If Israel fails to keep pace with the ever-more-demanding requirements of a modern country in the sensitive and vital area of education, how will we feel a generation from now if only a few of her citizens advance beyond high school and if even those few are unable to compete in international arenas? Can we accept the prospect of an educationally declining Israel without violating our own ethos and our traditional pride in education? The image of the Jew we cherished most is that of an educated person. I sincerely believe that we must help Israel fulfill her increasing educational needs, not only to assure her viability as a modern state but also to adhere to our traditional values.

The Making of a Nation

In the past 15 years, the UJA has been an active participant in rescuing our people and bringing them to Israel. We watched and abetted the slow, sometimes-erratic process of state-building: the emergence of an effective Israel Defense Force; the growth of a foreign service with more than 100 ambassadors around the globe; the building of factories; the expansion of the tourist trade; and many other components inherent to sovereignty.

But the progress Israel has made in *state*-building should not divert our attention from the far more complex task of *nation*-building: how to integrate immigrants coming from 70 other countries, speaking scores of other languages, with a wide variety of occupational skills (or none at all), and a tremendous array of cultural baggage and personal dreams. Solutions must be found or the entire experiment will founder.

Let me point out that a country-wide high school system is a tool for blending various groups and strains into a nation. If we look at the history of the United States in the 19th and early 20th centuries, we see the truth of that statement. The Poles and Germans, the Scandinavians and Italians, the Jews and Greeks, the Russians and Irish, the millions pouring into the United States every year, became Americans through the process of schooling. They learned the English language, American culture and mores, civics and democracy. The day and night schools those immigrants attended provided America with the foundation of a more or less homogenized citizenry.

We must not deceive ourselves. These tools do not exist in Israel today. More than a million people have been brought to Israel so far since the state was founded. They are there, free and safe. But a high percentage remain immigrants, divided into separate and distinct groups, many by their own traditions, many resentful and suspicious, underprivileged in their own minds and inferior in the minds of others.

Israel still lacks the character of a nation. To blend the population into some sort of homogeneity, we must have a network of high schools, and even with such a system, we must realize that the blending will take 20 or 30 years.

We have reviewed five major aspects of Israel's educational problem. Taken together, they point to a single conclusion: the nation's growth, phenomenal to this point, will soon be blunted unless educational levels are pushed higher and made universal. There is a great and real danger of Israel's becoming a small, Levantine state of three or four million Jews, with an elite superimposed on a poverty- stricken population.

I have no doubt that all of us would like to see a modern Israel, industrialized, well-defended, sustained in its economic progress by a literate, educated population. But it is clear to me that we will only see such a modern Israel if we come to her aid, if we accept our share of responsibilities in the vital, challenging field of education, by supporting the new Israel Education Fund being proposed to you today.

Following the presentation, the meeting proceeded to questions about the fundraising, a matter of great concern to the participants:

Q. How are we going to prevent donors from wanting to divert money they are now giving the UJA to this new fund, where they will get their name on a door?

A. If the Education Fund gift is a substitution for the regular annual gift, we won't take it.

Q. How firm is the conviction that gifts of less than $100,000 will not be accepted?

A. Night before last, the officers of the UJA voted on the $100,000 "floor" and recommended that amount to the executive committee, which meets next Monday. If the committee agrees, that becomes policy.

Q. Suppose a man who gives $1,000 annually to the regular campaign wants instead to give the IEF $10,000 for ten scholarships, and that would give him great pleasure. Would you take it?

A. No, no.

Q. Then you would be throwing some money away.

A. Yes, we might be, but we are trying to obtain two greater goods: first, large sums; and second, protection for the annual campaign. Those goals are more important than the smaller money we might lose.

Q. Assume a man gives you $100,000 and pledges to pay it in four years, and in the third year he goes to the federation and says, "I'm having some trouble this year and will have to reduce my federation gift in order to pay the $25,000 I owe on my IEF pledge." What would you do?

A. We have the responsibility of protecting the annual campaign to the maximum degree possible, but frankly we can't provide protection "unto the third and fourth generation." Although a situation like that might arise, experience with other large capital-fund campaigns, for hospitals, community centers, synagogues, etc., indicates that the number of such cases is not significant. For us to say that we would not accept a man's pledge because of some theoretical problem four years down the road wouldn't be realistic.

Q. Will Israel bonds be accepted in payment of IEF pledges?

A. Yes, just as they are accepted in payment of regular annual pledges.

Q. Will the bond organization be selling bonds on the basis that they will build schools with the proceeds of their sales?

A. No. Some speakers at bond meetings might try to refer to the educational problem in Israel, but the organization is not authorized to sell its investments for the purpose of building schools.

Q. It has been stated that, under the projected plan, secondary education will not be free. Is that right?

A. Yes. Before you can make any social service free, you have to make it available. We must first build the schools and train more teachers. Israel can't at the same time hope to raise enough money to provide a full operating budget, so that education can be free for every child. It will have to be on a tuition basis at the beginning. The average tuition for high school today is about $125 per year. That is a tremendous amount of money for a large, poor Moroccan family, with several children and average earnings of about $175 per month. Slowly but surely, as the government's ability to assume the school budget increases, the tuition cost of secondary education will dwindle to zero, or nearly that, for every child.

Q. You say that you do not intend to make the IEF a general appeal. Would you be willing to make it a 'restricted' appeal, approaching only those people who give to the UJA at least $50,000 annually? That means you would be approaching only 200 or 300 people in the whole country, and we wouldn't be so worried about our local campaign.

A. Yes, we have decided on a restricted campaign. We are not going to solicit the general public. Remember what we said about clearing the names of those to be approached. But restricted does not mean only people who already give $50,000. We in this room are all sophisticated in fundraising. We all know examples of individuals who give a fixed amount every year, and there is absolutely nothing anyone can say or do to obtain an increase. Take the person who gives his $5,000 every year with loyalty and enthusiasm, but that's it, not a penny more. Suddenly, he gives a half million to his university, or to a university in Israel, and the question on everyone's tongue is, "How come? Who got to him? Why did he do it?" That kind of thing happens rather frequently. So we will restrict this campaign to the smallest number of donors possible but will not put arbitrary dollar limits on the prospect pool. I hope we'll always be looking for, and occasionally find, such "sleepers."

Q. At a figure of $100,000, you are eliminating any solicitation of dozens of people in small communities. With the possible exception of one or two people, there would be no potentials in my own community.

A. It might very well be that two or three potentials in every community in the entire United States would be enough. A certain boldness and high imagination are required. Eagerness on our part to protect the regular campaign might seem to you to be an inhibition on the boldness. I don't think so. Let's ride the two horses and see how it goes.

It may be that a year from now, if we have turned down an overwhelming number of smaller gifts and shouldn't have done so, we will have to take a second look and change the ground rules. But for the beginning, this is how we visualize it.

Q. Is any consideration being given to contacting the non-Jewish world with respect to this new educational fund? I am referring to large foundations like Rockefeller and Ford.

A. The answer is definitely yes. Some of the large foundations might not be permitted, for example, to build a building, but they could get into teacher training, curriculum, language laboratories – the sorts of educational projects they have undertaken in many underdeveloped countries. Our intention is to seek them out and also to seek contributions from non-Jewish family foundations.

Following the successful public presentation of the plan, in many communities across the country, a National Leadership Conference on Education in Israel was convened in September 1964 at the Biltmore Hotel in New York. The choice of hotel, made by Ralph Goldman, is interesting. Goldman had served as David Ben-Gurion's assistant in the 1950s and adored B-G. The latter had chosen the Biltmore in 1943 as the site of a conference called to pass the first official Zionist resolution aiming at the establishment of a Jewish state. Goldman's emotional attachment to Ben-Gurion – and to the "Biltmore Resolution," as history terms it – led him to recommend that the resolution officially creating the IEF stem from the same hotel. I agreed, for my sentiments were identical.

At the opening dinner, Abba Eban, deputy prime minister and former minister of education, made a powerful, elegant plea for a massive re-invigoration of the education system. To our delight, Eban advocated concentrating on the pre-kindergarten and the secondary level as the two areas in most dire need of improvement. The more than 300 delegates from every major Jewish community in the United States, as well as many smaller ones, listened spellbound.

Dr. Harold Gores, president of the Ford Foundation's Educational Facilities Laboratories and a member of the study team that had investigated the problem earlier in the year, spoke in practical terms about enlarging the teaching pool, the difficulties of construction, and many related issues. Gores argued that if U.S. Jewry and its friends provided the necessary financial support, Israel had the talent, will-power, and energy to overcome all obstacles. His pragmatic approach gave way to an evangelical zeal as he described the advances that could be made and pleaded for a wide-spread, enthusiastic response. The audience reaction augured well for the future of the new fund.

The following morning, Joseph Meyerhoff opened the session with a statement of support. Then a panel consisting of the other members of the study team – Charles Bensley and Drs. Jansen and Wilson – offered brief opinions and suggestions. They supplied careful answers to the scores of questions that flooded from the floor. I followed with an outline of the plan and answers to the questions. Goldman and Abe Hyman answered questions as well.

The program finished at lunch with remarks by Edward M.M. Warburg, one of the most devoted and active leaders in Jewish philanthropy, the recipient of enormous respect because of his achievements, and a true intellectual. His unqualified testimonial of support for the new fund was of major value.

The meeting ended with a formal endorsement from U.S. Commissioner of Education Francis Keppel. He spoke lyrically about the role that free, universal education had played in the growth and strength of America and said that Israel would enjoy similar advantages if her educational system progressed along the lines we were contemplating. He offered whatever help and advice his office could give, whenever our evolving plans produced the inevitable dilemmas. His tone and manner were so genuinely friendly that they cast a warm glow from Washington over our proceedings.

The National Leadership Conference on Education ended on a high note. The delegates approved the concept and plan of operation, and dispersed to spread the word in their own communities. Goldman, Hyman, and I returned to our office to begin developing a prospect list. Our chief lay leaders, Bensley, Meyerhoff, and Zinman awaited their assignments for the first solicitations. An Israel-based director was appointed: Eliezer Shavit, who started out as the liaison between the IEF and the Jewish Agency and became over the years one of our most zealous and successful fundraisers. Every trip of Shavit's to the United States produced at least one or more large contributor. All in all, it was a strong, compatible, and motivated team of laymen and professionals.

The IEF's very first project showed the impressive imagination that we hoped would become the fund's trademark. It combined all of these disparate elements: the richly historic elements of Jerusalem, dramatic rescue from the Nazis, Christian nobility, and American Jewry at its best. Conceived by Bensley, the project included the following: building our first high school in Jerusalem, in the semi-slum section of Katamon, heavily populated by the North African Sephardic kids who most needed the new system; naming the institution "Denmark High School," in honor of the Danes who saved that nation's entire Jewish community (some 7,000 strong) on Yom Kippur eve, when the Nazis had planned to round them up and ship them to their death; and securing the funding from whatever number of donors was required at the standard level of $100,000 each.

When Bensley first suggested this idea to me, I loved its boldness plus the beauty of its symmetry: European Jews being rescued from physical death and African Jews being rescued from spiritual death – two celebrations with a single stroke. I congratulated him on his ingenuity. But I felt constrained to ask a bottom-line question: If he were to be the engine driving this plan to success, could he and would he make the first contribution himself – to give the program instant credibility? When his answer came immediately in the affirmative, my heart swelled. I knew that such a great and quick-starting project would galvanize the entire enterprise.

In Israel, Shavit got the engineers and bureaucrats working, and he soon relayed a vital piece of information. The mayor of Jerusalem, Mordecai Ish-Shalom, had given our plan his blessing and identified the requisite piece of land. The technical people had then come up with a cost of $1,100,000. That signalled a need for 10 donors, in addition to Charlie. He and the lay leaders went to work, and before long the donor group was formed.

Now the final element had to be put in place, namely, the approval of the Danish Government for the naming of the high school. Once again, Charlie had a smashing idea. He suggested that we should obtain for the entire group of eleven donor couples an audience with the Danish king and queen in the Royal Palace. The group would fly together to Copenhagen and then to Israel where they would announce that the Denmark School was a reality.

It worked. The royal couple hosted the group at a gala dinner in the palace and expressed their delight at the naming proposal. The entire venture was a public relations coup as well as a source of political harmony between the two countries and a means of providing a new life for hundreds of underprivileged kids. What more could anyone want from a single idea? Thus the first project demonstrated the huge potential of the Israel Education Fund.

TOTAL RESULTS of the IEF – 1964-1997
Total Raised during 33 years – $250 million
Equivalent Value in 1997 Currency – $750 million

Projects	Number
High Schools and Colleges	133
Sports Facilities	25
Community, Youth, and Cultural Centers	106
Libraries	33
Pre-kindergartens	304
Pre-kindergarten Nurseries	176
TOTAL	777

CHAPTER THIRTY

THE SIX-DAY WAR

Problems with water have been indigenous to Palestine-Israel since the beginning of agricultural development and tiny new settlements more than a century ago. The famous engineer Walter Lowdermilk surveyed the situation and, in 1944, recommended that all the water resources in the area now comprising Israel, Lebanon, Syria, and Jordan be unified and distributed to each country according to a mutually agreeable plan. That beautiful idea lay fallow until President Eisenhower appointed Eric Johnston to try to negotiate it into reality. After working for two years, Johnston thought he had an agreement that gave the Arab countries 60 percent of the water and Israel 40 percent. But at the last minute, the Arabs backed away, and the effort failed.

Ensuing events created tension that contributed heavily to the outbreak of conflict – the famous "Six-Day" War. In 1960, the Israelis started the construction of their own National Water Carrier, which was completed four years later. It involved drawing water from the Lake of Galilee and sending it southward through open channels and buried pipe (nine feet in diameter) all the way to the Negev Desert, with numberless capillaries along the route to provide irrigation down to the one-drop level.

When its Arab neighbors saw what Israel had achieved, they promptly decided to divert the headwaters of the Jordan by means of dams and tunnels, so that major sources of water would never enter the Jordan River system. Part would be diverted to flow into the Mediterranean and therefore be wasted; part would be channeled to flow into Syria.

Lebanon was reluctant to locate the diversionary projects on her territory, fearing Israeli reaction, with good reason. Prime Minister Eshkol and Deputy Defense Minister Peres both made it clear that denying Israel her share of the region's water would be regarded most seriously. Peres warned of "punitive action by the injured party," and Eshkol said that "any attempt to prevent Israel from utilizing her just share of the Jordan River system in accordance with the Johnston Plan would be considered as if it were an encroachment on our borders." The next three years, 1964 to '67, saw many military skirmishes on land and in the air, especially between Israel and Syria. In April 1967, for example, Syria lost several MIGs in a dogfight above the Sea of Galilee.

One did not have to be a soothsayer to sense the troubled air. In mid-May, Egypt had declared a state of emergency, and the next day Egypt and Syria declared themselves to be in "combat readiness." Such precise words might mean nothing, for overblown rhetoric and even bluff were almost standard elements of Arabic chest-beating. Yet on May 19, the UNEF (United Nations Emergency Force), which had been in place for almost ten years to monitor the armistice stemming from an earlier war, was officially withdrawn at the request of Egyptian President Nasser. That was ominous.

A premonition that war was imminent must have sent me to my office on Saturday night, May 20, 1967. War meant money, and I valued the time in a quiet office that would permit me to examine our accounts carefully. I was looking for cities or individuals owing the UJA large amounts from pledges previously made and not yet redeemed. About two-thirds of a given year's pledges were paid within that year. Most of the balance was paid off within the subsequent year. But that balance consisted of tens of millions of dollars, and if an authentic emergency arose, we would have to pull in as many of the outstanding pledges as possible.

The communities also had balances due the UJA in the form of allocations from previous campaigns. I wanted to scan the lists for the places with large amounts outstanding. I found about $20 million that I judged could be brought in quickly – within a few days, if truly necessary – and an additional $5 million that might take a couple of weeks and require some pressure.

Contemplating a possible $25 million, I started to make notes regarding assignments, that is, which UJA officer was best positioned to take which account. Suddenly the security officer outside my locked door called to announce that a visitor was seeking admittance with an urgent message. Francine alone knew where I was, and she would have given the information only to someone trustworthy. As it turned out, the visitor was Mike Arnon, Israel's consul-general in New York, a close friend. What the devil was he doing here late on a Saturday night?

Plenty. Mike carried a cable from Prime Minister Eshkol. It had come to the consulate in code, with instructions that Arnon deliver it to me in person. The cable asked if I could deposit in the Bank of Montreal $24 million to the account of the Jewish Agency, so that the money would be available to the agency at the start of business Monday morning. Money the UJA sent to the Jewish Agency for social-welfare use enabled the government of Israel to shift its funds to defense needs. President Johnson, for various and complex reasons, preferred that the sale to Israel of fighter aircraft not be made directly by a U.S. manufacturer, who would require an export permit license from the State Department. Instead, the sale would be made by a Canadian company manufacturing the identical aircraft under American license. The Canadian Government agreed.

In January 1964, Prime Minister Eshkol had met with President Johnson at the latter's Texas ranch. The main subject was Israel's security situation. Nasser was threatening to destroy Israel. Eshkol was pushing for offensive equipment, especially aircraft. Up to that point, the United States had not given or sold any such materiel to Israel.

Johnson interrupted their conversation, which was taking place in the ranch kitchen, sitting around the stove in rocking chairs like the two old farmers they were, because he wanted a breather from the pressure Eshkol was exerting. Johnson suggested they take a jeep ride around the spread, to see some of his prize herd. As they drove across the scrubby land, Eshkol noticed a rifle in a scabbard alongside Johnson's left leg and asked why that was necessary. LBJ replied that his ranch contained lots of coyotes – dangerous to the cattle – and that one always had to be prepared to deal with them.

When the conversation resumed over lunch, Eshkol made his bid for numerous Skyhawks and Phantoms, America's best military aircraft, pushing hard. And when Johnson asked why he needed so many, at such expense and so quickly, Eshkol said quietly that he had lots of coyotes in his neighborhood and had to be prepared to deal with them. Johnson chuckled, and Eshkol left for home with a firm promise – Israel's first ever – to get American aircraft. Now, three years later, the promise had yet to be honored, and those planes were desperately needed.

Eshkol also asked in the cable if I would come over to Jerusalem immediately. The word "war" was not used, but the implication was obvious. Mike was quiet, awaiting my reaction. At the same moment, Eshkol had been writing a cable on his yellow pad, while I was writing lists on mine – ESP operating at a distance of 6,000 miles! I wrote a return message for Mike to send: The money would be in the bank by the end of the day Monday, if not the beginning, and I was planning to leave for Israel immediately. By coincidence, I already had an appointment on Monday, May 22, with Pinchas Sapir, the finance minister, to discuss details concerning the implementation of the Israel Education Fund.

When I arrived at Ben-Gurion airport on May 21, I heard the rumor that Nasser was threatening to close the Straits of Tiran (which he did two days later), thus blockading the Gulf of Akaba and shutting down one of the two sea lungs through which Israel breathed. War suddenly seemed very real and close.

In Eshkol's office, the first fact I learned was one that had apparently shocked him more than any of the enemy threats. The chief chaplain of the Israel Defense Force, Rabbi Shlomo Goren (a major general) had asked the government to turn over to the army a large plot of land in Ramat Gan, near Tel Aviv, for use as a cemetery. Goren would consecrate the ground immediately as a sacred place for the interment of military and civilian casualties alike. Eshkol was familiar with the place and asked Goren why such a large plot was needed. The response: the Army anticipated – as a worst-case scenario, under massive, multi-nation attack – that the casualties might reach 40,000. That would amount to 2 percent of the entire population! Eshkol of course gave the permission; as it turned out, the casualties were far smaller. (Later the land was used to build a large sport stadium, dedicated to life, not death.)

The prime minister then briefed me on many other aspects of the situation. He concluded by suggesting that I go down to the Negev to see for myself how the Egyptian forces were massing in the Sinai desert and how the Israeli forces, increasingly mobilized every day, were training during this crisis period. I spent three days in the company of Col. Natan Zippori, commander of the artillery. He took me to a point on the Negev-Sinai border called Nitzana (El Auja in Arabic). It was as close as we could get. I was fascinated to learn that we were only a few kilometers from the famous oasis called Kadesh-Barnea, now on the Egyptian side, where Moses and the Children of Israel had spent 39 of their years in the desert before invading the Promised Land.

Standing on the highest dunes we could find, we could see clearly through binoculars the line of Egyptian tanks – T-55s from the Soviets, almost 1,000 in number – just about 3,000 meters distant. That is about the maximum range of a T-55's cannon, and if they had started firing at that moment, they could have hit us. Thus, they were deployed as far forward as they could be, in full view, filled with deadly intent and ready to spring.

I reported back to Eshkol and Chief of the General Staff Yitzhak Rabin, who with their staffs were now occupying the third floor of the Dan Hotel in Tel Aviv, in order to have key military and civilian personnel at hand. Filled with information and impressions, I was eager to return to New York to mobilize a massive, emergency war effort on top of the just-completed annual campaign, with all the proceeds earmarked for Israel.

I assured the Israeli officials it would be the largest campaign ever conducted, surpassing even that of 1948. I needed only one more thing; the approval of my UJA chairman, Max Fisher, who was in Athens at that moment, preparing to depart on an Aegean Sea cruise with friends. Eshkol, Rabin, and Louis Pincus, head of the Jewish Agency, all suggested bringing Fisher to Tel Aviv for a short visit, so he could feel the atmosphere for himself. Promising to do just that, I left for Athens, hoping to return in a few hours.

I met Max in Athens later that day (Friday, May 26) in his hotel, where he was accompanied by a friend of his whom I did not know. I learned later that the friend was Nathan Cummings of the famous Montreal family. I was tense, keen to get down to business with Max, nervous about each passing hour, and this stranger was wandering through the suite, in his bathrobe, frequently interrupting. Finally, impatient, I asked him to leave us alone, for his languid mood contravened my purpose with Max.

At last Max and I settled down, and I told him straight off that a big war was imminent. He was incredulous, suggested I was exaggerating, explained that he felt nothing in the air – wars did not suddenly emerge out of nothing – and tried to placate me as though I was an over-excited child, emotionally stretching some minor incident into a major catastrophe. I tried to be calm, and told him everything I had heard from Eshkol and Rabin, everything I had seen in the Sinai, and everything I felt about his and my responsibility to act. I recited Nasser's threats and the timetable of events since Egypt had declared a state of emergency nine days ago. We talked for several hours, during which I focused on one request; that he come to Tel Aviv with me, talk privately with the key players, and make his own evaluation. By now, Nathan Cummings was beginning to be impressed by the seriousness of the situation and ceased being annoyed by my unexpected interference with their holiday plans.

They were waiting for the arrival of Mrs. Fisher and Henry Ford and his wife, following which the whole party would embark on a chartered yacht for a cruise through the Greek Islands. Max did not want to disappoint his wife and the Fords by delaying the cruise for a day while he jumped over to Tel Aviv with me. By now it was late in the evening, and the Fords and Mrs. Fisher were due from Rome the next morning.

Max suggested we sleep on the matter. I agreed but racked my brain for any idea that might move him. I decided to call the UJA deputy chairman, Edward Ginsberg, of Cleveland, only to find that international telephone service had been cut by a *coup d'etat* a few hours earlier; a clique of colonels was trying to take over the Greek Government!

It took most of the night for me to get a call through, the difficulties being compounded by the fact that Eddie was out enjoying his 50th birthday party. That complication turned out to be helpful. Several of the UJA national chairmen were present at the party, and I was able to make my case to them as well as to Eddie. Those younger fellows, including Ollie Adelman, Barney Barnett, Paul Zuckerman, Mel Dubinsky, and Irving Bernstein, understood me better, knew I was not hysterical, appreciated my zeal and eagerness, and supported my contention that we were obligated to launch an emergency war campaign.

Next morning, to make certain Max understood the gravity of the Israeli situation, I recapitulated the sequence of recent events:

May 15 – Nasser ordered mobilization

16 – Egypt declared state of emergency

17 – Egypt and Syria declared themselves to be in "combat readiness"

19 – Egypt ordered UN force to withdraw, and Secretary General U Thant complied the same day

20 – Israel ordered partial mobilization

21 – Egypt had 80,000 troops in Sinai

22 – Nasser closed the Straits of Tiran

As it turned out, Max had changed his own mind after overnight reflection. His concern for Israel was genuine, and he understood that his cooperation was needed – all the more when I informed him of the support of Ginsberg and other UJA national officers. We then agreed to go to the Athens airport to await the arrival of the Rome contingent and ask for their cooperation.

As they descended from their plane, I took Mrs. Fisher aside and quickly obtained her acquiescence. Although Henry Ford and I were not close friends, we had known each other since we were classmates at Yale. Back in those antediluvian days of the 1930s, discipline rather than permissiveness prevailed, and seating in class was both alphabetical and fixed. That made Ford and Friedman close neighbors.

Henry now quickly agreed that it was Max's duty to hop over to Tel Aviv and that the loss of a day on the cruise was meaningless. With everything congenially arranged, Max and I took off for Tel Aviv, while the others went to the hotel in Athens. We were all a bit worried and edgy.

Max and I went immediately to the Dan Hotel to meet with Eshkol, Rabin, and Pincus. The full story unfolded quickly, and Max was convinced. It was not only the factual data, or the hours of brainstorming and devising different scenarios, but also the mood and atmosphere that swayed him. The highest officers of the general staff were in the next rooms, shaping their alternatives, while Rabin stayed with Eshkol and us to answer questions or offer opinions. There was a sense of strength and determination – deadly serious but not grim – in the way the military and civilian personnel handled the problems and made their decisions.

Pincus, the Jewish Agency chief, wanted an estimate of how much money we thought could be raised and how fast. When I said it was impossible to answer until I got back to the States and took the temperature in a number of communities, his demeanor was not agitated but understanding. I promised him an estimate in a few days.

To jump to the end of the story, the UJA share of the regular 1967 campaign, just then ending, would be about $75 million, and the emergency war campaign hopefully would run around $175 million. That total of a quarter-billion dollars would be the highest amount raised in UJA history, including the year Israel was born. Before the day ended, we had made numerous plans: to bring to the United States speakers whom we would dispatch throughout the country to tell the story; an hourly transmission from Jerusalem to my office, information that I could pass on through a nationwide telex network to our American communities; and to employ a brand-new piece of technology, the videotape.

The new device was most interesting and useful. At that time, Sony Corporation's American operations had only about 50 VCR's. We bought them all, placed them in federation offices throughout the country, and sent a daily, five-to-ten minute cassette to every city with a machine. It was a taped message, made in my office by an Israeli officer or political leader; a piece of film we got from Israel by overnight pouch; or an excerpt from a TV network-news department. To establish and maintain a mood of crisis and need, fast communication was mandatory.

Max returned to Athens and his cruise. I went to New York to get started on the fundraising. The next day, Sunday, May 28, the Israeli cabinet discussed the question of declaring war, and the vote was 9-9. No democratic nation goes to war on such a vote. Essentially, the cabinet decided to continue mobilizing to the full national potential and see whether Western support would be forthcoming.

From the very beginning of Israel's existence, Abba Eban's public life has been devoted to the promotion of her position on the international stage. As ambassador to the UN and the United States, as foreign minister and deputy prime minister, his voice had resonated around the entire globe, explaining, elaborating, elucidating, teaching, cajoling, pleading. He is an authentic intellectual, author of many books, commentator on television series that he himself has conceived and written. And although he has detractors inside Israel because of his liberal views on the Palestinian question and his Western manners, the high offices he has held remain solid testimony to the quality of his mind and lucidity of his speech.

Eban went abroad to assess the feelings among the three major powers, explain how Israel analyzed Egyptian intentions, stress Israel's sense of danger and range of possible responses, and seek political help in fending off an attack and material help if one came. The round trip would be completed in less than a week, and an evaluation of the results would determine Israel's next steps.

In Paris, de Gaulle was domineering, obstinate, totally unhelpful, and, as a matter of fact, threatening. He said that if Israel fired the first shot she would lose any chance of obtaining assistance from France. His stance was a clear foreshadowing of France's future intimacy with Arab states, which resulted in her supplying Iraq with the atomic reactor that Israel was destined to destroy in 1981. In London, Harold Wilson, the prime minister and well-known friend of Israel's Labor Party, pleaded poverty, explaining regretfully that England had declined into a mini-power that simply could not help, no matter how much she wanted to.

Finally, in Washington, a friendly and seriously interested Lyndon Johnson offered to round up a group of naval powers and create a multi-national armada that would challenge the Egyptian blockade of the Gulf of Akaba. Eban would surely understand, Johnson said, that the Vietnam bog was consuming more and more of his presidential energy; but he nevertheless would find the time to deal with Israel's needs and felt pretty certain that he could organize something within three weeks. Eban's reply indicated uncertainty whether Israel had three days, let alone three weeks. Johnson did try, but in the end the only nation he could persuade to join the U.S. challenge to Egypt was Holland.

When Eban returned to Israel and reported the essentially negative results of his probe, the cabinet voted 16-2 at its meeting on Sunday, June 4, in favor of going to war the next day, for it was clear that she would have to take her destiny into her own hands. There would be no timely help from the Western democratic powers.

The military had already decided that, if the government ordered a pre-emptive strike, it would come at 08:45 Israeli time – 07:45 Cairo time. There were five reasons for the time selection: Egyptian reconnaissance patrols that took off at dawn, as well as flights in readiness on the runway, were both standing down by this time; the Israeli pilots, who would have a long day's work ahead of them, could sleep until 04:00; the morning mist would have dissipated, the angle of the sun improved, and the air stilled; the Egyptian generals, commanders, and staffs begin work at 09:00 – so that at 07:45, they're still caught in the maddening Cairo traffic; the Egyptian pilots would have the morning sun in their eyes.

The ruling doctrine of the pre-emptive strike was to gain control of the air immediately. (Does that resemble the air-land doctrine of the 1990-91 Gulf War?) The primary objectives were to destroy Arab aircraft on the ground and render the runways inoperable. For the latter purpose, special bombs with delayed fuses had been designed to penetrate concrete and to keep exploding at pre-determined times, making runway repair very difficult, if not impossible.

At the appointed hour, Israeli aircraft flew about 50 feet above the ground, under the radar and therefore largely undetected, destroying the scanners as they came in. By early Monday afternoon, all 23 Egyptian radars (16 of them in the Sinai Desert) had been knocked out, as well as 22 airfields. 416 Egyptian aircraft were destroyed – 393 on the ground and 23 in dogfights.

All that took place in two hours and 50 minutes on the first morning. Another 53 Arab aircraft were subsequently shot down in dogfights. With total control of the air gained on the first day, the Israeli ground forces were free to concentrate during the next five days on destroying tanks and artillery. When they climbed the Golan Heights on the sixth day, the ground forces pushed the Syrians back to a point 25 kilometers from Damascus.

The Israeli airforce lost 46 planes and 24 pilots, half of them taken prisoner and the other half casualties. None of those losses occurred during dogfights; all resulted from ground fire or being "jumped" from above while concentrating on ground targets. The world's military professionals have attributed that remarkable record to the following factors:

1. Sixteen years of planning and practicing, largely under the command of Gen. Ezer Weizman, nephew of Israel's first president, a flamboyant, cheerful, morale-building, British-trained pilot who later became president in his own right.

2. Superb intelligence in every detail concerning the layouts of the enemy's air fields, the personnel files of its pilots, and anything else anyone could think of.

3. Total operational control – flight controllers always in touch with pilots, exchanging information – so that all planes in the air benefited from the experiences of all others.

4. A turnaround time of 7 1/2 minutes for refueling and re-arming, far, far below accepted norms, enabling pilots to fly many more sorties.

Randolph and Winston Churchill (son and grandson of Sir Winston) wrote an incisive report entitled simply *The Six Day War*. In a closing chapter, they recounted a fascinating post-war conversation with Ben-Gurion that included this exchange:

Question: "Do you see this great victory as being a turning point in your history?"

Answer: "In a way, yes, but if I could prevent this war, I would prefer to remain as we are, without any conquests, because we've paid a very high price for that; the best of our youth was killed, something like 700 people...I prefer peace to any war; even if the war is a beneficent one, it's too high a price." Ben-Gurion insisted that two requirements be satisfied before Israel would surrender any captured territory: The Arabs must recognize the state of Israel; and a genuine peace treaty must be signed. Such was the vision of this giant.

Back in the United States, the emergency war fundraising campaign needed only about five weeks to raise most of the $175 million it ultimately produced. The Jewish community was on fire. Spontaneity and generosity were the hallmarks. I often said, in subsequent years, that the UJA really did not "raise" the money, in the sense that we organized and stimulated and explained, in our customary fashion. On this occasion, the people simply stood up – and lined up – and gave: in synagogues, community centers, day schools, and federation offices, or to any individual known to be a community leader.

It was a heartwarming sight, and contained a deep element of relief that the awful fear of a national destruction had been avoided. No doubt, fear and the miraculous escape from danger were powerful stimulants. But the positive aspects of love for and identification with the people and land of Israel were equally strong, and as the fear slowly died, they constituted a heritage for the future.

The fundamental attitude of American Jewry toward Israel, which surged for a short time at the birth in 1948 but never took hold thereafter in any really solid and permanent manner, came to maturity with the Six-Day War, and has remained rock-solid ever since. Yes, there are disagreements with governmental policies: for example, not dealing with the Palestinians; heeding the religious parties and their demands; not loosening the controls of a centralized economy. But disagreements such as those, and others, do not weaken the overall ties that bind.

In the New York headquarters of the UJA, the fundraising was intense. Eddie Ginsberg led a wonderful team of lay leaders. He and I sat in my office wearing the Australian-type canvas campaign hats, with the upturned side-brim much favored by the Israel Defense Forces, working through long days and most nights in the board rooms where 50 telephones had been installed in only a few hours. The Israeli Government sent us Finance Minister Pinchas Sapir, former Chief of Staff Lt. Gen. Haim Laskov, Jewish Agency Chairman Louis Pincus, and others. They made their solicitations of selected donors, their videotaped speeches to be distributed, their airplane flights night and day. American Jews gathered at airports at two in the afternoon or four in the morning to listen to the message and pledge their money. The lay leaders volunteered countless hours, each one making dozens of calls per day, blanketing the country. Nobody refused to work or give.

Interestingly, we received only a single million-dollar gift – from Walter Annenberg. A million was then an unheard-of amount to a philanthropy that gathered funds every year; it was capital-gift, not annual-gift standard. Yet Annenberg, later to become U.S. ambassador to England, responded affirmatively to his friend Albert Parker, a New York lawyer, who called as a member of the telephone squad. Annenberg has remained ever since one of America's largest contributors to Israel.

American Christians and American blacks and even American Moslems gave. Children brought in their piggy banks. Women pawned jewelry. People mortgaged their homes. It was incredible.

Things quieted down toward the end of July, by which time many leading donors were requesting that a mission be formed. So Eddie and I took a large group to the Sinai, where we saw miles of burnt-out Arab tanks and trucks, and destroyed aircraft on the runways of four airfields. Our group took great satisfaction in that, and in a few days, every member became an arm-chair general, prophesying that the Arabs would never again challenge Israel's military prowess.

Only two months later, however, the Arab summit meeting was held at Khartoum in the Sudan, resulting in the famous "Three No's": no negotiations with Israel; no settlement; no peace. The no's meant more war, and that is exactly what I prophesied two months later at a quarterly meeting of the Council of Federations in Cleveland.

Representatives from all the major Jewish communities in the country were present. There was legitimate joy at the Israeli victory, and there was talk about planning the future, deciding what priorities now had to be faced, and whether money would be available after the recent massive outpouring. I rose to assert vigorously that Israel would be under fire again by next summer – nine months hence – and gave all my reasons for that conviction.

Further, I proposed a resolution that would authorize another emergency fund for Israel, the following year. The local communities would not share in the fund, because Israel would need every penny to maintain herself at a proper level of preparedness. That proposal brought a huge outcry, including shouts from the floor that I was a "warmonger" and was promoting war simply as a means of keeping campaign totals high, so that the UJA would look good. Some people charged that I did not care about what happened to the infrastructure of the local community services, only about Israel. The argument finally ended when a parliamentarian noted that the meeting had no authority to pass any such resolution.

That was perfectly okay with me. I had fired my shot across the bow. The proper resolutions were passed later in the proper forum. An emergency fund was authorized and raised in 1968, and the first artillery duels in what was later named the War of Attrition did indeed take place that summer.

CHAPTER THIRTY-ONE

GOLDA MEIR: MILLION-DOLLAR DINNERS AND SAVING JORDAN

The year 1970 brought two unusual events: one in fundraising, the other in Israel's geopolitical relation to the United States and the Kingdom of Jordan, respectively. Both events took place in September, and both involved the personal participation of the prime minister, Golda Meir. There was a third matter, not a defined event but rather the beginning of a trend: Jewish migration from the Soviet Union. It began in the middle of the year and reached a steady flow by the beginning of 1971. That migration was of major historic importance, and I will discuss it shortly.

As for the first item, I had been haunted since the emergency campaign following the Six-Day War by the fact that there had been no million-dollar contributions in the several subsequent years. I had entertained all sorts of mental explanations and rationalizations, admitting the extraordinary euphoria, adrenalin, and joy that followed the victory. Still, once a precedent had been set for seven-figure giving, I felt that the momentum would produce similar levels in following years. The problem consumed me, and I spent a great deal of time analyzing it from every angle – but failed to find the solution. I suddenly realized the futility of looking backward, seeking the clue to why something had not happened, instead of concentrating on how to *make* it happen in the future. My head began to swirl with creative ideas.

I had learned during the past 15 years of work in the UJA that when I wanted to achieve a new goal, I first had to plan the strategy down to the last possible detail and then personally determine the feasibility of the tactics. Thus, if I wanted to get big donors to accept million-dollar giving so that it would occur each year, I had to obtain such pledges in the framework of normal campaigning, without depending on the stimulus of war, immigration, or huge tragedy.

Easier said than done, of course. But at least I was now on familiar ground and could start figuring out how to put on a dinner for million-dollar prospects. I believe firmly in announcing in advance what was expected of those attending a fundraising function. When invitations were printed, I always insisted that the card carry a discreet notice indicating the level of expectation. The highest figure I had ever specified was at a luncheon for a small, select list at New York's 21 Club, where a note in a corner of the invitation read "$250,000 minimum." Now I had to create an event where each invited guest would know that he/she was expected to meet the level of one million.

After conceiving and rejecting a dozen complex formulas, I settled on a simple one: three dinner parties on consecutive evenings in private homes in cities with the nation's largest Jewish communities: New York, Los Angeles, and Chicago. The success of the plan would depend on these factors: the identity of the host, the names of the guests, the star who would grace the evening.

I decided that the star should be none other than the prime minister of Israel, Golda Meir herself, whose world-wide reputation was at its height. If she were willing to lend herself to the project, my chosen hosts would feel so honored they would almost certainly cooperate. After careful analysis, I decided that Meshulam Riklis' town house was the right place in New York, as were the Chicago suburban home of Colonel Henry Crown and the Beverly Hills mansion of Max Firestein.

Riklis migrated to the United States from pre-Israel Palestine as a young man, started life as a Hebrew teacher in Minneapolis, and became tremendously wealthy in real estate enterprises. Crown was head of the

General Dynamics Corporation, having served in World War II, with his military rank simply following him into civilian life. Firestein was head of the Max Factor cosmetic company; I had first met him in a stormy confrontation described in chapter 16. All three men were enormously wealthy and deeply devoted to Jewish/Israeli causes. They were already large donors to the UJA.

I visited each of the three, explaining at great length that they would be participating in a plan intended to trigger a quantum jump in fundraising on behalf of Israel. If we could make seven-figure gifts a normal level in the annual campaign, many more *six*-figure donors would be approachable for the higher amount, and five-figure giving would expand exponentially.

In other words, these men would be pioneers whose individual gifts in the amount requested, plus the use of their private homes enabling others to be drawn into the magic circle, would raise many, many more millions of dollars. All three understood what was at stake, agreed with the wide-ranging additional goals, and had large enough egos to relish the pleasure of being complimented by the prime minister as well as by their business and professional peers. Each man agreed to contribute the million and the home. The plan was launched. You can imagine my great satisfaction.

When Golda heard about the plan, she agreed immediately. I had obtained permission from the Federal Aviation Administration for El Al airlines to be granted one-time landing rights in Los Angeles and Chicago, so that the prime minister's customary level of security could be maintained. (Today such an exception would not be necessary, for El Al has regularly scheduled service to many U.S. cities; but at that time, it was a friendly American governmental gesture.) Golda would fly from Tel Aviv to Los Angeles for the dinner there on September 15, then to Chicago and New York on subsequent evenings. With her enrolled, the final element remained to be crafted: the list of invitees in each city.

Names suggested themselves, but research had to be done on such matters as financial standing; social background, especially concerning relationship to the host; and the number of close family members who would expect to be included if a family gift were contemplated. Because that was all delicate stuff, I did most of it myself. And once the short list of prospects was completed, I made yet another of my many trips to each of the three cities to solicit each individual personally.

At the dinner parties, I decided nothing was to be said concerning money. All the soliciting needed to be done in advance. It was tricky because the person I was talking with, face to face, was receiving only a conditional invitation. He and his wife (and perhaps other close relatives) were being invited to a most prestigious home to spend an evening in intimate conversation with the premier figure in the Jewish world – on condition that they make the minimum contribution. It demanded a stiff backbone to speak tactfully, yet straight to the point, to avoid misunderstanding. When all the solicitations were done, my sigh of relief was explosive.

Los Angeles resulted in three acceptances, in addition to the host, so it was a dinner for 12 persons that produced $4 million.

Chicago provided a completely different story. I stayed in town four days, and met with 24 persons, without obtaining one acceptance. At the end of that debilitating experience, for which I had no rational explanation, I visited once more with Col. Crown, told him the facts, and suggested that Mrs. Meir would overfly Chicago. I thanked him warmly, said that he should feel no obligation to adhere to the dinner conditions, and that a repetition of his previous year's gift of one-half million would be considered extremely generous. That's exactly what he did, and I assured him that we would arrange for him to meet with the prime minister privately on another occasion.

The New York effort was much easier because of the presence of William Rosenwald, the spiritual father of the UJA, the last of the trio whose signatures had created the UJA back in 1938. His unbroken association with its work, year after year, decade after decade, earned him the title of pre-eminent lay leader of American Jewry. He helped me cull and sift, and when all was done, the Riklis dinner produced four gifts besides the host's. Thus, New York and Los Angeles combined added nine million-dollar contributions to the normal 1971 campaign – a major breakthrough.

A word of tribute is due the hosts, whose role was indispensable. Their reward was not only their satisfaction at our success but also in the manner in which Golda bestowed her personal gratitude upon them. The setting of the two parties was perfect in its informality. One dinner table accommodated all guests in each home. The cocktail conversation was easy and natural, a sort of family gathering. After dinner, all sat around Golda in a circle of comfortable chairs and sofas, while she chatted, told stories, laughed and chain smoked. They asked questions, and she replied frankly, without diplomatic evasions. She treated them as insiders, colleagues and close friends.

Those who had had previous contact with her were quite familiar with the fact that she could be testy and abrupt, intolerant toward people who asked delicate questions; that she didn't suffer fools lightly; and that social chit-chat was not her long suit. Nevertheless, on those two evenings, she was tolerant as well as brilliant, at her sparkling best, and truly enjoying herself. She appreciated the extraordinary effort every guest had made to achieve a critical goal for Israel and the Jewish people. She even agreed, smiling all the while, to sit on a sofa for a separate "photo op" with each couple, however long it took. Some weeks later, the proud couple received the photo, personally autographed by her to them.

The second Golda Meir event was of a geopolitical nature. It took place on Sunday evening, September 20, at the New York Hilton Hotel. Once Golda had agreed to come to the United States for the fundraising dinners, I wanted to exploit her presence by exposing her to a much wider audience. So we planned a national dinner, with a closed-circuit cable hook-up to as many communities across the country as wanted to be tied in. We rented the transcontinental cable for one hour, and each community set up a location with an oversized screen to accommodate large numbers of viewers.

As it turned out, Golda spoke that evening to about 1,000 persons in the Hilton ballroom and another 20,000 in 40 cities across the country. The live audience was in a gala mood. The dais almost overflowed with top national and local Jewish lay leaders, as well as Israeli and American governmental figures. She began a comprehensive review of the past few years: the Six-Day War and War of Attrition; economic pressures; social welfare and educational problems; internal political affairs. Then she turned to future military needs and immigrant absorption, indicating that Israelis would have to accept higher taxes to handle the military problem, while American Jewry would have to respond even more generously to handle the civilian matters. Because we had booked the cable for a full hour, she timed her remarks carefully in order to cover her complete agenda.

About ten minutes before she was due to finish, I noticed some movement and whispering in the area behind the dais and learned that both the Israeli and American Secret Service agents were receiving messages through their earphones that the White House was trying to reach our honored guest. I sent a message to the two chief agents to tell the White House that she was in the midst of a nationwide, closed-circuit speech and would be finished shortly, and that she was due to leave immediately after the speech for Kennedy airport, where an El Al plane was being held for her departure; nonetheless, I would try to take her first to a room where she could return the call.

Here's what was happening: The PLO's Al Fatah military wing was planning a coup to take over Jordan, and the revolt the group organized had broken out two weeks before. Fighting and scuffling took place between Palestinians in refugee camps and the Bedouin troops loyal to King Hussein. Defense Minister Moshe Dayan and Gen. Ariel Sharon believed that the Palestinians deserved help. Gen. Aharon Yariv, the head of military intelligence, did not agree. After a week or so of skirmishing, rumors started that Syria would intervene on the side of the PLO – a serious threat to the Jordanian throne. At that point, King Hussein called Washington and asked Secretary of State Henry Kissinger for his assistance in persuading Israel to come to Jordan's aid.

That's why the White House was calling Mrs. Meir. Speaking on behalf of President Nixon, as well as himself, Henry Kissinger first briefed her on the most alarming developments: Syrian armored columns were crossing the Jordanian border and moving south toward the capital of Amman. Then Kissinger requested that Israel intervene militarily to deflect the Syrians and force them back, thus defending the integrity of Jordan.

The implications of that request were enormous. Jordan was an enemy. Why spill Israeli blood to defend her? How determined was Syria? Was she willing to fight Israel? And yet, this was the United States asking. How could Israel refuse her best friend and strongest ally?

I shall long remember that scene in the small room at the Hilton hotel; the tired woman slumped in a chair, worn down by a long hard week of traveling and fundraising and now having finished a tense, hour-long TV speech, to be faced with an agonizing request from Nixon and Kissinger.

She asked for time to think. Kissinger said there was precious little of that commodity: the Syrians were already marching. She said she wanted to speak immediately with her deputy, Gen. Yigal Allon, because she was about to board a commercial aircraft with no secure communication and would therefore be out of touch for 10 or 11 hours. Kissinger acquiesced. Golda reached Allon and told him that her instinct was to intervene.

She felt that she knew the King, whom she had met several times over 20-odd years, and that someday he would make peace with Israel. She asked Allon whether he had the capability to throw sufficient force across the Syrian line in time, and he replied affirmatively: brigades on the Golan Heights could be dispatched almost immediately. She ordered him to do so.

Returning to the White House phone, Golda took on a new bearing and demeanor. She was not the tired old lady slumping in the chair but the head of government, commander-in-chief of the army, a leader with her mind made up. With a crisp authority in her voice, she began by saying that, although she had given the order to stop the Syrians, no one knows how combat will escalate, where it will spread and to what degree. She therefore demanded American assurance on three points. The United States was to:

- Inform the Soviet Union why Israeli troops were on the move against Syria, a Soviet client state, and to say forcefully that the U.S. did not expect the Soviets to make a move, just as the U.S. was not making one to support *its* client, Jordan.
- Provide large-scale bombing maps of the entire region, which Israel did not possess and might need if the conflict spread to other countries. She suggested that such maps probably existed at U.S. Sixth-Fleet headquarters in Naples and could be flown to Tel Aviv in a few hours. She asked that the planes carrying them fly over Turkey, so that the Russians could see them.
- Replenish Israeli materiel, including the heaviest items such as tanks and aircraft. Further, the U.S. would come to Israel's aid in the event

that Egypt jumped Israel from the west or any wider conflict developed with other Arab countries in the region.

Nixon and Kissinger huddled, accepted those conditions, thanked Golda for her courage and speedy action, and wished her bon voyage. Upon arriving home, she was met by Gen. Allon, who passed on the good news that the Syrians, when they learned that Israeli troops were en route to interdict their columns, turned 180 degrees and headed back north. No shots were fired.

Shortly thereafter, King Hussein launched a massive attack against the PLO and Palestinian military camps in northern Jordan, scattering the PLO leadership and soldiers, most of whom fled to Lebanon. That country became home base until the 1980's, when the Israeli army drove them to Tunisia.

A few days later, Golda received a thank-you note from King Hussein.

LIVING THE DREAM

CHAPTER THIRTY-TWO

MOVING TO ISRAEL

In the late 1960s, I began to think seriously about making major changes in my life. I had worked for the UJA for almost 25 years: eight as volunteer chairman of the National Speaker's Bureau, while serving as rabbi of very large congregations in Denver and Milwaukee; and for the next 16, as chief executive officer, moving the annual campaign from $40 million to almost a half-billion dollars, while teaching and motivating the thousands of lay leaders who secured that achievement.

Those 16 years were intense. I created and developed the major UJA programs that functioned for the next decades: missions to European concentration-camp sites, to Israel, to North African countries; the Young Leadership Cabinet; the National Rabbinic Cabinet; the Israel Education Fund, and many others. I traveled tens of thousands of miles every year; made speeches in scores of cities; raised millions of dollars from major donors; poured great amounts of physical and mental energy into galvanizing my professional staff and lay leaders alike.

During that period, I was divorced and remarried, and fathered two sons to add to the three children of my first marriage. There were periods when guilt overtook me, because in times of crisis and extreme pressure (wars, huge immigration surges, political threats to some endangered Jewish community), my family saw me only fleetingly.

My second wife, Francine, and I determined to live in Israel. It was not enough that I visited that country several times a year in the course of my work and made innumerable speeches about the centrality of Israel in the collective life of the Jewish people. Since direct action was my forte, I felt I could no longer merely *talk* about Israel but must live there, among millions of other Jews. Perhaps I needed rejuvenation; or perhaps an elementary sense of mortality reminded me that it would be better to go now, while in my early 50s, rather than wait for some indefinite future time.

I started discussions with Irving Bernstein, my deputy for the past six years, and Edward Ginsberg, my friend of many years who was at that time UJA general chairman. Eventually, Max Fisher, the previous chairman, was drawn into the conversation. I explained Francine's and my reasons for wanting to settle in Israel and cited the ages of our sons, David and Charles. We wanted them to integrate smoothly with their peers in the Hebrew language, and as everyone knows, the younger the child, the easier for him or her to make a new language at least something like a mother tongue.

I outlined my plan for remaining at the helm of the UJA while residing in Israel. I had already created the main mechanisms and structures for the day-to-day operation of the annual campaign. This could be left to Irving, who understood the ideas behind each program and worked well with the various staffs. My future contribution would be in the realm of creative new ideas, suggestions, detailed plans to keep the organization fresh and abreast of changing conditions -- inside Israel as well as in the scattered countries where the Joint Distribution Committee was working.

I pointed out that since increasing numbers of American missions were coming to Israel, I could be useful there in planning itineraries and soliciting the bigger contributors through the systems I had previously inaugurated of "back-seat-in-the-bus" and "caucus-in-the-hotel."

When a busload of mission members were traveling on a day's itinerary, the back bench would be held empty, and selected individuals would be invited there one at a time for a private conversation with the chairman or myself to settle that individual's contribution to the current UJA campaign. After several days of such solicitations, we held a caucus in the hotel, with every individual speaking publicly about his/her feelings and opinions, and pledging the

personal contribution that had been decided earlier at the back of the bus. After
several hours of caucusing, during which emotions poured out and enthusiasm
compounded, many persons increased what they had committed to on the bus.
The caucus was a device for ventilation and self-expression. The best time to
convene it was the last day of the mission.

I noted further that living *in* Israel would expand my knowledge of the
government, the Army, and the Jewish Agency, as well as my friendships with
their leaders. Those leaders had been enormously helpful to the UJA in
running the U.S. campaign, and my more frequent contact with them in Israel
would strengthen their understanding of American Jews. Finally, I'd be
available to visiting American Jewish communal leaders to arrange social
meetings with top Israelis, which could only strengthen that nebulous but vital
concept called "Israel-Diaspora relations."

I therefore suggested that my moving to Israel would actually *help* the UJA.
The most important skills I possessed would remain with me, wherever I lived.

I suggested the logistical arrangements as follows:

1. Irving Bernstein would be based in New York as executive vice-
    chairman. Irving wanted that title badly, and there was no reason for
    him not to have it. I would have to invent a different one for myself:
    executive chairman, in contrast to the chief lay leader who was
    called general chairman.

2. I would be based in Jerusalem, occupying an office in the Jewish
    Agency building that David Ben-Gurion had used when he served
    as chairman of the agency in the days before statehood. I could not
    understand why that historic room had been neglected, often left
    empty, or utilized by a pool of clerical workers. To me, Ben-Gurion
    was the founder of the country, and his room was a shrine. Yet there
    was not even a small plaque to indicate its provenance. I later
    arranged for a proper memorial marker that paid tribute to the great
    man's vision. I was thrilled to enter "his" room every day.

    Irving and I would be in touch by telex and telephone – every
    day, if necessary. In addition, I would fly to New York each month

for one or two days to address problems, put out fires, exchange ideas, and discuss long-range plans.

3. Chaim Vinitsky, director of the UJA office in Israel, would remain in his office with his staff. Chaim was a skillful manager who opened doors to prime ministers, obtained rooms when every hotel was overbooked, and was dearly beloved by thousands of American lay leaders whom he had helped in personal ways over the decades.

4. I would invite a senior staff person to accompany me to Israel. Rabbi Matthew Simon of Washington, DC, jumped at the opportunity. He and his family rented quarters in Jerusalem.

I would thus remain as CEO, making the policy decisions and fashioning the outlines of each year's campaign as I envisioned it. Rumors about the Friedman family's intention reached Israel, even the prime minister's office. When the PM, Golda Meir, came to the United States in September, for the special program described in the previous chapter, she broached the matter to me in her customary, blunt style. There was absolutely no sense, she said, in my moving to Israel. Nothing I could possibly do there could be as important for Israel and the Jewish people as my remaining on duty at the UJA. I was a commander in battle and could be relieved only when a person of equivalent rank and experience was available. And so forth.

Everything she said was filled with praise and compliments, yet her inflexibility rubbed me the wrong way. And she resisted every explanation I tried to offer. Finally, in an effort to soften the tone of the argument, I reminded her, with a smile, that I would invoke my rights under the Law of Return – the Knesset (Parliament) legislation that gives any Jew the right to admission if he/she shows up at Israel's borders.

Golda turned away in annoyance. Our discussion was finished. I, of course, understood her position and was flattered at the high value she placed on my work. But I yearned to experience life in Israel with my family, and I was convinced that I could continue to lead the UJA from that base. Fisher, Ginsberg, and Bernstein agreed, and accepted my proposal.

Our family plans began to crystallize. Francine, who had made the first of several lengthy visits to Israel at age 19, strongly favored moving there. Her father, Charlie Bensley, a staunch supporter of the country, made a gesture that was generous beyond all expectation. He told his daughter that he would be happy to provide us with a home, in New York or in Israel.

That brought our dream to life. We opted for Israel and decided to build in Caesarea, on the Mediterranean coast, halfway between Tel Aviv and Haifa. A century earlier, Baron Edmond de Rothschild, dubbed *Ha-Nadiv Ha-Yadua* (the well-known benefactor), had purchased many thousands of acres in the region, enabling him to start several farm villages in a plan to colonize the Holy Land. The property had come down through inheritance to his grandson, also Baron Edmond, who decided to develop one section, namely the immediate area of Caesarea.

Once the Roman capital of Judea, the city had a rich and varied history. The famous Tenth Legion (*Fratensis*) was stationed there. King Herod had built Caesarea as a fabulous tribute to the Emperor Augustus and named it for the Roman Caesars. The shining marble columns thrusting seaward on the quays were a welcoming sight to the triremes coming from Rome, and the temples, theaters, amphitheater, and hippodrome served as fitting accoutrements to a city whose population at its height numbered a quarter-million Romans and Jews.

The Tenth Legion's corps of engineers had built an aqueduct, with two lines running down from the Carmel mountains 30 kilometers north, to bring fresh water to the city. Pontius Pilatus, the Roman governor who presided over the execution of Jesus, lived in the city. The legion marched 100 kilometers to Jerusalem, sacked it, and destroyed the temple. In 138 CE, after the Jewish Revolt against Rome failed, its leader, Rabbi Akiba, was flayed alive in the central square of Caesarea.

Some time thereafter, the city fell into ruins. Sand dunes drifted over everything, and no sound except the lonesome wailing of jackals was heard until the Crusaders arrived in the 13th century. King Louis IX of France built a fortress atop the Roman debris and surrounded it with a classic moat and drawbridge; Christian soldiers were based there until their final defeat by the

Moslems. Once again, the site was empty and desolate until the 19th century, when Moslems from Bosnia built a mosque and established a small colony.

Shortly thereafter, the original Baron Rothschild bought the large area that included the ruins, and it slowly began to be populated by the Jewish descendants of Akiba. In the mid-20th century, the young baron decided to develop Caesarea into what has become the most beautiful residential area in all of Israel.

He built a golf course in 1960 – still the only one in the country – and subdivided a tract into building sites. That year, I bought a site with an unobstructed view of the Mediterranean, the aqueduct, and the bougainvillea. The area between our property and the sea was reserved for future archaeological excavation, preserving it – and us – from any other construction. The half-acre plot cost $6,000 at the time.

In 1967, Francine and I began to talk in earnest with a Tel Aviv architect, Zvi Toren. I knew his work from the many schools and libraries he had built under the UJA's Israel Education Fund during the previous three years. A Czech by birth, Toren knew the Bauhaus style and, most important to us, had a paternal sense of responsibility for every building he designed. He supervised the construction on a daily basis, a process that was vital in the Israeli building industry of those times.

We discussed details with Toren, both in Tel Aviv and in New York, to which we invited him for a few uninterrupted days of consultation. He designed for us a stunning, two-story, modern structure. Both exterior and interior utilized white brick (almost unknown in an Israeli interior). The house featured large sliding glass doors leading out to terraces, a garden with swimming pool, fireplaces downstairs and up, many bedrooms and bathrooms – and a bomb-proof shelter, as required by law. The house was finished by Chanukah (December) 1969.

After the first summer of acclimatization, it became clear to Francine, with her practical sense of the support system necessary to supply our needs, that Caesarea could not serve as a permanent base. There was no school for the boys, no market for shopping, and a sense of loneliness pervaded the area when the owners of several of the other houses were absent traveling. We realized that, when we returned to Israel for good the following year, we would need a residence in Jerusalem. That meant finding a rental flat and coming to the villa by the sea on weekends and holidays.

Everything proceeded according to plan, and in June 1971, the Friedman family embarked on its new adventure. We came as temporary residents but with the intention of ultimately accepting Israeli citizenship, while retaining our American. By treaty, both the American and Israeli Governments allowed a person to be a national of both countries and hold both of their passports. In Israel, the process began with a three-year period of temporary residence, following which the government conferred its citizenship. If a person did not choose to accept it, for whatever reason, he/she could opt for status as a permanent resident.

Although eligible for the benefits and loans available to new immigrants, we decided not to seek or accept a single penny of Israeli public funds. We paid our own passage and freight, bought our house in Caesarea with our own funds, and intended to pay rent for our flat in Jerusalem.

We found an apartment in Rehavia, the most central residential area in Jerusalem, around the corner from the Jewish Agency headquarters where my office was situated and one block from the Gymnasium Rehavia, where we enrolled our two boys in elementary school. The third-floor apartment comprised 880 sq.ft. and a narrow terrace, while the Caesarea villa comprised 3,850 sq.ft. and four terraces. To reach the villa required a four-hour round trip – out of a 24-hour weekend – but the one day was worth the effort.

Slowly, life assumed a routine. Francine was the first to lead a "normal" Israeli existence. Ruth Dayan, wife of the famous general, Moshe Dayan, had helped new immigrants develop a craft industry and had founded a chain of stores – called Maskit – to display its products. Maskit lacked an outlet in Jerusalem, so Ruth invited Francine to construct a shop in a handsome old Arab house and then to manage it. This new American immigrant entered the complex business of negotiating a lease with the Catholic Church, which owned the property; then worked with architects (one of whom was Martin Holt, a friend of ours from Caesarea) and contractors on the interior and selected an appealing inventory of jewelry, rugs, clothing, and souvenirs. The result was an instant success, and Francine and Maskit-Jerusalem were launched.

All of us Friedmans had language problems. Our family policy was to speak English at home – so the young boys, having come to Israel with only rudimentary skills in reading and writing English, could develop that language properly. The flip side of the policy was to speak Hebrew in public, on the street, in Maskit, and in school. We adults would have to struggle only with Hebrew, while the boys would have to conquer both languages simultaneously.

A particularly vivid language episode occurred a few years after our arrival. Francine was at work, and the boys and I were strolling up the long promenade toward the entrance to the marvelous Israel Museum, speaking Hebrew, according to our policy. My voice is resonant and penetrating. My Hebrew was not as fluent as theirs. Apparently embarrassed by my errors, the boys suddenly turned to me and suggested firmly that I would do better to speak English, even in public.

My mind flashed back almost 40 years, to a day when I was walking with my father across the Yale campus. Even though his English was fluent, a Vilna-born accent must have been discernible, for I turned and asked him not to speak so loudly as to be overheard by my fellow students.

Wow! Here was a vivid turning of the wheel of Jewish history. From Lithuania to Connecticut to Jerusalem, generations of wandering Jews, struggling with new languages, cultures, mores, repeating the same experience in each generation, making adjustments and renewals – and blunt requests.

CHAPTER THIRTY-THREE

BREAKING THE DEAL: MY RUSSIAN PLAN SCUTTLED

The power of the UJA, and its appeal to the contributors, stemmed partly from the fact that it dealt with monumental crises and thus shaped history. Responding to historic challenge was the core of every speech, advertisement, rally, film, and conference that I had the authority to design. The power of the UJA also stemmed from two other sources: the sovereignty of the State of Israel, for the state had altered the basic condition of the Jewish people from weakness to strength – the strength to control its own destiny and the organization's ability to communicate to ordinary Jews that they, too, could influence both past and future history.

Let me give you an example. When the UJA said that the vessel "Transylvania" was leaving the port of Constanza on the Black Sea every Sunday, carrying 2,000 Rumanian Jews, disembarking them at Haifa three days later, then turning around and sailing empty to Constanza to reload, every concerned American Jew could do the arithmetic: 2,000 people per week times 50 weeks meant 100,000 immigrants in one year from a single country. When we whispered quietly what we had agreed not to publicize – that it cost $1,200 to spring every single soul – our supporters understood that we were spending $120 million dollars on exit permits alone. When UJA speakers described that situation, at closed meetings, every listener knew it to be the truth. The speakers would leave rhetorical questions hanging in the air: "Are you worth $1,200? Suppose it was you who needed to be rescued? Wouldn't you like to believe that some other Jew, somewhere in the world, would be willing to pay that amount to bring you to freedom and safety in a Jewish state?"

I knew instinctively that connecting the rescue of endangered Jews with its costs would produce maximum contributions. Why? Because ingrained in the consciousness of most American Jews were the basic elements of *tzedakah* (doing justly by one's brother) and *mitzvah* (holy commandment). Even highly assimilated Jews responded to those stimuli.

When a small but steady flow of immigrants from the Soviet Union began to appear, in January 1971, trickling out by train from various points and converging in Vienna, they were greeted by Jewish Agency and JDC officials who provided food, shelter, and information. Safe and protected, the tired, anxious travelers could relax and listen to the plans for their flights to Israel.

In New York, when I learned the details of that operation, I had a palpable feeling that it might be the realization of a sustained and compelling dream. My dream had envisioned the success of decades-long, underground efforts to "thaw" the Soviet Union, with hundreds of thousands of Jews escaping Soviet oppression and the UJA providing the necessary funds. An infusion of intelligent, well-educated immigrants would propel Israel to a new plateau of technological and economic advancement. Was this now beginning to happen? I had to see for myself, to probe the depth of the phenomenon, both in Vienna and Jerusalem, so that I could begin to plan the campaign that must follow.

I had often visited Vienna in the post-war years, charting the flow of refugees and DP's coming from far eastern reaches of the Soviet Union, on their way to the American Zone of Germany. Aliya Bet's man in Vienna was known by the code name "Artur," and he and I often met in the Bristol Hotel and the Rothschild Hospital. Only years afterward, when he was appointed Israel's first ambassador to Germany, did I learn that Artur's real name was Asher ben Natan. Here it was 25 years later, and I was once again in Vienna, appraising a flow of immigrants. This time, however, they were not en route to some dismal DP camp. They were going home. I flew with a planeload of them one night to Tel Aviv. What a wonderful feeling.

I traveled around Israel for a few days, watching the absorption process, which went very well. I made appointments with government and Jewish Agency officials in various departments to learn the plans for accelerating the construction of housing; see the charts for population dispersal; anticipate financial needs; and gather data and other facts with which to inform and inspire my lay leaders and staff.

That highly concentrated effort was shattered by a telex; my father had just died in his sleep at age 79. I left Israel within hours for New Haven, Connecticut, where he had lived. On the long flight home, I savored amid grief my many memories of the quiet, gentle man, always polite and helpful, who had worked so hard to provide for all of us.

He and my mother had lived peacefully and happily through the awful years of the Great Depression, facing crushing financial crises, including the foreclosure of their house, without ever losing hope or dignity. After almost 40 years of such a union, he was desolate when she died at a mere 61. She had always been the dominant personality, and he depended on her.

A few months after her death, he reminded his three sons of the Biblical injunction that man should not live alone and asked how we would feel if he remarried. As we knew, he had loved our mother dearly and certainly intended no disrespect to their past life together, but he could not face the future alone. At the end of the Jewish religion's customary year of mourning, he married a widow, Fanny Walhimer, who had been our mother's closest friend for the past 30 years and a constant visitor in my parent's home.

Now, after 14 comfortable years in that second marriage, he died in his sleep, as peacefully as he had lived, earning the "death by a kiss" that is reserved for the righteous. He had served the synagogue B'nai Jacob, earnestly and lovingly, throughout his life, as usher, board member, officer, and willing volunteer. Thus the synagogue was filled for his funeral service – a testimonial to the fact that virtue and goodness do receive recognition, even though the deceased may possess neither fame nor fortune. He was buried in the congregational cemetery, next to my mother. I placed in his casket a small sack of soil that I had brought from Mt. Zion immediately after receiving the news of his death. At the same time, I brought for my brothers two small Hebrew Bibles inscribed with the date of his passing.

After our move to Israel in June 1971, I began to organize a plan for the campaign of 1972, which I knew should be based on the now-clear prospect of a large influx of Soviet Jews. History was pounding on the door, thousands of immigrants were arriving every week, and it was obvious to me that this cherished opportunity must be impressed on every American Jew we could reach.

Events had converged in stunning fashion. The Soviet Government, succumbing to heavy pressure, was opening its doors. World opinion, expressed through Western political leaders at the very highest levels, was demanding free right of exit. Massive groups of Jewish students on every campus across the country were campaigning to "Let My People Go." A group of 36 English women, chaining themselves to the gate of the Russian Embassy in London, maintained a constant vigil and chanted similar slogans.

As the protests began to take effect, and exit visas were issued in larger numbers, the Kremlin made clear that it would look with disfavor on open publicity concerning the flow of immigrants to Israel. After all, the Cold War was at its peak. The two world powers had opposing clients. America was linked to Israel; the Soviet Union was supplying arms to the Arab states and would not welcome an Arab complaint that it was simultaneously providing manpower to Israel. Although the increasing emigration could hardly be kept a secret, the customary widespread information campaign necessary for fundraising was definitely out of the question.

The costs for emigration were very high: for a family of three or four persons, bribes, taxes, transportation, and final document – the exit permit itself – totaled many thousands of dollars. The would-be emigrants themselves could not possibly come up with that kind of money. Even if they were fortunate enough to sell the one or two rooms in which they lived, or their few pieces of furniture, they received only what a fire sale provided, for the buyers knew that the Jews would have no choice but to accept whatever was offered.

In addition to raising the money, we would need to create a channel inside the Soviet Union to get the requisite amount of cash into the hands of the migrants themselves. There was no Israeli Embassy in Moscow and no Israeli Consulate in other cities; the Soviets had severed diplomatic relations with

Israel after the Six-Day War, when its Arab clients had been thoroughly defeated.

Luckily, the historic link between the Netherlands and the Jewish people once again came into play. The Jews in long lines around the Dutch Embassy in Moscow were ushered inside and, after displaying all the required documents, were simply handed the necessary cash to cover permits and other costs. The migrants went from the Dutch Embassy to the Soviet OVIR (emigration) office, obtained their permits, and arranged for train tickets to Vienna. The Dutch were marvelously kind, and they handled scores of millions of UJA dollars with scrupulous honesty and accuracy.

The UJA's task remained. It had to organize the "secret" American fundraising campaign. Unable to utilize conventional methods of getting the story across to our constituency (through newspaper ads, brochures, posters, photo albums, TV interviews with Israel officials or our own speakers), I had to create a private communication network with the leading local donors. They would then fashion a sort of oral chain letter, asking ten people to pass the story on to ten other people, and so on down the line. After mulling over several variations on that approach, I decided that the strongest and simplest method was to let the immigrants themselves tell their stories about the harshness of Soviet life to as many influential American Jews as they could see.

Here is how I structured it in my mind:

1. 95 percent of American Jews resided in approximately 50 communities.

2. The calendar would be divided into four quarters.

3. One Russian immigrant, a new Israeli, would be posted in a community for one of those quarters.

4. During that 90-day period, assuming that both the immigrant and the local campaign officials worked hard, the former could meet 400 to 500 prospects, at the rate of five to six per day. If the appointments were made in the prospect's home, perhaps for breakfast or dinner, other family members and relatives could be invited to come and hear the story.

I could think of no stronger force than the emotional energy pouring out of a person who had gone through a nerve-wracking hell trying to get himself and his loved ones out of slavery to the freedom of Israel. Sitting at the dinner table, explaining, answering questions, plumbing the depths of human emotion, seemed the most effective way to implant the historic dimensions of this new Exodus in the minds of American Jews.

5. Staying in one medium-sized community for three months, our hero-immigrant could reach every potential contributor of $1,000 and higher.

6. In larger communities, the effort might have to last longer, for perhaps *two* quarters. That would require rotating visitors. In the very large metropolises, we might have to bring immigrants in and out throughout an entire year.

7. No individual Russian could be expected to remain longer than 90 days. After all, he/she had a family back in Israel, and being fresh new immigrants, they had many problems of adjustment and absorption.

8. Making a rough calculation, I was quite confident that a pool of 150 to 200 well-briefed and articulate Russians could cover the entire 50 communities during one full calendar year, participating in face-to-face solicitations of every $1,000-and-over prospect, and that this process would bring in at least 90 percent of the campaign goal.

9. I planned personally to search Israel from top to bottom for new immigrants who had the right personalities, sufficient command of English, interesting personal stories to tell, and enough motivation to succeed at this historic task. I was certain that I could find and mobilize the necessary number, work out the logistical arrangements with their families, and assign them to communities they'd find congenial.

That was my plan. It was logical to me. But not only was it rejected, it also proved the undoing of my entire, Israel-based arrangement with the UJA.

The above outline, expanded to include the multitude of details necessary to achieve successful implementation, was sent to Irving Bernstein, the new executive vice-chairman in New York. I was doing what I thought was my agreed-upon role. That is, I was setting policy – in this case deciding – that the eagerly awaited Russian migration was to be the theme of the 1972 campaign. I was also suggesting a method of executing that policy and providing on-the-spot assistance in Israel by recruiting the personnel who could make the whole thing work.

There was ominous silence from New York headquarters and rumbling from the UJA representative in Jerusalem, Chaim Vinitsky. It seems that Vinitsky felt that his authority was being threatened, since he was the person previously empowered by the UJA to procure speakers for the organization's annual campaign. Here was I, his superior, depriving him of an important function. He made his dissatisfaction known to Bernstein and Max Fisher, and they asked him to provide them with four Russian immigrants who would travel around the U.S. making speeches. In effect, they were vetoing my plan and simply disregarding the scale and scope of the historic challenge.

Those top UJA officials were refusing (or were unable) to recognize that a sudden new historic event was in process, that a new type of saturation campaign was necessary – to shock American Jewry into providing the volume of money required to **free** untold thousands of Russian Jews from the Soviet prison. Fisher, Bernstein, and Vinitsky were derelict in their duty by deliberately avoiding the challenge, or failing to understand that they must exploit the miracle of an open Soviet door.

According to my arrangement with New York, I was to fly over there for monthly tête-à-têtes, and I did so in September, October, and November, 1971. Each visit included an exhaustive discussion of my basic plan. Bernstein pleaded administrative inability to carry out such an ambitious scheme, saying at various times that his staff was inadequate, local federation officials would never arrange such a heavy schedule of appointments, some reporter would get hold of the story, etc., etc.

I could not determine what was going through Bernstein's head or psyche. Was he afraid of managing a project of this size? Did he fear failure? All of this arguing, month after month, made the whole discussion irrelevant. Time was simply running away, and finally it was too late to execute the plan.

When I went to New York in December, for the annual national conference of several thousand of the UJA faithful, I held a summit meeting with Fisher, Bernstein, and Paul Zuckerman, the new incoming chairman. Their mood was polite, but firm. They accepted the fact that I wanted to live in Israel, but they wanted the power center to remain in New York. They agreed that I could probably "run" the UJA from Jerusalem, by my definition, but if I did, their share in the decision-making process would be diminished.

I was not interested in waging war with them. They were making a personal issue out of what should have been an objective analysis of ways and means to confront a major and historic opportunity. The lay leaders, Fisher and Zuckerman, abetted by professionals Bernstein and Vinitsky, translated the matter into a power struggle and reached a personal, selfish conclusion that "power" had to remain with them.

In fact, my plan for handling the flood of Russian Jews did not differ because I was now based in Jerusalem. I was acting exactly as I had for the past 16 years: facing a problem and designing a solution. Were I based in New York, I would have devised the same plan. Yet they turned distance into a negative factor. The New Yorkers did not challenge my ability to fulfill the obligations I had undertaken, e.g., to find and train the 200 new Israeli-Russian volunteers necessary. Nor did they suggest an alternative plan that everyone felt was better than mine. They were simply reneging on our agreement. I could have kept fighting them, but decided not to expend the energy that a constant war would require. I wanted to look ahead to a new life in Israel. We had reached a parting of the ways.

I explained to my UJA colleagues that my respect for the organization would remain undiminished and that I would undertake any assignment in Israel they requested. But I would no longer confine myself solely to UJA activities. (I'm sure they did not mind hearing that.) Israel was a wide stage, with many interesting projects, and I would wander across it at will, searching for the kind of challenge I always needed in order to perform well. We discussed various financial matters, arriving at terms that I considered somewhat less than generous. I would remain on a retainer until 1975, enabling me to complete 20 years of professional service, now as then the longest term of any CEO in UJA history.

I confess to deep sadness at leaving a great organization that I had helped to build from a modest beginning to its present level. Compounding the sadness was concern about what my successors might be able to accomplish. Lying ahead were these daunting events: the continuing Russian-Jewish exodus; an Israeli election that might bring a change of government (always a delicate event); perhaps another Mideast war; and the usual number of internal social and economic problems. The times would require, at the helm of the UJA, a person and a team that could meet these crises with strength and conviction, cleverness and creativity, marketing skills, oratorical ability, and sharp judgment concerning lay and professional personnel. I prayed that those who were destined to follow me would measure up to the demands history would place upon them. But I was uneasy about the prospect.

CHAPTER THIRTY-FOUR

SETTLING IN

A rriving in June 1971, we began setting up the house in Caesarea, where we intended to spend the summer, and the rented apartment in Jerusalem which had to be ready for the opening of school on September 1, when the boys would begin their new life. During the summer they had the great joy of playing in the sand dunes, swimming in their own pool, and exploring the Roman ruins. Francine began to think of a career path, for which she had first to complete an ulpan course to learn Hebrew at a Jerusalem community center. I made the first moves of settling into what would be a new and very different routine.

All my previous years of having been so thoroughly engaged at the heart of the state-building activity made it impossible simply to sit in my "Ben-Gurion" office and think about the glorious actions of the past. What should I be seeking to do now? The answer shaped up in a very natural manner.

Over the previous years I had grown quite friendly with Pinchas Sapir, Finance Minister of Israel, and Louis Pincus, Chairman of the Jewish Agency. The connections between us were organic, deriving from my function in UJA to raise money and their function to spend it for the immigrant absorption and social welfare needs. The three of us enjoyed a closely interwoven pattern of actions which bonded us in a web of mutual reliance. When I learned that the chairmanship of the World Keren Hayesod was open, it seemed the most logical solution in the world for me to offer myself as an eminently qualified candidate.

The World Keren Hayesod was the global counterpart of the American UJA, and much older, having been proposed at the First Zionist Congress in 1897. The organization's campaigns extended throughout Canada, South America, Western Europe, many countries in Eastern Europe, Australia and South Africa. Although the capitals of all those countries had WKH offices, headquarters was in Jerusalem as well as the Chairman. The annual fund-raising results varied considerably, depending upon the energy and creativity emanating from headquarters. I felt I could do the job credit, especially if I applied the many innovative methods I had developed in the United States.

Therefore, I felt quite at ease in suggesting to Sapir and Pincus that here I was, now living in Jerusalem, with all the previous experience in fundraising, and available as a candidate for the WKH chairmanship. I knew a fairly wide cross-section of the top lay leadership in England and South Africa, in whose campaigns I had been invited to assist several times. And I had met some of the country directors in France and Austria. With all of this knowledge about these countries, and with some ideas in my head regarding improvements which I had observed as being badly needed, I presumed to predict to my two friends that I could triple the WKH income within the next three years. They were delighted at the prospect, very appreciative of the advantages in bringing UJA skills to WKH.

After several days, we met again and they raised the question, with some embarrassment, of my Zionist Party affiliation. I explained, quite casually and without any real understanding of the implications behind the question, that I was not a member of any party, that I was a non-political Zionist – i.e., a person who had supported and worked for the creation of an independent sovereign Jewish State since early youth, but had little interest in the political party aspect of my Zionist idealism.

Further, I had been alienated from that aspect during my years in post-war Europe. Working with the Aliyah Bet, I had witnessed the ugly in-fighting between the parties on such matters as dividing up the available places on immigrant ships. Each party demanded the number of places to which it felt itself entitled. I had been dealing with the rescue of human beings, and the party politicians were dealing with people only as their own future supporters. I was proud that I had always maintained my loyalty to an ideal, above and beyond the pettiness of party.

My colleagues were visibly disturbed by my reply and explained the facts of life. High positions in the Zionist apparatus "belonged" to various parties, according to a formula negotiated among themselves. The position of WKH chairman belonged to the Confederation of General Zionists (the Capitalist Party, in opposition to the Labor Party). Since I was not a member of that Party, I could not have the job. Professional qualifications, skills, experience, zeal or any other of the normal prerequisites simply did not count. Sapir and Pincus were upset about losing me, but were themselves bound up in the party system and could do nothing about circumventing it.

Thus I learned another lesson about the politicization of Israeli society. Months later the position was offered to a very nice gentleman, Ezra Shapiro, who migrated from Cleveland with the proper background of long membership in the Confederation. He moved into an apartment around the corner from us, and we became friendly, although we never talked about the WKH. Decades later I came to know his son Dan, a charming, capable leader, who became President of the UJA/Federation of New York, the very top position.

After these two setbacks with the UJA and the WKH, I left the world of fundraising and gravitated to my earlier career, the Reform Movement. Dr. Nelson Glueck, a world-famous archeologist, had established in Jerusalem a branch of the Cincinnati-based Hebrew Union College-Jewish Institute of Religion. In order to obtain the necessary building permit (which would have been fiercely opposed by the Orthodox establishment if it had been openly described as a Reform seminary), the institution was defined as an archeological museum and study center. The branch was situated on a premier plot of land, facing Jaffa Gate, in the very heart of the city. When I saw it for the first time, there were two buildings, flanked by a large wooded garden and much empty land for future expansion. On the other side of the empty space stood the Papal Biblical Institute and the French Consulate.

The two HUC-JIR buildings were dignified and impressive in their Jerusalem stone construction. The first contained a chapel (where various Presidents of Israel were happy in future years to receive honorary degrees);

several classrooms (where American Reform rabbinical students came for their obligatory first year of study, and Israeli students wishing to enter the reform rabbinate were subsequently trained); a library; and workshops (for the technical archeological work). The second building, named for Mrs. Rosalie Feinstein of Philadelphia, contained additional classrooms, a social hall, offices and an outdoor amphitheater for ceremonies and performances. I was given an office in that building, which became my base for the next three years.

Housed in an office next to mine was Rabbi Richard Hirsch, a life-long friend going back to the original Denver days, when he had occupied my pulpit after I left for the Army chaplaincy. We had never lost touch during all the intervening decades. His career had finally taken him to Israel to serve as President of the World Union for Progressive Judaism (WUPJ). In that capacity, he traveled the world helping to establish new and strengthen old congregations linked to the reform or liberal movement. A recent addition to his duties included the development on the Jerusalem campus of the HUC-JIR – an enlarged center for the World Union. So our paths were crossing once again, for the job into which I entered was precisely to help with that development. Dick and I henceforth worked very closely together.

Architectural plans for the various buildings being contemplated were drawn by world-famous Moshe Safdie. His rendering became the raw material for a handsome brochure I designed and wrote – *World Education Center for Progressive Judaism* – which accompanied me in my travels, to explain the concept and find the necessary funds. I sought them mainly in the United States and United Kingdom.

A real source of strength and full-scale participation in the concept and its execution emerged: Rabbi Alfred Gottschalk, President of the HUC-JIR, and his Board Chairman, Richard Scheuer, played extremely active roles. They not only developed plans for more classrooms and a large museum of archeology, but actually financed their construction. An apartment was prepared on the top floor of the main building, so that Dr. Gottschalk could live on the campus during his frequent visits to Israel.

The three years I spent in that pursuit were happy and productive. I was involved in the planning of the whole project, helping to spread word of it during fundraising trips, and still having time left over to be of service in many other ways. When the Reform Movement felt that it should establish its presence in Israel, not only by founding congregations, but also by establishing archetypal native Israeli institutions such as *kibbutzim*, I was able to help realize that objective. The director of the Agricultural Settlement Department of the Jewish Agency was Raanan Weitz, a far-seeing visionary and a good friend of mine.

It took only one long, serious conversation between us for Raanan to grasp the value to Israel of this group of Anglo-Saxon new immigrants being eager to replicate the country's oldest model of social organization. And when he offered 750 dunam (almost 200 acres) of land in the far south of the Negev desert, it was accepted with enthusiasm. Kibbutz Yahel was born and we were all delighted. It will soon be celebrating its 25th anniversary.

I also had time to serve in a volunteer capacity for the Foreign Ministry. Whether the Minister was Abba Eban, Yigal Allon or Golda Meir, all friends of mine from the very earliest years of the State's existence, or their successors, when the Ministry was overwhelmed with visitors from abroad, and the key staff needed additional help, they sometimes called on me. If an official visitor was forced to wait between appointments, I could fill in the time by answering questions, providing historical background information or explaining the nuances of some tricky current problem. Sometimes my "fill in" required an entire day, with travel. It was never my responsibility to discuss Israel Government policy matters, but rather to fill in the necessary background so that Senator or Representative X better understood the issues that would later be discussed with high governmental personalities. I valued these opportunities, and from the feedback which reached me, the visitors and the ministry apparently did too.

Another advantage of being situated in the HUC-JIR building was the opportunity of meeting with the first year rabbinical students. They were all college graduates, smart, devoted to an ideal – about which they still had an enormous amount to learn – and not really very clear about the nature of the rabbinical profession upon which they were embarked. I invited them in groups to my office to talk informally about the profession. I tried to explain some of the various areas of work:

1. <u>Congregational rabbi</u> – where they would have to be preacher, school
   principal, social worker, community worker, pastor, counselor to
   individuals, hospital visitor, and servant to hundreds of members who
   felt they had the right to call on the rabbi for any of their religious
   needs. The primary qualification for service in a congregation was an
   unusually thick skin.

2. <u>Hillel rabbi</u> – where they would be working with students on the college
   campus, in an effort to create strong Jewish identity feelings among a
   population which would be largely indifferent and Judaically
   under-educated. These students would be a determining factor in the
   future of the Jewish people in a permissive America, where
   assimilation was all too easy.

3. <u>Educational rabbi</u> – where they would be working in the area of day schools,
   or congregational "religious" schools, which needed major changes in
   order to be effective, e.g., increasing the hours of instruction from the
   current two or four per week, to at least 10 per week. This would take
   enormous leadership skill and heaps of political savvy.

4. <u>Organizational rabbi</u> – where they would be working in a policy-making
   and/or administrative capacity, at least to begin with, and lots of
   opportunity for advancement if they found the goals of the
   organization to be compelling and consonant with their own personal
   philosophy of Jewish life and destiny. Here, there is a possibility of
   making important contributions to the strength of the total Jewish
   community.

5. <u>Military rabbi (chaplain)</u> – where they would be working with young Jewish
   men and women who had voluntarily entered the armed forces, and
   who needed not just the religious presence of a rabbi, but perhaps
   more importantly the role model figure of the Jewish officer in
   uniform on the same level as the Catholic and Protestant. This fact
   balanced out the other fact that the number of Jewish personnel in
   any given unit would always be a small minority. The Jewish chaplain
   provided every Jewish soldier with a feeling of total equality. As for the

chaplain him/herself, there are excellent lessons to be learned and qualities to be developed that will be useful through an entire lifetime.

I also tried to impart the idea that, especially in the non-orthodox world these graduates would inhabit, they would not be called upon to serve as *halachic* (legal) experts (although they should learn as much as possible about Jewish law), but should primarily think of themselves as civil servants of the Jewish people, in the broadest sense possible. Their task might begin within the four walls of their synagogue, but certainly should not end there. They must inspire and lead the entire community, when it comes to the question, for instance, of building a communal day school, or day/high school. Should that issue arise in the community, the rabbi must immediately jump into the position of advocate, for more education is the only antidote we have to the ignorance and indifference which marks so many of our people today. You must speak for it, work on the curriculum committee, take part in the fund-raising. And above all, get involved in the financial structuring of the new school, to the end that tuition must be as low as possible, even merely token, in order to attract as many young people as possible. I described this as holy work, and they must be part of it.

Or, take another example. If a situation develops anywhere in the world which results in a wave of migration to Israel, and large numbers of lives must be saved, the affluent Jews of America must immediately mobilize behind the UJA, and you must take the lead in publicly urging all the Jews in town, not just the members of your congregation, to raise the necessary funds for the rescue operation. You yourself will have to volunteer as a solicitor, taking your share of names to ask for their contributions. You are a civic leader of the whole community, and you must act according to the demands of that role.

These discussions were always very spirited, and the arguments pro and con reverberated for days afterward. That was very satisfying, for I was trying to open the student's minds to a wider horizon, and by taking strong positions, I provoked fervent debate. I had always enjoyed and profited from that, and I was pleased to be able to pass it on to members of the upcoming generation of Jewish religious leaders.

CHAPTER THIRTY-FIVE

THE YOM KIPPUR WAR

At 2 p.m., Saturday, October 6, 1973, I was asleep in our Jerusalem apartment when the air-raid sirens awakened me with their wailing: War had begun. It was Yom Kippur, the Day of Atonement, the holiest day of the year. The enemy had deliberately selected it as the most fortuitous time for its two-pronged attack, since Israel would be off guard.

Francine's parents, Hilda and Charlie, were visiting from New York, having chosen the High Holy Day period as the best time to see their daughter and her family. After worshipping together at the morning service of the Hebrew Union College synagogue, Charlie and I walked home to take a nap, planning later to visit the Western Wall, our favorite place to read the afternoon liturgy and hear the closing blast of the *Shofar* (ram's horn).

That Yom Kippur afternoon we did not reach the wall. Instead, we hung by the radio and listened to the sound of Army trucks blasting their horns as they gathered tens of thousands of reserve soldiers at street corners. I was then 55, over the age for call-up.

The War had not been expected. Israel's citizenry was confused, and perhaps the Army was also. Only a few weeks earlier, a military intelligence report had pronounced the chance of war negligible. That assessment was made despite Defense Minister Moshe Dayan's previous instructions to the Israel Defense Force (IDF) to prepare for war by the end of summer. Perhaps

Secretary of State Kissinger had informed Dayan of King Hussein's whisper that the intense army exercises then being held in Egypt and Syria were <u>not</u> merely exercises, but preparation. No matter, Israel was caught unawares and the scale of the attack on this of all days left the population reeling in disbelief and fear.

Several days before Jerusalem's sirens sounded, another, related crisis had erupted. The steady flow of immigrants from the Soviet Union, which had started two years earlier and continued at a very welcome pace, had developed a smooth travel pattern. The Moscow to Vienna train arrived daily at that city's South Station, with the Jewish refugees concentrated in the last two cars. The Jewish Agency and Joint Distribution Committee (JDC) officials who met the train knew exactly where to stand on the platform in order to gather the travelers and their luggage, shepherd them to waiting buses, and bring them to the modest hostel known by the grand name of "Schönau Castle." The procedure was quick and calm. After a few days of sorting and registering, those headed for destinations in the West were taken to the seaside town of Ostia, outside of Rome, to await visas. The great majority was taken aboard El Al Boeings for direct flights to Ben-Gurion airport.

Suddenly, on October 1, the Moscow-Vienna train was attacked en route by Arab terrorists, inflicting casualties on Jewish immigrants and Austrian railway personnel. Austrian media protested that Austrian citizens should not be endangered because of a Middle Eastern struggle and demanded that Vienna not be used as a way-station by one of the adversaries. Chancellor Kreisky, a Jew who favored the PLO position, responded by threatening to close both the train route and Schönau Castle.

In Jerusalem, the Jewish Agency's Immigration Department called an emergency meeting. I was invited because of the possible financial implications and because, as a figure known to agency officials, my advice was respected. One of the government ministers present stated that a rumor was spreading through the prime minister's office that the PM herself intended to fly to Vienna to intervene with Kreisky. I thought that a bad idea and urged that she be dissuaded. My mind was focused on what I believed was a coming war.

Egypt's Nasser and Syria's Assad had been threatening for several years. They were intent on redeeming the humiliating defeat they had suffered in the

Six-Day War and recapturing the territory lost – the Sinai Desert and Golan Heights. They could now rely on a full arsenal of Russian equipment supplied during the intervening years. In sum, the two Arab leaders were eager and thought themselves ready.

Under such circumstances, it was inconceivable to me that Golda Meir should leave Israel. Yes, I told the assembled group, the possibility that the flow of immigration might be cut was very serious, because once cut, permission might not be restored. But other fully capable, top-level people could make Israel's case forcefully to Kreisky. I named Abba Eban, Yitzhak Rabin, and Shimon Peres. Those suggestions were forwarded to the PM's office, but she had decided to go to Vienna. Getting Jews out of Russia had been a hot button with her ever since she had made contact with them during her tour as Israel's ambassador in Moscow.

Her impulse was noble, based on her humane attitude toward rescuing Jews. It was practical too, a reflection of her desire to maintain the flow of well-educated immigrants who would add to Israel's strength. So Golda herself, fully aware of the pending military crisis at home, flew that same day to Vienna to joust with Kreisky. One theory has it that the attack on the train was aimed precisely at drawing her away from Israel at a critical moment. If so, that ploy succeeded.

Golda did succeed in obtaining an agreement: the train stoppage would be temporary, to allow Austrian public opinion to cool down; and once the flow resumed, the immigrants would be taken to a hostel in another part of town. She returned to Israel overnight Wednesday, October 3, and went immediately into a cabinet meeting to resume discussion of the impending war.

Thursday and Friday, October 4 and 5, were spent in an endless round of consultations with cabinet, defense ministry, general staff and intelligence officials, in an effort to evaluate Arab intentions and strength and to determine Israeli response. On Friday afternoon, Golda adjourned the cabinet, but asked all ministers, especially those who observed the Sabbath, to remain close and not to scatter to their homes all over the country – despite their natural desire to spend Yom Kippur with their families.

On Friday night, October 5, everything came to a head in Golda's kitchen. The PM made tea for her guests: Defense Minister Dayan, Chief of the

General Staff David Elazar, Israel Galili (one of her oldest and most trusted advisers), and American Ambassador Kenneth Keating, a well-known friend of Israel, who delivered a vital report. The Pentagon and State Department, Keating said, had uncovered the Arabs' intention to strike at 6 p.m. the following day – Yom Kippur. Henry Kissinger, speaking for President Nixon, had instructed Keating to advise the Israeli Government to absorb the first blow. That would make it patently clear that the Arabs were the aggressors, giving Israel the moral and public relations advantage, plus permitting her later to seek full U.S. support and re-supply of equipment.

Now the heart of the dilemma lay openly on the table. Heated discussion ensued. Mindful of a costly, false-alarm partial mobilization of the previous April, Dayan agreed only to a small, symbolic call-up of troops. Elazar pointed out that by this time (late Friday evening), radio and TV personnel were at Sabbath skeleton strength, so full mobilization would in any case be impossible. Regular IDF units had already dismissed personnel for the Holy Day, and the almost half-million reservists could only be reached by radio broadcasts, not available on Yom Kippur.

Elazar added, however, that the air force was always on full alert and could be activated immediately. He asked for permission to order a massive, pre-emptive bombing of all 25 Arab military airfields and their planes, to start at first light. Since it was now known that the Arab attack was scheduled for 6 p.m., that would give the air force 12 hours to work – enough time, Elazar indicated, to blunt the Arab air capability.

Golda and Dayan conferred and denied Elazar's request. They decided instead to go along with Nixon's reasoning and let the Arabs strike first. The most important factor in their decision was the matter of re-supply. Although no estimates could be made of prospective Israeli losses of aircraft, tanks, large-caliber ammunition, etc., the ability to obtain replacements quickly would be crucial.

Keating was present through the entire discussion and was pleased with the decision. Golda urged him to convince Kissinger to convey to Egypt and Syria Israel's decision not to strike pre-emptively, and further to urge them not to resort to war but to employ diplomatic means to achieve whatever objectives they might have. Kissinger made both calls, with no success. The two Arab leaders then spoke to each other by telephone (with the call overheard by U.S. intelligence) and agreed that, since the Israelis were expecting to be hit at 6 p.m., the attack should be moved up to 2 p.m., in the middle of Yom Kippur day. Half the country would then be in synagogue, the other half at the beach. A nation at prayer or at play would be easy prey.

During the morning of the 6th, the radio and TV were restored to full-staff status and the emergency mobilization broadcasts started. Trucks began to rumble, picking up reservists at street corners throughout the country. At 2 p.m., right on the Arabs' revised schedule, air raid sirens began shrieking throughout the land. The attack had begun.

Several weeks later, I learned from two participants the details of what had happened that night in the kitchen. Ambassador Keating, a former senator from New York, and I had met in the United States on several occasions. Now I was a guest at a reception in his residence in Herzlia Pituach, a lovely village on the Mediterranean, and a few us were invited to remain after the crowd dispersed. Keating felt like talking and told the story as I have narrated it above. He stressed the effort he had made, after returning from the kitchen meeting, to persuade the Pentagon and White House to begin the re-supply of equipment without waiting for the Arab strike.

Shortly after the Herzlia reception, I happened to visit General Elazar, and told him about the conversation with Keating. Elazar corroborated every detail, up to the point when he left the meeting after his request for a pre-emptive aerial strike was denied.

When war began, the Egyptians quickly breached the Bar-Lev line on the east bank of the Nile and poured two full armies (the Second and Third) and thousands of tanks across the river and into the Sinai Desert. Israel beefed up her Southern Command with the immediate recall to duty of several former chiefs of staff.

The Syrians simultaneously smashed across the full width of the Golan Heights. By the second evening, hundreds of Israeli tanks had been destroyed, and the Syrian forces stood at the western edge, looking through their gun sights at the civilian kibbutzim and settlements, sitting ducks in the valley below. Luckily, the Syrians had run low on fuel and ammunition and had to wait for fresh supplies.

By the third day of fighting, Israel had lost more than 500 tanks, thousands of soldiers dead and wounded, and 49 aircraft, victims of the Sam-2 and Sam-7 missiles Russia had supplied to Egypt. That day, General Dayan panicked and called the situation desperate: everything was lost, we must withdraw; this was the end of the "Third Temple." (Two previous temples had been destroyed, in 586 BCE by the Babylonians and 70 CE by the Romans.) A nuclear alert was ordered, and nuclear weapons were armed – but never used.

By the fourth day of heavy fighting on both fronts, the Sinai in the south and the Golan in the north, Israeli forces were facing the extremely urgent issue of re-supply. On Tuesday, October 9, they were out of heavy-caliber ammunition and had suffered severe losses in tanks and aircraft. In addition, the large numbers of soldiers killed and wounded lowered morale in both the Army and the civilian population, threatening the country's ability to fight back. Golda's kitchen cabinet decided to inform Washington of its nuclear preparations and to demand that the United States immediately start replacing arms and ammunition by airlift.

In *The Samson Option, Israel's Nuclear Arsenal and American Foreign Policy*, American journalist Seymour Hersh provides some details. One passage reads: "Kissinger described in his memoirs a series of urgent telephone calls from Simcha Dinitz, the Israeli ambassador to Washington, beginning at 1:45 a.m. on Tuesday, October 9, and again at 3.00 a.m., demanding to know what was happening with the resupply.... Kissinger, accompanied by Peter Rodman, his longtime assistant, and Dinitz, accompanied by General Mordecai Gur, the Israeli military attache, met at 8:20 a.m. in the Map Room of the White House, where Kissinger was told of the desperate situation and the need for more tanks and aircraft.... At one point, Dinitz insisted that he and Kissinger needed to be alone. Dinitz's message was that Golda Meir was prepared to come to the United States for an hour to plead with President Nixon for urgent arms aid. It was a request that Kissinger 'rejected out of hand... such a proposal could reflect only either hysteria or blackmail.' By that evening of October 9, Kissinger wrote, 'Israel had been assured that its war losses would be made up. Relying on this assurance, it stepped up its consumption of war materiel, as we had intended.'"

More arresting descriptions can be found in the narratives of those who participated in the dramatic events, as well as in the street gossip that inevitably circulates after such historic encounters. Particularly fascinating is the story that Golda's call to Dinitz, ordering him to put the heat on President Nixon for the delay in the promised airlift, included two injunctions: Nixon was to be reminded of his agreement via Ambassssador Keating that if Israel took the first blow she would receive timely American aid; and if he didn't remember that, she intended to fly over herself, remind him very forcefully, and also appear on American television to recite the whole story to the American public. Those who knew Golda recognized such a threat as consistent with her style and personality.

Another story has to do with the fog surrounding the basic question of who was responsible for the delay in shipping the materiel. Was it Kissinger or Secretary of Defense James R. Schlesinger? Kissinger's own description of his basic strategy – to let Israel win the war but bleed – would seem to place the blame on him. On the other hand, Schlesinger said at one point that Defense Department calculations indicated that the Israelis had sufficient supply for at least seven days of fighting; yet by the fourth day, they were already screaming for help. That would shift the blame to him.

No one outside the inner circle really knows. But a perhaps apocryphal story relates that when the matter came to Nixon's personal attention during the tense fourth day of fighting, he is said to have exploded: "Which one of my two damned Jews is responsible for this delay – Kissinger or Schlesinger? Get that materiel loaded and on the way immediately!"

Whatever the truth, by that same evening, at Langley Field in Virginia, huge transport aircraft were being prepared to fly to Israel. Meanwhile, frantic efforts were underway to secure landing rights for refueling, because those heavily loaded planes could not make the trip non-stop. No one had thought of that problem, but it made the previous *Sturm und Drang* pale into insignificance. Great Britain, Spain, and Germany all refused landing privileges, even though those countries housed American bases. France followed suit. Reasons were never stated publicly, but the private explanations were identical: nobody wanted to offend the Arabs by taking Israel's side – especially if the Arabs actually won.

Israel's very existence, America's reputation and political morality, and the world's conscience were all rescued by relatively powerless Portugal, which offered its base in the Azores. The lumbering transports set down there, refueled, and hurried on to Ben-Gurion airport, where long lines of trucks and tank transporters waited to ship the precious cargo to the fighting fronts.

Since I could do nothing in an active military sense, and most of the other men in our apartment house had gone off to the war, I took the responsibility of cleaning out the basement area that was theoretically designated as an air-raid shelter for the inhabitants of our building and two adjoining ones. I say theoretically because the basement's few rooms were completely cluttered with everyone's odds and ends: broken furniture, old bicycles, books, bales and bundles, the detritus of a consumer society heaped and jumbled together. Drastic discarding was necessary, and I did it.

Then the air vents had to be cleaned and tested, and food, water, candles, and kerosene for lamps had to be stocked. Sleeping mats and blankets, stools, tools, books, sweets for the children, and so forth were brought in. The work took two days – and produced a model shelter that was never used.

I started to think about the UJA back in the United States: would it be helpful to the organization's fundraising efforts if I made a trip to the fronts, even as the War raged, to gather impressions and forward them to my former colleagues? In New York they were delighted, for they knew I would deliver highly usable material. The IDF public relations office liked the idea as well, and a trip was quickly arranged to the Golan Heights, where the fighting was abating but still in progress. Charlie Bensley was eager to go along. So was Sidney Edelstein, a strong UJA supporter from New Jersey who happened to be residing in his Israel apartment, and one or two others whose names I don't remember but whom the UJA office in Israel wanted to include in the expedition. The Army supplied a small bus, an armed escort, and an itinerary that included meetings with various commanders at selected points. It was to be a long one day's journey from Jerusalem and back.

We drove north along the Jordan River valley, across the B'not Yaacov bridge, and started the climb up the Golan Heights. Our vehicle constantly wove between huge tank transporters going in both directions; some bringing down damaged and destroyed tanks for repair, others carrying up replacements. At the top, the first farm village we saw, Ramat Magshimim, had been overrun and partially destroyed. It was a religious kibbutz, containing a school, and as we poked among the ruins, I picked up a souvenir to take back – a volume of Maimonides punctured by several bullet holes.

In all political discussions pertaining to Israel's security, the right wing argues in favor of establishing settlements, filled with buildings and people, as a means of blocking invasion and attack. That argument has always seemed to me stupid and untrue. How can a small house block even a small tank? Seeing that first village, empty of people and full of smashed buildings, reminded me of the nonsense of the contention that civilian settlements could deter and delay enemy military aggression.

Heading north and east across the heights, the roads were reasonably clear, but the fields were littered with destroyed tanks, armored cars, command cars, assorted artillery pieces and rocket launchers – the debris of combat. In the distance, we heard the sound of tank fire. The tide of the War was changing direction as Israel's Air Force threw its full power into pushing the Syrians back.

We reached the ruined and deserted town of Kuneitra, the capital of the Golan, but went no further, for the road continued to Damascus, the Syrian capital. When the War ended some days later, Israeli forces had advanced beyond Kuneitra and been stopped by the cease-fire at a point only 15 miles from Damascus.

On our way back to a briefing at brigade HQ, we passed a spot where several burned-out tanks of a different size and shape sat by the side of the road. Walking among them, we discovered Russian markings. Syria's equipment was to a great extent supplied by Russia. I appropriated a long-handled shovel, strapped to one of the tanks, as a souvenir; I subsequently used it to garden and still have it. Those two items, a bullet-shattered book and a Russian shovel, are the memory-prodders that take me back to the northern front of the Yom Kippur War.

At the end of the following week, October 21 and 22, I made a similar trip to the southern front. The tide had turned there also. We crossed into the Sinai at Nitzana (near the oasis of Kadesh Barnea, where Moses and the Israelites spent 39 of their 40 years "wandering" the desert). The paved road was in good condition as we drove by the Israeli air bases of Jabel Libni and Bir Thamada, but from that point down through the Mitla Pass, the next 40 miles were most difficult to traverse because of the fighting and the burning equipment on the road. The Egyptians had thrown more than 2,000 tanks into the battles at the so-called Chinese Farm, skirmishes were still occurring, and Israeli infantry efforts to encircle the Egyptian Third Army were still in progress.

Interestingly, the road westward to the Suez Canal was easier to maneuver because the IDF had conquered the territory on the west (back) side of the Egyptian Third Army and Israeli troops were bringing water and pita bread to its Third Army prisoners. Israeli engineers had thrown some Bailey bridges across the canal itself and a new battle cry immediately surfaced – "On to Africa," as the exhilarating realization spread among the troops that they would be leaving Asia, and passing over to another continent.

Our journey ended on the Egyptian side, in Suez City at the southern end of the canal. We slept that night on the floor of a gymnasium and ate cold rations. The city blazed from Israeli artillery and bombardments, with the canal itself blocked by sunken vessels. Israel controlled the air, and large contingents of her troops were crossing the waterway. The United Nations passed a cease-fire resolution on October 22, but the Israelis stalled for two more days so they could consolidate their gains militarily.

After each of the visits described above, I sent the UJA lengthy reports incorporating human-interest features; places to visit when the missions again started coming over (the Women's Divisions arrived first); sets of photos to give some idea of what the mission participants would see; people to interview for good stories; military officers who could be invited to the United States for speech making; and as many statistics as I could accumulate in a short time.

After the war, an Israeli Government commission investigated the *Mechdal* (neglect, failure, default) of military intelligence and preparation that almost led to a catastrophic defeat. General Elazar, as the highest-ranking military officer, chief of staff, was declared responsible, a finding that was severely criticized by press and public as unfair. Elazar resigned in silence and sadness, and some months later suffered a fatal heart attack while exercising in a swimming pool. The political leaders were exonerated, but public pressure on them mounted, and a few months later, in the spring of 1974, Golda Meir and

Moshe Dayan resigned. The Labor Party appointed Yitzhak Rabin as the new prime minister.

The Yom Kippur War was finally won after 18 days of the hardest fighting Israel had ever endured. What started so badly ended with a bold victory, a tribute to the men and women whose hearts were brave and hands were skilled.

Sharing a glass of wine, 1972,with
Israel's third President, Zalman Shazar

The Yom Kippur War interrupted
the construction of Jerusalem's new
Maskit. The opening was finally held in
December, 1975. Left to right: Shimon Horn;
Francine; Ruth Dayan;
General Haim Bar-Lev.

In honor of the 10th anniversary of the founding of the UJA Young Leadership Cabinet, the
group's leaders presented me with a drawing. Left to right: Leonard Bell; Michael Pelavin;
Jim Nobil; Bob Schrayer; Gordon Zacks (in rear); Joseph Kanter.

On the occasion of Mathilde Brailove's 86th birthday in June 1986, several past national chairpersons of the UJA women's campaign gathered to pay tribute to her (third from left). Edward M.M. Warburg and I spoke. These top leaders are, left to right: Lea Horne, Bernice Waldman, Mathilde Brailove, Harriet Sloane, Sylvia Hassenfeld, Harriet Zimmerman, Judy Levy, Fannie Schaenen, Paulette Fink.

Mathilda Brailove on left, with Harriet Sloane, past national chairpersons.

Nan Goldberg Greenbaum, on left, long-time executive director
of UJA women's campaign, with Mathilda Brailove.

Carole Solomon, first woman ever to serve as nationwide campaign chair since the establishment of UJA in November 1938.

My conversation with Pope John Paul II in 1994 included
compliments for his work in continuing Catholic-Jewish
reconciliation started by Pope John XXIII.

Deep in conversation with Yitzhak Rabin, July 1995.

In 1992 at the winter retreat of the Wexner Heritage Foundation, the guest of honor was Israel's fifth president, Itzhak Navon, who gave a wonderful lecture on Sephardi history. At left is Rabbi Ramie Arian, Vice-President of Wexner Heritage Foundation.

Ezer Weizman, Israel's seventh president, livened up the reception of the Wexner group at the official residence in 1995. At right is Rabbi Nathan Laufer, president of the Wexner Heritage Foundation.

Abigail and Leslie Wexner

LOOKING BACK
ON THE UJA

CHAPTER THIRTY-SIX

HOW TO RAISE BILLIONS

During my career, I estimate that I've raised hundreds of millions of dollars in charitable contributions through personal solicitations of individual donors. Additional, untotaled millions resulted from countless dinners and other functions at which I spoke about Israel's current problems and the situation of Jews endangered in a variety of countries. I have no way of knowing whether my efforts produced the most that any individual raised in this century for Jewish causes, but in any case, it was a great deal of money.

Indeed, fundraising has occupied a major portion of my working life, roughly divided into three different aspects: the individual solicitations, usually for large sums; the creation of fund-raising ideas and their execution through the detailed planning that produces success; and perhaps most important, the teaching and training of others to sally forth onto the battlefield. Fundraising is more an art than a science and is therefore difficult to teach. One sometimes hears or reads the title "professional fundraiser," which would imply that the skill can be transferred to an apt student through classroom or laboratory exposure.

I'm afraid that is only partially true. What can be transferred is a certain amount of experience, i.e., what techniques work better than others, what mistakes must be avoided, how to present the case to a prospective donor, etc. While learning from the experience of others is helpful, the most significant assets in the fundraiser's arsenal are *knowledge* of the cause he or she is representing, a *passionate belief* in that cause, and a *strong self-confidence* that produces clear articulation, an easy manner, and an ability to rebound from rejection.

When seeking to turn someone into a successful fundraiser, it is possible to teach deep knowledge of the cause and even to instill the necessary passion, but the self-confidence is already there or not there. That characteristic is difficult, if not impossible, to impart.

In individual soliciting, I had my own method and taught it to any colleagues who felt strong enough to utilize it. First, I consulted with a committee of nine others to determine the amount I should request from the prospect. This process is called "establishing the rating," and is best conducted by a legal quorum of ten. A group of that size, called a *minyan*, is authorized in the Jewish religion as the minimum number for any substantive communal activity such as holding a prayer service, consecrating a cemetery, and establishing a synagogue.

Consultation with the *minyan*, whose members are selected for their familiarity with the prospect and financial ability, is a shield with which solicitors can defend themselves in case the prospect should ask, during the solicitation: "What right do you have to ask me to contribute such and such an amount?" The solicitor can then honestly reply, "It is not I doing the asking. The *minyan* has established this rating. The whole community is doing the asking."

Once the rating had been set, I would call the prospect and make an appointment to meet him in his office – asking him for 15 minutes, with his secretary holding all calls. He certainly knew why I was coming, but if the relationship between us was good, he also knew he couldn't refuse to see me.

As I entered the door and walked toward his desk, I immediately started speaking, stating that I had come to ask him for x dollars, the rated amount. A brusque opening, yes? But by the time I finished that announcement, I was seated in the chair across from him. And I did not say another word. One minute of silence in those circumstances seems like a century.

The ball was now in the prospect's court. His first response usually questioned my sanity in asking for so much. I then paid tribute to his intelligence, saying something like, You know all the salient data; I don't have to make a speech to you. I don't have to tell you how many poor Rumanian (or other) immigrants came into Israel needing help last month. Again I fell silent, leading to another unnerving moment. The prospect would try to entice me into conversation to give himself some time to decide how much less than my request he could get away with.

It was all very delicate. He knew I wanted more than last year; he thought the rating was exaggerated and tried to find that happy compromise between what he had in mind and what I had asked. So it ended either with his surrender and acquiescence to the rated number or his compromise figure, to which I would agree when I felt that was the most I could wring from him. The whole meeting usually took no more than 15 minutes – unless he wished to prolong it with general conversation. My parting word, spoken in good humor if I had been given less than I expected, was that it was okay. We both knew that next year I'd be back asking him to make up the difference.

I always felt that the strongest fundraising appeals were those resting on an ideological base, and mine was simple and straightforward: the sacredness of Jewish survival, for the sake of both the Jewish people and the world at large; the value of every Jewish life, especially now, in view of the genocidal Holocaust; the inestimable worth of Israel as a physical and spiritual center; the responsibility of every Jew for every other and for the homeland.

That rubric, short and sweet, had to be established, repeated, and woven through every speech, for once the underlying ideology was accepted, all that remained was a negotiation over the amount of the contribution. Raising money is really an exercise in educating the listener.

Throughout my entire professional career, whenever I was asked for the secret of fundraising, I answered that it lay in raising *people*. People raise money, and if you develop a cadre of workers, knowledgeable about and dedicated to the cause they espouse, they will do the job successfully. Therefore, my task was to teach the basic ideology, to enthuse, to inspire, to explain what the money would make possible.

Fundraising is a process built on a series of conditions and methods. I'll name four. First is the *cause*, which must penetrate deeply into the consciousness of the prospective donor. Outside observers often express amazement at the remarkable success of Jewish fundraising. They ask, how can this small group of Americans each year raise sums that almost equal those amassed by the Red Cross and United Way, which appeal to all Americans? The answer lies in the twin stimuli that comprise the motivation: rescue of endangered Jews anywhere in the world, and support of Israel.

Regarding this question of cause, I remember in the 1960s receiving a request for help from the State Department. Many colonial powers were then withdrawing from Africa, and new native governments were being formed. The United States was besieged with pleas from them for assistance. One was forwarded to me. Would I be willing to meet with a delegation from a large African country, newly independent, whose leaders were thinking of starting a philanthropic campaign among African-Americans to raise much-needed development funds? The State Department thought the Jewish record of success in fund-raising contained lessons that would benefit this delegation. I was of course willing.

The first questions I asked the group, as we sat around the table in my office, went to the heart of the matter. Did they have any reason to believe that black Americans were at least somewhat interested in this new country in far-off Africa? Was support of that country a *cause* that would galvanize American Negroes (the then-current term)? The chairman of the delegation was astonished at the question and dismissed it as unimportant.

He elaborated on the campaign plan his group had in mind. They intended to mount a large parade that would wind through the main streets of Harlem in New York City (and similar neighborhoods in several other large cities), flying the flags of the new country. Bands would play catchy music, pretty girls would wave from floats and flashy convertibles, with loudspeakers urging the onlookers to throw money into the slowly moving vehicles. He explained that this method would appeal to the crowds.

I listened in genuine distress at the naivete of these good men. Injecting a little humor, I told them that money tossing would not produce many bills, especially if the day were breezy, and probably not even many coins, although they could more easily be thrown on-target. In a serious vein, I explained again and again how they had to create a sense of the importance of their cause; build a base of knowledge about their new country; use the churches and clergy to awaken mass pride in the new freedom of millions of Africans once removed; develop a corps of American black lay leaders to undertake the big-gift individual solicitations on which a successful campaign is built; set up a unit to work with the major black national organizations and a similar unit to work with friendly whites who were potential contributors. At least two years of hard preparatory work would be required before they could launch their first fundraising function. Once an atmosphere had been created, a parade might be helpful.

The Jewish people, I pointed out, had spent 2,000 years shaping a frame of mind based on two Hebrew concepts: *tzedekah* (commonly translated as "charity," but more accurately as "justice" or "righteousness") and *mitzvah*. Every Jewish person, even the most assimilated, knows these two words. That doesn't mean all Jews contribute; but all know they should, because the religion teaches the simple principle that humans have a responsibility for other humans. An act of charity is not doing someone a favor but performing a deed of righteousness based on a moral imperative. You <u>must</u> act <u>justly</u> toward your neighbor. That intellectual and ethical infrastructure is the basis for individual and communal conduct. From this flows successful fundraising.

The delegation departed enlightened but not happy. They had hoped to acquire a magic solution to their problem – and the parade was clearly not it.

The second condition is a *set of operational rules*. Establish a dollar goal. Accept the fact that 80 percent of that goal must be achieved from 20 percent of the contributors. Thus the emphasis must be on big gifts that are best obtained by individual solicitations and on forming a nucleus of solicitors who first make their own gifts at an appropriate level before asking others.

With regard to that last point, William Rosenwald (of whom more will be said in the next chapter) developed a most sophisticated system. He was in perpetual demand as general chairman of the national UJA. When it came time for Bill to be asked to serve yet another year, he would ask me and Henry Bernstein, the New York City chief UJA executive, to select ten men as a committee to meet with him in his apartment on Park Avenue. The ten were themselves "heavy hitters" as donors, but Bill was ostensibly calling them together to discuss his remaining as general chairman.

Bill would set the stage, placing ten chairs in a semi-circle facing him. The committee members were invited to give their reasons why he must continue to lead the campaign. When they finished, he stated that he intended to go around the circle asking each person, one by one, what his gift would be for that campaign; he also indicated that he would be calling out publicly each person's *last* year's gift, thus making clear that he expected a proper increase this year.

To an outsider, the whole approach might appear rather brutal, even outrageous, and possibly provocative of rebellion. Yet that was not the case, because these men were all deeply devoted to the cause and accepted the procedure as loyal members of a fraternity of big givers who would be employing the same system toward others.

Then, establishing the "you-first rule," Bill would announce his own gift – a hefty increase, thus setting the pace for all to follow. And relentlessly but warmly, because he knew all these men well, he would say a few personal words to each. The result: ten top gifts recorded, ten top solicitors initiated into the circle. Only then would Bill stand to accept the chairmanship of the next campaign, expressing his happiness at having this committed core of workers. This pre-meeting, as he called it, was repeated four years running, always successfully.

Third are *techniques of individual soliciting* that begin with research on the prospect. Among the information sought are such telling factors as the names of his close friends, his country club, special interests, other philanthropic causes, unusual business successes, and attitude toward Israel and endangered Jews. The research was to be followed by choosing the proper solicitor and rating the prospect.

A variation on the above technique involved a good solicitor developing a small list of individuals whom he solicited year after year for very large gifts. With these people, it became a pleasurable game. I acquired gradually such a list of permanent "customers." They wanted to give, but the annual personal meeting became a friendly contest with high stakes. I especially remember one man, Morris Senderowitz. A member of the national campaign cabinet, he would call me when the individual big-gifts phase of a given campaign year was beginning. I didn't have to call him.

Morris and I had our game every early summer. He would send his car to pick me up in New York and bring me to his house in Allentown, Pennsylvania. I was to have done my homework on his financial situation and without a *minyan* (ten man legal team) made my own rating for him. If I asked for the correct amount, he would give it with a bit extra. If I asked him for too much or too little, I would be penalized, forced to pass the decision over to him, and he would give whatever he wished. Morris had given as much as $400,000 in some years and as "little" as $250,000 in others, and the range made the game interesting for both of us. The stakes were high.

Arriving around noon, I would walk up the steps to the front porch where Morris sat in his rocking chair, and he would impatiently shout – *Nu?*" (Yiddish for "Well?"). I loved to stall because that stretched out the game. I would ask for a lemonade and, sitting in the adjoining rocker, start a long story about the latest gossip concerning someone he knew. He'd grumble, eager to get into the money game. But I would stall further, saying I was hungry and wanted lunch. Morris would shout for his wife. After the meal we'd return to the porch for the denouement.

I would plead ignorance, saying for example that because I had not had time to do a background check on all his charitable donations of the past year, I could only suggest a contribution range, between x and y. He would look triumphant and insist I pick one figure. It was now after three o'clock; he was looking tired, we had to close. I named my figure – a reasonable 20 percent higher than last year. He smiled, said I was a little *too* high, but not seriously so, and he would give, say, 15 percent more.

We were both happy. The game ended to our mutual satisfaction. I was back in my office by 5:30, preparing a telex to a short list of top givers to announce that we now had one more contributor at the necessary increase.

Fourth is *the staging of events*, such as one the UJA held with 3,000 lay leaders from all over the country, to commemorate the tenth anniversary of Hitler's defeat. For that occasion we secured the participation of President Eisenhower, as well as of several former U.S. Army generals who helped resolve the displaced-person crises of a decade earlier. We also organized a national gathering of the Young Leadership Cabinet – 2,500 strong – in Washington every two years, an event that attracted the highest White House and

Congressional officials. We got Prime Minister Golda Meir as guest of honor at private dinner parties for million-dollar donors. We chartered a Concorde flight to Israel every August for $100,000 donors. We rented the co-axial cable for one hour for a closed circuit TV speech by Prime Minister Yitzhak Rabin linking 40 communities throughout the United States with a total audience of 20,000 influential listeners.

The above examples illustrate what could be called crescendo episodes, spread every so often judiciously to create excitement and send "juice" flowing throughout the fund-raising system. The events had to display imagination and power, while at the same time producing pace-setting gifts. They gave volunteer workers a conviction that the cause for which they were working was truly worthwhile. They imparted a sense of achievement and status, and that helped energize lay and professional workers alike.

Enough about how a campaign *should* work. Now for the men and women who must *make* it work. I'll present some profiles of them in the next two chapters.

CHAPTER THIRTY-SEVEN

ILLUSTRIOUS CAMPAIGN CHAIRMEN

I served the United Jewish Appeal (UJA) for thirty-five years, from 1947 to 1982. Fifteen of those years involved volunteer work as a lay leader, the other twenty as the professional CEO and executive chairman. I learned on the job, invented most of the programs that are still in operational use, and taught the organization's notably successful fundraising techniques to the national staff and many lay leaders. When I accepted the top position in 1955, the annual national UJA/Federation campaign was raising about $50 million. When I left the active leadership in 1975, the total was exactly nine times that amount.

A fundraising effort of any size is a complex machine with lots of interlocking factors. In many ways, including vocabulary, it resembles a military unit. The very word "campaign" is listed in the dictionary with two primary definitions: 1) a series of military operations with a particular objective; and, 2) a series of organized, planned actions for a particular purpose, as for electing a candidate – or, one might add, raising a large sum of money.

The general chairman of the organization is the commander in chief; the top professional serves as the chief executive officer. The particular purpose or objective is called the "target" or "goal," denominated in a dollar sum and decided upon by a duly constituted authority. As in the army, the five branches – G-1 for Personnel, G-2 for Intelligence, G-3 for Operations, G-4 for Logistics, and G-5 for civilian-military operations – must all function well if the fundraising campaign is to succeed. Further, the people who head the various "divisions" of the campaign are often called "captains." They are lay men and women who volunteer their time, energy, expertise and financial contributions in an effort to inspire others to support the campaign. They are aided by professional staff who make appointments with prospects to be solicited, write advertising copy, drum up attendance for large meetings, escort missions to overseas destinations (very important at the UJA), arrange speaking engagements in cities all across the country, and utilize a multitude of other skills to keep the campaign headed toward its target.

The lay leaders are the most important asset in the arsenal of any campaign. Their enthusiasm, personal generosity, and initiative make the difference between success and mediocrity. This truism was stunningly exemplified in the famous Operation Exodus of 1990 to 1995. During that period, a special goal of $1 billion was set – and raised – on behalf of the flood of Russian Jews emigrating to Israel and the United States. During the same years, the regular annual goal had to be met, at an average of $700 million per year, and it was.

The UJA often asked Leslie Wexner, chairman of The Limited, to take its general chairmanship, but for many reasons, he was never able to accept. He did, however, volunteer to kick off Operation Exodus, convening in his home the first meeting of approximately 15 top prospects; they contributed a total of more than $30 million. Two years later, Wexner gave Exodus another huge shot in the arm by repeating the process with twice the number of contributors and twice the amount raised. Aided by Marvin Lender, the indefatigable UJA chair, and Brian Lurie, the CEO, this one man produced 10 percent of the $1 billion goal in only two events.

Wexner put his heart, energy, and influence into the efforts that initiated and then sustained the five-year special campaign. No more compelling proof of the value of a single leader's dedicated effort could be offered.

The men who assumed the role of general chairman included, from the very beginning, individuals bearing the most aristocratic names in the American Jewish community. Each understood the hard work expected of him and did it with an élan and conviction that lifted the spirit of other volunteers and contributors alike. The Jewish public was delighted to acknowledge them as the prime leaders in the largest Jewish communal effort in the entire Diaspora.

Although Governor-then-Senator Herbert Lehman was never the actual chairman, he attended most of the inner, policy-making meetings, accepted his assignment of speaking engagements, encouraged participation by the other members of his social crowd, chaired many meetings so that everyone knew he supported the cause, and urged his family to join him in this public identification. He was prominent not only in New York and Washington but also world-wide, through his chairmanship of UNRRA, which provided help to the millions of displaced persons in Europe after World War II. The fact that there were a quarter-million Jews in those D.P. camps in Germany, where he visited personally, made him especially keen to ease their terrible burdens.

HENRY MORGENTHAU

Although the UJA started campaigning on January 1, 1939, some weeks after the infamous *Kristallnacht*, and continued all through the years of the War, large-scale fundraising was not launched until the War ended. The first chairman of international stature was Henry Morgenthau, Jr., who served with great dedication from 1946 until 1950. His father served as U.S. ambassador to Turkey, and he himself reached the pinnacle as secretary of the treasury under President Roosevelt, whose personal friend and neighbor he was in the farming country of Dutchess County, New York.

In a family history entitled *Mostly Morgenthaus*, Henry Morgenthau III analyzed his father's attitude toward his Jewishness. Those feelings became apparent during the arguments concerning the American plan for post-war Germany. Debating this issue at the highest level of the U.S. Government, with fellow secretaries and FDR, Morgenthau found himself the only one pushing hard for a policy that would prevent Germany from ever again plunging the world into war. While economic, political, and international factors obviously played a role in the discussions, Jewishness entered the equation when the secretaries of state and war accused him of taking a hard line against Germany because of his "race."

Morgenthau's feelings about de-industrializing Germany and reducing her economy to a pastoral condition were *very* strong, deriving in no small measure from his outrage over the Holocaust. The argument raged through several meetings. At times he thought he had the President on his side, only to see him waffle. One of Morgenthau's closest associates at Treasury, Harry Dexter White, suggested that he back down a bit and opt for the Ruhr to be internationalized instead of destroyed. Morgenthau responded angrily: "Harry, you can't sell that to me.... There will be an *Anschluss* and the Germans will go in and take it.... Just strip it down, every mine, every mill and factory, and wreck it... steel, coal, everything. I'm for destroying it first, and we will worry about the German population second."

Morgenthau lost the argument, and post-war Allied policy called for Germany's economic reconstruction. Stalin disagreed completely. In 1946, when I was stationed in Berlin and carefully followed the meetings of the four-power Allied Command, I learned of the speech made by the Russian representative, General Kotikov, who announced his country's intention to strip her zone of Germany of all factories, machine tools, coal, railroads, and anything else Russia could use, and to ship all that materiel back to the Soviet Union, to partially replace what Hitler had destroyed in his invasion.

When Harry Truman became president, he wanted his own appointees around him and selected Fred Vinson as secretary of the treasury. Morgenthau was out. Suddenly, his life seemed without purpose, his days not engaged, his agenda devoid of significant decisions to be made.

A loyal member of Morgenthau's former staff, Henrietta Klotz, found the solution. She got him involved with Henry Montor, executive director of the UJA. The national Jewish community urgently needed new leadership, and Morgenthau was a natural. The best-known Jewish political figure in the country, scion of a distinguished family, reasonably wealthy, experienced in shaping policy, and now possessing a heightened Jewish consciousness, he was invited to assume the UJA chairmanship. His new career was launched, and he remained in the chair for the next five years.

In the beginning, Morgenthau barnstormed the country in private planes, stopping in two or three cities every day. As I have related in an earlier chapter, he requested that I accompany him. Our first trip together spread over a whole month and led to numerous other ventures of a day or two. During those times, flying between cities, we had many long conversations. Thus I came to know Morgenthau as a person, as well as in his formal role of chairman. He felt deeply about the need to help people, grew more comfortable with the concept of a Jewish state, and often spoke about the UJA work as restoring to him a sense of the worth of his own life.

He went to Israel in October 1948, during the War of Independence, and while observing the enemy lines, saw mortar shells exploding just outside the Notre Dame Hospital. Later that month, Israeli officials bestowed on him the the highest honor the new state could confer by naming for him, in gratitude for his leadership, a new settlement down the hill from Jerusalem. Morgenthau in German means "Morning Dew," so the settlement was named in Hebrew "Tal Shachar," the exact translation of the German.

Morgenthau called that occasion "one of the greatest moments of my life." To the crowd at the dedication of Tal Shachar, he said: "You are showing the world that the Jew is a fighting man, and in that way you have raised the standard of the Jew in the eyes of the Christian world. Unfortunately, the young Republic of Israel has very few friends in the outside world. You will therefore have to depend on your own strong right arm." This was the kind of exultant militancy that inspired both the American and Israeli Jewish communities.

The annual sums raised during Morgenthau's chairmanship show his effectiveness:

    1945 – $35 million
    1946 – $102 million
    1947 – $124 million
    1948 – $148 million
    1949 – $127 million

When the Israel Bond Organization was established in 1950, as a new method of mobilizing capital for the fledgling state, Morgenthau moved from the UJA to the bond operation and assumed its chairmanship. Even though the switch triggered political and communal upheavals, Morgenthau took the attitude that he was continuing in seamless fashion to aid in the growth of Israel and the support of her people. Having given five years to the UJA, he was to give an additional four to the bond organization. Those nine years encompassed the displaced-persons crisis, Israel's birth, waves of immigration, and the beginning of Israeli financial expansion. He served longer than any other American Jewish principal leader in the half-century since the end of World War II.

EDWARD M. M. WARBURG

The Warburgs, by Ron Chernow, tells the family story. Father was Felix Warburg of the famous German banking family; mother was Frieda Schiff, daughter of Jacob Schiff, head of Kuhn, Loeb, & Co., a Wall Street prince second only to J. Pierpont Morgan. The marriage of Felix and Frieda linked two of the most influential German-Jewish families in New York and produced four sons and a daughter.

It was Felix, incidentally, who persuaded Julius Rosenwald, the head of Sears Roebuck, and John D. Rockefeller to contribute $9 million in the 1920s to the Agro-Joint, an enterprise that subsidized Jews on agricultural colonies in Siberia. Rabbi Stephen S. Wise, a prominent American Jewish leader, termed Warburg and group "Soviet dupes" and prophesied the project would be a failure, which indeed it turned out to be. Wise was angry with these arrogant, snobbish German potentates, as he perceived them, because they would not get behind the Zionist Movement with equal zeal.

Each of Felix's sons inherited some of his traits, so that collectively they added up to a portrait of their father. They had his lively, witty manner, engaging personality, and splendid sense of fun. When asked about the two middle initials of his name – M.M. – son Edward would explain that they meant "More Money." Actually, they stood for "Max Moritz." It was that son who inherited Felix's sense of social responsibility toward Jewish philanthropy.

"Eddie"'s lifelong interest in art started at Harvard – where he roomed with FDR's son, Jimmy, and the following year established the Society for Contemporary Art, concentrating on fresh, bold, rebellious artists such as

Picasso, Braque, Matisse, and Brancusi. Later, he was one of the founders of the American Ballet Theater and the Museum of Modern Art.

He taught art appreciation at Bryn Mawr after arranging to make a contribution to the college equal to his year's salary. And he often told a remarkable story about his acquisition of Picasso's famous "Blue Boy" in Berlin. The painting shows a pensive, downcast figure. That somehow appealed to Eddie, and he paid $7,000 for it. On the trip home, he worried about his father's reaction and decided – for future recounting – to reduce the amount he had paid by half.

Upon arrival, he told the customs officer that he had paid $3,500. The man gasped. "You mean you actually paid that much for this? Sonny, I'm going down to the dock, and when I come back, you change that to $1,000." His brother Paul ("Piggy"), was present to add comedy to the scene. "You see," Piggy explained, "the family finds it cheaper to let him do this than to keep him in a mental hospital." Decades later, Eddie sold "Blue Boy" for $1 million.

In World War II, Eddie enlisted as a private, because he wanted no special attention, and rose by merit to the rank of captain, landing in Normandy on D-Day + 7. He subsequently signed more affidavits of support than he could remember for refugees who wanted to come to America. He often did that at the request of the Museum of Modern Art, which helped many artists escape to the United States.

Everyone knew that Eddie could be counted on to find jobs for the immigrants as teachers or in other professions. His cousin, Bettina, a psychoanalyst, enabled more than 200 people in her field to reach America. Eddie once received a drawing from Marc Chagall inscribed, "With thanks." When he asked, "Thanks for what?," he learned that the Chagalls were among those whose papers he had personally expedited.

When he spoke at public meetings about refugees, or about Palestine, he did so with a conviction and intensity that moved his listeners to action.

Eddie became general chairman of the UJA in 1950, following Henry Morgenthau, and served until 1955. At the same time, he served as president of the Joint Distribution Committee (which cared for Jews in need the world over). No leader before or after has carried a double load of such magnitude.

He found such tasks as face-to-face solicitations distasteful, yet performed them with the grace and style that characterize nobility.

Indeed, the phrase *noblesse oblige* could have been invented to describe Eddie's attitude. He was shy – except when telling a joke, and then his friendliness poured out. He often used self-deprecating humor to lessen the sense of awe felt by his audiences, who recognized him as one of the handful of Jewish aristocrats.

Here is one such story. The original family name, in early 17th century Italy, Eddie said, was "del Banco," appropriate because the family ran a small bank that made loans to impoverished feudal barons. When circumstances caused the del Bancos to flee Italy, they went all the way to Germany, to a village outside Hamburg by the name of Warburg. As often happened, the family took the name of the location – and started from the bottom all over again. Stories like that put Eddie on the same level as his audiences of self-made men.

When I came to the UJA as the CEO, he was the chairman. We had met time and time again on the campaign circuit during the previous half-dozen years and now became close friends. His room at the UJA was right next door to mine. We saw each other constantly. I felt honored when, upon Eddie's death, his wife, Mary, asked me to participate in a memorial "Celebration of His Life." It was held in the old family house on Fifth Avenue that now serves as the Jewish Museum.

WILLIAM ROSENWALD

William (Bill) Rosenwald was a son of Chicago's Julius Rosenwald, owner of Sears Roebuck & Co., one of the great entrepreneurs and philanthropists of the 20th century. Bill established his own firm, American Securities, and made his own very large fortune, in addition to the inheritance from his father. Julius contributed scores of millions of dollars building universities – Howard, Tuskegee Institute, and several others – for "Negro" students. In addition, he built and endowed a great museum in downtown Chicago. He set a fine philanthropic example for his son. And Bill absorbed and observed it all throughout his life, which lasted into its tenth decade.

Bill Rosenwald came to the general chairmanship of the UJA from a long prior period as president of the National Refugee Service, which began many years before the UJA. He was one of the three persons who signed the original document that merged the three founding organizations (United Palestine Appeal, Joint Distribution Committee, and National Refugee Service) into one united campaign called United Jewish Appeal in November 1938. So when he arrived at the peak of the UJA in 1955, he had already been on American-Jewish active duty for more than 20 years.

He was strong, resolute, tireless, and clear-headed as to the UJA's goals. He remained general chairman, the most demanding job in the entire American Jewish establishment, for five years, a period that embraced one of Israel's wars, numerous waves of her immigration and settlement building, and assorted crises. He managed them with calm self-confidence and enthusiastic bearing.

Let me give you an example of how Bill worked. He agreed to solicit one of the bellwether contributors in the west, Herman Taubman of Tulsa, whose generous gift would have a major effect on many of his peers in that part of the country. Bill and I met Herman in his suite at the Waldorf-Astoria Hotel in New York. The breakfast table was set, and the conversation flowed easily, for we all knew each other well. After coffee, Bill got down to business. The numbers used in such intimate settings were spoken in a shorthand familiar to everyone: $100,000 was spoken of as "a hundred," $250,000 as "a quarter" (of a million); at that level, single digits like "five" could mean $500,000 or even $5 million.

Rosenwald asked Taubman if he remembered his last year's contribution and received the reply, "Yes, it was a quarter." Bill then requested "five" this year, and to make certain he was being clear, added, "I would like you to raise to 'a half,'" The two men went back and forth briefly, with Herman asking why so much more was needed and Bill replying from his endless reservoir of data.

Finally, Herman turned to Bill and played his own card (he himself was a skilled solicitor): "OK, I'll tell you what I'm going to do – I'll give five if you give five." Without any change in demeanor, and after a short pause for reflection, William Rosenwald of Sears, Roebuck fortune, turned to me, a salaried man, and said, in a tone and manner as though he were still negotiating with Taubman, "Well, Herb, it looks as though you're going to have to give five also, in order to make this circle complete. Herman will go to five if I do, and I'll go to five if you do."

I was stunned, caught completely by surprise, but a flash of insight told me that Bill was fulfilling the role of consummate chairman; that is, he was signaling Herman that <u>every</u> Jew was required to participate financially. My five would be $5,000, which was equivalent to their $500,000. I said yes – with my heart in my mouth, for that sum represented one-seventh of my annual salary. We finished the breakfast with a champagne toast. That was Bill Rosenwald at his very best.

PHILIP M. KLUTZNICK

With the passage of the great names – Lehman, Morgenthau, Warburg, and Rosenwald – the era of aristocrats came to an end. It was now better for the UJA to have as its head a person who could be a symbol to both the Jewish community and the rest of the American people, someone with a newsworthy name, as well as leadership abilities and cogent commitment to Judaism and Israel.

I looked into the ranks of government service, and one man stood out. A prominent Chicago attorney and businessman, Philip Klutznick, had devoted much of his life to public service in both domestic and international spheres. By the end of his public career, he had served in various federal posts under seven Presidents, from Franklin D. Roosevelt to Jimmy Carter. He was U.S. representative to the United Nations Economic and Social Council (UNESCO), with the rank of ambassador; vice-chairman of the Committee for Economic Development, dealing with economic problems in the Third World; commissioner of the Federal Public Housing Authority; and secretary of commerce under Carter.

Phil's career on the Jewish side was equally varied. He had been president of the World Jewish Congress and the Memorial Foundation for Jewish Culture; international president of B'nai Brith; an officer of the UJA, the Israel Bond, and many other Israel-connected organizations. He was one of the major builders of the first Jerusalem Hilton Hotel, as well as a prime planner of the deep-water port of Ashdod and the town's industrial center. He could perform such feats because his profession was real estate development.

I grew increasingly enthusiastic about the quality of his potential leadership. He had deep, emotional feelings for the Jewish people and Israel. His organizational skills were impressive, and his oratorical ability had been polished by several decades of public speaking. Happy at the thought of working with him, I made a formal request that he accept the general chairman's position. He acknowledged that we had a deadline – the first week in December, when our annual national conference would take place and when the incoming chairman would be presented to the delegates.

In a very short time, Philip came back with a positive answer, based on one condition. President Kennedy had his name on a short list for a high governmental post, and if the President tapped him for such a position, he would have to accept. If I wished, I could announce him as our new chairman, gambling that no offer would be coming from Kennedy. I thought the matter over carefully and decided to take the chance, for the qualities of leadership he could put at our disposal were too superb to turn down.

To broad public acclaim, Phil was installed at the national conference, where he made a stirring inaugural address, and we began to work on the plan for the 1961 campaign. Alas, I lost the gamble. Two months later, Kennedy appointed Adlai Stevenson as U.S. ambassador to the U.N. and Philip Klutznick as his deputy. Phil had previously worked closely with Stevenson when the latter was governor of Illinois, and the combination of Kennedy and Stevenson importuning him to get on the U.N. team was too much to resist.

So Philip Klutznick was the chairman of the UJA for only three months, the shortest tenure in the history of the organization. Although we parted company prematurely, we remained good friends; I saw him many times in later years and worked with him on several projects. But at that moment, I was in trouble, without a partner.

JOSEPH MEYERHOFF

Who could assume the mantle on short notice? A few of us huddled, and a very short list emerged: not many Jewish leaders in the entire country could match the caliber of the distinguished predecessors. Joe Meyerhoff was one who we thought could, and as we continued to compare and evaluate and judge, it became ever clearer to me that he would be the best choice.

I realized that I had actually made my judgment of Meyerhoff ten years earlier, at the Jerusalem meeting in 1950, when the Israel Bond Organization was born. Here was an infant government, just finished with a dreadful war of independence that had taken the lives of one out of every hundred citizens; a government now confronted with predictions that the financial contribution of American Jews would dwindle to a meaningless amount, and seeking to find a new avenue of economic support – namely, to offer that government's bonds for sale on the world market. Would it work? Could leaders be found? Would the UJA fight the bond organization? Would the local communities buy the bonds? The discussion went into a third day, with uncertainty and fatigue taking their toll.

All through the arguments and speeches, Joe Meyerhoff and I and a relatively few others kept stressing the point that the two ventures should function in parallel, dividing up the calendar and the staunchest of Israel's supporters in each community. The UJA need not wither, and the new bond organization could grow. Israel could have them both, if we kept our nerve and used our brains.

Then Joseph Meyerhoff stood and volunteered to prove that theory correct. He offered to chair the local UJA/Federation campaign in his home city of Baltimore; and after that was completed, to chair the city's first bond campaign. He would thus demonstrate the legitimacy of both efforts, defuse any opposition from the federation side, prove that enough manpower existed to fill the ranks of volunteers in both campaigns, and place an almost constant focus on Israel's needs throughout the entire year, instead of just the few months of the heretofore-single campaign. It was a master stroke on his part, dispelling the pall of doubt and uncertainty.

Looking to fill the empty UJA chair at the beginning of 1961, I therefore considered Joe Meyerhoff the very best prospect. When invited to become the general chairman of the UJA, he responded in typical fashion – quickly and affirmatively. In a matter of days, he took command and generated a surge of confidence among the staff and the lay committees. He had made a great success as a home builder and real estate developer because of his decisiveness, farsightedness, stubbornness mixed with idealism, compassion, and financial generosity. It was an awesome combination of characteristics. When some special need compelled a resolicitation of the biggest givers, he set an example straight off and asked others to follow. When a mission to Israel or to a concentration-camp site was planned, he announced at the outset that he would personally lead it.

Joe's attitude toward Israel was based on family ideology. Back in 1892, his father, Oscar, had traveled with a small group from his *shtetl* (village) in Eastern Europe to Palestine to investigate the possibility of settling there. The poverty, backwardness, filth, and poor health conditions turned them off (a brother-in-law died of typhus). The survivors returned to Russia, and the family joined the huge migrations to the United States at the turn of the century. As Joe grew to maturity, the Zionist effort to establish a Jewish state won his whole-hearted support.

He performed so well during his four-year stint that the UJA reversed a downward trend in annual contributions. And he received the greatest tribute possible from the previous chairman. At a dinner in December 1964, at the close of Joe's regime, Bill Rosenwald said the following: "We knew you as a congenial companion, as a respected and resourceful businessman, and as one consecrated to the ideal of working for your fellow man. But it was only after you showed us how good you really are that we realized that, high as our opinion of you had been, you had exceeded our expectations."

Joe Meyerhoff and I worked very effectively together. The chemistry was right, and I came to know the members of his wonderful family, who have maintained and even expanded his traditions. His son and daughters have made their own marks. Harvey (Bud) was chairman of, and the largest single donor to, the U.S. Holocaust Memorial Museum on the Mall in Washington. We have remained close friends to this day. One of *his* daughters, Lee Hendler, has become a scholar in Judaism and is in demand as a speaker and an advocate of adult Jewish education.

Two years after Joe left the chair, he became the second president of the Israel Education Fund, a special division of the UJA, and again performed brilliantly. As his own contribution to the fund, he accepted my recommendation that he build a chain of free public libraries throughout Israel. He knew how such a gift would help elevate the educational standards of the country.

When he died, at the age of 85, his funeral service filled Meyerhoff Symphony Hall, his gift to the city of Baltimore. Twelve hundred mourners, including the governor, mayor, senators, and many of the craftsmen who had worked with him, came to pay their last respects. I was invited to give a eulogy and based it on the passage in 2 Samuel 3:38, in which King David wept at the grave of Abner, his beloved general. And David said to his soldiers: "You well know that a great Prince in Israel has fallen this day." Joseph Meyerhoff *was* a great prince in Israel, a civil servant of world Jewry, and we remember him with love.

MAX M. FISHER

He was born in 1908 in Salem, Ohio, a small town west of Pittsburgh originally founded by Quakers and containing five Jewish families.

Max's Jewish environment was minimal. There was neither synagogue nor Hebrew school, so he had no Bar Mitzvah and learned little of basic Judaism. His father conducted a family Seder for Passover, and his mother lit candles on Friday night. The fundamental commandment of charity was represented by the traditional blue-white tin box of the Jewish National Fund standing on the kitchen shelf; a coin was occasionally dropped into the box to help plant a tree in Palestine.

Max was tall and husky, played center on the football team, and, despite shyness, was quite popular. The family moved to Detroit, where Max prospered and took his place among the community leaders, Jewish and non-Jewish alike. In 1957, he was appointed chairman of the city's Jewish Welfare Federation. At the same time, he came to the attention of the United Foundation, the general community's umbrella organization, whose leaders learned from Max the Jewish community's secret of "card calling" (the system of calling each donor's name publicly so that each stands to announce a contribution) as the best route to handsome campaign results. Soon Max became chairman of the United Foundation as well.

As he rose in prominence in Detroit, he became known to me at national UJA headquarters, and a fortuitous meeting occurred at New York's airport. We were booked on the same Pan-Am Clipper to London, and the plane's configuration included two private bedrooms, available for $500 more than first-class fare. Max had engaged one of them, and I was seated back in the coach section. Once aloft, I went forward to chat with him further. We talked in detail about his Detroit experiences, his impulses to work for the good of his fellow humans and the satisfactions he gained from that, his nervousness at speech-making, the concept of the leader's personal generosity as a stimulus to other givers, and on and on about the business of fundraising. Hours went by, and gradually the conversation shifted from Detroit to the national scene.

I began to weave the story of how the national UJA campaign was organized, how the single most important element was lay leadership, how I was always seeking new talent, how crucial it was for a national leader to have local roots – so that many other local leaders would be encouraged to expand their scope of activities. All that led me to the climax; a request that Max think about enlarging his own stage. Our conversation consumed almost the whole night, and in later years, whenever we would think of that fateful evening and where it had led him in his public career, Max would sum it up by saying that it had cost him $500 to lose a night's sleep listening to my seduction. But it worked, and from that moment, Max Fisher was on the path toward the UJA's premier position.

At that time, there was still considerable discussion among American Jews about dual loyalty; could one be loyal to a foreign country (Israel) – tied to it through any combination of emotion, religion, historic memory – while remaining a citizen of another country (the United States)? Was there not a fundamental conflict?

"Jews would come and argue with me," recalls Fisher. "They used to ask, 'If the United States attacked Israel, what would you do?' That's silly. The U.S. is not going to attack Israel. There's no hang-up there. I can be a good citizen of the United States and be a supporter of Israel at the same time. Israel is something that I love. It's something that the Jewish people have dreamed about; they wanted a homeland. Where's the dual allegiance?"

Because of his coolness and experience, Max moved to the peak of every major organization with unprecedented speed. After serving as UJA chairman, he went on to the presidency of the Council of Jewish Federations and Welfare Funds. Later, he became chairman of the reconstituted Jewish Agency in Jerusalem and of the executive committee of the American Jewish Committee. Wrote Abraham Karp, in his history of the Jews in America: "Fisher held leadership positions in all the power bases of the American Jewish community. He was ubiquitous. No major policy decision was made without him."

Max enjoys enormous political power in the U.S. Government through his Republican connections. Beginning with President Eisenhower, and resuming with Presidents Ford, Nixon, Reagan and Bush, he was the number-one American Jew consulted on matters involving the Jewish people or Israel. His opinions carried weight with top officials at every level – cabinet secretaries, chiefs of staff, top bureaucrats in the departments of state, defense, and treasury.

Max Fisher always gave whatever time and energy were required to serve his people and the Holy Land. No higher compliment can be given.

SUBSEQUENT CHAIRMEN

Following Fisher, there have been 14 chairmen, each serving a two-year term. Every one of them deserves a much more detailed account than space permits, for each gave maximum contributions of time, energy and money. Medals are not bestowed by the UJA, but perhaps they should be, for these men served far above and beyond the normal call of duty. Let me at least record their names for posterity:

Edward Ginsberg	1968-71	Lawyer, Cleveland
Paul Zuckerman	1972-74	Businessman, Detroit
Frank R. Lautenberg	1975-77	U.S. Senator, New Jersey
Leonard R. Strelitz	1977-78	Businessman, Norfolk
Irwin S. Field	1978-80	Manufacturer, Los Angeles
Herschel W. Blumberg	1980-82	Real Estate Developer, Washington, DC

Robert E. Loup	1982-84	Real Estate Developer, Denver
Alexander Grass	1984-86	Rite-Aid Drugstore Chain Chairman, Harrisburg
Martin F. Stein	1986-88	Businessman, New York City
Morton A. Kornreich	1988-90	Insurance Executive, New York City
Marvin Lender	1990-92	Baked-Goods Company Chairman, New Haven
Joel D. Tauber	1992-94	Investor, Detroit
Richard L. Pearlstone	1994-96	Investor, Aspen
Richard L. Wexler	1996-98	Lawyer, Chicago

CHAPTER THIRTY-EIGHT

WOMEN'S WORK:
WELL DONE, BADLY REWARDED

Jewish women in the United States have demonstrated an extraordinary capacity for successful philanthropic work. In addition to all the specialized women's organizations that attract their loyalty, plus the synagogue social-service groups and the local community agencies, they have contributed enormously to the success of the United Jewish Appeal. The results of their fundraising are spectacular – not sufficiently known or appreciated.

In December 1991, I wrote a major article for *Moment* magazine on the structure and functioning of the UJA, urging that women be promoted to the highest leadership positions. It was incomprehensible to me that educated, motivated, and experienced womanpower should be ignored rather than mobilized into the widest possible, multi-gender pool of potential leaders as well as contributors. Let me quote a paragraph from that article:

> Women have figured prominently in UJA and local Federation work from the beginning, having risen to the top as chairpersons of campaigns and presidents of local federations in the largest Jewish communities in the country, including New York and Los Angeles. And women have organized a National Women's Young Leadership Cabinet independent of the Men's

Young Leadership Cabinet, which had been formed years earlier. But all this has been women working with women.

The notable gap in this record of women's achievements lies at the apex of the national UJA structure. Not one female has been invited, in more than a half-century of work, to serve as national chair of the UJA, or chief executive officer, or president. This cannot be explained by lack of ability or inadequate commitment. Women's divisions over the decades of UJA's existence have raised almost $2.5 billion, more than 20 percent of the total. The UJA must bring more women into the executive committee, other key committees, and thus into the top positions of general chair and president of the board.

As this memoir was being prepared for publication, news arrived of a change in the previous lamentable situation. The first woman, Carole A. Solomon of New York City, had just been appointed general chair of the national UJA. I offer her my heartiest congratulations and look forward to her progress and achievements in office.

In an effort to understand the persistent decades of male exclusiveness at the UJA, I arranged a conversation with three of the organization's most-experienced and knowledgeable women: Matilda Brailove, women's division chair in the early 1950s; Harriet Sloane, chair in the 1980s; and Nan Goldberg Greenblatt, professional director of the division over several decades. They possessed all the necessary skills for soliciting contributions, organizing missions abroad, speech-making, training, inspiring new recruits. And above all, each had calmness, grace, and self-confidence.

The four of us gathered in my office around a tape recorder for many hours one spring day. We conducted a free-wheeling discussion, focusing on questions I had given them to stimulate their thoughts.

The trigger questions were:

- What is the rationale for a separate women's campaign? Except for single women or for business and professional women who earn their own money, aren't the contributions coming from the same family pocket?

- Why has there never been a woman general chair of the national UJA campaign (as has occurred in many local federation campaigns and in the national Council of Federations)?
- Relate some of the major achievements in women's division history.
- How is women's fundraising conducted? Are there dollar-level meetings? Wealthy-widow meetings? Face-to-face solicitations?
- How do Women's Division missions to Israel fare?

Beginning with a brief account of how the Women's Division got started, here is what my three interviewees told me:

After World War II, when the shattering facts of the Holocaust became widely known and the gathering of survivors into displaced-persons camps made it possible to visit them, the first American Jewish woman to do so was Adele Rosenwald Levy, the sister of one of the UJA's three founders. Levy returned filled with electricity and energy, determined to traverse America to arouse the sympathy of women by describing what she had seen, and urging them to raise money to alleviate the hunger and suffering. Women's audiences responded beautifully. By 1946, a wide-spread operation was in full swing.

It was decided to base the UJA women's campaign on luncheons charging a minimum contribution of $100 per person. In those days that was a lot of money for a woman to spend on philanthropy. And in the first year, with Adele Levy speaking at scores of luncheons, about $13 million was raised. The total campaign for that year achieved $102 million, so the women's share was almost 13 percent – a tremendous beginning.

The best estimate is that during 45 years of work (1946-1991), the Women's Division raised $1 billion in the first 35 years and another $1 billion in the next ten. That kind of acceleration was due to the increased efficiency of the operation, as the division's operatives learned better techniques and worked harder.

But, my three guests said, we know we are responsible for additional large amounts that never showed up in the totals, simply because new gifts from men brought in by women were credited to various men's divisions. We may have been responsible for garnering even more contributions from men than we did from women. We know, from innumerable conversations with our officers and workers, how that happens.

The woman sits at the family dinner table and relates what she did for the campaign that day. Her enthusiasm and the aura of warmth she has about herself as a result of the good she is doing, reach out to her children and husband. And that subtle stimulus often carries over to fundraising meetings, when the husband, responding to his name being called, rises and announces that he had planned to contribute X, but his wife has influenced him to give more. So there's no way to keep track of the *total* amount women raise.

There is a rationale for having a separate women's campaign. In many Jewish households, a woman has disposable income of her own. Either she earns it herself, or she manages the household budget; either way, she makes many financial decisions. Some people of course believe that, although there may be two earners in a family, there should be only a joint contribution to the campaign. A married couple acts together, handling its finances jointly, the argument runs, and that approach should also govern its charitable activities. A countervailing viewpoint considers that attitude a great loss, not only in dollars to the UJA, but also in the quality of life in the family involved.

Some years ago, in Tampa, there was a case that illustrates this issue. A young couple, both substantial earners, well disposed to the campaign, still insisted on the joint-family, single-gift approach and lobbied for the dissolution of Tampa's separate Women's Division. It was dissolved. Within three years, the overall-campaign results had dropped so precipitously that the division was re-instated, and by the end of the fourth year, the results had returned to previous levels. The determining factor was the number of volunteer workers. Without the stimulation of an organized women's division, large numbers of female volunteers gradually drifted away, leaving all the work to the men.

The key to successful campaigning is the philosophy that every Jew – man, woman, and child – is commanded by Jewish law and tradition to make his/her personal contribution to the welfare of our entire people. In Biblical times and for centuries thereafter, every Jew in the world was expected to contribute 1/2 shekel (1/2 ounce of silver) per year to the Temple in Jerusalem. In today's world, young adults often inherit large sums from a parent or grandparent and are not educated in the principle that they, like their forbears, should make contributions proportional to their means.

The philosophy and need for education applies also to widows who inherit large sums. If throughout their married lives they had left it to their husbands to make joint family gifts, widows would not develop the necessary emotional and intellectual grasp of their personal responsibility. Had they been making their own gifts, they would have developed the capacity to deal in widowhood with philanthropic matters.

An additional piece of evidence validates the thesis that individual giving promotes a stronger total Jewish community. That evidence is found in Project Renewal, which was established some years ago to link American donors to projects in Israel's urban slums. The Women's Division came up with the idea of awarding to every woman who gave the project an extra $2,500 an unusually handsome, calligraphed scroll testifying to her personal commitment to the people of Israel. The division sent out almost 10,000 such scrolls – representing $25 million raised.

Examples such as Project Renewal have convinced me that caring women learn the joy of giving and sharing. Women who work on the campaign grow personally in important ways. They gain confidence in themselves – in their independence, judgment, and abilities.

When I asked my three interviewees why there had never been a female general chair of the UJA (the interview preceded the selection of Carole A. Solomon), they gave a forthright answer. They recalled one instance in which a woman had been briefly considered as a possible chair; the all-male selection committee quickly dropped the idea. The Joint Distribution Committee later found her so able that it made her chair of its international board. There is, my experienced trio told me, a fundamental lack of consideration, perhaps even a denial, of the value of women at the helm. The discrimination, they noted, starts well below the exalted position of chair: women are not given leading roles at national conferences or any opportunity to demonstrate their abilities as successful national campaigners.

Further, the three women said, the UJA male officers have simply thought of the Women's Division as an autonomous constituent group that runs itself very well and can be left alone. The positive side of that attitude is that the officers don't interfere with the women's organization. Staff members are left to create and execute their own programs and ideas. They just keep getting better at what they do, their structure gets stronger, and occasionally they're recognized. For example, when a general meeting of all UJA officers is called, several women can be seen; and of 70-odd national vice-chairs, about ten are women.

If one asked a group of experienced women campaigners why such a situation existed, a variety of answers would be heard: "Oh, those men haven't gotten out of the Dark Ages"; "Well, perhaps it's just benign neglect"; "We don't protest – they leave us alone to do our work, and we leave them alone."

One of the women I interviewed offered a personal experience to illustrate the problem: "The UJA public relations office was preparing a campaign booklet to be distributed nationwide, and I was sent some material for my comments. The booklet contained a very long section on major gifts, detailing the various kinds of functions being planned to solicit them. In the Women's Division, we have four different kinds of major gift events, at the levels of $5,000, $10,000, $18,000, and $25,000, and not one of those was listed. I protested vigorously. The explanation given was that major gifts come under the direction of one of the assistant vice-presidents, and since he doesn't supervise the Women's Division, there was no reason for any of its events to be included in that section. The director was told she could list the Women's Division's major gift events in the separate section where all the other women's material was gathered!"

The woman who chaired the division in 1973 pushed for a women's mission to Israel immediately after the end of the Yom Kippur War. She organized the mission quickly. Speed in seizing a historic moment is one of the crucial aspects of leadership, and she possessed it. The men were furious, complaining that they should be going first, but since they were nowhere near ready, off the women went. They took with them what caring mothers would take: handmade woolen helmets, warm sweaters, and warm socks to help the troops who would be remaining on snowy Mt. Hermon above the Golan Heights through the winter.

The mission was tremendously successful. Both shocked and inspired, the participants gathered material for future speeches and geared up for a huge campaign to start as soon as they got home. Just before the return trip, several of the women went to dinner in Jerusalem at the house of Israeli friends, a general and his wife. The wife asked the American visitors what they had brought and was told about one who had brought eight dozen pairs of socks. The general said: "That woman is smart. She ought to be the chair of the Women's Division." One of the Americans replied: "She's already been that. You could have said, general, that she should be chair of the national UJA."

The national women have developed a unique, eight-day mission to Israel. They invite both the women's division chair and professional director of the 40 largest American-Jewish communities to join them. In so doing, the national leaders help their community counterparts plan the local campaigns according to local problems and needs and, in the process, gather data for national use in the months ahead. And, of course, all 80 of the mission members are solicited for their own gifts during the visit to Israel.

The Women's Division also utilizes a number of other methods of solicitation that have been developed jointly with their male counterparts:

- The *caucus*, an open meeting of any group with an especially high degree of commitment or state of emotion (such as mission returnees). The members of such a group seek not merely to publicly announce their gifts, but also to ventilate their emotions and motivation. It is a spiritual experience, in addition to a financial one.
- "*Calling the cards*," a classic method that consists of convening a meeting and calling aloud the name of every woman in the room. Each one stands, in response to the call, to announce her gift. This is a voluntary action; the woman knows the process in advance, and by attending, she agrees to be part of it. But calling the cards comes with a caveat; the meeting must be preceded by pre-solicitation of some of the attendees. The person at the podium calling the cards must skillfully call in succession three or four people whose gifts she knows will be impressively larger than last year's – and then call several persons who have *not* been pre-solicited. The latter usually fall into line; that is, having heard several big gifts announced, they tend to

follow that trend. (As a rule of thumb, at least one-third of the
attendees must be pre-solicited.)

- The *face-to-face* solicitation. Although the most effective method, this
one finds the fewest workers both able and willing to do the job. It's
the best because it affords the opportunity to uncover grievances,
rebut the usual excuses, sell the case with detailed arguments, and to
send some solicitors to other cities to invoke the ultimate power – the
personal friendship between solicitor and prospect. But the approach
requires great self-confidence; easy-going charm, even charisma;
verbal skill; lots of knowledge about the worldwide condition of Jews
and Israel; and a thick skin so that a refusal by one prospect doesn't
incapacitate the solicitor for the next prospect. The Women's Division
has inspired and trained a cadre of about 80 good solicitors who can be
sent not only to prospects in their own community, but also to
strangers in far-off cities.

I asked my three Women's Division sources about the degree of success of
Division missions to Israel. Their combined response added up to the
following:

"When we run them, the missions are all very successful from the point of
view of both inspiration and financial results. That's true despite the fact that
we have to work harder each year to recruit the number we would like to have
on any given mission.

"Why is that necessary? Because the number of opportunities to *go* on
missions keeps expanding. In the beginning, only the UJA, which pioneered
with the mission concept, was capable of arranging the logistics. Now almost
every federation in the country runs its own mission, as do the regional
organizations. And both of those operations accept husbands and wives, which
we do not. Synagogues run them, too, and the UJA's Young Leadership
Cabinets sponsor them for both men and women. Nonetheless, ours continue
to do very well."

UJA women play another, vital role: it is they who transmit the Jewish
tradition of philanthropy to their children. Without that, the tradition – and
therefore the philanthropy itself – would be in danger of extinction.

Now that one woman has broken through the UJA's "glass ceiling," we can expect that others will follow. That can have only a beneficial effect: a surge of female pride that strengthens women's leadership across the country and increases the fundraising totals. As a result, the entire cause – from Israel's security to an enhanced sense of pride in Jewish identity in the United States – will be strengthened.

CHAPTER THIRTY-NINE

VALEDICTORY: AN ORGANIZATION WORTH MORE THAN MONEY

It is appropriate in this final chapter on the UJA to describe the intellectual and philosophical concepts that motivated me in my work there. But I will do so using practical examples rather than abstractions. Let me talk about the objectives and long-range goals I had in mind when I accepted the leadership of the organization. All the ideas I planned to introduce required a combination of creative planning and energetic execution. Looking back over the decades, almost all were quite successful, some in the short run and others over a longer period. Specific programs evolved from the following precepts:

1. The UJA should teach American Jews how to give money; all Jewish causes would benefit as ever-larger sums are raised.

Someone once asked for an elaboration of the above point, and I answered using the example of Dr. Abram Sachar, who served as President and Chancellor of Brandeis University for many decades. He really laid the foundation and could be called the creator of today's school. "Abe" Sachar, as he was affectionately known by the thousands of people whom he solicited, personally raised tens of millions of dollars – one of the most remarkable individual success stories of 20th-century fundraising. Lay leaders, board members, and others of course aided that enterprise, but Sachar's energy drove it.

One of his favorite techniques was to urge an individual being solicited to think of him/herself as a graduate of this new university and to make an "alumnus/alumna" gift of $1,000 annually. In the 1950s and 60s, that was a very large amount to bestow on an untried venture. Besides, most of the people approached had graduated from other schools, long before Brandeis was founded. Thus there was a double helping of chutzpah in the request.

His approach was prompted, Sachar once told me, by the fact that the UJA was teaching people how to give money, and as a result, nobody was shocked at receiving such a request. Not everyone would or could give at that level, but the necessary climate had been created. And once people grew accustomed to writing thousand-dollar instead of hundred-dollar checks, *hundred-thousand-dollar* gifts became feasible among those few prospects who could afford them.

Universities, hospitals, schools, community centers, homes for the aged, every necessary social institution benefited after the UJA raised the levels on behalf of Israel and other Jews in need worldwide. Courage had been imparted to solicitor and donor alike.

2. The UJA should teach the centrality of Israel.

UJA leaders were to stress the fact that Israel stood at the center of the existence of the Jewish people, which was born in that land and would end there, when the Messiah arrived. Love of Israel, dependence upon it for our spiritual dimension, reliance upon it for physical security – all those blended in the mega-concept of people, land, and faith as one.

The main vehicle for that image would be group missions to Israel for American Jews. The first mission of 12 persons was dispatched in 1954, a year before I took the UJA helm. Small and experimental, it was deemed a success when measured by the reactions of the participants. I decided to expand that program as much as possible because I felt intuitively that, if we ran it properly, we could eventually create links between thousands of people that would have a powerful multiplier effect; more missions to meet more people in an ever-increasing web of relationships that would produce vacationers, future students at Israeli universities, or even people going on *aliyah* (immigrating).

Once an American Jew was caught up in that web and had clear memories – of an idealistic person encountered on a kibbutz, a squad of soldiers on border patrol, a new immigrant struggling to learn Hebrew, or a bus driver who pointed out every Jewish cow along the road – the American tourist would have fallen in love with the Israelis.

The same would happen with the land itself. It is truly beautiful, with an incredible variety of scenery – desert, sea, mountains, wilderness, orchards, villages – all of which can be seen in just a few days. After a bit of travel, most visitors fall in love with the country. That occurs principally when the guide is knowledgeable and charismatic enough to tie the land of today to the land of the Bible – the kings, prophets, temples, Romans, and Maccabees – so that they come alive, and fascinated visitors hardly know in which century they stand. But they certainly do know that this is part of their heritage, the homeland of their people, going back almost 4,000 years.

In addition to the varieties of people and landscape, the plan called for mission members to be exposed to contemporary problems. That meant taking them to army bases and borders; seeing planes and tanks and hearing military analyses of the last and possibly next war. It also meant stopping at a reception center for new immigrants, hearing from the most recent wave their experiences in reaching Israel and their worries about obtaining housing and jobs. And it meant visiting an old-folks home or hospital to hear harrowing tales of escape from the Nazis or pleasant ones about ending their days peacefully in the midst of flowers and gardens.

The missions were to sell Israel, its importance, its people, and its problems. After a few years, when the program was solid and sending as many as a thousand people a year, I would take a further risk. I was convinced that, if we actually solicited contributions during missions, we would obtain very good results under the emotional impact of what our members were seeing and hearing.

Other voices warned me against that. Word would spread, they argued, and people would avoid coming on missions for fear that they might be pressured for a contribution. In my view, the potential gains outweighed the possible losses, and I decided to press forward with solicitations on missions, designing a procedure consisting of two elements: the "back of the bus" and the "caucus."

In the first, solicitors would invite prospects to come to the rear seats of the bus, deliberately left vacant, at a fitting moment during a day's journey. In a conversation of moderate length, the prospect was asked to donate an amount that had been determined in consultation with his/her community leaders back home. We called that sum a "rating" and calculated it to involve an increase the prospect could afford and one likely to serve as a bellwether for others to follow. If the prospect was ready to make a commitment on the spot, the solicitor would call the *next* prospect to the back and use the former's generous response as a pointed example to the latter. If the first person asked for time to ponder the matter, the solicitor graciously agreed, expressing the hope that a commitment be made before the mission ended. So it went, hour after hour, on bus after bus, with the "jungle telegraph" whispering the news through hotel lobbies at the end of the day as to who had contributed what.

The caucus was a session held in a hotel on the next-to-last day, in order to accommodate everyone who wished to express emotions, opinions, impressions, personal feelings – and hopefully end with a pledge. These meetings lasted at least three or four hours because *almost everyone* wanted to speak, to ventilate. Some people actually cried when reciting a particularly poignant experience they had had during the mission week. And almost every contribution was notably larger than a normal solicitation would have produced back home.

The caucus thus became a sort of therapy session. The participants gave money, to be sure. But in the caucus setting, that was merely the means of reasserting their identity, tightening their links with land and people, restating their loyalty, and reaffirming their very existence. The whole, successful system has been continued to this day.

As for the original fear of dissuading mission-goers if we solicited them for gifts, attendance eventually increased to as many as ten thousand per year. Not even war lowered the numbers substantially. As everyone knows, when Jews believe in something, they are very stubborn. Apparently they believe in missions, are willing to go to the back of the bus, and actually like the caucuses.

Arousing emotions in the course of explaining Israel to our constituency was one thing, but another ingredient had to be added: knowledge. The thin layer of top leadership, both in the local federations and the national UJA organization, represents the major strength of the campaign. Only a few thousand strong, this cadre of principal figures must be thoroughly steeped in a continuous UJA educational system: missions that would enable them to see and feel for themselves; hearing high-ranking Israeli speakers; reading long, personal letters from me a half-dozen times a year; receiving constant analyses of current events in Israel and throughout the Jewish world. Knowledge is indeed power. It leads to conviction, and power and conviction are the main elements in leadership.

Even knowledge is not enough. Passion is the ingredient that lights the flame of relentless action. During my years as a volunteer speaker, before I took the formal position with the UJA and certainly after, my speeches were fiery performances intended to stir the listeners, to bring them literally to their feet. My style was fervent, emphatic, emotional, designed to create a sense of excitement and start the adrenalin flowing. That was passion. Passion multiplies and amplifies the power that knowledge creates.

For me, however, more important still was clear-cut sincerity. My audiences knew that I believed with heart and soul every word I spoke. They knew that my whole purpose was to convince them to join the crusade on behalf of the Jewish people worldwide and the renascent Israeli state. I sought their advocacy for these causes and wrapped my arguments in the cloth of cogency, warning of the consequences of failure on our part and, conversely, of how history would praise our generation if we performed our duties faithfully and well.

3. The UJA should help build community strength in the United States.

Aside from the negotiations over how to apportion the campaign proceeds, I had no quarrel nor ideological difference with the local federations. On the contrary, I sought to strengthen them, for the stronger the federations became, the more money they would raise. "Stronger" in this context meant clearer goals, more inspiration, greater emphasis on Judaic values, more cooperation with local synagogues and rabbis, more effective speakers, and so on.

I had no intention of becoming involved in internal community problems, but I took the right to express my opinion concerning priorities for the communal agenda. Fighting anti-semitism was relatively low on my list because I did not see it as a significant danger in America; day-school education was high for I saw it as an agent to enhance strong Jewish identity. Major support to hospitals was low; community-supported summer camps, high.

You can see the drift. I was urging communities to spend their money on educating their citizens in Judaism, for that would guarantee survival and serve as the only dependable bulwark against assimilation and eventual disappearance. If we might need community campaigns 25 years hence, we had better educate that next generation in the values of Judaism and explain convincingly why we must work to exist as a separate and distinct people. Communities that have developed a good Jewish educational system, for adults as well as children, will remain strong and productive for a long time. I not only preached that but also offered to help create and nurture it wherever I could.

4. The UJA should build a cadre of leadership through a specific training program for both young and older leaders.

The Young Leadership Cabinet, whose story I told in an earlier chapter, is a prime example of how an idea can be transformed into reality by means of an enormous investment of energy and money. Identifying, recruiting, and teaching individuals with leadership ability and motivation was to me a matter of primary importance. I firmly believed the axiom that people raise money, and the primary task of the professional fundraiser is to raise the people who will take on the task. Raising people demands an intensive, tutorial approach to one individual after another, inspiring, coaxing, and instructing in the nuances of salesmanship and creating an *esprit de corps*. I took that to be a basic obligation of the national UJA and started to work on it as soon as I took office.

Incidentally, the young leadership idea spread widely outside the UJA/Federation system. Almost every Jewish organization in America adopted the nomenclature, as did other fundraising organizations in Europe, Latin America, South Africa, and Australia. I never had the slightest objection.

I was often invited to a city to lead a class in a Young Leadership series. That visit was my opportunity to see from the inside the caliber of the people the federation was choosing, the seriousness of the curriculum, the skill of the teachers, etc. By and large, I was pleased with the quality of the work I witnessed, and came away convinced that these training programs constituted a valuable addition to the arsenal of community organization.

5. The UJA must always emphasize long-range historic goals and place them before American Jewry.

Making the distant future a matter for current concern served to impress on our constituency long-range challenges. Those challenges, I emphasized, might present themselves with little warning (in the form of a war, for example), or might grow slowly in the womb of history. I also stressed that we can actually *shape* history, that our victories assure our very survival. Such an approach, I think, empowers ordinary people with inner strength to accomplish extraordinary tasks. Let me take Soviet Jewry as an example.

I had started thinking about the matter of Soviet Jewry in 1954, a full year before coming to the UJA post. The trigger was a conversation with Moshe Sharett, then prime minister of Israel. Sharett's brother-in-law, Shaul Avigur, whom I had met in Germany when he was working on Aliyah Bet, was now a member of the Mossad, in charge of the effort to get Jews out of the Soviet Union. That involved a two-pronged project of maintaining the spark of Jewish identity in the heart and soul of activists inside Russia, as well as directing an outside propaganda effort to "let my people go."

Prime Minister Sharett used to tell me stories of how Avigur worked. One of the best involved smuggling sacred but allegedly "seditious" literature to the deprived Soviet Jews. For example, a hand-written calendar bearing the dates of the Jewish holidays was a precious object – and a dangerous one, because the secret police considered it a piece of "anti-state propaganda." The Mossad nonetheless spirited such calendars into the Siberian labor camp at Vorkuta, enabling the Jewish prisoners to celebrate holidays secretly. Tiny Bibles, prayer books, Psalm books (such as Anatoly Sharansky was to cherish during his years in prison) were also smuggled in, and they served to maintain the flame of Jewish identity and loyalty. It is incredible, in a way, to think of something the size of a match box containing that much emotional power. But the first atomic bomb was relatively small also, wasn't it?

Once I received a letter from a dear friend, Rabbi Morton Berman, formerly of Chicago, now lying in the cemetery on the Mount of Olives in Jerusalem. He was writing a book of memoirs and asked me the following question: "Was your decision to accept the UJA post motivated by your desire to help Jews get from Russia to Israel?"

I replied: "My main motivation was to help build the new State of Israel and to expedite the gathering of immigrants from many countries. In my UJA acceptance speech in 1955, I made strong reference to the ultimate dream of re-uniting the Jews of Russia with Israel and the entire Jewish people, but it was a speech of pure vision. There was no shred of empirical evidence at that moment to believe that such a possibility could come true. Yet the thought of rescuing that most important segment of the Jewish nation was uppermost in my mind from the beginning."

I also recall a conversation with Rabbi Ely Pilchik of Short Hills, New Jersey, who asked me in 1955 why I had left the practicing rabbinate to take a "mere" fundraising job. I tried to explain the history-making possibilities inherent in that fundraising position and used the example of bringing millions of Jews from Russia to Israel. He looked blank at first, but slowly his facial expression changed, as he caught on to the incredible notion. He asked if I thought it was really possible, and I told him what Shaul Avigur was doing in his amazing, secret operation, then stated my faith in that tiny program. Pilchik realized it was all a dream on my part. But in later years, when the emigration was underway, he complimented me on such far-sighted vision.

Meanwhile, I talked about the great historic possibility, in order to keep the idea alive. No matter what the subject of any particular speech, I would deliberately include a warning to my audience that "someday those Russian doors will open, and every one of you listening to me will be responsible for meeting that huge challenge."

For 15 years, no matter what pressing problem held my attention, I repeated my mantra that the Russian Revolution in 1917 had not killed the Jewish instinct for survival, nor could it. The Soviet Union could impose the most severe restrictions imaginable: synagogues could be turned into stables; learning Hebrew could be forbidden by law; atheism could be forcibly preached according to communist doctrine; meetings of Jews in groups larger than three people could be labeled as conspiracies against the state, and individuals could be imprisoned just for attending them. The Jewish spirit would nonetheless remain alive inside Russia and eventually express itself. My exhortations became an almost religious act of faith, held up as a shining hope that sustained morale, a future challenge and a reward we would receive if we did our present work faithfully and effectively.

In setting up a long-range goal, and keeping it constantly before the Jewish public, I was employing an important lesson in psychology. Giving people an ideal in which to believe, one that may come to fruition only in a distant future, provides a sense of comfort that we will all live to see that future and prepares us to make the necessary sacrifices when the time for action does arrive. Keeping an idea alive keeps hope alive.

The fact that, year after year, we were assisting the Jews in country after country to migrate bolstered my assertion that someday we would get the chance to rescue Soviet Jewry. The essence of the speech was simple: "The instinct for survival burns, the chance will come. Can I prove it? No. It is an act of faith. Get ready. You think you are being asked for a lot of money now. Wait until 1975 or 1985, or whatever year they start coming. Then you will be asked for ten times as much."

"Then" has of course come, and the Jews of the Diaspora, as well as the Israelis, are responding marvelously, with no sign of weakening. We see a magnificent display of Jewish solidarity and awareness and determination not to fail.

Long-range goals will contribute to the maturity of the American Jewish community and switch its thinking away from the question: "What is this year's crisis? What are we giving our money for?" There may very well be a "this year's" war or an immigration or housing crisis, and those must be handled. But taking the long view guarantees sustained, visionary attention, and I find that a strong and healthy attitude.

Because I believe so fervently in the value of placing new challenges before American Jewry, I will offer an agenda I would attempt to carry out, were I the chief executive officer of the UJA today.

• *Rebuild a national Jewish community in the former Soviet Union*

After almost a million Russian Jews have migrated to Israel and another one-third million to the United States, an estimated two (perhaps three) million still remain in the former Soviet Union (FSU). The JDC, Lubavitch Chabad, and World Union for Progressive Judaism (Reform) have all been working hard to fill in the 75 year gap during which it was forbidden to teach or practice Judaism. The success of their efforts is the best evidence that large numbers of Russian Jews are receptive to new programs and institutions designed to teach them the rudiments of the Jewish heritage. It will take a generation and billions of dollars to create the infrastructure of schools, synagogues, centers, rabbinical seminaries, training colleges, and even universities needed to restore a sense of full Jewish identity in the FSU.

There are two good reasons for persevering. Those who remain in the FSU will become practicing and knowledgeable Jews; and those who continue to leave in the years ahead will be better Jews in Israel, the United States, or any other new home. This is a huge, historic challenge: creating a new Jewish community in a territory that had been a Jewish desert for almost a century.

• *Establish a major program in the United States for teaching Hebrew*

It is the international Jewish language of the future. Just as Yiddish and Ladino were languages that in past centuries served to link Jews spread over wide geographic areas, so Hebrew must serve from now on. Such a program will mean mobilizing thousands of teachers from Israel, and establishing permanent classes with flexible schedules in every major American city. Again, this will require scores of millions of dollars and huge organizational effort. But it will link Israel and the American Diaspora much more closely.

• Build hundreds of Jewish schools at the elementary, middle, and high levels throughout the United States

The need for such schools is now widely recognized to combat ignorance which leads to assimilation. The salutary effect of day school education is also well known. But the effort involved to create a network of such schools demands a national initiative that only the UJA can provide. Very low tuition, perhaps none at all, must be the foundation of this program, with a major teacher-and-principal-training program also a mandatory component.

• Provide technical and financial assistance to help solve two fundamental problems in Israel and the Middle East as a whole: too few universities and too little fresh water

Progress in these two areas will go far toward cementing relationships between and among the fractious Middle Eastern nations. Population growth in Israel and all neighboring countries will create a demand for more universities in the coming generation. A system permitting Arab students from the region to matriculate at modern Israeli universities would have advantages for both sides.

Increasing the flow of fresh water – most quickly achieved with desalination plants – will alleviate one of the region's most bitter issues. Israel, assisted by American Jews, can be the great provider. Water pipelines, crossing national borders, can become as common as oil pipelines.

• Provide an Israel Experience for American-Jewish young people, from ages 15 to 25

Much research testifies that a well-programmed experience in Israel is invaluable in shaping the pride and identity of young Jews. But so far all efforts, however sincere and well meant, have been fragmentary, partial, and diffuse. Alas, no national approach standardizing such a program exists. Nor is there a national Jewish treasury to guarantee that scores of thousands of youth can be given the Israel experience at a token cost. In the last chapter, I will discuss in detail how to carry out such a program.

• *Maintain a world-watch for endangered Jews*

There are fewer places in the world nowadays where danger lurks for Jews. But because one cannot be sure that situation will continue, we must have a permanent, quick-response capability to mobilize both manpower and financial resources to deal with emergencies. The Joint Distribution Committee (JDC) has done this work well for almost a century. It is one of the most respected Jewish organizations working internationally. Its ability to detect problem areas far in advance enables it to handle new crises, as it has done so well for so long. The JDC and all international Jewish organizations, such as ORT, Lubavitch Chabad, HIAS, and others, working in the fields of direct relief rehabilitation, and rescue, must always be provided with whatever sums they need to function at the highest levels of professional efficiency.

I observe the UJA from afar now. I think of its formative years and exciting growth during the decades of my administration and also its later moments of glory. Those include the sharp increase of funds raised in response to the Yom Kippur War; the steady support maintained throughout the '80s; and the spectacular success of Operation Exodus during 1990-95, when an extra billion dollars was contributed to facilitate the flood of Soviet Jews to Israel and the United States. That was in addition to the annual achievement of raising three-quarters of a billion annually during the same period.

Then, sadly, two developments suddenly overwhelmed the leadership and preoccupied its attention. First came the appearance of a 1990 population study showing an American Jewish intermarriage rate of 52 percent and many other statistics demonstrating a low rate of synagogue attendance, philanthropic participation, and other ethnic identification. A new word, "continuity," concerning fear of continued Jewish existence in America, seized center stage. "Continuity" committees blossomed throughout the land as the leaders struggled for consensus as to what could be done to counter the threat of continuous shrinkage. No national program of action or actions emerged, only a torrent of wordy resolutions.

Second, almost simultaneously, was the appearance of another phenomenon also remarkable in its pre-occupation with words, committee meetings, and abstractions. I refer to the effort to find a formula for linking the two largest organizations – United Jewish Appeal and Council of Jewish Federations. It is hard to understand why that purely administrative problem suddenly became the most urgent matter on the national agenda. Perhaps, in some deeply psychological sense, the fear engendered by ongoing assimilation, and the failure to respond to it with a strong action program, sparked the thought that perhaps a "merger" of the two big organizations would somehow produce a vigorous re-strengthening of the communal will to survive.

The tinkering continued over a two-year period. The merger proposal was shot down, and an alternative word emerged – "partnership." No one is quite sure what that will mean in practical terms. A new office has been found to house both organizations, but that fact alone cannot assure improved grappling with the future. Although it might save some administrative expenses, that is not enough.

Concern with "continuity" and "administrative tinkering," in my opinion, were diversionary, time consuming, and bereft of any authentic solution. Challenges of historic dimension demand responses of equivalent weight. If the national and local leadership of American Jewry felt seriously challenged by diminishing numbers and a weakened future community, it was obliged to create a vigorous response, in actions, not words.

There are remedies, after all: a greatly expanded Jewish educational system, innovations in the synagogue system, and broader links with Israel, to name a few. All require a huge outpouring of money stemming from a sense of emergency. Experience over the past 60 years has taught us that American Jews, when spurred on by danger or given an opportunity to save lives, have always responded quickly and generously. More committee meetings, more wordy resolutions, more administrative tinkering are not likely to awaken that sense of emergency.

The fundraising establishment, national and local, entered a period of cloudiness in dealing with the two phenomena described above. That is, the establishment failed to issue an emergency call for action based on specific programs that could counter-attack assimilation, ignorance, and indifference.

I tried to stimulate a response. In March 1995, I asked for and received an invitation to address the UJA executive committee and senior staff. I prepared charts showing successful responses to various challenges over the past decades. I extended compliments for the success of Operation Exodus and urged that its completion be immediately followed by an announcement of another one-billion dollar <u>extra</u> campaign. That one would run from 1995-2000 on behalf of the Israel Experience for American-Jewish youth between the ages of 15 to 25.

The campaign slogan, I said, could be "Now We Must Rescue Our Own Youth." A set of programs would be organized in Israel according to the interests of different age groups. All youth would be invited to participate at community expense. I made a short concluding speech, with passionate conviction, that the "slam-dunk" enthusiasm of the Exodus success would jump-start the next big project. Energy is transferable. American Jews have proudly helped to bring and absorb more than two million Jews from 70 different countries into Israel. Now it's time to turn to three-quarter of a million of our own young people and bring them into full acceptance of their own Jewish identity. This bold challenge would be consistent with UJA's rescue role.

The reaction was untidy and disappointing: a few desultory questions; a comment that $30 million to $40 million might be a feasible target; limited approval from one or two persons; negative from one who stated that his community's capital fund campaign for an old-folks home, postponed in favor of Exodus, could not be postponed again (the perennial problem of the relative needs of youth vs. age).

The group showed no vitality, let alone fervor. The chairman said I would hear from them and proceeded to the next item on the agenda. I was trying to generate a crusade-type of mentality, and they were dealing with an agenda type. I left with an eerie feeling of dislocation. Soon thereafter, when the incumbent CEO left (by pre-arrangement), the vital post remained vacant for months, while the administrative tinkering proceeded.

To the time of this writing, there is no carefully engineered master plan to include and coordinate efforts by the nation's Jewish leaders. I am not saying that idealism has been lost. It is simply not being harnessed to a large, all-inclusive goal. Some communities are trying to direct additional funding to their synagogues; an individual major personality has made the strengthening of Hillel on the college campus his domain, and is working hard at it; some billionaires are trying to direct a few tens of millions into new day schools; a few visionaries are trying to lower tuition costs. All of the above, as well as other single efforts, are well meant, but not equal to the massiveness of the problem. We are moving through a period of witnessing individual tactics, but no large strategy.

On the other hand, my faith in the UJA runs deep. I maintain contacts with its leaders, both professional and lay, and make suggestions that I believe could restore the organization to its former condition of articulating historic challenges and meeting them with vigorous planning and action. I outline those suggestions in chapter 43. There is no objective reason why the UJA cannot continue to expand, take on new causes, raise more money and more leaders, and thereby fulfill the prime reason for its existence: to be one of the main guardians of a strong Jewish future in the United States and a resolute partner with Israel in the prophetic mission of improving the world for all humankind. The UJA as an instrument is potentially just that important.

FIGHTING FOR
THE FUTURE

CHAPTER FORTY

JERUSALEM ACADEMY:
A DREAM DEFERRED

In the early 1970s, I had a seemingly simple but sublime idea: to build in Israel a school called the Jerusalem Academy. I had found the motto to be emblazoned on its shield in chapter 1, verse 2 of the Biblical *Book of Proverbs*, written by Solomon, the son of David, King of Israel:

> "For learning, wisdom and discipline;"

In Hebrew, the line reads – "*l'daat chochma v'musar.*"

"Wisdom" – *chochma* – refers to a knowledge of <u>basic principles.</u>

"Discipline" – *musar* – came to stand for practical morality and refers essentially to the shaping of <u>character.</u>

In his widely acclaimed commentary, Rabbi Gunther Plaut wrote: "The *Book of Proverbs* makes the basic assumption that knowledge leads to proper behavior.

"To create a knowledge of basic principles, and to develop character through values: this is the stated aim of the Book of Proverbs."

Thus the stated aim of my dream: to build in Jerusalem a school of excellence for a carefully selected body of gifted and talented students, half from Israel, half from the Diaspora, young men and women with bright futures as leading figures in the Jewish and general communities around the world. To achieve that, a good deal of infrastructure was obviously required, and I moved to establish it.

In March 1974, I created The Jerusalem Society for the Advancement of Education and Culture, which was registered with the Israeli Ministry of the Interior as a non-profit Ottoman Society (based on old Turkish law.) Today such a body is called, in Hebrew, an *Amuta*, simply an Association. The co-founders were myself as chairman, and Hertzel Fishman as deputy chairman. The other members of the society were drawn from a broad cross-section of the Israeli leadership and included: Mrs. Ayala Zaks Abramov, governor, International Museums; Avraham Agmon, director-general, Delek fuel oil company.; Dr. Avraham Avichai, chairman, World Keren Hayesod; Ambassador Walter Eytan, first director-general, Foreign Ministry; Erwin Frenkel, editor, *Jerusalem Post*; Teddy Kollek, mayor of Jerusalem; Lt. Gen. (reserve) Chaim Laskov, former chief of staff, I.D.F.; Israel Pollack, owner and director-general of Polgat Industries; Eliezer Shavit, representative of the UJA's Israel Education Fund; Maj.Gen.(reserve) Aharon Yariv, director, Jaffee Institute for Strategic Studies; and Yitzhak Navon, who later became president of Israel.

An international academic council was also formed to advise on curriculum, student regulatory policies, faculty qualifications, and similar matters. Its members included:

> From France – Raymond Aron, professor, *Ecole des Hautes Études en Sciences Sociales*;
>
> From the United States – Saul Bellow, Nobel laureate in Literature, University of Chicago; Henry Rosovsky, dean, Faculty of Arts and Sciences, Harvard University; Eugene Rostow, dean, School of Law, Yale University, and former under-secretary of state; Theodore Sizer, headmaster, Phillips Andover Academy;

From Israel – Abba Eban, former deputy prime minister, foreign
   minister, education minister, and president of the Weizmann
   Institute.

From England – John Thorn, headmaster, Winchester College.

The Jerusalem Society was established with the enthusiastic endorsement and
encouragement of the Israeli minister of education, Aharon Yadlin. He
formally requested that the Israel Lands Authority lease to us, on reasonable
terms, an area of 450-500 *dunam* (112-125 acres) of land for the school.
Successive ministers of education, Zevulun Hammer and Yigal Allon,
reaffirmed their wholehearted support for the project.

   The campus would be a world unto itself – situated on a hilltop in the
Judean mountains, 15 miles from the center of Jerusalem, at the head of the
Valley of Elah, where David fought Goliath, and 22 miles from Tel Aviv, with a
stunning view of the Mediterranean sea to the west on a clear day. Surrounded
by trees, rock outcroppings, and a boundless sky, a small village would rise to
house all the appropriate facilities. The buildings would be built of red brick
and tawny Jerusalem stone. Outdoor sculptures, fountains, green grass would
abound.

   The Jerusalem Academy was to be a residential, co-educational secondary
school for 480 gifted and talented students, ages 14 to 18, with admission based
on rigorous exams, essays, and interviews, plus outstanding references. The
academy would seek to develop in its students sound scholarship, desirable
moral character and self-reliance, as well as a commitment to work for the good
of the Jewish people and all mankind.

   The creation of a strong sense of Jewish identity in each student, based on
the twin foci of the State of Israel and the meaning of Judaism, would be
fundamental factors in the school's philosophy. The students would become
immersed in an environment that enabled them to understand and love the
heritage of their people and its contribution to the human race.

   All of that, of course, would be in addition to the secular courses of study
required for admission to any of the great universities of the world. The British
standards of "A" level, American standards of SAT scores, Israeli standards of

Bagrut (matriculation), and similar standards for the French Sorbonne and the leading German universities would all have to be met – not just minimally, but at the most advanced level. Intermingling the Jewish and general studies in a demanding curriculum was a natural framework for students of high intelligence who would be expected to become leaders in the Jewish and general worlds.

In a brochure I prepared for parents and contributors, I described student life. Two passages follow:

> Each student will belong to and live in one of eight dormitory clusters. A dormitory would consist of apartments, not single rooms. Each apartment will house four students, two Israeli and two Diaspora. They will learn each other's language, psychology, cultural habits, and hopefully will become life-long friends whose families will visit back and forth as the years go on. Israeli-Diaspora relations will improve based on mutual understanding between students.
>
> Faculty members living in each cluster will act as counselors to an assigned group of 15 students, offering the personal touch, for which there is great need at the crucial teen-age years. Accessible in the dormitory, in the classroom, at athletics and extra-curricular activities, at meals and in the evening, these teachers will offer strong support and often act in *loco parentis*.
>
> Athletics will figure prominently…with plentiful tennis courts, various large fields for ball games, outdoor and indoor gymnasiums, swimming pools, etc. A full program of social events will be interspersed – movies, dances, concerts, plays. There will be frequent trips throughout Israel, as well as trips to Europe, particularly to learn about Greek and Roman civilization, in addition to the modern nations.
>
> The Sabbath will be a major institution at the Academy. It will be spent in prayer, song, Torah study, ceremony, and recreation. Guest speakers will come. Celebrations will be created. The Jewish traditions and holidays will be honored. The dietary laws will be observed.

To make the academy dream a reality, I enlisted the services of my architect friend, Zvi Toren. He drew hundreds of pages of blueprints; met often with the regional council to solicit their enthusiasm for the project and with the National Planning Council to obtain the necessary building permits; and came with me to the United States for a tour of several boarding schools and colleges to check his ideas and obtain new ones. Zvi was endlessly patient. He and I went over the plans again and again in detail, right down to deciding the width of corridors and the type of wood for staircase railings. He was a tower of strength, in professional and personal terms. I loved collaborating with him.

I worked even harder – and traveled a lot more – than Zvi. I requested a grant of $1 million from the State Department's agency called American Schools and Hospitals Abroad (ASHA). I spent months in the United States tackling my request on the political level. I had to explain the concept of the school to the Senators and Representatives who were members of the relevant appropriations committees and whose votes I needed to obtain the State Department grant. There were about 20 individuals to be seen, and I pursued them from New Hampshire to New Mexico, back and forth from Washington to their home locations, making and remaking appointments. It was an exhausting effort that took me finally to the topmost administrator of ASHA, Peter McPherson. He became increasingly interested in the Jerusalem Academy as a vehicle that would produce graduates who, in the years ahead, would grow into positions of responsibility in both the U.S. and Israel, and who would understand each other's mentality, to the advantage of improving relations between the two countries, in conformity with American policy to maintain tight links between two allies. He promised $1 million toward the first stage of construction, knowing that four stages were required for full completion. He knew I would be back with a similar request for each stage, and his responsive attitude toward continuing support encouraged me mightily.

I worked with the Internal Revenue Service and a law firm, Willkie, Farr and Gallagher, to obtain tax-exempt status, which was mandatory if we were to raise American money. We received the exemption letter in August 1977.

I raised funds in large and small amounts. Hiring lawyers in the United States and Israel, buying airplane tickets, hotel rooms, and food, took relatively small sums, while maintaining a simple office in Jerusalem on Abarbanel St.

took larger ones, and supporting Zvi Toren's design work larger ones still. The process of fundraising was endless.

I did all that without staff or personal salary over a three-year period. To earn a very modest income, I had to arrange speech-making tours in the United States.

In the end, we achieved a great deal. We raised approximately $7 million in payments or pledges toward the $10 million needed for the first stage; we secured all the necessary permits (an incredible achievement in view of the Israeli bureaucracy) and the proper administrative, legal, and tax status. Even the geological omens were good: Preparation of the site, we learned to our relief, would not require heavy blasting of rock.

Yet the project did not materialize. There was no Jerusalem Academy. If the idea was so good, and if we worked so hard to develop it, what went wrong?

I have tried hard to analyze the complex variety of reasons, but the bottom line is this: <u>I closed the project down of my own free will, without pressure from any one.</u> In retrospect, the following five factors all played a part in my decision:

1. Personal fatigue and loneliness.

After working seven years on the project, from mid-1975 to mid-1982, largely alone except for Toren, I was simply tired, broke, and discouraged. My family and I returned to Manhattan in 1978. I rented a small office on East 55th Street to continue working on the academy. I had one assistant, Moshe Leshem, an old friend, a former ambassador in Israel's Foreign Ministry, who had moved to New York. Eventually, I couldn't afford even his humble salary, and went to that office every day and sat alone, working the phone, trying to raise the money to keep going. Harder still was keeping my own spirit alive and my own morale from cracking.

2. Failure to establish a functioning organization.

Working as a one-man show made it impossible to build an organization, lay and professional, that could move systematically toward creating the living reality. I needed a strong group of lay leaders to canvass the list of major contributors and simply did not have the time to organize such a group. Nor did I have any of the following three important components: a publicity operation to spread the news of the school; a staff to contact the educational systems in major American cities to solicit their cooperation; or a committee of lay leaders to approach families whose children we would hope to attract. All of my time and energy were spent on fundraising and architectural planning.

3. Insufficient Funds.

I did manage to raise about $750,000 in cash and more than $6 million in pledges (to be paid during the two- or three-year construction period). Three gifts of $1 million each came from ASHA, Charles Schusterman of Tulsa, and Harvey (Bud) Meyerhoff of Baltimore. Stanley Sloane of New York was chairman of our American Friends group, and he tried hard to inspire others. His gift was in the six-figure range, as were those of Leonard Strelitz of Virginia and Alex Grass of Pennsylvania. Scores of friends replied in the four- and five-figure range. All of them responded because they believed in the concept and were expressing their respect for and confidence in me. But it was not enough. We simply did not have sufficient funding to continue.

4. Decision Not to Seek Jewish Agency or Government Funds.

I made that decision, for the very basic reason that the Academy had to be totally free and independent of bureaucratic interference. Compliance with the plethora of Israeli Government regulations and criteria, as well as pressure from religious sources that might not agree with our philosophy and operation, would consume time and energy better employed in keeping the academy running smoothly.

I did intend to work closely with the Ministry of Education, asking for advice and welcoming suggestions. But that was different from accepting public funding that would obligate us to adhere to rules and regulations that might inhibit or even prevent us from acting in the best interests of our school. We would of course welcome inspection by the Ministry. After all, this school was not being built on the moon, and half its student body would be Israeli youngsters. But freedom and independence were crucial, and we paid the price for them in forgoing public funds which would probably have been available to some extent.

5. Building Smaller Would be Unfair to the First Students.

The operating plan contemplated the construction of two dormitories and two classroom buildings, to accommodate a total of 120 students in the first stage. It was therefore suggested that we start by building half of the planned first stage, i.e., facilities for 60 students instead of the proposed 120. That plan would require only one dormitory complex and one classroom building plus a smaller dining hall, fewer faculty houses, and so on. Such a "compromise" sounded reasonable to many board members. After careful thought, I decided against on pedagogical and psychological grounds. I feared it might turn out to be unfair to the first 60 students admitted.

I was afraid that if we started in a weak financial position, we might remain there, unable to gather momentum, condemned to be a stunted school with no future, thus prejudicing the status of the 60 pioneer students. We could not carry them responsibly to graduation four years later, for we would not be able to maintain the faculty and superstructure necessary to nourish their growth – especially since admission to first-rate universities was the goal.

On the other hand, if we built for 120 entering students, and suffered the bad luck of becoming stalled at that level, we would have enough faculty to carry the 120 all the way through to graduation, without harming their future. Then, if forced to, we could close down. The basic question was a moral one, and I felt there was only one answer; not to start at all, rather than make a weak start with fewer teachers and students that could not maintain a full curriculum, thus jeopardizing the future of the students.

In addition to the reasons stated, I may have made two strategic errors. The first concerned a conference center, which I planned to build on the Academy grounds. Facilities of that type contain residential as well as educational buildings, so it was quite logical to place the Academy and the center together. The center could serve as an inn for families visiting their youngsters at the Academy; as a haven for adults seeking to study in a campus environment; and as a base for missions and groups from abroad, offering them the technical and academic infrastructure needed for their programs.

With hindsight, it is clear that skillful marketing would have drawn to the center a steady stream of institutional customers such as the UJA, Federations, congregations whose rabbis bring groups to Israel every year; national organizations that hold assemblies of their members in Israel on behalf of universities, bond drives, hospitals, and museums. We would also be attractive to the whole spectrum of local Israeli associations – business, military, academic, medical, legal, and so forth – that are constantly seeking locations for meetings. A conference center that succeeded commercially, making a profit, would become an additional source of funds for the Academy.

Yet in my enthusiasm for the Academy itself, I did not concentrate on the conference center, viewing it as a good project to be undertaken down the road. Instead, I should have assigned one or two individuals the task of building the center. It would have been completed a year or more before the school and might have served to accelerate fundraising. (Incidentally, Israel still remains without a first-class conference facility.)

The second strategic error involved market research. During our fundraising discussions, it was often suggested that we launch a research effort to determine whether we would, in fact, be able to find enough admissible students whose parents were willing to let them travel great distances to attend boarding school at such young ages. I recognized that market research would be a valuable asset to the planning process. But I could neither undertake such an effort myself at that juncture nor pay to have it done professionally. So I kept postponing action.

Another shortcoming in my thinking was that I thought of student-raising in terms of the same methodology as fundraising. It was best done through a one-to-one approach with a pre-selected list of families obtained from a variety of reliable sources. Canvassing those sources was in itself a massive task involving many personal visits in many cities. And then a second round-robin of visits to families seemed likely to consume a year or more. On the other hand, enrollment of high-quality students was the key to the reputation of the school. The visits could have come during actual construction, when I could be absent, for I had complete faith in Toren's ability to supervise the building contractor. During that period, I could have been out raising more funds and recruiting students.

When a great dream falters, struggles, and finally falls, the people most closely affected are left shattered. Personal recovery is often slow but can be accelerated by an immediate plunge into another activity. That therapy was available to me, and I seized it: Tel Aviv University had been courting me to accept the presidency of its American office, and I accepted.

But in this case, true therapy is the hope that the dream might be realized by a later believer. And that hope has truly sustained me. The plans for the Jerusalem Academy are carefully preserved in tall aluminum tubes standing in the architect's cellar, and the land in the Judean hills remains vacant to this day. I hope I live to see the dream re-activated and brought to fruition, as I am certain it will be, since the essence of it is so compelling.

CHAPTER FORTY-ONE

THE WEXNER HERITAGE FOUNDATION

Leslie Wexner is a remarkable person: bright, friendly, soft-spoken, idealistic, so non-aggressive he is often described as shy. Yet he also possesses a powerful entrepreneurial drive that has propelled him into the front rank of America's merchants. He has built his empire – principally The Limited clothing stores – laying block on block, risking, almost failing, recovering, always planning carefully. A remarkable sense of fashion and design, an almost painful attention to detail, and the ability to see far ahead are among his outstanding talents.

On the non-business side, Wexner has a finely developed sense of social obligation to a wide area of interests: his local community of Columbus, Ohio; his university, Ohio State; the welfare of the Jewish people, in Israel and throughout the world. He serves those causes devotedly, even though his personal participation in any specific project is often limited by the demands on his time.

I describe this man with deep affection and admiration because his vision is so large and long, his heart so big, his purse so generous. He is unique in that he eschews the conventional acts of accepting titles, sitting on committees, presiding over an endless series of dinners, speaking formulaically. His leadership asserts itself through remote control and role modeling.

We met first in the winter of 1983, brought together by Gordon Zacks, a long-time friend of us both. Gordon, who lived in Columbus, called me about Wexner's idea of inviting several local Jewish young men of extraordinary promise as his guests on a four-day mission to Europe. They would accompany him on his private jet in the hope that they would be inspired to participate intensely in Columbus' annual Federation/UJA campaign. Wexner asked Zacks to recommend someone to arrange an itinerary that would expose the group to current Jewish history, with emotional impact.

Gordon hoped to persuade me to construct an agenda, contact the key personalities abroad, and lead the group. Although I was then serving as President of the American Friends of Tel Aviv University, I decided it was worth taking the time off to enjoy a change of scenery and perhaps even produce a new bunch of young leaders. So I said yes to Gordon and the as-yet-unknown Mr. Wexner.

The plan was to take off from Columbus on a Thursday at 4 p.m. and to touch down at Columbus by 4 p.m. on Sunday. This was the week of Chanukah, so I took a pocket menorah, some candles, and a song sheet. There were ten of us aboard. In the blackness of night, over the Atlantic, we could see the lights of another aircraft not far away. I requested that our interior lights be darkened; then we lit the candles and hoped that they, in the other plane, would be touched by the magic of seeing our tiny lights across the sky. Reciting the blessings, singing the songs, telling the story of the Maccabees (the heroic family whose five sons led a successful revolt against the Greek occupiers of Judea), we felt the hand of history in that very special setting.

Landing in Vienna, we met with the Israeli ambassador and heard the inside story of the Austrian flirtation with the Palestine Liberation Organization and Austria's simultaneous grant of permission for Israel to use its capital as a staging area for the Russian migration. The paradox illustrated the Viennese reputation as the espionage center of Europe, where all sides met.

In the afternoon, we went to the South Station to see groups of Russian Jews who were passing daily through the city on the train from Moscow. We walked to the very end of the platform, for I had learned that the Jews gathered in the last two cars. As they descended and assembled their luggage, we exchanged greetings with them in several languages, and followed them to their Jewish Agency hostel. It was exciting for me to feel once again the pulse of a large wave of migration.

That night we had dinner with Simon Wiesenthal, the famous Nazi hunter, in the Imperial Hotel. We had the feeling of brushing against a historic figure. Wiesenthal's life was a roller-coaster of emotions: great successes, tremendous frustrations, horrendous fights over claims he made about having uncovered this or that top Nazi. The claims were sometimes disputed by others, including Israeli officials. We knew our guest was a man of fantastic devotion to his cause. Although he lived in Vienna, his monument was in Los Angeles, where an impressive and important center carried his name.

All of the above agenda took place on the first day after leaving Columbus, Ohio, which already seemed part of another planet.

Next morning, we flew to Linz – still in Austria – the city of Hitler's birth. A quick bus ride deposited us at the gate of Mauthausen, one of the notorious Nazi camps, where scores of thousands were worked to death in the quarries, and other multitudes were gassed and burned. The stone ramparts, cruel and fearsome, chilled our hearts, more than the December cold and snow chilled our bodies. We passed through the buildings, from chamber to chamber, furnace to furnace, and saw the rooms where experimental operations were done, where gold teeth were extracted from corpses, where unspeakable torment was invisible to the outside world. And then, silently, we walked across a frozen field to a small monument where we laid our wreath, said our *kaddish* (prayer for the dead), and returned to the bus in mournful silence.

The next stop was Munich, the city in which Hitler tried his beer-hall putsch in 1923, where he grew his movement into millions of Brown Shirt storm troopers and Black Shirt Gestapo killers, from which he went to Berlin in 1933 to become chancellor of the Third Reich. We went to see Hitler's brown house, from whose balcony he harangued crowds with tirades against the Jews. Around the corner was a large public building in which the infamous meeting with Neville Chamberlain took place. I knew Munich well, from my postwar years of living and working there. And as we walked from place to place, I talked about that work and my memories of the city.

The last stop of the day was Paris. We went from dreadful past to present pleasure; a reception at the home of Baron David de Rothschild, son of Baron

Guy, who would someday inherit his father's positions as head of the *Consistoire* (the governmentally recognized Jewish religious establishment in France). David was about the same age as the young Americans in our group, which created an immediate rapport amid the palatial splendor. Dinner followed at the esteemed Pre Catelan restaurant, where the kitchen had been prepared in kosher fashion, so that the Grand Rabbi of France, the Israeli Ambassador, and local Jewish notables could join the party. The meal was lovely and the conversation sparkling.

On Sunday morning we drove to Belleville, a crowded suburb of Paris, populated heavily by Sephardic North African Jews who had emigrated in the 1960s. Most of their relatives from Morocco and Tunisia had chosen Israel as their new home, while most of the Algerians, because of their colonial ties to France, had elected the latter. We went to their synagogue and participated in a Chanukah service and party, full of joyous singing, tasting the spicy *latkes* (pancakes) and sugary *sufganiot* (jelly doughnuts). Talking with the people in a mixture of languages, we got an inkling of their experiences in the Arab countries from which they had fled. Then a quick bus ride to Orly Airport, wheels up at 12 noon Paris time, wheels down at 4 p.m. in Columbus.

The flight home provided plenty of time for the group to huddle, ask questions, obtain answers. The seven invitees (besides Les, Gordon, and myself) were all super-charged, eager to get to work in the community. With the exception of one person who moved away, all six have made serious contributions of time and money to a variety of activities over the past decade and more. Gordon and I were very pleased, and so was Les. The example of this kind of intense exposure to the perils of the Jewish condition in the real world left an impression on him. The effects of the trip reverberated in many of our future conversations.

Throughout 1984, Les and I enjoyed a series of luncheon meetings. He wanted to explore ideas related to one basic question; what was the most important thing he could do to strengthen the American Jewish community? I replied that the *single* most important thing was to create a cadre of specially selected lay leaders who would be intensively educated in their Jewish Heritage and imbued with the desire to improve the Jewish communities in which they lived. That would require paying serious attention to the words "educated" and "improve." If we were skillful and creative, those words would explode into actions that strengthened the national Jewish polity.

Decades earlier, I had conceived the same idea, called the Young Leadership Cabinet (YLC) of the UJA, which was based on the premise that the indispensable prerequisite for successful fundraising was a program for "people-raising." No matter how valid the cause – and in the late 1950s, rescuing endangered Jews plus building a strong Israel to absorb them was the most valid of causes – the fundraising capability would be weak without an adequate pool of motivated manpower.

Thinking back about the demands we made on those selected for the prestigious cabinet, I can see that they were limited. The minimum required of a cabinet member was to solicit ten pledges in the campaign of his home city; to make one trip per month for a similar solicitation in another city; to read one book we sent every month, and to join one mission to Israel per year. Thus the effort was almost entirely campaign oriented, and although I have just labeled that as limited, it was also so innovative and aggressive for its time that its methods and even its name were copied by every organization in the Jewish world.

At the time Les Wexner and I were having our philosophical discussions about creating a new generation of leaders, I was thinking of a different agenda. I was not concentrating primarily on fundraising, although that is unavoidable in any program designed for progress and change, but on a strong injection of background knowledge for those whose early Jewish education had been so thin and fragmentary.

I have always believed that there exist antidotes to a diminishing Jewish consciousness and have passionately advocated certain remedies throughout my long professional life. If properly designed and executed, the following programs can build a Jewish identity firm enough to overcome the ignorance and indifference that lead to a destructive assimilation: offering a Jewish day-school education through high school; providing for adults a body of text-based knowledge; outlining a set of priorities for communal action; and urging parents to expand ritual and religious participation in their family life. Those elements would go very far toward strengthening Jewish identity in this free country that provides so many temptations for people simply to discard, slowly and imperceptibly, their Jewish skins.

Talking with Wexner, I recommended that we attempt to discover and recruit a cadre of mature, sensitive men and women who still retained a sense of the uniqueness of the Jewish people and were willing to enlist in the cause of preserving it in their own lives and communities. They had to be willing to study in order to increase their own knowledge; advocate the creation of a day-school network; and develop a system of practicing the rituals and customs of the Jewish tribe.

Leslie and I debated the philosophical question of whether leaders are born or could be made from conventional clay. He believed that leaders of the first caliber can only be born. I agreed – if we were speaking of political leaders at the summit – a Lincoln or a Churchill. The weakening condition of the Jewish people could not, however, wait for the occasional genius to appear. We had to search for the best human material we could find and mold it into leadership. Our discussion was fascinating and intense. Finally he said, "Okay – let's try it." And in 1985, the Wexner Heritage Foundation was born.

Every Sunday during July and August of that year, Gordon Zacks and I met with Les at his home in Columbus, working out the principles and operational details for the new project. Then we discussed where to begin, and I suggested tackling four Midwestern cities simultaneously. Les replied that when he planned to open a new type of store, he started with one, honed and polished it, ironed out all the inevitable wrinkles, and, when satisfied, considered opening 40 in the following year. I took his meaning immediately, and recommended Columbus, which was his intention all along.

So I began selecting Columbus students, and by the end of September we had 16 of the very best (including several who had been on the four-day super-trip two years earlier) sitting around the large boardroom table at the Leo Yassenoff Jewish Community Center. I served as a faculty of one and flew from New York to Columbus every two weeks for the entire academic year.

During the middle of the year, we had to decide whether or not to expand the following year. Les was extremely pleased with the feedback he was getting, and asked me which four cities I had in mind. I said Pittsburgh, Detroit, Milwaukee, and Minneapolis. He approved, and we went full steam ahead.

★   ★   ★

Let me describe the structure systematically:

The *program*, aimed at Jewish community activists, men and women in the 32-42 age range, is holistic. That is, it conceives of a community in its totality and thinks of leaders as people who serve any and all aspects of communal life. It presents a balanced offering of materials, helping members form an ideology or point of view. The ability to engage in objective critical analysis assists them in policy and decision making. Making decisions, while if possible avoiding community collisions, is the special responsibility of leadership. The pursuit of knowledge bonds the participants into a group whose activities benefit both their communities and themselves.

At the beginning, the *staff* consisted of myself and a secretary. The following year, Nathan Laufer, an orthodox rabbi (and lawyer) joined us, along with another secretary. Ten years later I became president emeritus, and the full staff consists of three rabbis: Laufer, now president; Avram Arian, Reform; Shoshana Gelfand, Conservative; a conference and publication director, Lori Baron; and four support persons.

Members are admitted to the program through a rigorous process. Candidates do not apply on their own; nominations are solicited from a wide network of professional and lay leaders in each community we take on, and are given the general profile of the type of member we are seeking.

The *nominees*, often hundreds in number from the larger communities, are invited to complete a 10-page questionnaire, which is carefully evaluated. The most promising, up to 60-or-so persons, are interviewed individually in their own communities by two of our staff. Selection of the right candidates is the single most important element in the program. This highly personal approach gives it the reputation of being very serious and elite. And it gives us the proof we seek that the candidates accepted are truly committed to the future of the Jewish people.

The candidates chosen are formed into a seminar group of about 20 – the largest number that can be seated comfortably around one table. Some cities produce one group; larger cities wind up with two, even three groups. During the personal interviews, we explain that we impose strict discipline. Students are expected to attend all 19 of the bi-weekly evening seminars (2 cuts allowed) and to arrive on time. Each seminar requires the reading of 50 to 75 pages of material.

Individual affiliation to Reform, Conservative, or Orthodox movements is not relevant. The Wexner Heritage Foundation believes in religious pluralism and therefore has a multi-denominational staff, faculty, and student body.

While seminar members are selected individually, they are encouraged to share the readings and discussions with their spouses. Further, spouses are invited to attend retreats and institutes at their own travel expense, and most do.

The *faculty* consists of leading rabbis and Jewish educators and lecturers. Fifty-one (of the total 100 individuals we have employed over the years) are teachers by profession. All are engaged in public life and deeply aware of the nature and condition of present-day American Jewry. All are employed elsewhere, and we are grateful that they carve out time to teach for us.

In addition, we have enjoyed over the years the participation of approximately 45 Israeli lecturers, here and there. The very top of the Israeli hierarchy has responded, including Presidents Navon, Herzog, and Weizman; Prime Ministers Rabin, Peres, Begin, and Netanyahu; Cabinet Ministers Eban, Beilin, Sharansky, and Sneh; Mayors Kollek, Olmert, and Lahat. We have also had, with great pleasure, two Israeli Arabs, Hashim Mehameed, a member of the Knesset (parliament), and Newwaf Masalha, a deputy minister of health; and two Palestinians, Elias Frej, mayor of Bethlehem, and Saib Erekat, deputy to Yasser Arafat and head of the PLO negotiating team.

Our students are constantly impressed by the quality of the faculty, three or four of whom appear at different times during the academic year to keep student interest fresh.

The *curriculum* is divided into four large subject areas, spread over three summer institutes and two academic years:

a) Basic Judaism – covered in a summer session of five or six days, before the students in a given city start their Year One seminars in September. The classes focus on theology (God, Covenant, Messiah, etc.), the meaning and observance of rituals and holidays, and similar subjects.

b) The History of the Jewish People – covered in Year One, from Abraham (ca. 1750 B.C.E.) to the present. Students receive an overview: not a great deal of detail, but at least the main events. They learn how we were formed and how we got to where we are today.

c) The Thought of the Jewish People – covered in Year Two; a study of the major texts and ideas that have formed the intellectual and legal foundations of our basic philosophy. Because the texts, which include the Bible, are basically unfamiliar, students struggle with this course. But as often happens, they find that what is hard to digest is all the more appreciated.

d) Contemporary Issues – covered in the "Summer Institutes," which last six to eight days and are held in resort conference centers. Locations have included Snowmass and Aspen, Colorado; Lake Tahoe, California; Snowbird, Utah; and Caesarea and Jerusalem, Israel. Using a combination of plenary sessions and workshops, bringing in many outside lecturers and experts, holding seven hours of classes daily plus evening lecturers, we explore the complex challenges facing Israel and American Jewry today. Israeli issues include: a constitution for Israel?; Arabs in Israel – are they second-class citizens?; can the conflict between religious and secular Israelis be compromised? Among the American-Jewish topics: conflicts between Orthodox and non-Orthodox; allocation of funds between local-community needs and overseas needs; re-shaping of national organizations; creation of an enlarged day-school network.

Miscellaneous

a) In addition to his singular financial generosity, Les Wexner also extends personal hospitality. When the foundation holds a Basic Judaism Institute or Summer Institute in or near Aspen, he invites the entire assembly – sometimes hundreds of people – to his ranch home for a late afternoon barbecue on the terrace facing the western range of mountains. He has even done that on occasions, the most recent in 1996, when those institutes were held back to back, so that he threw one party on Thursday and another on Sunday.

b) At the end of Year Two, for the student groups that have completed the curriculum, we hold graduation during the Summer Institute. The ceremony is simple but touching. The members mount the platform to the tune of Elgar's *Pomp and Circumstance* and receive their diplomas individually from Les (which permits a "photo op"), and he sometimes makes a short speech. Then the whole class performs a funny sketch or song, usually "roasting" the staff. The mood is light and upbeat. The low-key text of the diploma alleges no extraordinary achievement, but good intentions by the recipient.

c) In September 1997, Los Angeles, last in the foundation's Round I of cities, began its Year One, presenting the foundation with a cross-roads decision: Where do we go next? I posed four possibilities:

1. United States – Start again with Round II, because there is a new generation of the right age, and we could spend the next 10 or 12 years revisiting the same cities plus adding a few new ones.

2. Canada – Toronto is certainly worthy of the program, and Montreal and Vancouver may be also.

3. Israel – We looked into this possibility a few years ago, but decided to complete Round I in the United States before going abroad. Israelis would welcome the program because everyone is aware that, as paradoxical as it may sound, the Jewish identity of modern, secular Israelis may be just as weak as that of assimilated American Jews.

4. Former Soviet Union – After 75 years of communism and several years of near-turmoil, it appears that, despite the huge migrations to Israel, the F.S.U. will still include 1.5 to 2 million Jews who are now more aware of their Jewish heritage but have no knowledge of the ways in which Judaism defines them. A small but growing infrastructure of synagogues, schools, and community centers is in formation. However, an educated leadership, by our criteria, does not exist and must be created from scratch. Several cities are candidates. Kiev, St. Petersburg, Moscow, and Khabarovsk (in far eastern Siberia) come immediately to mind.

The decision was made to include Canada – interviews were completed in the three cities mentioned above, and the Basic Judaism Institute was held in July, 1998, with Year One classes starting in September.

★ ★ ★

Many outstanding achievements have resulted from the insights gained through, and motivations aroused by, the Wexner Heritage Foundation educational program. Here is a representative list:

• <u>Chicago</u> – A new synagogue, Aitz Hayim, has been born in the northern suburbs. The "parents" are two Wexner Heritage alumni and their spouses whose personal energy and generous funding enabled the baby to grow. Some 200 families have already joined them. Their holiday celebrations are innovative, seeking to duplicate the environment and atmosphere of Biblical times, using nature outdoors instead of a room indoors. They write study pamphlets and invite scholars for week-ends. In addition, they cooperate closely with the Federation during campaign time. It is a creative, intelligent model of a vibrant new synagogue – one without its own building but with a school. The synagogue rents space whenever necessary.

- <u>Atlanta</u> – Two new day schools have been established: an elementary school whose first through third grades are already functioning; and a high school in the organizational stages, with a headmaster and administrative director already hired. The former is the personal project of a member and spouse, whose extended family, long-time reform leaders, have backed him generously. The latter has a lay chairman and several board members from the Wexner group, and they are moving ahead rapidly.
- <u>Long Island</u> – a Solomon Schechter High School is up and running, along with four Schechter elementary schools that serve as feeders to assure a constant flow of students. The schools are in the third year of operation, and several Wexner graduates are among the most influential leaders.
- <u>Boston</u> – A new Jewish high school opened in September 1997 with 48 students in grades 9 and 10 and a faculty of 20. Two key people – the headmaster, Rabbi Daniel Lehman, and his assistant, Sara Heitler, an honors graduate of Yale – were at work for a full year before the school opened. This smart move enabled a curriculum to be designed, faculty recruited, and students attracted.

  Several Wexner alumni were forceful and faithful advocates of the new high school, participating in many of the important practical chores. I, too, was involved in many planning meetings, and I'm pleased to say that my suggestions were accepted.
- <u>Denver, San Diego, Ft. Lauderdale</u> – Those cities are at various stages of planning high schools, all with Wexner people acting as prime or secondary movers. The high school activity is quite remarkable: before it began, fewer than a dozen Jewish high schools existed in the entire country, outside of the Orthodox yeshiva network.
- <u>Columbus</u> – An elementary day school, with a traditional orientation has long been in place. Several Wexner alumni felt the need for a pluralistic communal school, now in the active planning stage. All three denominations mingle, and Leslie has played an active role with both advice and financial support.

• <u>Manhattan</u> – boasts two new community centers, as these institutions are known throughout the country, but in New York are called YM/WHAs or Y's for short. One, located on 14th St. in a remodeled building, has a Wexnerite as executive director; she runs the place with financial help from UJA/Federation. The second, on the Upper West Side, will be a large new facility and is operating meanwhile in rented space; the foremost lay leader plus several board members are Wexner graduates, determined to create an institution that will produce a program of Jewish identity-formation among the scores of thousands of Jews living in the area.

• <u>Boca Raton, Florida</u> – a large campus, with an elementary school, old folks' home, and community center, has been created during the past several years to serve the rapidly growing Jewish population. Wexner people are among the project leaders already planning an expansion onto a new site. In addition, an interesting phenomenon has developed: a thrust toward political office. Two Wexner graduates of the Boca Raton group have recently won elections. One has become a U.S. Congressman, another a state senator. Both men have strong, open Jewish personalities and are good prospects to go far in politics.

• <u>Testimonials to success</u> are almost endless. The phrase "this program changed my life" is heard most often. Scores of Wexner graduates have entered their own children in day schools in their communities; altered their family's lifestyle with regard to Shabbat and holiday rituals; continued their Jewish studies at their own expense; taken on heavier workloads at their Federations and synagogues; joined community missions to Israel. As the years pass, the cumulative effect of their enhanced Jewish consciousness and their understanding that action must flow from their convictions will help achieve the long-range goal that prompted Les Wexner to ask me years ago: "What can I do to help strengthen the American Jewish community?"

That single question launched a dozen years of work for me and Rabbi Nathan Laufer. The effort to date has involved enormous intellectual and emotional input on the part of the dozens of teachers and lecturers who have educated almost 1,000 Wexner graduates in 30 cities from coast to coast.

The benefits that will result in the century ahead cannot yet be imagined, but hopefully they will be revolutionary. Leslie Wexner can and should be very proud. *I* am certainly proud that he trusted me to shape and administer such a noble enterprise.

CHAPTER FORTY-TWO

THE FOUR-CENTURY SAGA
OF AMERICAN JEWRY

BEGINNINGS – 1654

The fascinating story of the very beginning of a community destined to become the most powerful Diaspora in history is especially well told by Dr. Howard M. Sachar, of George Washington University, in his magisterial, 1,000-page *A History of the Jews in America*. It is written in an engrossing style, combining narrative with detailed fact.

Sachar begins with the large colony of Sephardic Jews living in Recife, Brazil, on the Atlantic coast. This was a Dutch colony that had offered a haven to Jews displaced from Spain and Portugal a half-century earlier under the impact of the Catholic Inquisition and two politically minded monarchs. The Jews prospered under the Dutch, until Portugal, one of the most powerful nations in the world at that time, conquered Brazil and introduced the Inquisition to the New World. That was the signal for the Jews to flee once more.

In early September 1654, the Ste. Catherine, a French barque carrying 23 Jews, sailed into the Hudson River in North America, hoping to land at the tiny village of New Amsterdam, whose very name evoked the hope of a friendly reception. Holland had been hospitable toward Jewish refugees since their expulsion from Spain in 1492.

But if the small group – four men, six women, and 13 children – had anticipated a friendly welcome, they were sharply disappointed. They arrived penniless, having been stripped by Spanish pirates of all their possessions, except clothes and furniture. Then, at New Amsterdam, unable to pay the captain of the vessel for their passage, they lost their furniture to him at public auction. The Dutch governor, the later-famed Pieter Stuyvesant, was already hostile to Jews because of a previous experience in Curaçao, where he had argued with local Jews over their aversion to farming and preference for commerce. So Stuyvesant resisted this group's settling in New Amsterdam. He wrote to the board of the Dutch West India Company, asking for permission to expel the refugees, since Jews were notorious for "their usury and deceitful trading with Christians."

The minister of the Dutch Reformed Church in New Amsterdam supported Stuyvesant and added his own letter saying that "as we have here Papists, Mennonites and Lutherans, also many Puritans and Atheists and various other servants of Baal among the English, who conceal themselves under the name of Christians, it would create still greater confusion if the obstinate and immovable Jews came to settle here."

The forlorn Jews had contacts of their own back in Holland, including several important stockholders in the West India Company, and the refugees appealed to them. The stockholders reacted immediately, reminding the company that the fugitives had "risked their possessions and their blood in defense of the lost Dutch colony of Recife" and that Jews brought economic benefits wherever they settled. The board instructed Stuyvesant to allow the Jews to remain, and to worship and to trade in New Amsterdam, provided "the poor among them shall not become a burden to the Deaconry or the Company, but be supported by their own nation."

The group settled in, working as butchers, importers, peddlers, metal workers, fur traders, and retailers. Although at the beginning they were not allowed to bear arms, within a year they were sharing in the defense of the village against the Algonquin Indians and the British. When it was felt necessary to build a defense wall across Manhattan Island, the Jews assisted in the construction work along what is today called Wall Street. Gradually, most of the Jews sailed away, some to various Caribbean islands, and in 1663, nine years after their arrival, the last group carried its Torah scroll back to Holland. Of the pioneer settlers, only Asser Levy remained.

SEPHARDIC WAVE – 1600's to 1700's

The Dutch seized the Caribbean island of Curaçao from the Spanish in 1634, and Samuel Coheno, interpreter for the Dutch naval commander, became the first Jew to set foot there. Seventeen years later, Joao d'Yllan, who had lived in Dutch Brazil, led a small group of Jews from Amsterdam to Curaçao, and the two adventurers promptly established Mikve Israel synagogue, the first in the Americas. For centuries, Curaçao Jews have scattered sand imported from the Holy Land on the floor of the synagogue. A nearby cemetery, whose earliest tombstones date from 1668, holds 5,500 graves.

Curaçao had the largest and most vibrant Jewish community in the Americas until the early 19th century, and even today its vigorous Jewish population numbers about 500. Hebrew words have crept into the native language; beautiful old colonial homes in pastel colors stand as reminders of a once-affluent center of 3,000 Jews that extended financial support to other Jewish groups in Jamaica, Panama, St. Thomas, and Newport, Rhode Island.

Dutch Jews, who had been re-admitted to England in the mid-1600s, also started migrating to British-held islands in the Caribbean, where they lived full and openly Jewish lives. Jamaica had five synagogues by 1776. Alexander Hamilton was a student in Nevis' Jewish school, having been denied admission to its Anglican parish counterpart because he was an illegitimate child. When Ezra Stiles, president of Yale College in Connecticut, wanted to learn Hebrew (the new college had been founded as a divinity school), he took Hebrew lessons from Rabbi Haim Carigal, who had migrated to New England from the Caribbean. For eleven years, Stiles preached the baccalaureate sermon at Yale in Hebrew. The Yale seal is emblazoned with two Hebrew words, *Urim v'Thummim*, and their Latin equivalents, *Lux et Veritas*.

A small migration resumed to New York from Amsterdam and the Caribbean, and by the end of the 1600s, 250 Jews had settled there. The city's first Sephardic synagogue, Shearith Israel, existed without rabbinical leadership. Not a single ordained rabbi came to America during the colonial period. In 1685, a layman named Saul Pardo arrived in New York to serve as cantor, and he adopted the title of "Reverend."

Philadelphia in those decades was home to 100 Jews; close behind were Newport, Savannah, and CharlesTown (now Charleston, South Carolina). Sachar writes: "Not a single law was enacted in British North America specifically to disable Jews....They were free not only to engage in any trade, in any colony, but also to own a home in any neighborhood. In New York and Rhode Island, Jews could attend university....By 1776, the 2,000 Jews of colonial America unquestionably were the freest Jews on earth."

In the Revolutionary War, many remained loyal to the British, but many more assisted the colonists. Haym Solomon of Philadelphia brokered fairly useless Continental currency in exchange for stable Dutch and French currencies, enabling the Continental Congress to buy European goods that were shipped back to New York in Jewish-owned vessels.

Despite his efforts, Solomon died insolvent, owed more than $600,000 – a great fortune – by the Continental Congress. The money was never paid to him or his family. He had to be content with the title "Broker to the Office of Finance of the United States."

Approximately 100 Jews performed military service for the Continental Army during the Revolution. Additionally, Jews who owned ships ran the British blockades. Others manufactured rifles, worked as surgeons in the Army, and supplied various other goods and services.

Upon George Washington's inauguration as the first President, several Jewish congregations sent congratulations. He replied to Newport's congregation with a letter that became famous, for it officially established religious freedom for the Jews in the new United States of America. Writing in the ornate style of that era, Washington stated:

> It is now no more that toleration is spoken of, as if it were by the indulgence of one class of people that any other enjoyed the exercise of their inherent

natural rights. For happily the Government of the United States, which gives to bigotry no sanction, to persecution no assistance, requires only that they who live under its protection demean themselves as good citizens, in giving it on all occasions their effectual support. May the children of the Stock of Abraham, who dwell in this land, continue to merit and enjoy the good will of the other inhabitants, while everyone shall sit in safety under his own vine and fig-tree and there shall be none to make him afraid.

ASHKENAZIC WAVE – 1800s
German and Central European

By the early 1800s, the United States was absorbing millions of European immigrants. Their brawn and brains helped satisfy the voracious demands for manpower of a nation looking westward across a continent ripe for the taking. The Louisiana Purchase had provided millions of square miles of additional land, from the Gulf of Mexico almost to the Pacific Ocean. Between 1815 and 1875, three million German-speaking Europeans, among them Ashkenazic Jews, arrived in this vast region. They represented the second wave of Jewish migrants, different from the Sephardic wave in language, culture, religious practice, and occupational skills.

By 1847, for example, an estimated 50,000 German Jews resided in the United States, and about 15,000 of them gravitated to various trades connected with the clothing industry, especially to peddling. That was a uniquely Jewish phenomenon, based on a chain-letter-like operation. Jewish manufacturers of clothing in such Eastern manufacturing centers as New York, Rochester, and Philadelphia sold their products to Jewish wholesalers in Cincinnati, St. Louis, and Chicago. The wholesalers supplied small-town Jewish retailers; and they in turn provided goods on consignment to Jewish peddlers who fanned across the Ohio, Mississippi and Missouri river valleys to reach isolated villages and farm families all the way to the Midwestern and Southern states.

The peddler worked fiercely hard. He often carried 50 to 80 pounds on his back and walked many miles every day, seldom knowing exactly when he would eat or where he would sleep. The best solution was a friendly farmer's offer of supper and a bed of hay in the barn. A peddler who managed to husband his meager profits could acquire a horse and cart, easing his physical burden and enlarging the inventory of goods he could carry. After more years of crisscrossing his territory, he might even be able to rent a small store at a highly traveled cross-road, and there his wandering would cease. R. H. Macy and Co., the world's largest department store in its heyday, started as a tiny Georgia shop that was founded by Lazarus Strauss, an erstwhile peddler.

By 1880, department stores had begun to flower all over the land: Garfinkle's in Washington; Thalheimer's in Little Rock; Goldsmith's in Memphis; Sakowitz's in Houston; Rich's in Atlanta; Kaufman's in Pittsburgh; Gimbel's in Philadelphia and New York, and, of course, Macy's in New York. That store's name came from its location: a building owned by a retired whaling boat captain, R.H. Macy. The U.S. Jewish population (largely German) had reached one-quarter million, with a third of it in New York City.

Between 1860 and 1880, the manufacture and sale of clothing throughout the United States formed the backbone of the nation's German-Jewish economy. The immigrants who plied the clothing trade found success because they arrived with some formidable qualities: a good education, a dignified bearing and proper manners, a sense of *Ordnung* (orderliness), and the prevailing, 19th-century belief in rationalism, scientific inquiry, and mercantilism. Add to this the Victorian habits of dress and behavior, and the typical German immigrant appeared as a person seeking to live as an emancipated citizen in a free country in the modern world.

In addition to clothing, investment banking emerged as a strong economic factor in the acculturation of the German-Jewish wave. Names familiar today began to surface: Joseph Seligman; Heinrich Lehman; Marcus Goldman and Samuel Sachs; Abraham Kuhn and Solomon Loeb; Jacob Schiff; the Warburgs; Meyer Guggenheim; and many others.

And then came practitioners of the arts and sciences: Joseph Pulitzer, Oscar Hammerstein, Leopold Damrosch (father of Walter), Dr. Simon Baruch (father of Bernard), to name a few among an increasing multitude of talented people.

Despite George Washington's letter of a century earlier, bigotry and discrimination certainly existed, including a social rejection of even the most successful German-Jews. One of the most shocking examples occurred in 1877 and involved the banker Joseph Seligman, who was a personal friend of President Grant, and had been offered the position of secretary of the treasury. He was, in fact, the most prominent Jew in the United States.

When Seligman and his family arrived in Saratoga, in upper New York State, a major resort catering to the country's high society, they expected to be accommodated in their usual suites. Instead, the desk clerk at the Grand Union Hotel greeted them with a prepared statement: "Mr. Seligman, I am required to inform you that Judge Hilton [the hotel's administrator] has given instructions that no Israelite shall be permitted in the future to stop at this hotel."

Seligman sent a scathing letter to Hilton, released it to the press (where it made front-page news) and organized a boycott of Saratoga's Stewart department store, whose proprietor also owned the hotel. There was a huge outcry, with many prominent persons taking Seligman's side. In rebuttal, many other top-scale hotels instituted similar restrictions, going so far as sponsoring newspaper advertisements saying "Hebrews need not apply" and "Jews excluded."

The war spread to social clubs. Jesse Seligman, brother of Joseph, both of them among the founders of New York's celebrated Union League Club, suffered a terrible rebuff when his son Theodore, an attorney of renown, was blackballed for membership there. The natural result was the formation of Jewish clubs, such as the Harmonie in New York and the Standard in Chicago.

One of the striking features of the Jewish drive toward emancipation in mid-19th-century Germany was the revolutionary change in the practice and theory of Judaism. The process had begun a century earlier, when Moses Mendelsohn translated the Bible into German, so that Jews could learn and adopt that language as one method of gaining acceptance from the majority in whose midst they lived. The assimilation process was so successful that, even though Mendelsohn himself was a traditional, observant Jew, his family produced no Jewish descendants.

The religious reformers of the 19th century had no such radical results in mind. They advocated shortening the liturgy, introducing music and some prayers in German; eliminating references to rebuilding the Temple with its animal sacrifices or rebuilding Jerusalem; seating men and women together; and other, minor changes.

The desire to Reform and modernize included a change of attitude toward ancient rabbinic *halachah* (religious law). Strict observance of the Sabbath, maintenance of dietary laws *(kashrut)*, obedience to the laws of marriage and divorce, and many other normative rules of behavior that had prevailed for millennia, all began to crumble. A reaction arose from those who believed that any accommodation to modernity was dangerous and destructive to basic Jewish values that had endured for so long. The traditionalists called themselves Orthodox and organized into a separate movement. Thus, two new denominational structures were created, one after another, within a few years of the mid-1800s, where nothing similar had occurred during the past 19 centuries.

A third way was shortly born, a compromise calling itself Conservative. This group made some concessions to modern life, but did not utterly disregard the authority of the *halachah*, as Reform had done. The three movements, so familiar to American Jews today, were all born in Germany less than 150 years ago. Today there are more than 3,000 synagogues in the United States, representing *four* organized movements, the latest being the Reconstructionist, founded in this country and occupying a niche between Conservative and Reform.

About 10,000 Jews served in the armies that fought the American Civil War, roughly 60 percent of them on the Union side. Eight Jews became generals in the Union forces, four in the Confederate. Yet there was anti-Jewish sentiment in the ranks, even at top levels. Judah P. Benjamin served in Jefferson Davis' cabinet as attorney-general, secretary of war, and finally secretary of state. Nevertheless, he became a target. Vice-President (later President) Andrew Johnson accused Benjamin of improprieties as secretary of war in connection with certain shortages of ammunition. After Lee surrendered at Appomatox, Benjamin fled the United States for England, where he remained until his death.

In addition, on December 17, 1862, General Grant issued his famous Order No. 11 expelling all Jews from the Military Department of Tennessee (which included Misssissippi and much of Kentucky) within 24 hours. Grant cancelled the order at President Lincoln's demand.

As president, however, Grant changed his colors completely. When the Rumanian Government issued harsh anti-Jewish regulations and encouraged mob attacks on Jews, Grant listened to protests from prominent American Jews and intervened. He appointed the president of B'nai Brith as U.S. ambassador to Rumania with the following message: "The United States, knowing no distinction of her citizens on account of religion, naturally believes in a civilization the world over which will secure the same universal views." Grant's intervention succeeded in quieting the situation.

Following the Civil War, most German Jews supported the new Republican Party – the party of free soil, free men, and vigorous business enterprise. In that spirit, the solidly established, financially secure German-Jewish leadership started to organize the network of charities that would fortuitously be in place when the overwhelming wave of East European Jews from Russia and Poland soon crashed on American shores. Among groups formed were the Educational Alliance, Jewish Welfare Board, Hebrew Free Loan Society, Burial Society, and welfare funds in many cities across the United States. To extend the philanthropic hand overseas, Felix Warburg created the American Jewish Joint Distribution Committee. Popularly known as the Joint, it has been the premier organization bringing material assistance, professional personnel guidance, and medical aid to Jews and non-Jews who suffer from hunger and disease, natural disasters, and man-made persecution.

In a way, America's German-Jewish philanthropists were schizophrenic. They felt obligated as Jews to aid the incoming masses of brethren from Poland, Galicia (a part of Poland), Russia, Ukraine, and the Baltic states. Yet they were basically put off by these Eastern newcomers, who arrived loudly speaking their Yiddish jargon, many wearing unfashionable black garments and long earlocks, practicing an antiquated religion, bereft of manners and civilized behavior. One of the motives for helping those folk was truly idealistic; another was to Americanize them as quickly as possible.

ASHKENAZIC WAVE – 1881 to 1914
East and North European

Czar Alexander III encouraged anti-Jewish pogroms, sending brigades of peasants rampaging through the Pale of Settlement. The Pale occupied much of the area between Poland and Russia, where hundreds of thousands of poverty-stricken Jews had been compressed into tiny villages called *shtetls*. The peasants roamed from shtetl to shtetl, burning and looting, killing and maiming. The Jews had no means of defense. By the end of 1881, thousands had been killed, 20,000 left homeless, and scores of thousands of others had fled southwestward toward the border of Galicia, then under the control of the Hapsburg Monarchy.

The following year, the Czar decreed that no Jew could settle in any rural area, even within the Pale, or purchase a house or land there. Small towns were reclassified as rural settlements, closing them off to Jews. Hundreds of thousands of Jews were thus forced from the countryside into the congested city slums, where there were no jobs for country bumpkins without skills. Hunger, disease, and despair overwhelmed the masses.

The large majority of Jews in the beleaguered areas chose the road of migration. In spite of the difficulties and hardships involved, more than two million came to the United States between 1882 and 1914, when Atlantic Ocean civilian shipping almost ceased in the face of Germany's World War I submarine attacks. The *Goldene Medina* (golden land) of America was the ultimate goal.

The exodus was generally heart-rending. Multitudes simply left shack or tenement behind and walked, sometimes pulling a loaded cart filled with bedding, children, some food, and a few prized books of photos or prayers. Others were lucky enough to buy a horse and wagon, so that women and old people could ride and some clothing or even a sentimental piece of furniture could be salvaged. A well-to-do few left in style, by train, to pre-selected destinations beyond the reaches of the czar, where they could rest and plan their futures. Many of those families chose to settle in Western Europe – Germany, France or England.

Whatever the status of the emigrant, most forms of flight were traumatic. There was danger on the road in the form of bandits seeking valuable loot or peasants overturning carts for food or clothing. Daily tasks like eating, sleeping, personal hygiene, and safety became daunting. Disease and even death were hard to avoid. But the pulsating columns kept moving, animated by fear and anxiety about the unknown next day and pushed by the agitated throng behind.

The human flood headed toward a town named Brody, which sat on the border between Germany and what is today the Czech Republic. This was the narrow end of the funnel, and hundreds of thousands of weary travelers had to pass through it. Identification papers ranged from primitive to proper to nothing. But papers hardly mattered: The border officials could not control the surging crowds and soon abandoned the effort altogether.

Once across, the streams of refugees split in several directions. One human river flowed to the North Sea ports near Hamburg and other smaller points. Another headed toward Berlin, with the intention of going no further. And the third aimed for Liverpool, which entailed the longest land journey but offered the cheapest "Schiffskarte" (transatlantic ticket) at $29 per person, steerage class. A similar sailing from Hamburg cost $39.

The scene at each port was chaotic. Huge crowds milled around, selling items they had dragged across Europe in order to buy the tickets, screaming for children lost in the shuffle; searching for toilets and for kiosks to buy food and water, enduring long lines at the tables where ship's personnel were trying to write passenger lists. Con men sold steamship "tickets," urging weary migrants not to wait in the lines. Most of the tickets were false, and when purchasers were refused boarding at the gangway; they screamed for help – but no police responded. Frustration; fear; tears.

At the train station in Berlin, officials of the Jewish relief organizations offered food and water, but then tried to persuade the migrants to return to their starting point or to continue further west and not remain in Germany. The proud and proper German Jews did not want these motley ragamuffins infiltrating their society, affecting the status and reputation of the native Jews. Nor did they want the burden of subsidizing unskilled Ostjuden (Eastern Jews), who would never get decently paid work and would thus have to be supported for years until they advanced to the level of German standards.

The ocean voyage itself was excruciating. Passengers spent two weeks or more below decks in steerage, packed like sardines. Sometimes there were planks for beds, and sometimes nothing. People slept on each other, curled up in fetal positions. The air was fetid. Lines for the single feeding of the day snaked through all the holds, and it took hours to reach the food station, only to receive some stew slopped into a bowl. Most of the vessels, carrying several hundred passengers each, were outfitted with only two toilets. When the seas became rough and seasickness overtook most of the passengers, vomit spewed from all sides over everyone. There was no reaching an upper deck, where one could find relief over the rail. One's neighbor became the rail.

At the entry ports in the United States, whether Castle Garden and Ellis Island in New York harbor, or Baltimore or Galveston, there was somewhat more order. Names were altered by inspectors who could not pronounce them in Polish and Russian; so Aronowicz became Aaronson (my mother's maiden name) and Frydmann became Friedman (my father's name). Health officials focused particularly on examining eyes and lungs. Any indication of glaucoma, cataracts, or tuberculosis resulted in the immigrant being rejected and deported on the very next departing vessel.

To diminish the large numbers settling in New York ghetto areas, American Jewish relief agencies sent volunteers to the hinterlands, particularly the Midwest. Although not skilled farmers, most of the volunteers came from shtetls in rural areas and were passably familiar with agricultural life. In addition to trying to move their largely unwilling clients to distant towns, the agencies started wholly Jewish agricultural settlements. Of the original 16 settlements, only one succeeded, in Toms River, New Jersey. My uncle Meir learned chicken farming there, became quite expert, and in the early 1920s migrated to Palestine to join Kibbutz Merchavia; one of his fellow workers there was also an American, named Golda Meyerson, later famous as Golda Meir.

The first decades were the hardest for the immigrants: living in crowded tenements in an alien and often-unfriendly culture, scrambling for work, struggling to learn English, accommodating to a wholly unfamiliar system. Twentieth-century industrial expansion eased their transition. Many of the newcomers went into the sweatshops and factories, there to become members of the newly forming trade unions, where Jews were prominent as organizers and recruiters. It was a natural attraction. The social-justice ethic expressed by the ancient Biblical prophets, bred into the Jewish consciousness for millennia, tied in nicely with a union creed promising to strengthen the poor and weak, to provide for the widow and orphan.

Many others preferred the mercantile route. They opened small shops, selling all types of basic household needs, working unimaginable hours to make a few pennies of profit. Mothers and even children struggled to keep such businesses alive. Often the venture would fail, but sometimes success would lead to a larger store in a better location, and that would become the base for financial stability. It would also open related opportunities: wholesaling, distributing, manufacturing.

Gradually, the family's housing improved, children's education brought joy and pride to the parents, and the burden of being strangers in a strange land slowly diminished. The appetite for a higher standard of living replaced the previous hope for mere survival.

The climb out of crowded, often-squalid urban quarters became a broad American phenomenon in which the Jews participated avidly. In the decade following World War I, the trek to "suburbs" began. Developers and builders quickly responded. Small projects got underway, slowed down during the Depression years, and restarted vigorously after Roosevelt's New Deal began to repair the economy. Major cities acquired adjuncts: middle-class Levittown in Long Island and upscale Scarsdale in Westchester, both near New York; Shaker Heights in Cleveland; Glencoe, north of Chicago; Beverly Hills in Los Angeles. As automobile ownership expanded, and highways were built accordingly, hundreds of subdivisions grew. Whether modest or extravagant, all offered green grass and trees.

The first generation of Jews born in the United States, children of the immigrants who spoke no English, reached out for higher education. They were strongly encouraged by their parents, because a fierce value was placed on education in the average American Jewish family. The value stemmed from two sources: the traditions that labeled us "People of the Book"; and the feeling that only education would accelerate the long road to social acceptance and economic independence. A high school diploma was already a common goal in the 1930s, and a college degree equally common by the 1960s.

As a result, the fourth generation born in this country, hard at work today, is almost entirely professional in character, possessing second and even third academic degrees. The ranks of current American Jewish breadwinners include professionals of all sorts – not just the doctors and lawyers of folklore and even jokes, but also architects and accountants, computer engineers and programmers, artists and journalists, authors and musicians, scientists and politicians, professors and researchers, financial managers and investment counselors, environmentalists and astronomers, and on and on in hundreds of specialties. It has been an explosion, a revolution that has placed the average Jewish family relatively high on the socio-economic scale and eased the way to friendly relations with non-Jewish neighbors living on the same street or co-workers in the office, because they share so many things in common. Bagels have become as familiar on the American breakfast table as doughnuts. Assimilation into a secular American life-style follows a smooth path, especially as the steady "Judaization" of America continues, with the Chanukah menorah as a familiar companion to the Christmas tree in TV shows and newspaper ads.

The most natural jump has also been made: entry into the American intellectual world. Jews write many of the nation's books, and sit at the top of companies that publish them. Jews own newspapers, and not only *The New York Times*, as well as major TV networks. Jews have dominated the cinema industry almost from its beginning – as studio owners, producers, directors, writers, musicians, and in some cases, star actors. Jews have built great art museums, performed as celebrated musical soloists, ranked among the leading dramatists and producers and directors of the legitimate theater, and penetrated deeply into the academic world, achieving the presidencies of several of the most prestigious universities in the land and sending more than 50,000 men and women into academe as professors during the last half-century.

Great-grandfather worked in a clothing sweat-shop or rolled cigars for $2 per week, lived in two rooms with four or five other people, and barely spoke the language. He persevered on the strength of a deep hope for the future and retained his strong sense of Jewish identity through ritual observance, kosher diet, and at least some religious practice. Today's great-grandson has earned a master's degree in business administration or civil engineering, enjoys a six-figure income, lives in an eight-room house in a leafy suburb, attends synagogue a few days a year (if at all), contributes something to the UJA, talks about visiting Israel but hasn't done it yet, and loves his non-Jewish daughter-in-law. That admittedly truncated summary describes the odyssey of the East European immigrants from the beginning to the end of the 20th century.

During the last decade of this century, about 400,000 new Jewish immigrants from the former Soviet Union have entered the United States, and more will come in the several years ahead. Not enough is known yet about their adjustment, economic status, Americanization, geographic distribution, religious education, participation in the Jewish community, etc., to provide an accurate group profile. In addition to addressing their material needs for housing, jobs, and language, the main Jewish agencies responsible for their absorption into this country have made valiant efforts to integrate them into the Jewish community as well. Jewish day schools, community centers, and synagogue afternoon schools have offered free tuition and memberships.

Because the American Jewish population is diminishing through intermarriage and other forms of assimilation, the addition of large, new numbers is a very welcome development. It is urgent that, wherever they settle, as many of these new immigrants as possible be quickly integrated into an enveloping Jewish environment. Fortunately, they are on the whole intelligent, well educated, and capable of making rapid adjustments. The speed with which they master English is amazing. They become American citizens as soon as the law permits. Within that five-year waiting period, can they also become knowledgeable, identifiable, proud American Jews? If so, the diminution of the American-Jewish community, such a fearful prospect, could be slowed down.

★   ★   ★

Thus we have explained the birth and growth of the American Diaspora during the past 350 years. As tectonic plates crack and shift in the earth's mantle, altering the shape of continents over geologic time, so do Jewish population shifts occur, but in the relative blink of an eye. Think of the amalgam of tribes and languages and cultures that compose the American-Jewish polity of today. Yet out of the jumble, one striking fact occurs. A show of hands by today's fourth-generation, American-born Jews, regarding the ancestry of their families would yield a 90 percent majority grown from Russian-Polish roots.

They and their Jewish brethren from other roots have earned their place in America; been blessed by its freedoms and bounties; contributed to its greatness; and are thoroughly at home here. The main uncertainty lies in their future. Will they maintain a vibrant practice and knowledge of their Jewish tradition, or will they permit the precious heritage to evaporate in the welcoming warmth of America's embrace? I offer my opinion and advice on that – the existential question – in the next and final chapter.

CHAPTER FORTY-THREE

WHITHER AMERICAN JEWRY?
TO LIVE ON OR TO DIE OUT

Three hundred fifty years after its pioneers first appeared on New World soil, American Jewry faces its greatest crisis. The crisis is, ironically, of its own making and is so severe that by 2054, the 400th anniversary of Jewish settlement on this continent, American Jewry may be seriously diminished, reduced to less than one-half of one percent of the total population. There are those who derogate such predictions, countering with defiant slogans that a "renaissance" is in the making. Proof is offered in the form of increased day school enrollments, synagogue rejuvenation, wider adult education programs, and expanded Jewish consciousness on college campuses. All this is indeed positive, helpful, lovely to witness – and yet is hardly a renaissance. That term suggests a sweeping surge of creativity in all areas of Jewish activity – and does not describe the present condition of American Jewry.

Large numbers of Jews are simply drifting away from Judaism because they aren't living and thinking *as* Jews. They are living instead as single-identity persons (Americans only). They don't know much about Judaism, nor practice its rituals, nor relate to Israel in any way – not even as tourists. Worse, perhaps, they seem not to care. They marry "out" (of the faith), and most don't even try to bring their mates and children "in." The inevitable result: a combination of ignorance, indifference, and intermarriage leading to total assimilation and disappearance into the culture of the majority.

Everyone in the American Jewish establishment knows what's happening. The chief fundraising organizations, United Jewish Appeal and Council of Jewish Federations, know it; the local federation system knows it. The synagogue system feels it. The national organizations suffer from it. Even far-off Israel knows it.

Intellectuals and writers have already covered the subject. Alan Dershowitz's latest book is entitled, *The Vanishing American Jew*; Seymour M. Lipset and Earl Raab have addressed *Jews and the New American Scene*; Rabbi Arthur Hertzberg recently wrote *The Jews in America: Four Centuries of an Uneasy Encounter*; and Elihu Bergman, a Harvard demographer with a long view, predicted 25 years ago that the Jewish population of the United States in 2076 would consist of fewer than one million.

Bergman used 2076 as his benchmark because that will be the 300th anniversary of the Declaration of Independence. I prefer to use 2054 because that will be the 400th anniversary of the landing of the first Jewish settlers on this continent.

Nevertheless, I accept Bergman's population estimate. It is shocking to realize that the golden age of American Judaism, which has produced the most powerful and successful Diaspora community in the entire 3,700-year history of the Jewish people, may well be expiring as the anniversary of its fourth century in America approaches.

For many casual readers, it is difficult to accept such a prediction, for they see all around them an affluent, educated, prominent group of Jews who appear anything but "endangered." A modern paradox makes the confusion understandable. American Jewry today exhibits two faces, two facets, two definitions of itself. One is strong, vigorous, thrusting forward to new creative heights in every field of human endeavor; the other is weak, indecisive, stumbling toward a self-inflicted immolation.

The strong face has many features:

- Departments of Jewish studies functioning in more than 200 American colleges and universities, registering tens of thousands of students, Jews and non-Jews alike. Oddly, the largest of these departments – in terms of endowed chairs, books published, outside lecturers brought in, students enrolled – exists at the University of Indiana, in the American heartland.

- Nine Jewish Senators, 25 Congresspersons, two members of the Supreme Court.
- A Reform Jewish day school in Los Angeles enrolling more than 3,000 students in grades K-12.
- A Conservative synagogue in New York welcoming thousands of enthusiastic members to overflow services every Sabbath evening and morning in a great singing and dancing congregation, which meets in a nearby Methodist church because its own building is too small.
- A fundraising philanthropy, the UJA, rating in 1996 as the fourth-largest public charity in the entire country, just behind the United Way and the Red Cross.
- Almost 400 national Jewish organizations dedicated to promoting various areas of culture, education, community relations with other groups, overseas aid, Israel-related projects, religion, and social welfare. In addition, hundreds of Federations are linked to thousands of local agencies.

It would thus appear that the relatively small Jewish community, a mere 1.8 percent of the total U.S. population, is thriving in the political, social, cultural, economic, and religious spheres. Yet the other face is equally impressive in its negative aspects:

- *The National Jewish Population Study* of 1990 indicated that more than 50 percent of American Jews have exogamous marriages – that is, with non-Jewish partners.
- In the late 20th century, only 38 percent of the Jews in this country belong to synagogues at various points in their lives. Life-long members form a much smaller percentage.
- Only 25 percent contribute to Jewish charities.
- The rate of ignorance of Judaism is incredibly high.

- The number of children in Jewish day schools (not counting the Orthodox network) is incredibly low – a national total of 35,500.
- Only one-quarter to one-third of American Jews have visited Israel during its 50 years of existence.
- The number of Jews considered "active" or "caring," that is, participating in aspects of the community's existence, is estimated at only 25 percent.

If the negative prediction of a constantly diminishing number of Jews during the coming half-century does indeed come true, specific and serious changes will result. One million Jews, scattered in small numbers throughout the nation's cities and towns, will be insufficient to maintain the infrastructure necessary for communal existence. There will not be enough people to support the institutions, professional staffs, and annual budgets of the local and national agencies, to say nothing of the needs of less fortunate Jews overseas.

Such support amounts to billions of dollars every year. Without it, almost all of the Jewish infrastructure – synagogues, federations, centers, schools, homes for elderly, and so on – will gradually crumble as operations lose the money and/or the people-power to maintain them. Forget about supporting the JDC and ORT and all the Israeli universities and hospitals and museums and immigrant-absorption centers: They will be the first to suffer.

One million Jews, in a total American population that may easily reach 350 million by 2054 or 2076, will constitute such an insignificant factor that the final process of disintegration will accelerate. There will be no reason to hang on, and nothing to hang on to. Some portion of the core group itself may well emigrate to Israel.

The Orthodox community believes that its observance of ritual, obedience to the ancient unchangeable code of law (*halacha*), and emphasis on a parochial school education of at least 12 years for its youngsters will guarantee its survival, no matter what happens to the other 90 percent of the American Jewish population. Israel Zoberman, in a review in the Summer 1997 issue of the *Jewish Spectator* of a book by Seymour Martin Lipset and Earl Raab, entitled "Jews and the New American Scene," wrote: "Is the Orthodox Jewish day school the magic bullet that will lead to Jewish survival?... Research indicates that a stronger commitment to a higher level of Jewish education and observance leads to a lower level of intermarriage (not more than 2 percent) and assimilation....Choosing ritual observance is likely to lead to Jewish education, which in turn is likely to lead to choosing a Jewish spouse, which is likely to lead to providing a stronger educational and ritual base for one's children, who then perpetuate the cycle."

Although that reassuring theory may well be accurate for the Orthodox world, it does not fit the huge number of non-Orthodox Jews who have chosen alternative forms of religious expression. Many analysts argue that the minimal education now given to the great majority of children who receive *any* form of Jewish education is hopelessly inadequate and must be radically reshaped. The argument has validity, and there are faint signs that it is gaining wider acceptance among communal leaders.

Rabbi Arthur Hertzberg, a scholar and community leader, offers the following trenchant observation: "It is possible in this new age of America to evaporate out of being Jewish without making a decision to be anything else. In fact, the drift of life in contemporary America is toward free association. The older generation of Jews still finds most of its friends among other Jews; the young do not. They remain 'proud to be Jews,' but they are less and less likely to live their lives within the ethnic community."

Lipset-Raab acknowledge the problem but appear to be less apocalyptic: "Given the inexorably integrative forces of American society and the resultant parallel trends among Jews, it is reasonable to predict that the Jewish community as a whole will be severely reduced in numbers by the middle of the next century. The extent to which the remaining core will endure, or even possibly recoup, will depend on intrinsic factors....The religion-connected aspect of Jewish life provides the strongest deterrent to the swift or complete dissolution of American Jewry. It also is the most credible basis for the prediction that, while the Jewish community will be much reduced in size, it will not have disappeared and may even have reached some relatively stable plateau....

"'Fragile remnant' is a term Benjamin Disraeli applied to Jews in the 19th century. The remnant of American Jewry, both the more devout and the fellow-travelers, will tend to be those who feel somehow connected to the religious core of their tribal identity.... As a result, the remaining body of American Jewry may well be significantly less fragile than it is now. Yet, even that religious core cannot be durably nourished by isolationist remedies. The tribal dilemma in America is not to be solved for most Jews by requiring them to forgo those exceptional qualities of American society that have so beneficently created that dilemma."

Lipset-Raab seem to me to be fudging the question. They may be overly optimistic in their hope that a connection with religion plus an attenuated tribal loyalty will keep a diminished population Jewish, especially since they freely admit that Jews will not isolate themselves from a free, permissive, welcoming American society that will only become more so.

Dershowitz concludes that there is only one weapon with which to fight the dissolution – a new kind of education. He dismisses several alternatives offered by other observers:

- *Religion* is not the wave of the future for most young intellectuals. Today's American Jewish community is secular.
- *Israel* is not Judaism's salvation. Most American Jews want to remain where they are.
- *Jewish ethics* cannot be transmitted to children without living a Jewish life (which most American Jews do not do).
- *Fundraising and charity* cannot ensure the Jewish future.

Dershowitz' singular solution; an educational system of a different kind.

Jewish education today is controlled almost entirely by the religious component of Jewish life and has been one of the great failures of the American Jewish community....We will have to loosen the monopolistic hold that rabbis have over Jewish education so that we can compete effectively in the marketplace of ideas for the minds and hearts of our Jewish youth.... We will have to educate our children differently, select our leaders differently, allocate our charitable giving differently – even define our very Jewishness differently. Jewish life will have to become less tribal, more open, more accepting of outsiders, and less defensive.

A new Jewish leadership must emerge to supplement the traditional rabbinic and political leadership of the Jewish people. Judaism has been led by kings, priests, rabbis, politicians, and philanthropists (in various epochs). Today a new leadership must be added to this pantheon of heroes. We need a leadership of Jewish *educators* who can address the pressing issue of Jewish illiteracy and ignorance. We need teachers who can inspire – who believe in Jewish education for its own sake – not for any other reason.

The Judaism I am trying to defend and enhance is a Judaism of ideas, attitudes, skepticism, justice, compassion, argumentation and inclusiveness. That kind of Judaism can survive, indeed thrive, in an open and welcoming world into which Jewish ideas can cast a beacon of light. That kind of Judaism does not depend on who is a Jew or whether one's father or mother is a Jew, or whether one is a 'whole' Jew or a 'half' Jew. That kind of Judaism is the power of Jewish ideas to educate, influence and repair the world. Every Jew who cares about our future must join in building the foundation for this new Judaism.

In my view, neither books nor authors will decide the destiny of American Jewry. That lies in the hands of the great leaders who are accustomed to dealing with crises and shaping solutions; their powerful organizations which formulate action plans and carry them out. They lead the mass of Jews to understand a particular emergency in historical terms and urge the mass to react in a certain manner.

All of that constitutes leadership in action. One has a right to expect action, but there is stunning silence instead. That is, there's a massive *failure* of leadership. We see a plethora of meetings, an outpouring of resolutions, discussions ad nauseam of the "continuity" problem, an outcry of lamentations, a restless formation of committees in every city in the country, all regurgitating the same data and repeating the pious statements that "education" is the solution.

The texts of resolutions passed by every local task force on continuity sound weirdly similar. And the culminating report of the National Continuity Commission of the Council of Jewish Federations, the result of a two-year effort, turned out to be an empty bladder of wind, over-wordy and non-specific. Was that the mighty battle cry to mobilize the country? Both chairpersons, Marvin Lender and Shoshana Cardin, veterans of many monumental projects, who rank among our most able national leaders, confessed to me their frustration in being unable to emerge with a strong, revitalizing program. What should have been a huge *shofar* blast, summoning the nation to support a detailed plan of action, emerged as the weak bleat of a kazoo, a dull, pallid, bureaucratic failure.

It should be noted that during this very tense period, when great and urgent policy should have been formulated on a live-or-die question, the leaders of the two most important organizations, the United Jewish Appeal and the Council of Jewish Federations, spent their time tinkering over administrative matters: "merger" or "partnership"; one board or two; one executive director or two. From groups whose duty it is to shape the future, that amounted to a nauseating display of irrelevancy.

Never has the Biblical sentence of Proverbs 29:18 been more relevant.

בְּאֵין חָזוֹן יִפָּרַע עָם
"Where there is no vision, the people break loose or perish"

In sum, the present generation of leaders has failed so far to provide vision, and the people have broken loose. The end of the process, if unreversed, must inevitably be to perish.

To prevent that calamity, vision must be coupled with reality. The UJA provided such a vision in rescuing the Jews fleeing the former Soviet Union. The organization's leaders named the action plan Operation Exodus (which resonated with the entire Jewish community), calibrated it to raise $1 billion between 1990 and 1995, and succeeded brilliantly. That brief description hardly describes the quantity of brainpower, the number of personnel, the involvement of all sorts of experts in communication, the logistics of speakers going all over the country, the mobilization of some of the richest Jews in the country. All of that was simply the execution of the vision and its attendant plan. Alas, that essential combination is missing today, and without it, there is nothing.

In March 1995, as Operation Exodus drew to a close, I proposed to the UJA executive committee a vision plus an action plan for the next historic challenge facing the American Jewish community, namely, the rescue of our own youth. We helped rescue Russia's Jewish young people – why not our own?

Specifically, I suggested that the UJA raise $500 million to $1 billion in additional funds during the next five years to support an Israel Experience for all 15- to 25-year-olds at community expense. I had in mind a missionary-like approach that would galvanize the entire UJA/Federation system into "Judaizing" our own American kids. An Israel Experience is not merely a trip but a carefully designed program for getting under the skin of impressionable youth. The evidence showed that, when properly crafted, an exposure to the depth of Israel has instilled in thousands of young people a sense of commitment to Judaism and to Israel.

The UJA response? The leaders ignored the idea, without explaining why or suggesting any alternative for awakening the languid constituency.

If the UJA and Federation system understood the danger and mobilized all the strength they possess in both money and manpower, it might be possible to alter the course of the war of attrition and defeat that now confronts us. The American Jewish public, including its youth, has always responded in time of crises and emergencies. It is essential that its top leadership respond as well.

In addition, the Federation system must join with the synagogue system to fill the pews and classrooms with a new generation seeking Judaism. Such a commitment to new programs, backed by the necessary funds and the creative genius of the best lay and rabbinical minds, might well trigger the knowledge, enthusiasm, and commitment of a larger number of new members.

Make no mistake. The task is huge. Hundreds of schools must be built and thousands of talented teachers must be found, for children and adults alike. Tuition must be absolutely token, even free where necessary. Every college campus where more than 100 Jewish students reside must have a fully staffed Center for Jewish Life (a.k.a. Hillel) to provide constant stimulation. Every young teen should be exposed to a Jewish summer camp for several summers, again at a token cost. And in high school or college, every American Jewish youth should be given an Experience in Israel at communal expense.

The dimensions of such a program are so huge, so unprecedented, so demanding, and so expensive that no concerned Jew would remain unaffected by its scope. Fifteen billionaires could kick off the fundraising and thereby set the appropriate levels down the line; 150 Federated communities, currently sitting on almost $5 billion in endowment or foundation funds, could use them as collateral to borrow ten times that much.

Funds would be quickly gathered to give momentum to this vast educational enterprise. The education itself would pose no problem. The reservoir of academics in all the hundreds of departments of Jewish studies in this country's colleges and universities is sufficiently large to provide teachers for all the subjects that need to be taught.

As an aside, let one point be very clear: the weakening or diminution or even withering away of the American Diaspora would not doom the Jewish people as a whole. A long look at Jewish history, studying the rise and fall of previous strong Diaspora entities in Babylonia, Egypt, Spain, Iran, and Poland (to name a few) teaches us that even as old communities erode, new seeds are being planted in other lands, on other continents. Those seeds sprout and flourish to produce – in time – a new and vigorous Jewish environment that will absorb the wandering fugitives from the old ones.

Should the spectacular American Diaspora come to a self-inflicted, tragic end in the coming century, those remaining Jews whose self-identity demands a robust Jewish environment can seek fulfillment in Israel, a land strong and capable of welcoming them to a new home whose seeds were sown two centuries earlier. Such is the magic of this hitherto unbreakable chain. The song *"Am Yisrael Chai"* (The People of Israel Live) embodies the core conviction. Even if some of its limbs and branches wither and disappear, the people as a whole is indestructible, immortal.

If its life in the United States can be invigorated and strengthened, there is no limit to the creative potential of an inspired Jewish community. I mean potential for its own benefit and that of the larger world, including the possibility of helping the American nation as a whole regain the moral values it so desperately needs and seeks. Thus, the ability to overcome a mindless assimilation becomes the major task of the next two generations of American Jews. In an optimistic vein, we can hope and pray that our leadership will understand, respond to the challenge, make the plans and mobilize the funds to spark the renewal, and give birth to the renaissance.

American Jewry's national organizations plus America's thousands of synagogues must produce the electricity to light up the entire system. That can be done by crafting a national set of long-term strategic goals, publicizing them, blanketing the country with advertisements, videos, speakers, forums, and slogans to make it clear that all components of the total battle plan are linked and interwoven to achieve one common objective. We must educate every Jewish man, woman, and child we can reach with the desire to preserve Judaism and not drift away from it. There are nine elements, or individual goals, that form a complete mosaic designed to save our people and its mission. Here is what is specifically needed:

1. <u>A widely expanded, communal, trans-denominational day-school system covering K-8</u>, with scores and scores of such schools to be added within the next decade. Modeled after the best private schools in every community, these institutions must be of sufficiently high quality to attract the most secular parents as well as modern, Orthodox families. Annual tuition for the family should be a token $100 per student. The total cost of the school system is a communal responsibility.

2. <u>A high school system covering grades 9-12</u>, with a strongly Judaic curriculum plus a secular one of such quality that the school's graduates can gain admission to the finest universities in the country; plus exciting extra-curricular activities and a wide array of athletic facilities. Again, annual tuition should be a token $100 per student. Total cost is communal. The full network – one or more such high schools in every city – must be up and running within the next 15 years.

3. On every <u>college campus</u> containing more than 100 Jewish students, a fully staffed Center for Jewish Life to provide constant programming and stimulation. Most campuses will require much larger staffs than they currently maintain, as well as new or renovated buildings. Since the Jewish students are present in large

numbers (approximately 400,000 on 100 to 150 campuses), the need here is immediate.

4. An Israel Experience, providing a variety of programs for students between the ages of 15 to 25. Younger kids would spend four to eight weeks at a summer camp; tenth graders could spend a whole year in an accredited high school, and receive credit at their home-town high school; college students could spend junior year at an Israeli university, also for credit back home. Graduate students could spend two years in Israel working toward a master's degree. To succeed, the initiative needs a sufficient volume and variety of attractive programs in Israel; enough trained personnel to carry them out; pre-departure study to enrich the experience, and post-return courses to capitalize on the enthusiasm and establish a future pattern of Jewish action and living; universal and almost-free financing; and a major advertising program to inform everyone – parents and youth alike – that the opportunity exists and should be seized. Here again, the cost of whatever program is chosen, is at communal expense, with a family token of $100 to $500. This communal expense is an investment to secure our future.

5. A summer camp in the United States for every young Jewish person between the ages of 10 and 15. Few American camps excel at instilling Judaic influences while providing pleasurable recreational pursuits. At present, the Reform movement runs nine camps and the Conservative movement six. Each movement should have between 25 to 50 – at a tuition of $100 for the summer.

6. For adults, a widespread duplication of the Wexner-type seminar program, which, as I have pointed out, is the most serious adult Jewish education program in the country. Wexner students pay nothing; Leslie Wexner himself shoulders all expenses. Every city in America even with only a small or medium-size Jewish population should duplicate his approach, programmatic as well as financial. Each community can find its own local Leslie Wexner.

7. <u>Family educators</u> who can help create, in the home, a Jewish environment of holiday observance, songs, and stories, as well as the historic knowledge to enable understanding of the Sabbath and holidays. These skilled professionals function best when employed by the synagogue system and assigned to service new member families. One good approach is to organize a group of such families, including children for a mission to Israel. Communal funds must be used to add such educators to the synagogue staffs.

8. <u>A redesign of synagogue programs</u> to offer educational series that will increase the present small number of participants. This is a large subject that cannot be detailed in a few sentences, but well-intentioned rabbis and synagogue officers could come up with many suggestions. As it is, the best ideas are usually discarded because they cost too much. If additional funds are required to supplement what the synagogue can afford, the community should provide them.

9. <u>Welcoming the intermarried</u> in every possible fashion. I don't consider union between a Jewish person and a non-Jew who converts to Judaism an intermarriage: According to Jewish law and history, the convert has the same status as the born Jew. (Contemporary arguments in this area relate to the credentials of the clergy performing the conversion. It's a sort of turf war, because even when non-Orthodox clergy observe all the requirements of Orthodox law, they still are considered suspect.) The sincerity and long period of study required often make the convert a more knowledgeable Jew than his or her Jewish-born mate.

When I speak of intermarriage, I am talking about a Jewish person and any non-Jewish person, not necessarily a Christian. Since millions of Americans are no longer *practicing* Christians, many so-called intermarriages involve American Jews who are marrying simply other Americans. Unfortunately, the Jewish partner usually takes no steps to enroll this "neutral" person, who might well be amenable to conversion. In that situation, everyone involved – and potentially involved – is lost to Jewry: the Jewish partner, the mate, and any children they may have.

Every effort must be made – in honest, patient wooing and welcoming – to "rescue" the members of such families. Make the non-Jew feel comfortable, wanted, at home in the synagogue, the center, the federation, the social group, the vacation club, the bridge club, the mutual-fund club, the PTA, every institution with a niche into which to fit a new neighbor.

In the list of goals above, I have repeatedly indicated that communal funding is indispensable. Most middle-class parents simply cannot pay for Jewish primary and high schools, no matter how much they might want their children to attend them. Although it's impossible to estimate the costs of all the above items, it could easily run into billions of dollars.

We should not be frightened by such a number. Our people's life is at stake. In such a predicament, what meaning does money have? When catastrophe threatens, society spends whatever it must.

How do we obtain those huge sums? In the same way we obtained them for the earlier emergencies I have described. The UJA and all the Federations together must raise the rescue banner so widely, urgently, compellingly, skillfully, and constantly that they mobilize the entire organized Jewish community to a degree never before seen. The goal of the annual campaign must be pushed up into the billions.

Seventy-five percent of the American Jews – millions of people – are now not contributing a dime; they must be reached. Seventy percent of the wealth of this nation is in the hands of widows; they, too, must be reached. Communal property must be mortgaged. The billionaires must come forward, with sums they have never dreamed of, let alone contributed. Great *non*-Jewish foundations must be approached for "heavy" money; I predict a favorable reaction from them because their intelligent leadership will understand the immense impact that the disappearance of our talented people would have on America.

And the final resource; the gigantic nest egg that has been growing for the past quarter-century or more in the endowment funds, by whatever name they are called, of the country's Federations. As noted above, that amount has reached about $5 billion and is constantly growing. Individuals have donated that money and taken their tax deductions, but they retain the right to advise the Federations how their funds should be used. We need to urge those individuals to recommend that *some* of their billions be used on school tuitions, or the Israel Experience, or the other programs suggested above. What governing body would refuse such a recommendation? None.

Bottom line: I'm not really worried about where the money needed to do a proper job would come from. In my opinion, it's available; it simply needs to be excavated. The endowment funds could also serve as collateral for borrowing – to quickly put several billion dollars at the disposal of a national master plan.

One other money matter: how the funds raised in the annual campaigns are to be allocated and specifically how the allocations would affect Israel. Most of the usual formulas used by the UJA and the local Federations would have to be substantially altered. Israel must be informed, openly and officially, that American Jewry has embarked on a long-range effort to save itself from self-destruction. Detailed discussions would then take place with Israeli officials, as to their essential needs and how much could be supplied to them.

I'm certain the Israelis would understand and cooperate. Why? Because of a conversation I had with Prime Minister Yitzhak Rabin in New York in late October, 1995, two weeks before his tragic assassination. His closest aide, Eitan Haber, was present at that meeting. I asked Rabin how he would feel if the UJA took $50 million off the top of the usual allocation to Israel and used it to finance an Israel Experience for 10,000 American Jewish kids. He asked in return how anyone could be certain the money would actually be used for that purpose. When I assured him that the UJA would monitor the operation carefully, he agreed wholeheartedly because he understood and wholly sympathized with the underlying motive. Sadly, the project discussed with Rabin never materialized.

The crucial, underlying question, then, involves will power. I speak now to the generation of leadership today, men and women in their 60s and 70s who still remember the horrors of the Holocaust and the glories of statehood. I speak also to the younger generation, in its 40s and 50s, whose members have been acquiring some Jewish sensibility and understand what is at stake. Do all of you, amounting to tens of thousands across the entire country, feel the weight of history? Are you – especially you leaders – ready to give this effort your total conviction, dedication, commitment? In other words, is your will power fully energized?

If your answers are "Yes!," act fast, even at the risk of making mistakes. *Not* acting is the only unacceptable response.

Jewish leaders, it's your call. If you go to work quickly, with vigor and imagination, you can succeed brilliantly. Bear in mind that eternal existence is decided anew every 40 years with each new generation. A people 3,700 years old must regularly renew its claim to exist. If you protect your heritage, it will protect you.

The value of Judaism to every Jew is that it provides a proud identity and a meaning to life by linking you to an ideal greater than yourself. The value of Judaism to the whole world is that it represents the greatest civilizing moral force man has ever known. Thus you are part of something that immeasurably enriches both you and the world around you. What more can one man or woman desire?

Through you, this people will be "rescued" again and again, as often as necessary, into eternity.

Brother Stanley as Navy ensign, 1943.

Brother Sam
in tank corps, 1943.

Working my way through Yale at
Sam's smoke shop, 1935.

My parents on a visit to us in Denver, 1948.

I'm holding Joan as we all, Elaine, Judy and Dan
leave Milwaukee for New York in 1955.

Francine and I with David, on her right, and Charles
in Caesarea, summer 1969.

Back in my beloved west, with David and Charles,
on the road to Los Alamos.

Francine with her brother Norman Bensley,
25 years after the dedication of the
Denmark school, 1993.

Francine with Charles, standing,
and David, on her 60th birthday.

My daughter Joan Bentsen with her partner Erik Olsen.
Both perform in Danish children's theater and TV.

My granddaughter
Rachel Unice graduated
high school in 1996.

How gratifying to officiate at the
marriage of my granddaughter Debby
to Daniel Levenson in August, 1997.
On the right is my daughter Judy Unice.

My son Dan and his wife Margie with Lizzie and Ben.

What a treat to travel through Israel with
my grandson Ben and his father Dan.

Francine and I celebrating our 33rd anniversary on a mountaintop
near Aspen, 1996.

APPENDICES

SPEECHES GIVEN AT UJA CONFERENCE HELD IN WASHINGTON, D.C.
ON JUNE 3-5, 1955

Rabbi Philip S. Bernstein

It was a matter of historic significance and something for which we have the greatest gratitude that Joe Schwartz was the head of JDC in Europe, and later the UJA in America. Because of Joe's early rabbinical training, because of his closeness to East European Jewish life, because of his innate kindliness and warmth of heart and sympathetic understanding and vast competence and ability to get people to like him, these made him ideally equipped to do the job he had to do, and it was, I repeat, a historic job.

I for one, and here I speak with strong feeling and personal knowledge, am highly gratified that Herbert Friedman is now going to take his place. In a sense I can say that he is my boy. I helped to guide him into the chaplaincy. I helped him to get an assignment in Europe, so that he could serve both in his military capacity and at the same time become one of the succorers of his people. I came upon him in Berlin in early 1946 doing a tremendous job there, and I persuaded him later to leave Berlin and come back to Frankfurt with me to be my aide and my colleague in the unique responsibilities that were ours. I watched him grow step by step as he undertook new responsibilities, and I tell you that in all America, the Jewish community, you could not find a better person for this job than Rabbi Herbert Friedman. The work of the United Jewish Appeal is in good hands.

I went to Europe in the spring of 1946 to be the adviser on Jewish Affairs to General McNarney, Eisenhower's successor.... I have never known a finer human being. I have never known a man with more genuine goodness of heart. I have never known a person in a position of historic responsibility with so much innate humaneness and kindliness as General McNarney displayed.... I had a feeling that I was going to encounter in the DP population a beaten people, an abnormal people, a neurotic people, and after a few weeks of listening and coming close to their lives and hearts, I found I was dealing with a vital people with perennial, unquenchable sources of faith and hope and courage.... Herbert Friedman and I went to Warsaw and stood on the ruins of that ghetto. Looking out at what had been the teeming center of Jewish life in Eastern Europe, we saw there wasn't a single building standing. There was every reason to despair as we looked out on that terrible destruction. Tonight our mood is not despair but gratification, because *Am Yisrael Chai*, the Jewish people live. Somehow they found hope and courage, somehow they retained their faith, somehow they went on toward a better life, a freer, more dignified life, for themselves and for all mankind.

We salute tonight the Jewish will to survive. We salute tonight the essential decency and goodness of the American people and their leadership. We reaffirm the inner kinship of Israel and the United States, the oldest and the newest of democracies, the greatest and the smallest of democracies, held together by a common faith in the free and dignified way of life.

Tonight we reaffirm our faith in the future of mankind. If a little decimated people such as we encountered just ten years ago could rebuild its life, could so quickly establish something out of the ashes of the old, could so soon bring a functioning democracy into existence, why should we despair of the future of mankind? Why should we despair of the future of peace and freedom? Israel points the way, Israel holds out, not to Jews alone, but to all mankind, the beacon and the promise and the hope of what men can be. Yes – hope.

General Joseph T. McNarney

As I recall it, I was on my way to address a UJA conference in Wernersville, Pennsylvania, when the weather closed in and my plane was grounded....You called on a young man who used to do some work for Phil Bernstein and myself in Germany, and who had also just arrived from there, to say a few words in my stead. He made such a remarkable impression on you then – and has continued to do so for the past several years – that you have just elected him to be executive vice-chairman of your great humanitarian organization. I refer to my friend and former associate in Germany, former chaplain and captain in the United States Army, assistant to the Adviser on Jewish Affairs, Rabbi Herbert Friedman. Along with all of you here, I want to express to Rabbi Friedman my heartiest congratulations on his new assignment and to wish him that full success which I know he will attain.

I look, and today there are no displaced Jews left in Central Europe. Meanwhile, on the far rim of the Mediterranean, on the soil where thousands of years ago their forebears worked and built and thought of God and created the Book of Books, there exists the young democratic state called Israel. And in this new Israel, peopled by a proud and freedom-loving citizenry, every fifth person was once an inmate of a DP camp, and thousands bear as a badge of remembrance the number which the Nazi tyrants tattooed on their arms. Finally, I know too that it would not take me very long to discover in any large city of our own country many industrious, useful, well-integrated and loyal Americans whose address but a few short years ago was Feldafing, Foehrenwald, Landsberg, or some other DP camp in the heart of Germany or Austria. For example, I note with pleasure the presence here of Dr. Samuel Gringaus, who so ably led the Central Committee of Displaced Jews when I was in Germany.

There are words in the English language that have lost their original freshness because, like a worn and dull coin, they have been passed around too often. One of these is the word "miracle." But if you have stood, as I have stood, in the midst of a just-liberated hell of hells called a Nazi concentration camp; if you have seen, as I have unbelievingly seen, the unburied Jewish dead stacked like cordwood in such terrible places; if you have been, as I have been, numbed beyond words before crematoria in which tens of thousands of innocent people were gassed and their bodies burned; if you have gazed, as I have gazed wonderingly, upon those who remained alive, those living skeletons we found in the camps who seemed about to draw their last breath; yes, if you had witnessed all these things, then you would know the full and awesome meaning of the word "miracle," as you contrasted them with what has since come to pass.

Who would have thought it possible that in a matter of a few short years the Jewish DP problem would be well on the way to solution. When I served in Germany, the DPs adopted a decorative symbol which expressed their innermost hopes. This symbol showed the stump of a mighty tree which had been cut down, and out of this stump there sprouted a lone but living twig. Today, it is obvious that the twig has grown again into a sturdy trunk fed by roots that are deep and undying.

I have often asked myself, "How did this come about?" I believe the answer rests, in part, with the fact that the American people and the American Army were led by men to whom it was a matter of the utmost moral responsibility that the fullest possible aid be extended to those who had suffered most at the hands of the Nazi tyranny. Perhaps it was more than an accident that Presidents Truman and Eisenhower are men who, among other things, were brought up in an atmosphere where the Bible is an important symbol of man's finest hopes and aspirations. For my own part, I regard it as a great privilege to have been able to make a contribution to the work of saving and restoring the Jewish displaced and persecuted. I was happy to be able to recognize and give official status to the Central Committee of Liberated Jews in Germany. I am happy that I was able to issue the order that Jewish persecutees from Eastern Europe would be admitted to haven and sanctuary in the American Zone of Germany. I am happy that, with General Clay, I was able to help make possible the publication of the Talmud in the land where Hitler once ordered it burned. And I am happy that the Army was able to help in the material sense of providing housing and food.

It seems to me that what the Army did in Germany through its humane treatment of these people, and what you have done since that time, represent very real contributions to the winning of the peace. The Army and the

American people demonstrated to millions of Germans, in a manner which I believe they will never forget, that democracy is more than a word and the United States is more than a mechanized civilization, but affords the average man the opportunity to live in dignity, safety, and to share in the good things of life.

General John H. Hilldring

I was whole-heartedly in favor of a solution which would mean that the homeless Jews of the DP camps and the pioneer Jews of Palestine would be given an opportunity to live their lives in a country they could call their own. I told you at your UJA Conference in Atlantic City, in December 1947, that I was confident that this new state "would emerge a virile, prosperous, and happy land."

Therefore, I pay tribute to you, and to the courageous citizens of Israel, for what they have done and what you have helped to bring about. And I am proud that the Government of the United States has done its part in granting great material aid to democratic Israel. Since the prediction I made in 1947 has turned out so well, I will dare venture another tonight: that Israel's people will reach their goal to stand on their own feet, stable and self-sufficient within their borders, and they will do it with your help. I feel confident that Israel's present leaders will work unceasingly toward the establishment of peace in their part of the world. I trust that the other leaders in that area will reciprocate.

Meanwhile, as men and women of conscience, you know your job and you will do it as well as you have always done. I am glad to pay tribute to you, the leaders of this fine united effort.

Honorable Abba S. Eban

This decade has been the story of a spasm in the life of a people which counts its generations in thousands of years. Never will it find any period which can compete with this, in the poignancy of its suffering or in the sublime heights of its exaltation.

The United Jewish Appeal has not been an idle spectator of these great events. It has attended all of these turbulent changes with its vigilance, its sustenance, and its love. It has mourned the dead, consoled the bereaved, lifted up the fallen, healed the sick, sustained and revived the ancient pride of the Jewish people, laid the foundations of a homeland, guided and reinforced its infant steps. It has brought the Jewish people from the threat of its total extinction into the absolute certainty of a proud and sovereign survival, amidst the dignity of statehood and the youthful exuberance of its newly won freedom....

It would be wrong, however, to recall the liberation of Europe by Allied armies as the only turning point in this dramatic and turbulent story. The military victory was not the end of the danger. As the nations of the world gathered in your great city of San Francisco in the aftermath of the War, to form a new world organization, the world came perilously near to a disgrace more heinous than any which had been overthrown in the successful assault upon Nazism. The blueprint of the new international order would exclude the Jewish people upon whose very blood and tormented flesh the edifice of human freedom had been constructed.

Ten years ago, at San Francisco, it appeared to be that freedom and sovereignty were the inheritance of all people except ours. Next month the United Nations again reconvenes in San Francisco, but this time the international community has gained a new dimension. This time we shall be there, and the fact that our flag now takes its place among the banners of free nations – symbolizes one of the few genuinely moral achievements of these past ten years. The UJA was not merely the architect of survival for hundreds of thousands of individuals; it was also the builder of a state, the architect of a nation. [Author's note: Mr. Eban today, at age 82, is the last person alive from among those who raised the flag of Israel in front of the UN headquarters in 1951.]....

We have passed in a single decade from a world in which the existence of a free Israel seemed inconceivable into a world which is inconceivable without its existence.

In my recent consultations in Israel, I elicited as the main conclusion of our governmental and public mind the fact that we are passionately dedicated to the primacy of American friendship as the central focus of our aspiration.... Partnership and friendship between these two peoples who hold so many ideals and purposes in common is in the interests, the welfare and to the advantage of both....We attach great importance to the treaty which Israel and the United States initialed yesterday and which makes them partners in the peaceful use of atomic energy. Ever since President Eisenhower took his statesmanlike initiative in this question a year and a half ago, our people, our government, and especially our scientific community, have been exhilarated by the thought of what this uncannily compact and transportable fuel might mean in terms of an accelerated strength and solvency for Israel.

Look back with gratification upon the rich tapestry of Israel's achievement. We advance with bold steps to the toil and challenge of the future. You have lingered piously and reverently tonight in the avenue of memory, but after all, the Jewish people has now become far more than a memory. It has a monument, it has a citadel, it has the pride and the opportunity of a home over that citadel. Across the monument and above the roofs of our home flies the banner of David, the proud symbol of Israel's resurrected statehood. Let us assemble at the foot of that banner. Let us hold it aloft. Let us strengthen its honor. Let us permeate it forever with the love and grace of our undying devotion.

Honorable Herbert H. Lehman

In 1945, when we were seeking the appropriation of the second U.S. contribution of $1 billion 350 million, which we were morally obligated to the 43 other nations in UNRRA to do, we were held up for a considerable time in Congress in securing these funds which were so sorely needed for the suffering millions of refugees who depended on our help. I was not then a member of the Congress, nor did I at that time know as much about Congressional Committees as I do now, but day after day my associates and I appeared before committees with pleas for prompt action. The situation was critical. Our resources were nearly exhausted.

On Thanksgiving Day of 1945, General Eisenhower left a sick bed to appear before the Foreign Affairs Committee of the House of Representatives. I recall that day very well indeed. It was mean, cold, and blustery. General Eisenhower, though ill, nevertheless came and dramatically told the story of the displaced persons camps and the great help that UNRRA was giving in repatriating millions of people to their homes, and caring for those who no longer had any homes. It was a powerful appeal to the Congress and the nation, and it greatly helped to bring about early and favorable action by the House. My friends, I shall never fail to be grateful to General Eisenhower for the humanity he showed on that and many other occasions.

Dr. Zalman Grinberg

My friends, I come to you as a living witness. It is not difficult to recall the hour of liberation when the dedicated forces of the American Army broke open the notorious Dachau Concentration Camp...The noise of the oncoming American troops visibly disturbed our German guards. As the noises grew louder, the master race tightened up with fear. They couldn't decide on a course of action. Finally, in a frenzy, they started to flee, but opened a last reckless burst of machine-gun fire, and in the very last minute before the Americans crashed in, there were 136 more Jewish victims of German bullets.

A group of us, physicians, started to give first aid to the prisoners still living. We gathered the sickest and wounded and carried them off to a nearby monastery, St. Ottilien, where there was a German military hospital. We turned this into the first Jewish DP hospital, with a capacity of 1600 beds. Liberation takes time. You fed us and made us physically well. You clothed us, not merely with garments, but with dignity and self-respect. You lifted our eyes, so that we could see the sun once again. You set out to destroy the odor of the concentration camps that tenaciously held on to the membranes of our nostrils. Before too long, we had a book on our shelves, a newspaper in our pockets, and an argument upon our lips. We were once again swirling in the world of thoughts and ideas, on the way to a full and complete liberation....

We came home, home to the land of Israel, home to a new beginning. It was a difficult beginning but then we learn in life that birth and creation bursting forth to the new horizons, tackling dreams, these are the most difficult of man's enterprises. We began, and with you, to build the land, and at the same time we built our own liberation. The fields themselves must have heard of our coming. They gave up their desolation and flowered with grain. Waters were harnessed, power was extracted, wheels turned and the city dreamed. Each bit of progress was a source of satisfaction and inspiration. I remember the day the first automatic traffic light was hung in the street of Haifa. I was intrigued. I had seen many traffic lights before, but not in Haifa. I drove around the square two or three times to watch it blink and to rejoice even in this bit of progress. My dear friends, we have become free. The rays of the sun now warm us. The horizons excite us and the language of the waters of the Mediterranean against our shores is music to our ears. The liberation of our people must continue. We are now free, made free by what you are and what you have done. We join hands with you in the task that remains to be done. At this time, however, let my purpose be merely to bring to you, from the desolation and despair of Dachau 1945, and now from the life and hope of Jerusalem 1955, a humble word of thanks to you Americans, and to you, my Jewish brethren of America, for a decade of humanitarianism which is our liberation.

Dr. Samuel Gringaus

I personally had the privilege of working continually with Rabbi Philip Bernstein and his wonderful team of Abe Hyman, now director of the World Jewish Congress, and Rabbi Herbert Friedman, now your executive vice-chairman. The names of Bernstein, Hyman, and Friedman are connected with the greatest achievement in the field of refugee policy, the opening of the gates of the American Zone of Germany to the infiltrees. By this act, about a quarter-million Jews were saved... In this connection I deem it appropriate to mention the splendid work accomplished by the field workers of the Joint Distribution Committee (JDC). Their work in the years after the War adds a glorious page to the history of this humanitarian organization....

And now some words about the DPs themselves. They dissolved themselves through emigration to Israel, U.S., and other countries. However, out of the deep experience of oppression and injustices, we developed certain emotional and intellectual ingredients of an ideology...which we brought with us into the new countries of our settlement, and these are the five articles of faith of the *shearith ha-pleitah* (surviving remnant) as they emerged in the years after the liberation.

First: We wanted to preserve the memory of the great catastrophe.

Second: We knew from our experience that where Communism rules, Judaism must die.

Third: It was our deep conviction that the great catastrophe was not ordinary, but a structural upheaval, bringing about a complete transformation of the Jewish global set-up, a transformation requiring particular responsibility on the part of Jewish leadership.

Fourth: Out of the depth of their tragic experience, the *shearith ha-pleitah* brought home an ardent desire for Palestine.

And last: The experience of totalitarian persecution taught us that there must be resistance to evil, which is exemplified by the heroic uprising in the Warsaw Ghetto and the noble rescue operation of the Danish people. Free society has to defend itself against the propaganda of hate in the same way as it defends itself against other crimes, by national and international laws entailing individual punishment and collective indemnification.

These are the articles of faith set forth almost a decade ago. I daresay that they have retained their validity for the present days and for the years to come.

Ladies and gentlemen, we express the hope that American Jewry will face the years to come with the same firm determination to continue contributing to the welfare of the Jewish people and of the free world at large.

Dr. Joseph Schwartz

You know, as I listened to Dr. Grinberg, whom I have known and admired over the years, I heard him use an expression which impressed me. He said the DPs were looking for a <u>place</u>, in addition to medical assistance and help of all kinds. They wanted a place, and it occurred to me that in the Hebrew language, which has many words and expressions for the Deity, there is one which employs the term *Ha-Makom*, which means "the place." The Hebrew word for place is also a name of God.

To those people in Germany, it certainly had a divine ring. This place we are building, this Israel, this home is not just a new territory. It is not just a new political entity. It is not just a monument. It is a place which has a deep spiritual role to play and is important to the preservation of everything that is dear and holy to us in our long history....

We must see to it that that edifice which we have started to build is completed, that the work which we have undertaken with so much dedication in 1945 is continued without interruption, until it is brought to a successful conclusion.

For whatever part I have had in this effort, I am deeply grateful. I am grateful to the American Jewish community which had the confidence to take me and give me this opportunity of serving in the JDC and the UJA, and I am grateful to the Jews of the United States and to the people of Israel for having placed this additional burden (Israel Bonds) upon me, which I hope with your help is a burden that can be lightened. And, finally, I am deeply grateful to all of you in this room and to my dear friends around this table. Everything that has happened in these sessions deals in symbols, and I suppose it is symbolic that others have received an ancient oil lamp but I received a desk set. It means that I am expected to continue to work, and I look forward to the fact that you will work along with me.

William Rosenwald

Rabbi Friedman is very familiar with Israel. I met him there in 1951, heading a group of rabbis. Before that he attended the Jerusalem Conference in 1950, which eventuated in the Israel Bond Drive, and he was again, as a representative of the UJA, at the Jerusalem Conference in 1953, from which flowed the Consolidation Loan. He also knows our campaign very well, because he has traveled all through this country making speeches for us as national chairman of our speakers bureau.

It is quite striking that, at the age of 37, he is the youngest person ever to head our campaign. He shows a wisdom far beyond his years, and we already know his fine personality, his contagious enthusiasm, and his great talent of presentation. I should like to read a cablegram we have received from the prime minister of Israel: "To know Herbert Friedman is to know that the UJA has in him a devoted, able, and inspiring man, whose work is guided by an encompassing knowledge of Jewish affairs and by a passionate responsibility for the welfare of the Jewish people. Looking forward to cooperation with Rabbi Friedman and to his forthcoming visit to Israel, my warm regards to all associated with you in the magnificent work of the UJA" – signed, Moshe Sharett.

Rabbi Herbert A. Friedman

I am glad to be getting into the UJA and especially to being put there by Bill Rosenwald's hands. The general chairman of the UJA is a person who sits at the summit of Jewish life in America, and for us to know that we have one such as he is reassuring. The knowledge that he is possessed of the strength and conviction which are his, gives us the firm feeling that we are under the captaincy of a man who knows well how to lead the major enterprise of American Jewish philanthropy. To have been installed in office by him is something which I shall not forget.

I will try to bring a message to the young Jews of America, try to explain to them the meaning of the 17 years of work since the UJA was created, the billion dollars of money which was raised, the two and a half million people who were helped, the million people resettled. I don't know if anyone can understand or grasp what such huge figures as these really mean. Try to think of one family settling into one house, and then enlarge the picture to a whole village of 80 families, and so on. Think of all the Jews of Morocco who must be brought from the mountains of the Sahara to the mountains of Judea. The UJA has had a record of standing at historic moments and assuming historic tasks. For this year and next, the task will involve the Jewry of French North Africa. They will come from the vastnesses of the Atlas Mountains and the squalor of the

Casablanca *mellah*. They will come because there is an irrepressible urge to be resettled in the land of their forefathers. They will come because history has its own dynamics and the Jews are starting to leave. Momentum will accumulate, the tempo will increase. And the role of the UJA is to stand at the side of any man or woman who says they want to or need to go to Israel. There we shall resettle all who ask.

What of the Israel to which they go? This gallant, beleaguered nation has, without a moment's hesitation, taken every single person who knocked at her doors. This Israel has problems which are continuous. This Israel cannot endure a sporadic or erratic response from us. If the problems are continuous, our response must be continuous. It is the height of immaturity and irresponsibility to make one or two gigantic spurts of response at one or two peak years, and then to slough off the job undone, partially done, done well up to an extent, but by far, not really done.

If the record of service of 17 years has any meaning at all, it means that there lie within it the seed of 17 more, should that be necessary. Let not the people of Israel in the land, nor the children of Israel outside the land, ever be worn down. Let us go on, day by day, year after year, building settlements on the borders that will house the newcomers, flinging pipe across the land that will bring water, for water brings life. We will build houses and seat people at the tables in the houses, whether the question of war or peace is settled or not.

There was a beautiful custom among the medieval rabbis in France. They used to study at long tables, and when they died, those very tables were fashioned into coffins. This was their immortality, their resistance to death. I should like to reverse this procedure. I should like us to fashion tables to put in the houses for our children of the future, out of the coffins of our martyred dead of the past. Each generation has two responsibilities – backward toward its predecessor and forward toward its successor. Our predecessor generation has gone to its coffins. Our successor generation shall go to its tables to live and work and eat in peace, and by their side, for whatever time shall be necessary, will stand this pious and devoted fraternity, as Mr. Eban characterized us last night, this UJA from whose constituent strength shall flow the love and the emotion and the life which will keep the people of Israel and the land of Israel surviving for all eternity. So shall it be, with your will.